Building Resilient Energy Systems

I0028110

This book explores an ongoing puzzle: why don't catastrophic events, such as oil shocks and nuclear meltdowns, always trigger transitions away from the energy technologies involved?

Jennifer F. Sklarew examines how two key factors – shocks and stakeholder relationships – combine to influence energy system transitions, applying a case study of Japan's trajectory from the time of the 1970s oil crises through the period following the 2011 Fukushima Daiichi nuclear disaster. Examining the role of diverse stakeholders' resilience priorities, she focuses on how changes in stakeholder cooperation and clout respond to and are affected by these shocks, and how this combination of shocks and relationship changes shapes energy policies and policymaking. From Japan's narrative, the book derives unique and universal lessons for cooperation on innovation and energy system resilience applicable to communities and nations around the globe, including implications for transitions in the context of the COVID-19 pandemic. The book also places energy system resilience and innovation in the broader context of the food-energy-water-climate nexus.

Building Resilient Energy Systems: Lessons from Japan will appeal to all levels of readers with an interest in energy policy, energy technologies, and energy transitions: experts and specialists; academics and students; and practitioners and policymakers.

Jennifer F. Sklarew brings 30 years of energy policymaking and analysis to her research and teaching as a professor of energy and sustainability at George Mason University. National Public Radio (NPR) has quoted her as an expert on Japanese energy policymaking. In the U.S. Department of Commerce's Office of Japan, she collaborated on Japanese electricity and gas deregulation and served as a Mike Mansfield Fellow in Tokyo. She previously served as an energy policy consultant to Japanese utility companies and a policy analyst for the Japan Nuclear Cycle Development Institute. Her broader food-energy-water-climate resilience interest appears in this book and a coauthored book, *Managing Challenges for the Flint Water Crisis*.

Routledge Explorations in Energy Studies

Energy Cooperation in South Asia
Utilizing Natural Resources for Peace and Sustainable Development
Mirza Sadaqat Huda

Perspectives on Energy Poverty in Post-Communist Europe
Edited by George Jiglau, Anca Sinea, Ute Dubois and Philipp Biermann

Dilemmas of Energy Transitions in the Global South
Balancing Urgency and Justice
Edited by Ankit Kumar, Johanna Höffken and Auke Pols

**Assembling Petroleum Production and Climate Change
in Ecuador and Norway**
Elisabeth Marta Tómmerbakk

International Law and Renewable Energy Investment in the Global South
Avidan Kent

Local Energy Governance
Opportunities and Challenges for Renewable and Decentralised Energy in
France and Japan
Edited by Magali Dreyfus and Aki Suwa

Local Energy Communities
Emergence, Places, Organizations, Decision Tools
Edited by Gilles Debizet, Marta Pappalardo & Frédéric Wurtz

Building Resilient Energy Systems
Lessons from Japan
Jennifer F. Sklarew

For more information about this series, please visit: www.routledge.com/Routledge-
Explorations-in-Energy-Studies/book-series/REENS

Building Resilient Energy Systems

Lessons from Japan

Jennifer F. Sklarew

Routledge
Taylor & Francis Group

LONDON AND NEW YORK

earthscan
from Routledge

Cover image: Jennifer F. Sklarew

First published 2023
by Routledge
4 Park Square, Milton Park, Abingdon, Oxon OX14 4RN

and by Routledge
605 Third Avenue, New York, NY 10158

Routledge is an imprint of the Taylor & Francis Group, an informa business

© 2023 Jennifer F. Sklarew

The right of Jennifer F. Sklarew to be identified as author of this work has been asserted in accordance with sections 77 and 78 of the Copyright, Designs and Patents Act 1988.

All rights reserved. No part of this book may be reprinted or reproduced or utilised in any form or by any electronic, mechanical, or other means, now known or hereafter invented, including photocopying and recording, or in any information storage or retrieval system, without permission in writing from the publishers.

Trademark notice: Product or corporate names may be trademarks or registered trademarks, and are used only for identification and explanation without intent to infringe.

British Library Cataloguing-in-Publication Data
A catalogue record for this book is available from the British Library

ISBN: 978-1-032-13087-3 (hbk)
ISBN: 978-1-032-13083-5 (pbk)
ISBN: 978-1-003-22758-8 (ebk)

DOI: 10.4324/9781003227588

Typeset in Goudy
by Apex CoVantage, LLC

This book is dedicated to my wonderfully supportive, encouraging family:

my spouse, Dann, and my children, Ben and Jasmine.

In memory of Ko Sugiura, whose lifelong dedication to U.S.-Japan energy cooperation continues to inspire me.

Contents

Acknowledgments

My journey to this book began in Japan, where the first years of my life created a lifelong interest in U.S.-Japan cooperation. I have many friends, colleagues, mentors, and family members to thank for their roles in the path that has led me here.

I could not have undertaken this project without Tsuyoshi Maruyama. He has my deepest appreciation for his encouragement, guidance, and willingness to exchange views on Japanese energy policy throughout this project and the decades that preceded it. I wish to thank him and my other colleagues from my time at Japan's former Power Reactor and Nuclear Fuel Development Corporation (PNC) for their collegiality, and for the many opportunities they provided to learn about Japan's energy system and the role of U.S.-Japan cooperation in mutual energy security.

I am grateful to the U.S. Department of Education for generously supporting my data collection in Japan through a Fulbright-Hays Doctoral Dissertation Research Award (DDRA), and to George Mason University's Office of the Provost for the generous funding to complete the initial phase of this study.

Many thanks to numerous colleagues who exchanged views while I worked on this study and traversed the path that led to it: Kent Calder, Taro Kono, Giulia Bisconti, Tom Terbush, Gail Marcus, Daniel Aldrich, Jim Platte, Jane Nakano, Geovanni Castano, Scott Sklar, Llewelyn Hughes, Dick Samuels, Adrienne Vanek, and Micah Himmel. I also am indebted to many other colleagues in Japan and Washington, DC, who kindly exchanged views and provided data and contacts for this project.

Sincere thanks to David Hart, Christopher T. Hill, and Todd M. LaPorte for their invaluable guidance and support during the initial phase of this project during my studies at George Mason University. Many thanks also to Thomas Birkland at North Carolina State University for his insightful feedback and encouragement.

I would like to thank the colleagues from each of the places along my path to this book: George Packard and Michael Green for sharing their insights during my studies at Johns Hopkins University; Bill Martin for his encouragement and insights during my time at Washington Policy & Analysis, Inc.; my U.S. government colleagues for collaborating with me on Japanese electricity and gas market liberalization during my time in the U.S. Department of Commerce's Office of Japan; the Maureen and Mike Mansfield Foundation for enabling me to gain new insight into Japanese policymaking processes through a Mike Mansfield Fellowship; and former and current Mansfield Foundation colleagues Paige Cottingham-Streater, Niharika Joe, Chie Igarashi, Teruyo Kuramoto, Gordon Flake, and Ryan Shaffer for their friendship and support.

Thanks to Katrin Anacker, Christine Pommerening, and Benjamin Sovacool, who shared their insights on the book publication process.

I am grateful to Routledge's editors, Annabelle Harris and Caroline Church, and editorial assistants, Jyotsna Gurung and Matthew Shobbrook, for their support with book publication. Special thanks to Elsevier's *Energy Research and Social Science* for enabling reuse of the data and analysis from my article published in their 2018 Special Issue on Energy Infrastructure and the Fate of the Nation. Additional thanks to Stephanie McMillan for allowing me to include her poignant cartoon, and to Springer editor Summers Scholl for her guidance and recommendation to publish this book with Routledge.

Deepest gratitude also goes to my husband, Dann, and my children, Ben and Jasmine, for their indispensable years of emotional and physical support, for accompanying me to Japan, and for their enthusiastic interest in my work. Many thanks also to my parents and extended family for their years of encouragement and support throughout my journey to this book.

Figures

Tables

Abbreviations

ABWR	Advanced Boiling Water Reactor
AEC	Japan Atomic Energy Commission
ANRE	Agency for Energy and Natural Resources
ANS	American Nuclear Society
BWR	Boiling Water Reactor
CRIEPI	Central Research Institute of Electric Power Industry
EGC	Electricity and Gas Market Surveillance Commission
FBR	Fast Breeder Reactor
FEPC	Federation of Electric Power Companies
FIT	Feed-in Tariff
FIP	Feed-in Premium
GW	Gigawatts
IEA	International Energy Agency
IAEA	International Atomic Energy Agency
JAEA	Japan Atomic Energy Agency
JAERI	Japan Atomic Energy Research Institute
JAERO	Japan Atomic Energy Relations Organization
JAIF	Japan Atomic Industrial Forum
JANTI	Japan Nuclear Technology Institute
JCO	Japan Nuclear Fuel Conversion Co.
JNC	Japan Nuclear Cycle Development Institute
JNES	Japan Nuclear Energy Safety Organization
JNFL	Japan Nuclear Fuel, Ltd.
JNOC	Japan National Oil Corporation
JPDC	Japan Petroleum Development Corporation
KEPCO	Kansai Electric Power Company
LDP	Liberal Democratic Party
LNG	Liquefied Natural Gas
LWR	Light Water Reactor
MAFF	Ministry of Agriculture, Forestry and Fisheries
METI	Ministry of Education, Culture, Sports, Science and Technology
MEXT	Ministry of Economy, Trade and Industry
MITI	Ministry of International Trade and Industry

MLIT	Ministry of Land, Infrastructure and Transport
MOE	Ministry of Environment
MOX	Mixed Oxide Fuel
NEDO	New Energy and Industrial Technology Development Organization
NISA	Nuclear and Industrial Safety Agency
NRA	Nuclear Regulation Authority
NRC	Nuclear Regulatory Commission
NSC	Nuclear Safety Commission
OCCTO	Organization for Cross-Regional Coordination of Transmission Operators
OPEC	Organization of Petroleum Exporting Countries
PNC	Power Reactor and Nuclear Fuel Development Corporation
PRA	Probabilistic Risk Assessment
PWR	Pressurized Water Reactor
RITE	Research Institute for Innovative Technology for the Earth
RPS	Renewable Energy Portfolio Standard
STA	Science and Technology Agency
TEPCO	Tokyo Electric Power Company
TMI	Three Mile Island
UNFCCC	United Nations Framework Convention on Climate Change

1 Introduction

The Resilience Puzzle

The COVID-19 pandemic has highlighted the global effect that shocks – or catastrophic events – may wield on energy systems, altering production and consumption patterns for oil, gas, solar power, and other energy supply sources.[1] At national and local levels, energy policy responses to shocks such as pandemics, accidents, natural disasters, resource shortages, and price disruptions vary widely. Understanding the factors behind these variations can illuminate the potential for change and innovation when shocks to an energy system occur. Resilience has become the new global mantra, but each national and local government, in conjunction with its energy stakeholders, is conducting an individual struggle to define a resilient energy system.[2] Resilience generally refers to a system's ability to absorb shocks and continue operating,[3] but policymakers, energy industry decision-makers, and consumers may include other features, such as environmental sustainability, cost-effectiveness, and social justice, in assessing the resilience of their system. Thus, to develop a holistic understanding of each unique energy system's resilience and innovation environment, we need to examine these variations in resilience priorities and perspectives, as well as the catalysts for and barriers to energy system adaptation aftershocks occur. Such understanding will enable us – whether energy policymakers, industry professionals, community leaders, or consumers – to identify ways to collaborate to achieve our energy system resilience goals before, during, and after shocks.

To this end, this book explores an ongoing puzzle: why don't catastrophic events, such as oil price shocks and nuclear meltdowns, always trigger transitions away from the energy technologies involved? Such catastrophic events have yielded a variety of policy responses around the globe. These responses tend to fit into one of two categories. We might observe the emergence of new policies and innovations to address the challenges to use of the relevant energy technology, thus perpetuating and strengthening resilience of the existing system. The U.S. government's policy response to the 1970s oil crises – including development of a Strategic Petroleum Reserve and diversification of oil import sources – provides an example of this type of response.[4] The government of Ukraine's continued reliance on nuclear power to provide the nation's electricity, even more than three

DOI: 10.4324/9781003227588-1

Figure 1.1 Word cloud composed of words commonly associated with energy system resilience.

decades after the Chernobyl nuclear disaster, offers another example.[5] Alternatively, we might observe policies aimed at divestment of the relevant energy technology, coupled with innovation toward a more resilient system based on different technologies. The Japanese government's policy response to the 1970s oil crises reflects this type of shift, demonstrating a transition away from oil-based electricity supply and addition of energy conservation and efficiency measures to reduce energy demand. Chapter three of this book discusses this transition in more detail. By contrast, very few examples of dramatic energy system transitions after domestic technological disasters exist, and this book will shed light on some of the reasons, drawing lessons for innovation to balance the diverse resilience priorities of various stakeholders.

We can view both of these types of responses to shocks as promoting energy system resilience in different ways. The first, innovation and change within the existing system, reflects modification of the system to prevent and respond to future shocks. The second, innovation and transition out of the existing system toward a new one, reflects redesign of the system to divest from challenging technologies and refocus on others that appear more secure and sustainable. Understanding the variations in these responses to shocks and definitions of resilience requires examination of the institutional factors that shape them. As we examine these factors, we will identify insights for stakeholder collaboration and ways to overcome conflict.

When systems reveal a lack of resilience to shocks – manifested in widespread power grid shutdowns; serious damage to environment and health; or other threats to economic, environmental, and energy security – barriers to change can result in policy and system stasis. We can refer to such stasis as "lock-in." A vast number of studies on system lock-in, also termed path dependence, describes how energy systems – and other systems such as transportation and telecommunications systems – become entrenched. Chapter two of this book contains an overview of studies of lock-in and the ways in which this book builds on them to provide lessons for energy system innovation and resilience. It also contains an overview of studies focusing on factors that can break such system lock-in. One of these sets of

Figure 1.2 Disasters and Energy Transitions Cartoon
Credit: Stephanie McMillan, 2010.

studies addresses the role of shocks or catastrophic events. The other set of studies examines stakeholder relationship changes as a factor in energy system development and change. To build resilient energy systems, we need to understand how catastrophic events and stakeholder relationships affect one another. We also need to recognize their combined influence on energy transitions, resilience, and innovation.

Thus, this book examines the influence of stakeholder relationships on the transformative capability of shocks, applying a case study of Japan's trajectory from the time of the oil crises through the period following the Fukushima Daiichi nuclear disaster. The analysis focuses on how changes in stakeholder cooperation and clout respond to and are affected by these shocks, and how this combination of shocks and relationship changes shapes energy policymaking.

What Resilience and Innovation Lessons Can We Learn from Japan?

Japan's situation has drawn global attention. Since the Fukushima Daiichi nuclear disaster occurred a decade ago, policymakers, reporters, energy industry professionals, students, academics, and others around the world interested in energy policy repeatedly have questioned why Japan has not transitioned away from nuclear power and toward renewables. If we look back 50 years instead of 10, we can observe that Japan has experienced several major shocks to its energy system, offering an opportunity to derive lessons on how shocks, relationships, and resilience priorities combine to influence energy system resilience and innovation. The book analyzes Japan's experiences over a period of five decades, during which government relationships with the electric utilities and the public combined with three external shocks to national energy systems: the 1970s oil crises, technological and institutional failures in the 1990s and early 2000s, and the 2011 Fukushima nuclear disaster. Many nations have faced the same or similar shocks, and examining Japan's case offers lessons for policymakers and energy industry decision-makers in nations and communities that may face such shocks in the future.

Japan's energy policy and energy policymaking processes have not changed in the same way after each shock. Japan's narrative explains how these divergent responses reflect ways in which stakeholder relationships can alter a catastrophic event's ability to generate change in such policies and processes, as well as changes in electricity market structure and regulatory structure. Recognizing that important relationships exist between many types of stakeholders, this book focuses on the government's relationships with the public and the electric utilities as the primary relationships that influence energy system change and define the environment for resilience and innovation after a catastrophic event. In particular, each empirical chapter examines the electric utilities' and public's relationships with energy policymakers, politicians, economic regulators, and safety regulators. This analysis also considers each group's resilience priorities. This understanding of the ways in which these relationships and priorities may affect responses to catastrophic events can help to promote cooperation and mitigate conflict across policymakers, energy industry decision-makers, and citizens, fostering an environment for innovation toward greater energy system resilience.

This book presents Japan's narrative in three phases, divided into separate chapters.

The narrative begins with the 1970s oil shocks. Chapter 3 examines how the shocks did not alter the Japanese government's cooperative relationships with or clout over the electric utilities and the public. These groups' resilience priorities and risk perceptions also aligned. The book then explores how this continued cooperation and government clout led to energy policy change in Japan, but no immediate changes to the policymaking process or regulatory structure.

In the second phase, the electric utilities gained clout over time, contributing to a scenario in which a series of technological and institutional failures in the 1990s and early 2000s did not result in Japanese energy policy change, policymaking process change, or impactful regulatory or market structure change. Chapter 4 examines how the regulatory change that did take place aimed to appease conflict between the government and the public, though the government retained clout. Parallel trends in Japanese electricity market liberalization and climate change mitigation took place concurrently in the 1990s and early 2000s. These institutional shifts added elements that enhanced both conflict and cooperation in the Japanese government's relationships with the electric utilities, as well as a struggle for clout. A notable switch in political leadership followed this period, indicating growing public clout over and conflict with the government. Underlying these relationship shifts are the increasingly divergent resilience priorities and risk perceptions of each group.

Finally, Chapter 5 examines the 2011 Fukushima Daiichi nuclear disaster. The accident occurred in this environment of tenuous balance between cooperation and conflict, coupled with the battle for clout. The photograph in Figure 1.3 reflects this ongoing struggle. This book suggests that three factors drive whether this shock leads to long-term policy change along with policymaking process change: the conflict/cooperation axis of the government's relationships with the electric utilities and the public; public, government, and utility clout; and alignment or divergence of these groups' resilience priorities and risk perceptions. Electricity market liberalization and global climate change have continued to influence these factors. Ten years after the disaster, the relationships remain in conflict, and the government has aimed to balance rebuilding public trust with the utilities' resilience goals. As a result, slow, incremental changes to Japan's energy policies have emerged, accompanied by major and minor Japanese policymaking process and structural changes.

Understanding the factors behind these energy system trends helps us to better comprehend energy policy lock-in and identify the tools to promote cooperation and innovation toward energy system resilience.

Japan's culturally driven paternal government-public relationship may appear to make the Japanese case an outlier. Even during the data collection for this book, electric utility and government interviewees depicted Japan as an exception based on electric utilities' close relationship with policymakers and tension

Figure 1.3 Antinuclear protest tents in Tokyo, 2013.
Photo credit: Jennifer F. Sklarew.

with regulators, as well as the public's zero risk tolerance. However, Japan's parliamentary system of government, in which the bureaucracy plays a leadership role in Japanese policymaking along with the political parties, parallels policymaking structures in many other developed and developing nations, including the United Kingdom, Sweden, Australia, New Zealand, Denmark, India, Malaysia, and Thailand. Politicians' close relationships with the electric utilities resemble similar relationships in many other democratic, industrialized nations like the United States and Germany. The tensions and transitions in electric utilities' relationships with safety and economic regulators also reflect trajectories in other nations. Japan's lack of indigenous fossil fuel resources also enables this book's analysis to offer insights for other nations facing a similar challenge.

What, then, can we learn from Japan's energy system narrative over the past 50 years, since the oil crises of the 1970s? This book derives lessons on ways to turn shocks into opportunities for policy innovation, build resilience into energy systems, and promote stakeholder collaboration on innovation that enables incremental or dramatic transitions out of unsustainable energy systems. The book also applies these lessons to the broader context of resilience in the food-energy-water-climate nexus.

Key Concepts

This book's analysis employs several key concepts pertinent to shocks and stakeholder relationships. Defining them here will help to ensure that we are speaking the same language when we refer to cooperation and conflict, power balance or clout, and energy policymaking and processes. An explanation of various types of energy system resilience appears in the next chapter.

Cooperation and Conflict

Existing studies often frame stakeholder relationships as characterized by cooperation and/or conflict. These studies generally use the term "cooperation" to describe various stakeholder groups' coordination or collaboration on policy action, and conflict to describe lack of such coordination. Existing studies also identify trust in stakeholder relationships as a major underlying factor determining cooperation (e.g., Farrell, 2004, 2005; Gillebo and Francis, 2006; Pirson and Malhotra, 2007; Farrell, 2009; Aldrich, 2013; Abbas et al., 2014; Parkins et al., 2017). In particular, trust comprises a major component of public cooperation with changes in government policies and can precipitate changes in policymaking processes. Cooperation between government agencies and electric utilities includes trust but also transcends it to include direct collaboration and consultation on policy development. As a result, in this study, government cooperation with the public and the electric utilities is measured by a combined factor of trust and level of coordination on energy policies. Conversely, conflict is measured by lack of trust and lack of coordination on government policies.

Power Balance/Clout

In addition to cooperation, existing studies of stakeholder relationships and advocacy coalitions also highlight power balances between groups, or relative clout of these groups, as a factor affecting policy change. These studies reflect the notion that shifts in power balance or clout resulting from a shock, or other catalyzing event may alter policy outcomes differently than economic considerations alone would suggest. Some energy policy studies have incorporated this concept of stakeholder clout, particularly as it applies to shifts out of existing energy systems (e.g., Birkland, 1997; Hirsh and Sovacool, 2006; Stefes and Laird, 2010; Aklin and Urpelainen, 2011, 2018). While these studies do not measure power balance/clout directly, they establish a precedent for including it as a factor representing relationship change that affects energy policy.

This book analyzes qualitative interview data to determine shifts in relationship power balance or clout. Since the term "power" appears frequently in this book in the context of electricity, the term "clout" will be used in assessing relative influence of government subgroups versus the electric utilities and the government versus the public. Clout is measured by the amount of input the public and electric utilities have on government policies, either through formal channels or informally.

In this book, per Figure 1.4 below, relationships are measured in terms of cooperation and conflict using a four-point scale developed for this study: conflict, conflict outweighs cooperation, cooperation outweighs conflict, and cooperation. Relationship power balance or clout is measured on a three-point scale developed for this study: electric utility and/or public clout over the government, equal power, and government clout over electric utilities and/or the public. Qualitative assessment of the interview data determines placement on the scale.[6]

Energy Policies and Policymaking Processes

This book examines the effects of shocks and stakeholder relationship shifts on energy system transitions, characterizing such transitions as changes in energy supply policies and energy policymaking processes. Policymaking processes

- **Cooperation vs. Conflict**

Conflict	Conflict > Cooperation	Conflict < Cooperation	Cooperation

- **Clout**

Government < Utilities/Public	=	Government > Utilities/Public

Figure 1.4 Scales to measure cooperation versus conflict and relative energy policymaking clout in government relationships with the electric utilities and the public (Sklarew, 2015).

analyzed here focus on the formal and informal roles of government entities, the electric utilities, and the public in development of energy supply policies and regulations. Analyzing changes to energy policies sheds light on energy system stasis and transformation. By also analyzing changes to policymaking processes, this study broadens an understanding of the ways in which shocks and relationship changes can impact energy systems, even when policies do not change. Structural changes to the government and electric utilities also can influence the energy policymaking process. Such changes include alteration of the electric utility industry structure, as well as shifts in energy policymaking and regulatory bodies. Accordingly, the analysis also includes changes to these structures. Analyzing whether changes in energy supply policies, policymaking processes, and structure occur also enables a more complex analysis of how stakeholder relationships can limit certain kinds of change while catalyzing others after a shock occurs.

Japan's Narrative: Shocks, Cooperation, Conflict, and Clout

Applying these concepts as defined here enables us to identify ways to promote stakeholder cooperation and innovation, mitigate conflict, and achieve diverse groups' energy system resilience goals. Thus, to answer the question of why catastrophic events don't trigger transitions away from the energy technologies involved, this book explores several subsidiary questions on the impact of stakeholder relationships on energy policy and policymaking processes. When relationships between government agencies, electric utility companies, and the public move from cooperation toward conflict, what happens to energy policy and policymaking after a shock such as a resource price spike or technological disaster? As clout shifts from one group to another, what happens? What role do these groups' resilience priorities play in relationship changes and policymaking? How do these relationship elements combine to affect changes in energy policy and the policy-making process? This book considers how the answers to these questions influence energy policy and the policymaking process.

Data Collection and Analysis Parameters

This book's analysis emerges from data collection that took place in Japan, including 80 interviews: 21 government or former government officials involved in energy policymaking, 23 executives from electric utility companies and affiliated energy organizations, 7 NGO or public interest group representatives identified by the government to represent public opinion and journalists covering public opinion, and 7 academics researching Japanese energy policymaking and public opinion. One-fourth of these interviews were conducted in Japanese, and the remainder of the interviews were conducted in both Japanese and English. Quotations that appear in the book preserve interviewees' original English statements where possible. Translations of interviewees' Japanese statements were confirmed and supplemented by interviewees' English recapitulations.

Government interviewees, referred to as "G" followed by a number to preserve anonymity, included current and former officials from the Ministry of Economy, Trade and Industry (METI); the Ministry of Environment (MOE); the Cabinet Office; the Japan Atomic Energy Commission (AEC); and the Japan Atomic Energy Agency (JAEA).

Members of the Diet – Japan's parliament – have become increasingly involved in Japanese energy policymaking during the period covered in this project. Thus, interviewees also included two Diet members with active influence on energy issues.

Electric utility interviewees, referred to as "I" followed by a number, included current and former executives from Tokyo Electric Power Company (TEPCO), Kansai Electric Power Company (KEPCO), Tohoku Electric Power Company, Chubu Electric Power Company, J-Power, and the Federation of Electric Power Companies of Japan (FEPC). Other energy industry interviewees included executives and officials from the Japan Atomic Industrial Forum (JAIF), and Japan Nuclear Fuel, Ltd. (JNFL), and the Research Institute for Innovative Technology for the Earth (RITE), as well as analysts from the Central Research Institute of Electric Power Industry CRIEPI), the Japan Electric Power Information Center (JEPIC), and the Institute for Energy Economics Japan (IEEJ).

NGO and media representatives, respectively referred to as "P" and "M" followed by a number, included journalists from three energy think tanks, one public interest group, and three major news outlets. Academic interviewees, referred to as "A" followed by a number, came from five well-known Japanese universities and two well-regarded research institutes.

Additional data analyzed includes Japanese documents from the periods just prior to and following the 1970s oil crises, the 1990s nuclear accidents, and the March 2011 Japanese nuclear disaster. These documents include public opinion polls on trust in the government before and after the three shocks, energy industry statements, and government documents such as policy statements and white papers on energy policy.

Parameters for Lessons Learned

Four research parameters shape the lessons emerging from this book's analysis. First, existing studies suggest that governmental relationships with electric utilities and the public can directly influence national energy policymaking and the possibility of change (e.g., Samuels, 1987; Verbong and Geels, 2007; Stenzel and Frenzel, 2008; Mah et al., 2017). Other studies suggest that government relationships with the media and manufacturing industry influence government relationships with the public and electric utilities. However, these studies indicate that government-media relations do not directly alter policymaking. They also suggest that the manufacturing sector typically competes or coordinates with, but has not typically trumped, the electric utilities for influence over energy policymaking (e.g., Vietor, 1987; Gamson and Modigliani, 1989; Walgrave et al., 2008; Sengers et al., 2010; Birkland, 2011; Heras-Saizarbitoria et al., 2011; Hess, 2019). The increasingly prominent role of IT firms and other large energy consumers in energy transitions over the past decade suggests the need to examine these stakeholders' relationships with governments,[7] but even these large energy users can gain useful insights from an analysis of government relationships with electric utilities and the public. Thus, this proposed book focuses on governmental relationships with electric utilities and the public, with brief discussion of media and manufacturing sector roles in the concluding chapter.

Data from the interviews demonstrated a need to subdivide the government into four groups to holistically understand relationships with the electric utilities: energy policymakers, politicians, economic regulators, and safety regulators. Energy policymakers include bureaucrats responsible for energy policy decisions. Politicians include elected officials involved in energy policymaking. Economic regulators are officials designated to handle the electricity market structure. Safety regulators are officials responsible for power plant and electricity grid safety. The interviews confirmed that the relationships of these groups with the electric utilities are not homogenous, and the differences impact changes to energy policy and policymaking processes.

Existing studies reflect the relative power of these groups in Japan's policymaking process (e.g., Samuels, 1987; Moe, 2012; Samuels, 2013; Sklarew, 2018). Policymakers in Japan's bureaucracy have both formal and informal relationships with the electric utilities. Both kinds of relationships directly affect energy policy changes, as well as process and structural changes, thus dominating changes to energy systems. Politicians' relationships with the electric utilities hold equal weight, since they influence energy policy directly through legislative changes, and they also indirectly impact energy policy by affecting policymakers' interactions with bureaucratic policymakers. Economic and safety regulators' relationships with the electric utilities affect energy system stasis or change, but their impact is bounded by policymakers' and politicians' dominance in policymaking. While policy processes and relationships between these groups in other nations may differ in various ways, we can derive relevant lessons from Japan's similar experiences with relationship shifts and shocks.

The interview data collected for this book confirms that intragovernmental relationships are intertwined with government relationships with the public and the energy sector. The book largely reserves the analysis of intragovernmental relationships as an important topic for future study. This said, it analyzes the relative power of these four groups' relationships with the electric utilities to determine the overall effect when the relationships yield conflicting influences on energy policymaking. Since the data also reflects the Japanese public's tendency to view the government as a monolithic entity, this book examines the public's relationship with the government as a whole, rather than with the three subgroups.

The data further demonstrates the importance of the government's relationship with the manufacturing sector, as well as the media's relationships with the government and the public. In providing a deep analysis of government relationships with the electric utilities and the public, this book does not deeply analyze governmental relationships with the manufacturing sector and the media, and their inclusion would provide even a deeper understanding of the complex interactions between stakeholder relationships and catastrophic events in promoting energy system change toward resilience and innovation.

Second, media sources in Japan have political affiliations that can bias their poll data. To correct for this internal validity challenge, poll results from the source cited in the book were cross-checked with data from media organizations with different political affiliations.

Third, the study features historical grounding in events occurring in the 1970s through early 2000s, allowing us to draw lessons from these events and the periods following them. However, the most recent lessons may evolve due to continued shifts in governmental, private sector, and public relationships and positions in the aftermath of the Fukushima disaster.

Finally, understanding how economic and safety considerations influence stakeholder relationships' role in energy policy entrenchment and change constitutes an important element of the study. Interview questions thus probed the roles of efficiency, cost, and safety as values that contribute to energy policy developments.

Book Overview

The second chapter of this book places Japan's narrative in a broader geographical and historical context by providing an overview of other studies of the framing concepts for this analysis: energy system lock-in, the roles of shocks and stakeholder relationship changes in breaking system lock-in, cooperation and clout in stakeholder relationships, resilience definitions, and shocks and relationships' combined effects on innovation and resilience. This broader framing helps us to connect globally to the concepts and frameworks examined through Japan's lens and apply Japan's universal lessons for promoting cooperation toward energy system resilience and innovation.

Chapters three, four, and five describe how shocks and stakeholder relationships have affected Japan's energy policy and policymaking processes from the time of the oil crises through the aftermath of the Fukushima nuclear disaster. Chapter three examines this effect after the 1970s oil crises, establishing a foundation for chapter four, which analyzes the series of nuclear accidents and a scandal that took place during the 1990s and early 2000s. This chapter connects the patterns from the post-oil crises era with the trends during this period and explains how they contributed to the chapter on the Fukushima disaster. Chapter five examines the roles of the Fukushima nuclear disaster and institutional relationships in defining policy and policymaking process change and stasis. These pieces of Japan's narrative provide tangible examples of stakeholder cooperation and conflict, clout, and their effects on energy system innovation and resilience.

The book's final chapter consolidates and links the conclusions from chapters three, four, and five into a unified narrative and offers broader lessons for cooperation on energy system resilience and innovation. These lessons center on innovating from disasters, building resilience into energy systems, and innovating out of problematic or unsustainable energy systems. The conclusions also explore how Japan's narrative on the roles of stakeholder relationships and shocks may provide lessons and implications for nations' energy system resilience and innovation after the COVID-19 pandemic. Finally, the conclusions examine applications of these lessons to the broader context of resilience in the food-energy-water-climate nexus.

Notes

1 Shocks are defined here as focusing events such as crises, catastrophic events, or disasters, in accordance with the vast bodies of literature on shocks, as well as work based on John Kingdon's concept of focusing events. For examples, see Frank Baumgartner and Bryan Jones, 1993; John Kingdon, 1997; Thomas Birkland, 1997; Christoph Stefes and Frank Laird, 2010; Michael Aklin and Johannes Urperlainen, 2018.
2 Amory Lovins' work has raised the issue of energy system resilience for decades, starting with his article in *Foreign Affairs* in 1976. See Amory Lovins, 1976.
3 See Haimes, 2009; National Academies, 2012; Gasser et al., 2019.
4 See Department of Energy, Government of the United States. History of the Strategic Petroleum Reserve. www.energy.gov/articles/history-strategic-petroleum-reserve
5 For Ukraine's nuclear energy supply and policy trends, see World Nuclear Association. Nuclear Power in Ukraine. www.world-nuclear.org/information-library/country-profiles/countries-t-z/ukraine.aspx; and International Energy Agency, 2020, Ukraine Energy Profile www.iea.org/reports/ukraine-energy-profile.
6 Analysis of the data consisted of coding the initial interviews for themes that guided the secondary interviews. To formulate systematic responses to project research questions, analysis identified data trends across all interviews. Conclusions were based on analysis of the complete data set for each case and across all three time periods to create a holistic narrative.
7 See, for example, Hess, 2018.

References

Abbas, N., van der Molen, I., Nader, M., and Lovitt, J. (2014) 'Trust and Cooperation Relations in Environmental Management of Lebanon.' *European Scientific Journal*, 2 (June), 274–284.

Aklin, M., and Urpelainen, J. (2011) 'The Strategy of Sustainable Energy Transitions: Political Competition and Path Dependence.' *SSRN eLibrary*, February. http://papers.ssrn.com/sol3/papers.cfm?abstract_id=1754742.

Aklin, M., and Urperlainen, J. (2018) *Renewables: The Politics of a Global Energy Transition*. Cambridge, MA: MIT Press.

Aldrich, D. (2013) 'Rethinking Civil Society – State Relations in Japan After the Fukushima Accident.' *Polity*, 45, 249–264.

Baumgartner, F.R., and Jones, B.D. (1993) *Agendas and Instability in American Politics*. 1st ed. Chicago, IL: University of Chicago Press.

Birkland, T.A. (1997) *After Disaster: Agenda Setting, Public Policy, and Focusing Events*. Washington, DC: Georgetown University Press.

Birkland, T.A. (2011) *An Introduction to the Policy Process*. Armonk, NY: M.E. Sharpe.

Department of Energy, Government of the United States. 'History of the Strategic Petroleum Reserve.' www.energy.gov/articles/history-strategic-petroleum-reserve.

Farrell, H. (2004) 'Trust, Distrust and Power.' In Hardin, R. (ed.), *Distrust*. New York: Russell Sage Foundation.

Farrell, H. (2005) 'Trust and Political Economy: Institutions and the Sources of Inter-Firm Cooperation.' *Comparative Political Studies*, June, 459–493.

Farrell, H. (2009) *The Political Economy of Trust Institutions, Interests, and Inter-Firm Cooperation in Italy and Germany*. Cambridge: Cambridge University Press.

Gamson, W., and Modigliani, A. (1989) 'Media Discourse and Public Opinion on Nuclear Power: A Constructionist Approach.' *American Journal of Sociology*, 95 (1), 1–37.

Gasser, P., Lustenberger, P., Cinelli, M., Kim, W., Spada, M., Burgherr, P., Hirschberg, S., Stojadinovic, B., and Sun, T.Y. (2019) 'A review on resilience assessment of energy systems.' *Sustainable and Resilient Infrastructure*, 6 (5), 273–299.

Gillebo, T., and Francis, C. (2006) 'Stakeholder Cooperation in Sustainable Development: Three Case Studies in Norway.' *Journal of Rural and Community Development*, 2 (1), 28–43.

Haimes, Y. (2009) 'On the Definition of Resilience in Systems.' *Risk Analysis*, 29 (4), 498–501.

Heras-Saizarbitoria, I., Cilleruelob, E., and Zamanillob, I. (2011) 'Public Acceptance of Renewables and the Media: An Analysis of the Spanish PV Solar Experience.' *Renewable and Sustainable Energy Reviews*, 15 (9), 4685–4696.

Hess, D. (2018) 'Energy Democracy and Social Movements: A Multi-Coalition Perspective on the Politics of Sustainability Transitions.' *Energy Research & Social Science*, 40, 177–189.

Hess, D. (2019) 'Coalitions, Framing, and the Politics of Energy Transitions: Local Democracy and Community Choice in California.' *Energy Research & Social Science*, 50 (April), 38–50.

Hirsh, R., and Sovacool, B. (2006) 'Technological Systems and Momentum Change: American Electric Utilities, Restructuring, and Distributed Generation Technologies.' *The Journal of Technology Studies*, 32 (2), 72–85.

International Energy Agency. (2020) 'Ukraine Energy Profile.' www.iea.org/reports/ukraine-energy-profile.

Kingdon, J.W. (1997) *Agendas, Alternatives, and Public Policies*. 2nd ed. New York: Addison-Wesley Educational Publishers, Inc.

Lovins, A. (1976) 'Energy Strategy: The Road Not Taken.' *Foreign Affairs*, October, 65–96.

Mah, D.N.Y., Wu, Y.Y., and Hills, P.H. (2017) 'Explaining the Role of Incumbent Utilities in Sustainable Energy Transitions: A Case Study of the Smart Grid Development in China.' *Energy Policy*, 109 (October), 794–806.

Moe, Espen. (2012) 'Vested Interests, Energy Efficiency and Renewables in Japan.' *Energy Policy*, 40 (January), 260–273.

National Academies. (2012) *Disaster Resilience: A National Imperative*. Washington, DC: The National Academies Press. www.nap.edu/catalog/13457/disaster-resilience-a-national-imperative.

Parkins, J.R., Beckley, T., Comeau, L., Stedman, R.C., Rollins, C.L., and Kessler, A. (2017) Can Distrust Enhance Public Engagement? Insights from a National Survey on Energy Issues in Canada. *Society & Natural Resources*, 30 (8), 934–948.

Pirson, M., and Malhotra, D. (2007) 'What Matters to Whom? Managing Trust Across Multiple Stakeholder Groups, Working Paper No. 39.' The Hauser Center for Nonprofit Organizations, Harvard University.

Samuels, R.J. (1987) *The Business of the Japanese State: Energy Markets in Comparative and Historical Perspective*. Ithaca, NY: Cornell University Press.

Samuels, R.J. (2013) *3.11: Disaster and Change in Japan*. 1st ed. Ithaca, NY: Cornell University Press.

Sengers, F., Raven, R.P.J.M., and Van Venrooij, A. (2010) 'From Riches to Rags: Biofuels, Media Discourses, and Resistance to Sustainable Energy Technologies.' *Energy Policy*, 38 (9), 5013–5027.

Sklarew, J.F. (2015) *Shock to the System: How Catastrophic Events and Institutional Relationships Impact Japanese Energy Policymaking, Resilience, and Innovation*. Arlington, VA: George Mason University.

Sklarew, J.F. (2018) 'Power Fluctuations: How Japan's Nuclear Infrastructure Priorities Influence Electric Utilities' Clout.' *Energy Research & Social Science*, 41 (July), 158–167.

Stefes, C., and Laird, F.N. (2010) 'Creating Path Dependency: The Divergence of German and U.S. Renewable Energy Policy.' *SSRN eLibrary*, August.

Stenzel, T., and Frenzel, A. (2008) 'Regulating Technological Change – The Strategic Reactions of Utility Companies Towards Subsidy Policies in the German, Spanish, and UK Electricity Markets.' *Energy Policy*, 36 (7), 2645–2657.

Verbong, G., and Geels, F.W. (2007) 'The Ongoing Energy Transition: Lessons From a Socio-Technical, Multi-Level Analysis of the Dutch Electricity System (1960–2004).' *Energy Policy*, 35, 1025–1037.

Vietor, R. (1987) *Energy Policy in America Since 1945: A Study of Business-Government Relations*. Cambridge: Cambridge University Press.

Walgrave, S., Soroka, S., and Nuytemans, M. (2008) 'The Mass Media's Political Agenda-Setting Power: A Longitudinal Analysis of Media, Parliament, and Government in Belgium (1993 to 2000).' *Comparative Political Studies*, 41 (6), 814–836.

World Nuclear Association. Nuclear Power in Ukraine. www.world-nuclear.org/information-library/country-profiles/countries-t-z/ukraine.aspx.

2 Framing Concepts
Energy System Lock-In, Shocks, Stakeholders, and Resilience

Existing studies of energy system lock-in and factors that can break it provide relevant concepts and context for the analysis of Japan's trajectory and its lessons for cooperation on energy system innovation and resilience. These studies generally comprise three categories. One of them focuses on the factors that contribute to energy system lock-in. The second set addresses the role of shocks, or catastrophic events, in disrupting entrenched systems. The third set of studies examines institutional or stakeholder relationships – including changes in cooperation and clout – as a factor in energy system development and change. To build resilient energy systems, we need to understand how catastrophic events and stakeholder relationships affect one another. We also need to recognize their combined influence on energy transitions, resilience, and innovation. The concepts we will define here and apply to Japan's case include energy system lock-in or path dependence and the factors contributing to it: reliance on infrastructure, interrelatedness and complexity, institutional support, momentum, and uncertainty and risk. We also will define factors that can break such lock-in. These factors include critical junctures, focusing events, disasters, crises, and power balance. Finally, we will examine the diverse definitions of the concept of resilience.

Energy System Lock-In

Historical sociologists, political scientists, innovation systems theorists, and energy system theorists all examine the roles of actors, institutions, and organizations in creating lock-in. This work collectively suggests that certain features of energy systems make them prone to lock-in. As mentioned, these features include reliance on infrastructure, interrelatedness and complexity, institutional support, momentum, and uncertainty and risk. We will examine each of these features briefly, applying them later to the analysis of Japan's narrative.

Many studies observe that infrastructures that develop around large systems promote lock-in of existing technologies (e.g., see Hughes, 1987; Hughes, 1993; Berkhout, 2002; Foxon, 2007; Markard and Truffer, 2006; van der Vooren and Alkemade, 2011; Lovio et al., 2011). In his extensive research on energy system transitions, interdisciplinary scientist Vaclav Smil describes this feature as inertia

DOI: 10.4324/9781003227588-2

(Smil, 2010, 2016). Smil observes that the need to recoup infrastructure investments discourages transitions to other technologies, especially those that may require investment in new infrastructure. Smil and others explain that such infrastructure development designed around existing technologies also creates barriers to new technologies that are incompatible with the existing infrastructure (Kemp, 1994; Foxon, 2007; van der Vooren and Alkemade, 2011; Smil, 2016). The most frequently cited examples emerge from transportation and energy systems, including automobile and railroad infrastructure, as well as nuclear, coal and hydropower generation, and transmission infrastructure. Some studies frame this infrastructure accumulation as redundancy that comprises an element of system resilience (e.g., Molyneaux et al., 2016). Infrastructure thus represents both a requirement for resilience and an inhibitor to change when shocks occur.

Energy system and electricity production analysts observe that large investments in energy systems infrastructure, including power plant construction and connections to electricity transmission and distribution grids, create vested interests in perpetuating an existing system (e.g., Kemp, 1994; Lovio et al., 2011; Moe, 2012; Sklarew, 2018). These vested interests prioritize returns on investment, posing challenges for changes that may result in stranded assets or infrastructure cost increases.

Infrastructure investment contributions to system lock-in are linked to a related factor: interdependence within systems. A number of studies attribute energy system lock-in, especially in electricity production systems, to the interdependence of components, organizations, and institutions in these systems (e.g., Unruh, 2000; Markard and Truffer, 2006; Lovio et al., 2011). They describe network effects resulting from system interrelationships, which make system change more difficult since a shift in one part of a system necessitates changes in other components of the network. In their study of energy system resilience, Molyneaux et al. frame this connectedness as a contributor to system integrity or efficiency that minimizes responses to external fluctuations (Molyneaux et al., 2016). They observe that this same efficiency can contribute to system resilience. They further describe the tendency toward incremental system change in uncertain environments such as when shocks occur (Molyneaux et al., 2016). Gregory Unruh connects the depiction of the coevolution of technological systems and institutions with lock-in of fossil fuel use in energy systems, as well as the network of systems that utilize energy. He describes interactions between technologies, organizations, and institutions that create path dependence in a carbon-based energy system (Unruh, 2000). Research on innovation processes in energy systems also links interdependence with system path dependence. Markard and Truffer note that interdependent components and organizations within electricity production systems lead innovation processes in these systems toward the incremental rather than the radical (Markard and Truffer, 2006). In their analyses of fossil fuel lock-in, Unruh, Berkhout, and Lovio et al. come to similar conclusions regarding the possibility of system change and the rate of such change (e.g., Unruh, 2000; Berkhout, 2002; Lovio et al., 2011). Smil discusses energy system complexity as a key factor behind system inertia, asserting that in "complex energy systems the most important inertial considerations are not only the cost of existing set-ups but also their scale and complexity, as well as the predictability and reliability of prevailing arrangements" (Smil, 2016). This slow rate of change in energy systems and electricity production subsystems thus is linked to risk and uncertainty, with implications not only for system growth and momentum, but also for shifts in the direction of energy systems and innovation.

Much of the discussion on lock-in or path dependence in institutions and technological systems suggests that they combine to form interlinked technological and institutional lock-in (e.g., Pierson, 2004; Unruh, 2000, 2002; Foxon, 2007; Nelson and Sampat, 2001; Musiolik and Markard, 2011; Sklarew, 2018; Trencher et al., 2020). Some studies posit that the energy sector is particularly susceptible to such coevolution of technological and institutional systems, due to its dependence on infrastructure and public goods (e.g., Unruh, 2000; Foxon, 2007; van der Vooren and Alkemade, 2011; Seto et al., 2016; Sklarew, 2018). The development of civilian nuclear power programs by different nations such as the United Kingdom, France, and Japan reflect this notion of lock-in that results from combined interactions between technological systems and governing institutions. Existing studies suggest that governmental support policies reinforced the dominance of nuclear power in these nations' energy portfolios (e.g., Cowan, 1990; Delmas and Heiman, 2001; Sanden and Azar, 2005; Hymans, 2011; Kingston, 2014; Sklarew, 2018). Other studies have focused on the same coevolution of fossil fuels (e.g., Unruh, 2000, 2002; Perkins, 2003; Sanden, 2004). While many studies cite these interrelated technological and institutional frameworks as barriers to renewables development, some have countered that such tandem frameworks for renewables have yielded success (Jacobsson and Bergek, 2004; Sanden and Azar, 2005).

Institutional support also can lead an energy system toward lock-in. Existing studies suggest that institutional policies can override market forces such as efficiency, which might otherwise limit expansion of an energy system. Robin Cowan's study of the light water reactor's (LWR) ascension to global dominance in the nuclear power sector serves as an example of this phenomenon. Cowan attributes the LWR's worldwide dominance largely to U.S. government subsidies intended to promote the developing technology over other domestic and overseas technologies (Cowan, 1990). My prior work on Japanese energy infrastructure prioritization and resilience finds that governments' framing of energy system goals can promote infrastructure investment in ways that either hinder or create flexibility for future infrastructure adjustments and technology shifts (Sklarew, 2018).

Aligning with these studies' findings on the role of institutional support in energy system lock-in, the framework of historical institutionalism posits that policies and institutions can generate positive feedback in systems. In their comparison of German and U.S. policy environments for renewables transitions, Christoph Stefes and Frank Laird describe positive feedback as "a circumstance in which groups and individuals involved in that policy get more benefits the longer the policy stays in place and the more deeply it is entrenched," generating incentives to perpetuate it (Stefes and Laird, 2010, 7). This dynamic can lead to system entrenchment.

Staffan Jacobsson and Anna Bergek cite legitimization of a new technology as a key to its success or failure. Recognition of the legitimacy of institutional support for an existing technology can prevent new technological systems from emerging. They offer the example of institutional support for nuclear power in Sweden as a reason for relatively poor legitimization of renewable energy. In contrast, German opposition to nuclear power enabled legitimization of and institutional support for renewable energy, contributing to development of a renewable energy system (Jacobsson and Bergek, 2004, 826). Institutional support mechanisms involve advocates that generate and perpetuate them. Various studies refer to these advocates by different terms, including sponsors, advocacy coalitions, and supporters (e.g., Westrum, 1991; Sabatier, 1988; Birkland, 1997). Sociologist Ron Westrum observes that such support is necessary for successful adoption of a technology, and it also shapes the development of the system that surrounds it.

Technology historian Thomas Hughes suggests that energy system momentum combines with interrelatedness with other systems to perpetuate system continuity (Hughes, 1987). As systems absorb elements of their environment, reducing system uncertainty, these expanding, influenced networks of actors, technologies, and processes contribute to system perpetuation. Again, the energy sector serves as a widely cited example. A number of studies by Hughes and others examine the U.S. electric utility system as an example of momentum (e.g., Hughes, 1993; Hirsh and Sovacool, 2006). The development of incremental technologies such as improved steam turbine components and alternating current (AC) technologies contributed to electric utility system momentum. In addition, institutional mechanisms such as creation of regulatory oversight of utilities also played a role (Hirsh and Sovacool, 2006). Unruh links system interrelatedness, institutional support, and positive feedback to momentum. He observes that increasing returns to technologies and institutions that support them can lead to rapid expansion and entrenchment of the technological system they create (Unruh, 2000, 2002).

Historical institutionalism applies the concepts of sequencing and institutional change to explain institutional and policy lock-in, as well as occasional change. Creation of particular institutions at specific points in a system trajectory contributes to the paths these systems follow. Paul Pierson explains that the sequencing of processes can impact whether future options are removed from political possibility (Pierson, 2004, 12). The order of events thus takes precedence over their size in shaping processes, and small events early in a sequence can have a greater impact on the future than dramatic events occurring later. Studies by historical institutionalists such as Peter Hall, Kathleen Thelen, and James Mahoney build on this idea, positing that inefficient paths can result from earlier choices (Hall and Thelen, 2009; Mahoney and Thelen, 2009).[1] As systems build around technologies, problems that arise later in the life of a technology are less likely to result in termination of the technology and the system around it. This idea suggests that while technological safety and efficiency issues contribute to initial decisions on development of a technology, as systems grow around the technology, safety, and efficiency problems arising once a system is established are unlikely to derail the system entirely.

An array of empirical examples suggests that as reduced uncertainty reinforces investments in a technology and promotes its expanded use, it also leads to less emphasis on risks, including safety risks (e.g., Hughes, 1987; Cowan, 1990; Unruh, 2000; Sanden and Azar, 2005; Lovio et al., 2011; Smil, 2016). Institutions play a role in reducing uncertainty, and they also can reinforce existing risk perceptions. In their study of the U.S. electric utility system, Hirsh and Sovacool highlight the rule of regulatory oversight in reducing uncertainty for the electric utilities (Hirsh and Sovacool, 2006).[2] Unruh offers the case of electric utility regulators' tendency for risk averseness based on fear of blackouts. He posits that this fear leads to investment in dominant power supply and plant technology designs rather than potentially riskier alternatives (Unruh, 2000, 825). When perceptions of increased risk arise from shocks to such incumbent energy systems, governments may opt to make incremental changes within the system, rather than face the uncertainty of dramatic transformation. Kishimoto describes such internal system modifications during the same periods analyzed in this book (Kishimoto, 2017).

Since technological systems emerge from and coevolve from the societies that generate them, these energy system traits – reliance on infrastructure, interrelatedness and complexity, institutional support, momentum, and uncertainty and risk – that contribute to lock-in manifest themselves differently across societies. While many empirical studies of energy system lock-in reference these drivers, few examine how they influence responses to shocks that might otherwise break system lock-in. In this book, we will examine this phenomenon and its implications for energy system resilience and innovation.

Breaking Energy System Lock-In

We can better understand Japan's energy system trajectory and the roles of the aforementioned drivers if we first examine highlights from prior studies identifying factors that can break energy system lock-in. Studies of disruptions in entrenched systems examine the nature of critical junctures that can destabilize energy systems. Political scientists Ruth Berins Collier and David Collier define a critical juncture as a "period of significant change, which typically occurs in distinct ways in different countries . . . and which is hypothesized to produce distinct legacies" (Collier and Collier, 1991, 29). Political scientists John Kingdon and Thomas Birkland frame critical junctures as events that galvanize the policy community to consider change (Kingdon, 1997; Birkland, 1997). Political scientist Paul Pierson depicts critical junctures as "critical moments or junctures that shape the basic contours of social life" (Pierson, 2004, 18–19). Such junctures, which emerge from a confluence of exogenous and endogenous factors, can move policies toward lock-in or break it.[3]

Building on the ideas proposed by Kingdon and Pierson, a number of studies define critical junctures as periods of opportunity for changes to policy paths, which can break existing path dependencies or lead to new ones (e.g., Yoshimatsu, 2014; Eikeland and Inderberg, 2016). These studies generally focus on the role of either external shocks or incremental changes in institutions or stakeholder relationships in fomenting system shifts when critical junctures occur. Examined alone, these two factors each partially explain how to break energy system lock-in, as recognized by some studies (e.g., Hogan, 2019). In this book, analyzing both external shocks and shifts in stakeholder relationships as factors behind system change offers a more holistic view of how energy system stasis, incremental change, and transformation occur.

The Role of Shocks

One set of studies addresses the role of shocks or catastrophic events in breaking system lock-in. These analyses include duration of such shocks and timing of policy responses to them as factors that influence system change. The concept of focusing events initiated by Kingdon, and elaborated upon by Birkland and others, involves exogenous shocks that occur during brief time periods, providing a catalyst for change. Kingdon depicts focusing events such as crises or disasters as mechanisms that push problems to the forefront, opening "policy windows" that can lead to policy change. Disasters, which Birkland defines as sudden, catastrophic events that reach the public and the policy world at the same time, can serve as focusing events or trigger critical junctures.

In contrast, crises, which emerge from within organizations, build over time. Birkland explains, "A crisis can be internally generated or it can be the result of a disaster or some other undesirable event that strains an organization's adaptive capacity" (Birkland, 2006, 5). When an organization is adequately prepared for potentially disastrous events, disasters may not result in crises. In his examination of large technological systems, Hughes describes a similar "confluence of contingency, catastrophe and conversion" that can alter system momentum (Hughes, 1987, 470–471). Kingdon and Birkland describe how shocks serve as focusing events that can become critical junctures when they succeed in spurring the policy community to consider change (Kingdon, 1997; Birkland, 1997).

Birkland develops a framework for examining why certain events are focal and how their effects can vary across seemingly similar policy domains. The framework analyzes the features of events that determine how focal they become, including suddenness, rarity, level of impact on the public, and timing of public and policy maker awareness of the event. Birkland examines large oil spills and serious nuclear power plant accidents as examples of sudden, rare events that significantly impact the public and are not easily concealed. These characteristics make these events focal, sparking "mobilization of bias" to drive communities toward policy change (Birkland, 1997, 79). Birkland suggests that significant human-induced events such as large oil spills can accelerate long-term social change, which influences policy change. He describes the focal power of an oil spill as an attention driver that expands interest and concern, alters the status quo opposition to strict environmental regulation, and offers a window of opportunity for an organized environmental community to push for new policies. Examining the case of the Exxon Valdez oil spill, Birkland observes that it garnered significant Congressional and public attention, which led to policy change within 18 months, after nearly 14 years of deadlock on revision of oil pollution laws. House of Representatives members preferred a uniform national law, while members of the Senate supported individual state laws. The Exxon Valdez spill broke the legislative stalemate and enabled federal legislation that included a compromise between the House and Senate positions (Birkland, 1997). Other examples of manmade disasters that have led to public policy change include the levee flooding from Hurricane Katrina and the Three-Mile Island nuclear accident.

Studies of the policy process and lock-in by Birkland and others suggest that focusing events alone may not engender policy action, and action from within the policy community must support the effect of such events in order to make them focal (e.g., Baumgartner and Jones, 1993; Kingdon, 1997; Birkland, 1997; Stefes and Laird, 2010). Birkland highlights the degree of organization and polarization within the policy community as factors affecting the impact of focusing events on policy change. Baumgartner and Jones posit that changes in policy images and/or realignment of institutional jurisdiction over an issue can destabilize policy equilibrium. Birkland suggests that human-induced disasters such as oil spill are more likely to galvanize policy entrepreneurs opposed to existing policy, rather than defenders of the status quo (Birkland, 1997). Supporters of policy change capitalize on issue expansion, while defenders of the status quo rely on issue containment to minimize the need for policy change. Birkland observes that Exxon failed to tell its story quickly enough after the Exxon-Valdez oil spill, and attempts to minimize the spill and reassign blame backfired. TEPCO's belated efforts to explain the Fukushima Daiichi nuclear disaster met a similar fate. In studies of renewables development in the United States, Denmark, Germany, France, the United Kingdom, Spain, China, and India, political scientists Michael Aklin and Johannes Urpelainen assert that shocks can foment policy changes over a long time period (Aklin and Urpelainen, 2018).

While these observations help to explain the transformative power of exogenous shocks, little to no scholarship exists on institutional features that limit the ability of exogenous shocks, even those that meet the criteria for focusing events, to break lock-in. Such studies would help to explain why shocks do not always lead to energy system transformation. This book serves as one such study.

The Role of Stakeholder Relationship Changes: Cooperation and Power Balance

Studies that examine stakeholder relationship changes as a factor in energy system development and change can shed light on the ability of shocks to break system lock-in. Existing studies often characterize stakeholder relationships as featuring a balance of cooperation and conflict, as well as power or clout. These balances affect how these relationships impact system entrenchment and collapse. Examining how these stakeholder relationships and external shocks combine to contribute to development and deterioration of lock-in in the energy sector can illuminate some of the puzzling inertia emerging aftershocks that seem likely to catalyze innovation and system transformation to improve resilience.

Studies grounded in comparative politics, historical institutionalism, and innovation systems theory suggest that institutions influence strategic interaction between system actors. Institutions thus can serve as constraints, but system actors can turn them into supportive structures, and internal forces can elicit incremental institutional change (Hall and Thelen, 2009; Mahoney and Thelen, 2009).[4] Institutions' positive or negative impact on system lock-in features such as infrastructure, interrelatedness and complexity, institutional support, momentum, and uncertainty and risk can determine whether lock-in is preserved or broken. For example, Jacobsson and Bergek mention the role of institutions in fostering infrastructure and interrelatedness of energy systems in Germany, Sweden, and the Netherlands. They also cite failure of institutional support for a shift as a reason for continued lock-in (Jacobsson and Bergek, 2004). Unruh cites institutional influence on expectations and uncertainty as a driver behind technological system stasis or change (Unruh, 2000).

Some studies suggest that institutional structures and government priorities can combine to form a national energy policy that can support or alter an energy system (e.g., Hughes, 1993; Pierson, 2004; Jacobsson and Bergek, 2004; Verbong and Geels, 2007; Hall and Thelen, 2009; Karatayev et al., 2016; Sklarew, 2018). For example, Verbong and Geels describe how the government prioritized energy saving over renewables development in crafting the Dutch electricity system (Verbong and Frank Geels, 2007). Karatayev et al. explain how policy and regulatory frameworks focused on continued support for fossil fuels inhibit achievement of renewables deployment targets in Kazakhstan (Karatayev et al., 2016). My own prior study of Japanese energy policymaking explains how the Japanese government's prioritization of nuclear energy infrastructure created vested interests that shaped national energy and electricity market policies (Sklarew, 2018).

Prior studies of Japanese energy policy also indicate the role of government priorities as drivers that affect the direction of policy change in response to shocks (e.g., Valentine and Sovacool, 2010; Duffield and Woodall, 2011; Moe, 2012; Sklarew, 2015). These works mention how the Japanese government's priorities impacted energy policy responses to particular shocks or institutional shifts. They also reference either shocks or stakeholder relationships as forces behind policy development (e.g., Morse, 1981; Kohl, 1982; Samuels, 1987; Cohen et al., 1995; Pickett, 2002; Valentine and Sovacool, 2010; Hymans, 2021). This book joins these works in analyzing Japan's energy policy development as shaped by both exogenous shocks and stakeholder relationships. In particular, it builds on Richard Samuels' historical account of the institutional relationships influencing Japanese energy policy development from the end of World War II through the oil shocks period (Samuels, 1987) and later work examining the Fukushima Disaster (Samuels, 2013). This book's analysis and lessons also will expand on my own prior work, which examines how the Japanese government's priorities have contributed to changes in utility clout, influencing energy system change aftershocks (Sklarew, 2018).

Existing studies of institutional and inter-organizational relationships describe cooperation between stakeholder groups and relative power balances between them as factors affecting the nature and influence of these relationships (e.g., Baumgartner and Jones, 1993; Orru, 1993; Berardo and Scholtz, 2010; Lubell et al., 2010; Birkland, 2011; Peters, 2012; Yarahmadi and Higgins, 2012).

Analyses of stakeholder relationships often frame them as characterized by cooperation and/or conflict. These works generally use the term "cooperation" to describe inter-institutional coordination or collaboration on policy action. Mainstream theoretical and empirical work analyzing cooperation has highlighted trust between groups as a major underlying factor determining cooperation (e.g., Farrell, 2004, 2005; Gillebo and Francis, 2006; Pirson and Malhotra, 2007; Farrell, 2009; Abbas et al., 2014).

Studies of stakeholder power balance include literature on advocacy coalitions, a framework developed by Paul Sabatier and Hank Jenkins-Smith (Sabatier, 1988). The advocacy coalitions framework (ACF) they created defines advocacy coalitions as groups of policy participants who "share similar policy core beliefs" and "engage in nontrivial degree of coordination" (Weible and Sabatier, 2007). Some of the studies applying the ACF examine the impact of advocacy coalitions on energy policymaking (e.g., Hsu, 2005; Jacobsson and Lauber, 2006; Nohrstedt, 2008; Nohrstedt, 2009; Markard et al., 2016; Sklarew, 2018). A subset of these studies explores the role of advocacy coalitions aftershocks occur (Markard, 2016; Sklarew, 2018). In one such study, Markard et al. find that stable pro-economy and pro-ecology advocacy coalitions in Switzerland since 2000 contributed to a lack of policy change, despite the government's proposed nuclear phase-out following the Fukushima nuclear disaster. As described in Chapters 4 and 5, my own prior analysis of Japanese energy policymaking finds that the coalition supporting nuclear power did not shift or lose power after a series of accidents and a scandal that occurred in the 1990s–2000s. The much larger shock associated with the Fukushima disaster did disrupt this pro-nuclear coalition, but other factors have complicated the prospects for an energy system transition (Sklarew, 2018). Some theoretical and empirical studies of institutional relationships emphasize the importance of considering power balances that may produce different outcomes than economic considerations alone would suggest (e.g., Cumbers et al., 2003; Acemoglu and Robinson, 2008; Armstrong and Bernstein, 2008; Moe, 2010, 2017). For instance, in a comparative study of the United States, Denmark, Japan, Germany, and China, Espen Moe finds that coalition formation and vested interests explain fluctuations and variations in wind power installations. Studies of energy policy and institutions also incorporate the role of power balance, which some characterize as clout (e.g., see Birkland, 1997; Hirsh and Sovacool, 2006; Stefes and Laird, 2010; Aklin and Urpelainen, 2011; Zedan and Miller, 2017). In their comparative analysis of energy system shifts toward renewable energy, Stefes and Laird refer to "political clout" of the renewable energy industry in Germany, and lack thereof in the United States. Zedan and Miller identify stakeholder power as one of the key factors affecting energy efficiency in Australian buildings (Zedan and Miller, 2017).

Analyzing these two elements – cooperation versus conflict and power balance/clout – offers a holistic view of institutional relationships. This book thus will link these two criteria to determine the nature of changes in the institutional relationships examined, as well as their impact on energy system stasis and change aftershocks occur.

Cooperation, conflict, and clout in stakeholder relationships can hinge on the overlap and differences in perspectives across stakeholder groups. My prior work finds that these perspectives include definitions of energy system resilience (Sklarew, 2018).

Defining Energy System Resilience

As mentioned in the previous chapter, the generally accepted definition of resilience centers on a system's ability to absorb shocks and continue operating. Within this broad definition of system resilience, scholars, practitioners, and policymakers differ regarding the nuances. Examining some of these variations in perspectives on resilience characteristics can help us to better understand why different stakeholder groups may conflict over energy system resilience goals and related actions to address system disruptions.

In 1973, C.S. Holling framed the traditionally accepted definition of resilience, depicting a system's post-shock ability to resume normal operations as engineering resilience (Holling, 1973). Holling distinguishes this concept of engineering resilience, which focuses on system efficiency and a return to a prior stable state, from a second type of system resilience, which he terms "ecological resilience." Ecological resilience prioritizes preservation of system operations over system efficiency (Holling, 1996; Dalziel and McManus, 2004). Holling aligns ecological resilience with the unpredictability of complex adaptive systems. He further describes such systems' ability to absorb disturbances in ways that enable the system to continue functioning, but with the potential for various stable states rather than just one (Holling, 1973). Stakeholder cooperation and conflict can hinge on stakeholders' perspectives regarding the effects of these various stable states on stakeholder priorities and goals.

More recent studies that build on Holling's work divide system resilience into five categories: engineering, ecological, social, hybrid socio-ecological, and economic resilience (Gatto and Drago, 2020; Ahmadi et al., 2021). Molyneaux, et al describe these categories a bit differently, grouping them into ecological resilience, psychological resilience, risk management, energy security, and tolerance to attack (Molyneaux et al., 2016). Energy security includes elements that also could align with ecological, social, and economic resilience. Recognizing that resilience definitions may be divided into these various categories, which may overlap or conflict, can help us to examine how different stakeholder groups may prioritize some aspects of resilience over others.

Current studies' applications of engineering resilience focus on the return of system infrastructure to normal operations. A number of studies focus specifically on these technical aspects of energy system resilience (e.g., see Flynn, 2008; Roege et al., 2014; Liu and Bie, 2016; Gholami et al., 2018). Some studies equate engineering resilience with system robustness (e.g., Sharifi and Yamagata, 2016; Jesse et al., 2019). Critical infrastructure and supply chain resilience scholar Stephen Flynn identifies four factors required for resilient systems: robustness, resourcefulness, rapid recovery, and the ability to absorb lessons from shocks (Flynn, 2008).

Flynn's definition of robustness parallels many others' depictions (e.g., Shinozuka et al., 2004; Rees, 2010; Sharifi and Yamagata, 2016; Ahmadi et al., 2021), focusing on "the ability to keep operating or to stay standing in the face of disaster" (6). Flynn highlights the importance of substitutable or redundant systems for robust energy systems, as well as a need for investment in and maintenance of critical infrastructure to enable system survival of low probability, high consequence events (6). Flynn describes resourcefulness as the skills needed for disaster management, including prioritization of responses and communication of decisions to disaster responders (6). Resourcefulness is closely linked to rapid recovery, which Flynn explains as "the capacity to get things back to normal as quickly as possible after a disaster" (6).

While this book does not delve into technical details, we will examine how a focus on engineering resilience may elicit stakeholder conflict or cooperation after catastrophic events, depending on the ecological and social aspects of the system's resilience.

Studies of energy systems that apply ecological resilience build on Holling's definition. Some of these add other features such as pre-disaster preparation (Erker et al., 2017), as well as variability, which incorporates adaptation, diversity, and the previously described redundancy (Molyneaux et al., 2016). Molyneaux et al. describe diversity as the availability of alternatives to meet an energy system's requirements when vulnerabilities challenge system continuity. Diversity includes, for example, diversification of fuel supply types and sources, which embodies some aspects of the concept of energy security. Adaption is discussed in greater detail later. McClellan et al. link ecological resilience to sustainability, which they define through the five factors framework of natural, social, human, manufactured, and economic capital (McClellan et al., 2016). They describe natural capital as "the natural environment, including all environmental services and environmental quality," and social capital as "the networks or organizations that connect individuals" (McClellan et al., 2016). Their definition of human capital includes the concept of well-being and its links to education and health.

These five sustainability factors overlap with social resilience factors highlighted by others, including energy resource availability, accessibility, and acceptability (e.g., see Hughes, 2015; Sharifi and Yamagata, 2016; Molyneaux et al., 2016). Availability refers to the presence of energy resources for use, while accessibility describes the ability of all community members to access these resources. Acceptability pertains to social acceptance of energy technologies and facilities. Along with these energy justice issues, social resilience includes system operation and disruption effects on communities. Shalanda Baker, Deputy Director for Energy Justice and Secretary's Advisor on Equity at the U.S. Department of Energy in the first Biden Administration, has written extensively on energy system impacts on communities and the need for incorporation of this factor into definitions of system resilience (Baker, 2019).

Rees cautions that emphasis on the social aspects of resilience can harm overall system resilience if the ecological aspects are ignored (Rees, 2010, 9). Many studies depict combined socio-ecological resilience as "adaptive resilience" (e.g., see Sharifi and Yamagata, 2016; Jesse et al., 2019; Underwood et al., 2020). This definition of resilience incorporates stakeholder learning and system adaptation. It does not require a system's return to a previous stable state (Jesse et al., 2019; Ko et al., 2019). Ecology scholar William Rees characterizes socio-ecological system resilience as "the capacity of the system to assimilate disturbances without crossing a threshold into an alternative and possibly less 'friendly' stable state" (Rees, 2010, 5). Brian Walker, with Hollings, Carpenter and Kinzig, suggests two alternatives for change to achieve socio-ecological resilience: system adaptation to the new circumstances or, in cases where adaptation is not possible, system transformation (Walker et al., 2003). Erker et al. describe the latter as "transformative resilience," in which shocks can change a system's "logic and functions by creating novel configurations, pathways and mechanisms" (Erker et al., 2017). Molyneaux et al. emphasize system adaptation and improvement based on measurement and monitoring of system operations, which contribute to an adaptive system that can anticipate variable risks. They suggest that adaptive capacity depends on a system's balance of efficiency, redundancy, and diversity, and that more structured, efficient systems may face more constraints on change. They also align psychological resilience with the capacity to cope with and capitalize on shocks as opportunities for system improvement (Molyneaux et al., 2016).

Rees adds to the resilience definition the ability to maintain quality of life for citizens through continued provision of goods and services, reflecting the wellbeing component of human capital in the previously described five factor sustainability framework. This characterization also incorporates some elements of economic resilience, as supply chain continuity influences this goods provision. We can see this most clearly during the COVID-19 pandemic, when disrupted and altered supply chains across the globe resulted in reduced access to many goods and services, such as milk and toilet paper, as well as price changes based on the supply-demand imbalances created by these disruptions (e.g., O'Hara and Toussaint, 2021; Kamsiime et al., 2021; Thulasiraman et al., 2021). Some industry and academic studies observe that pandemic supply chain disruptions also affected access to components such as solar panels and wind turbine blades (see SEIA, 2020; Eroglu, 2021; Guidehouse Insights, 2020). And yet, studies of electricity systems in European nations and the United States found limited disruptions in electricity supply during the pandemic (e.g., Halbrugge et al., 2021; Ruan et al., 2021). Some studies have found that while electricity supply remained stable, vulnerable populations faced challenges to electricity access due to worsening of financial constraints during the pandemic (e.g., Fefferman et al., 2021). These trends reflect the complex interaction between factors that shape social, ecological, and economic resilience.

Factors included in economic resilience, which can align or conflict with social and ecological aspects of resilience, include economic loss (e.g., see Zhang and Peeta, 2011) and affordability of energy resources and electricity (e.g., see Hughes, 2015; Sharifi and Yamagata, 2016; Molyneaux et al., 2016). For example, in Brazil, as a result of the government's isolation measures during the COVID-19 pandemic, electricity distribution companies faced massive economic losses and shifts in demand from commercial and industrial consumers to residential consumers (Costa et al., 2021). Globally, reductions in electricity demand and prices spurred oil and gas price volatility that has challenged utility companies in many countries, as well as oil and gas exporting enterprises, especially in developing nations (OECD, 2020). From the consumer perspective, as mentioned previously, financial strain due to unemployment and other pandemic-induced financial hardship affected some populations' ability to pay for electricity.

Integrating the element of resource scarcity, Adam Rose distinguishes between static economic resilience, defined as "efficient allocation of remaining resources at a given point in time," and dynamic economic resilience, which involves repairing and reconstructing resources to facilitate recovery from a shock (Rose, 2007, 383; Rose, 2017, 56). Molyneaux et al. embed these aspects of economic resilience in the broader context of energy security (Molyneaux et al., 2016).

The aspects of energy system resilience discussed thus far align with a system's capacity for preservation when shocks occur. However, some definitions of resilience incorporate change as a healthy – even necessary – element of resilience. For instance, the National Academy of Sciences (NAS) includes in its resilience definition the ability "to more successfully adapt to adverse events" (National Research Council, 2012). Gatto and Drago also incorporate adaptation into the resilience concept, as well as accompanying learning. They define resilience as "the adaptive capacity of improving performance, as a result of learning and adaptation, informed by continuous change" (Gatto and Drago, 2020, 1). Some stakeholder groups thus may view a resilient energy system as one that adapts and transitions when shocks occur, even if such change shifts from the existing system to a different one.

Shocks and Stakeholder Relationships' Combined Effects on System Innovation and Resilience

Existing analyses of external shocks and stakeholder relationships offer many insights for energy transitions. However, they do not adequately explain why exogenous shocks do not always result in energy system transformation, nor how stakeholder relationships and resilience priorities can contribute to this effect. While existing studies indicate that the size of a shock can affect the changes that result from it, size alone may not predict the impact on an energy system. Small shocks can lead to big changes, and large shocks may not result in much energy system change at all. For example, the 1979 accident at Three-Mile Island did not precipitate permanent shutdown of the U.S. nuclear reactor fleet. Studies of nuclear power trends in the United States show that the accident merely compounded an existing economically driven downward trend in nuclear plant construction (e.g., Cohen, 1990; Hultman and Koomey, 2013; Csereklyei, 2014).

Existing analyses of external shocks and shifts in stakeholder relationships suggest that both of these factors partially explain disruptions in locked-in energy systems. In joining these two factors and examining the connections between them, we derive a more complete understanding of why and how they contribute to energy system transitions. Energy system resilience priorities influence these factors. Definitions of resilience affect stakeholder relationships, and they also influence the effects of shocks on energy systems. These factors in turn shape energy system resilience and prospects for innovation to address resilience challenges.

Applying the concepts described in this chapter, we will analyze how stakeholder relationships combine with three shocks to Japan's energy system: the 1970s oil crises, technological and institutional failures in the 1990s and early 2000s, and the 2011 Fukushima nuclear disaster. These concepts will provide a foundation for the lessons we derive on energy system resilience.

Notes

1 Thelen summarizes the historical institutionalist view of path dependence that develops during "crucial founding moments of institutional formation that send countries along broadly different developmental paths" (Thelen, 1999, 387). This perspective also appears in work by Pierson, Streeck, Steinmo, and others (Pierson, 2004; Streeck, 2010; Steinmo, 2010).
2 Not surprisingly, the set of actors and organizations Hirsh and Sovacool mention as contributors to electric utility system momentum overlaps greatly with those identified by Hughes as prominent in creation of momentum in the broader electric power production system. Both systems receive support from interactions between networks of regulators, utility managers, financiers, component manufacturers, academic institutions, and customers.
3 Followers of Kingdon and Pierson differ on the time frame and precipitating factors behind these critical junctures. Kingdon and other policy process scholars note specific points in time when external shocks become critical junctures that punctuate a stable system. Institutionalists and evolutionary theorists frame critical junctures as phases that can range from days to a decade, rather than one-time occurrences pinpointed on a calendar. These phases can include an exogenous shock, but they are driven by institutions and shifts in them over time that lead to gradual change in established paths. For example, see Peter Hall and Kathleen Thelen, 2009; James Mahoney and Kathleen Thelen, 2009; Sven Steinmo, 2010.
4 More recent institutionalists such as Pierson, Hall, Thelen, and Mahoney view institutions as products of dynamism stemming from current actors' interactions that influence institutions created and changed by previous actors (Pierson, 2004; Mahoney and Thelen, 2009; Streeck, 2011).

References

Abbas, N., van der Molen, I., Nader, M., and Lovitt, J. (2014) 'Trust and Cooperation Relations in Environmental Management of Lebanon.' *European Scientific Journal* 2 (June), 274–284.

Acemoglu, D., and Robinson, J.A. (2008) 'Persistence of Power, Elites, and Institutions.' *American Economic Review*, 98 (1), 267–293.

Ahmadi, S., Saboohi, Y., and Vakili, A. (2021) 'Frameworks, Quantitative Indicators, Characters, and Modeling Approaches to Analysis of Energy System Resilience: A Review.' *Renewable and Sustainable Energy Reviews*, 144 (2021), 110988.

Aklin, M., and Urpelainen, J. (2011) 'The Strategy of Sustainable Energy Transitions: Political Competition and Path Dependence.' *SSRN eLibrary*, February. http://papers.ssrn.com/sol3/papers.cfm?abstract_id=1754742.

Aklin, M., and Urpelainen, J. (2018) *Renewables: The Politics of a Global Energy Transition.* Cambridge, MA: The MIT Press.

Armstrong, E.A., and Bernstein, M. (2008) 'Culture, Power, and Institutions: A Multi-Institutional Politics Approach to Social Movements.' *Sociological Theory*, 26, 74–99.

Baker, S.H. (2019) 'Anti-Resilience: A Roadmap for Transformational Justice Within the Energy System.' *Harvard Civil Rights-Civil Liberties Law Review*, 54 (1), 1–48.

Baumgartner, F.R., and Jones, B.D. (1993) *Agendas and Instability in American Politics.* 1st ed. Chicago, IL: University of Chicago Press.

Berardo, R., and Scholtz, J.T. (2010) 'Self-Organizing Policy Networks: Risk, Partner Selection, and Cooperation in Estuaries.' *American Journal of Political Science*, 54, 632–649.

Berkhout, F. (2002) 'Technological Regimes, Path Dependency and the Environment.' *Global Environmental Change*, 12 (1), 1–4.

Birkland, T.A. (1997) *After Disaster: Agenda Setting, Public Policy, and Focusing Events.* Washington, DC: Georgetown University Press.

Birkland, T.A. (2006) *Lessons of Disaster: Policy Change After Catastrophic Events.* Washington, DC: Georgetown University Press.

Birkland, T.A. (2011) *An Introduction to the Policy Process.* Armonk, NY: M.E. Sharpe.

Cohen, B.L. (1990) *The Nuclear Energy Option: An Alternative for the 90s.* New York: Plenum Publishing Corp.

Cohen, B.L., McCubbins, M., and Rosenbluth, F.M. (1995) 'The Politics of Nuclear Power in Japan and the United States.' In Cowhey, P.F., and McCubbins, M. (eds.), *Structure and Policy in Japan and the United States.* New York: Cambridge University Press, 177–202.

Collier, R.B., and Collier, D. (1991) *Shaping the Political Arena: Critical Junctures, the Labor Movement, and Regime Dynamics in Latin America.* Princeton: Princeton University Press.

Costa, V.B.F., Bonatto, B.D., Pereira, L.C., and Silva, P.F. (2021) 'Analysis of the Impact of COVID-19 Pandemic on the Brazilian Distribution Electricity Market Based on a Socio-economic Regulatory Model.' *International Journal of Electrical Power & Energy Systems*, 132, 107172.

Cowan, R. (1990) 'Nuclear Power Reactors: A Study in Technological Lock-In.' *The Journal of Economic History*, 50 (3), 541–567.

Csereklyei, Z. (2014) 'Measuring the Impact of Nuclear Accidents on Energy Policy.' *Ecological Economics*, 99 (March), 121–129.

Cumbers, A., MacKinnon, D., and McMaster, R. (2003) 'Institutions, Power and Space: Assessing the Limits to Institutionalism in Economic Geography.' *European Urban and Regional Studies*, 10 (4), 325–342.

Dalziell, E.P., and McManus, S.T. (2004) 'Resilience, Vulnerability, and Adaptive Capacity: Implications for System Performance.' Presentation to the International Forum for Engineering Decision Making (IFED), Stoos, Switzerland, 6–8 December.

Delmas, M., and Heiman, B. (2001) 'Government Credible Commitment to the French and American Nuclear Power Industries.' *Journal of Policy Analysis and Management*, 20 (3), 433–456.

Duffield, J.S., and Woodall, B. (2011) 'Japan's New Basic Energy Plan.' *Energy Policy*, 39, 3741–3749.

Eikeland, P.O., and Inderberg, T.H.J. (2016) 'Energy System Transformation and Long-Term Interest Constellations in Denmark: Can Agency Beat Structure?' *Energy Research & Social Science*, 11, 164–173.

Erker, S., Stangl, R., and Stoeglehner, G. (2017) 'Resilience in the Light of Energy Crises – Part I: A Framework to Conceptualise Regional Energy Resilience.' *Journal of Cleaner Production*, 164 (Supplement C), 420–433.

Eroglu, H. (2021) 'Effects of Covid-19 Outbreak on Environment and Renewable Energy Sector.' *Environment, Development and Sustainability*, 23, 4782–4790.

Farrell, H. (2004) 'Trust, Distrust and Power.' In Hardin, R. (ed.), *Distrust*. New York: Russell Sage Foundation.

Farrell, H. (2005) 'Trust and Political Economy: Institutions and the Sources of Inter-Firm Cooperation.' *Comparative Political Studies*, June, 459–493.

Farrell, H. (2009) *The Political Economy of Trust Institutions, Interests, and Inter-Firm Cooperation in Italy and Germany*. Cambridge: Cambridge University Press.

Fefferman, N., Chen, C.F., Bonilla, G., Nelson, H., and Kuo, C.P. (2021). *How Limitations in Energy Burdens Compromise Health Interventions for COVID Outbreaks in Urban Settings*. SSRN: https://ssrn.com/abstract=3833000 or http://dx.doi.org/10.2139/ssrn.3833000

Flynn, S.E. (2008) 'America the Resilient.' *Foreign Affairs*, 87 (2), 2–8.

Foxon, T. (2007) 'Technological Lock-in and the Role of Innovation.' In Atkinson, G., Dietz, S., and Neumayer, E. (eds.), *Handbook of Sustainable Development*. Northampton, MA: Edward Elgar Publishing, 140–152.

Gatto, A., and Drago, C. (2020) 'A Taxonomy of Energy Resilience.' *Energy Policy*, 136, 111007.

Gholami, A., Shekari, T., Amirioun, M.A., Aminifar, F., Amini, M.H., and Sargolzaei, A. (2018) Toward a Consensus on the Definition and Taxonomy of Power System Resilience. *IEEE Access*, 6.

Gillebo, T., and Francis, C. (2006) 'Stakeholder Cooperation in Sustainable Development: Three Case Studies in Norway.' *Journal of Rural and Community Development*, 2 (1), 28–43.

Guidehouse Insights. (2020) 'COVID-19 Impacts the Wind Power Market.' 22 May. https://guidehouseinsights.com/news-and-views/covid-19-impacts-the-wind-power-market

Halbrugge, S., Schott, P., Weibelzahl, M., Buhl, H.U., Fridgen, G., and Schopf, M. (2021) 'How Did the German and Other European Electricity Systems React to the COVID-19 Pandemic?' *Applied Energy*, 285, 116370.

Hall, P.A., and Thelen, K. (2009) 'Institutional Change in Varieties of Capitalism.' *Socio-Economic Review*, 7 (1), 7–34.

Hirsh, R., and Sovacool, B. (2006) 'Technological Systems and Momentum Change: American Electric Utilities, Restructuring, and Distributed Generation Technologies.' *The Journal of Technology Studies*, 32 (2), 72–85.

Hogan, J. (2019). 'The Critical Juncture Concept's Evolving Capacity to Explain Policy Change.' *European Policy Analysis*, 5 (2), 170–189.

Holling, C.S. (1973) 'Resilience and Stability of Ecological Systems.' *Annual Review of Ecology, Evolution, and Systematics*, 4, 1–23.

Holling, C.S. (1996) 'Engineering Resilience Versus Ecological Resilience.' In Schulze, P.E. (ed.), *Engineering Within Ecological Constraints*. Washington, DC: National Academy Press.

Hsu, S.H. (2005) 'Advocacy Coalitions and Policy Change on Nuclear Power Utilization in Taiwan.' *The Social Science Journal*, 42 (2), 215–229.

Hughes, L. (2015) 'The Effects of Event Occurrence and Duration on Resilience and Adaptation in Energy Systems.' *Energy*, 84, 443–454.

Hughes, T. (1987) 'The Evolution of Large Technological Systems.' In Bijker, W., Hughes, T., and Pinch, T. (eds.), *The Social Construction of Technological Systems*. Cambridge, MA: MIT Press, 51–82.

Hughes, T. (1993) *Networks of Power: Electrification in Western Society, 1880–1930*. Baltimore: Johns Hopkins University Press.

Hultman, N., and Koomey, J. (2013) 'Three Mile Island: The Driver of US Nuclear Power's Decline?' *Bulletin of the Atomic Scientists*, 69 (3), 63–70.

Hymans, J. (2011) 'Veto Players, Nuclear Energy, and Nonproliferation: Domestic Institutional Barriers to a Japanese Nuclear Bomb.' *International Security*, 36 (2), 154–189.

Hymans, J., and Uchikoshi, F. (2021) 'To Drill or Not to Drill: Determinants of Geothermal Energy Project Siting in Japan.' *Environmental Politics*, 2 June.

Jacobsson, S., and Bergek, A. (2004) 'Transforming the Energy Sector: The Evolution of Technological Systems in Renewable Energy Technology.' *Industrial and Corporate Change*, 13 (5), 815–849.

Jacobsson, S., and Lauber, V. (2006) 'The Politics and Policy of Energy System Transformation – Explaining the German Diffusion of Renewable Energy Technology.' *Energy Policy*, 34, 256–726.

Jesse, B.J., Heinrichs, H.U., and Kuckshinrichs, W. (2019) 'Adapting the Theory of Resilience to Energy Systems: A Review and Outlook.' *Energy, Sustainability and Society*, 9 (1), 1–19.

Kamsiime, M.K., Tambo, J.A., Mugambia, I., Bundia, M., and Owuor, C. (2021) 'COVID-19 Implications on Household Income and Food Security in Kenya and Uganda: Findings from a Rapid Assessment.' *World Development*, 137, 105199.

Karatayev, M., Hall, S., Kalyuzhnova, Y., and Clarke, M. (2016) 'Renewable Energy Technology Uptake in Kazakhstan: Policy Drivers and Barriers in a Transitional Economy.' *Renewable and Sustainable Energy Reviews*, 66, 120–136.

Kemp, R. (1994) 'Technology and the Transition to Environmental Sustainability: The Problem of Technological Regime Shifts.' *Futures*, 26 (10), 1023–1046.

Kingdon, J.W. (1997) *Agendas, Alternatives, and Public Policies*. 2nd ed. New York: Addison-Wesley Educational Publishers, Inc.

Kingston, J. (2014) 'Japan's Nuclear Village: Power and Resilience.' In Kingston, J. (ed.), *Critical Issues in Contemporary Japan*. London: Routledge, 107–119.

Kishimoto, A. (2017) 'Public Attitudes and Institutional Changes in Japan Following Nuclear Accidents.' In Balleisen, E., Bennear, L., Krawiec, K.D., and Wiener, J.B. (eds.), *Policy Shock: Recalibrating Risk and Regulation after Oil Spills, Nuclear Accidents and Financial Crises*. Cambridge: Cambridge University Press, 269–304.

Ko, Y., Barrett, B.F.D., Copping, A.E., Sharifi, A., Yarime, M., and Wang, X. (2019) 'Energy Transitions Towards Low Carbon Resilience: Evaluation of Disaster-Triggered Local and Regional Cases.' *Sustainability*, 11 (23), 6801.

Kohl, W.L. (1982) *After the Second Oil Crisis: Energy Policies in Europe, America, and Japan*. Lexington: Lexington Books.

Liu, Y., and Bie, Z. (2016) 'Study on the Resilience of the Integrated Energy System.' *Energy Procedia*, 103, December, 171–176.

Lovio, R., Mickwitz, P., and Heiskanen, E. (2011) 'Path Dependence, Path Creation and Creative Destruction in the Evolution of Energy Systems.' In Wüstenhagen, R. (ed.), *The Handbook of Research on Energy Entrepreneurship*. Cheltenham, UK: Edward Elgar Publishing, 274–301.

Lubell, M., Henry, A.D., and McCoy, M. (2010) 'Collaborative Institutions in an Ecology of Games.' *American Journal of Political Science*, 54, 287–300.

Mahoney, J., and Thelen, K. (2009) *Explaining Institutional Change: Ambiguity, Agency, and Power*. 1st ed. New York: Cambridge University Press.

Markard, J., Suter, M., and Ingold, K. (2016) 'Socio-technical Transitions and Policy Change – Advocacy Coalitions in Swiss Energy Policy.' *Environmental Innovations and Societal Transitions*, 18, 215–237.

Markard, J., and Truffer, B. (2006) 'Innovation Processes in Large Technical Systems: Market Liberalization as a Driver for Radical Change?' *Research Policy*, 35 (5), 609–625.

McClellan, B., Zhang, Q., Farzaneh, H., Utama, N.A., and Ishihara, K.N. (2016) 'Resilience, Sustainability and Risk Management: A Focus on Energy.' In Ettingoff, K. (ed.), *Ecological Resilience: Response to Climate Change and Natural Disasters*. London: Routledge, 223–249.

Moe, E. (2010) 'Energy, Industry and Politics: Energy, Vested Interests, and Long-Term Economic Growth and Development.' *Energy*, 35 (4), 1730–1740.

Moe, E. (2012) 'Vested Interests, Energy Efficiency and Renewables in Japan.' *Energy Policy*, 40, January, 260–273.

Moe, E. (2017) 'Does Politics Matter? Explaining Swings in Wind Power Installations.' *AIMS Energy*, 5 (3), 341–373.

Molyneaux, L., Brown, C., Wagner, L., and Foster, J. (2016) 'Measuring Resilience in Energy Systems: Insights From a Range of Disciplines.' *Renewable and Sustainable Energy Reviews*, 59 (2016), 1068–1079.

Morse, R.A. (1981) 'Introduction: Japan's Energy Policies and Options.' In *The Politics of Japan's Energy Strategy: Resources-Diplomacy-Security*. Berkeley, CA: Institute of East Asian Studies, 1–14.

Musiolik, J., and Markard, J. (2011) 'Creating and Shaping Innovation Systems: Formal Networks in the Innovation System for Stationary Fuel Cells in Germany.' *Energy Policy*, 39 (4), 1909–1922.

National Research Council. (2012) *Disaster Resilience: A National Imperative*. Washington, DC: The National Academies Press.

Nelson, R.R., and Sampat, B.N. (2001) 'Making Sense of Institutions as a Factor Shaping Economic Performance.' *Journal of Economic Behavior & Organization*, 44 (1), 31–54.

Nohrstedt, D. (2008) 'The Politics of Crisis Policymaking: Chernobyl and Swedish Nuclear Energy Policy.' *Policy Studies Journal*, 36 (2), 257–278.

Nohrstedt, D. (2009) 'Do Advocacy Coalitions Matter? Crisis and Change in Swedish Nuclear Energy Policy.' *Journal of Public Administration Research and Theory*, 20, 309–333.

OECD. (2020) *The Impact of Coronavirus (COVID-19) and the Global Oil Price Shock on the Fiscal Position of Oil-Exporting Developing Countries*. Paris: OECD Publishing.

O'Hara, S., and Toussaint, E.C. (2021) 'Food Access in Crisis: Food Security and COVID-19.' *Ecological Economics*, 180 (C) 106859.

Orru, M. (1993) 'Institutional Cooperation in Japanese and German Capitalism.' In Sjöstrand, S.E. (ed.), *Institutional Change: Theory and Empirical Findings*. Armonk, NY: M.E. Sharpe, 171–198.

Perkins, R. (2003) 'Technological "Lock-In".' In E. Neumayer (Ed.), *Internet Encyclopedia of Ecological Economics*. Manchester, UK: International Society for Ecological Economics.

Peters, B.G. (2012) *Institutional Theory in Political Science: The New Institutionalism*. 3rd ed. New York: Bloomsbury Academic.

Pickett, S. (2002) 'Japan's Nuclear Energy Policy: From Firm Commitment to Difficult Dilemma Addressing Growing Stocks of Plutonium, Program Delays, Domestic Opposition and International Pressure.' *Energy Policy*, 30 (15), 1337–1355.

Pierson, P. (2004) *Politics in Time: History, Institutions, and Social Analysis*. 1st ed. Princeton, NJ: Princeton University Press.

Pirson, M., and Malhotra, D. (2007) 'What Matters to Whom? Managing Trust Across Multiple Stakeholder Groups, Working Paper No. 39.' The Hauser Center for Nonprofit Organizations, Harvard University.

Rees, W.E. (2010) 'Foundation Concepts: Thinking "Resilience".' In *The Post Carbon Reader*. Santa Rosa, CA: Watershed Media in Conjunction with the Post Carbon Institute.

Roege, P., Collier, Z.A., Mancillas, J., McDonagh, J.A., and Linkov, I. (2014) 'Metrics for Energy Resilience.' *Energy Policy*, 72, September, 249–256.

Rose, A. (2007) 'Economic Resilience to Natural and Man-Made Disasters: Multidisciplinary Origins and Contextual Dimensions.' *Environmental Hazards*, 7 (4), 383–398.

Rose, A. (2017) 'Construction of an Economic Resilience Index.' In Paton, D., and Johnston, D. (eds.), *Disaster Resilience: An Integrated Approach*. 2nd ed. Springfield, IL: Charles C. Thomas, 55–78.

Ruan, G., Wu, J., Zhong, H., Xia, Q., and Xie, L. (2021) 'Quantitative Assessment of U.S. Bulk Power Systems and Market Operations During the COVID-19 Pandemic.' *Applied Energy*, 286, 116354.

Sabatier, P. (1988) 'An Advocacy Coalition Framework of Policy Change and the Role of Policy-Oriented Learning Therein.' *Policy Sciences*, 21 (2–3), 129–168.

Samuels, R. (1987) *The Business of the Japanese State: Energy Markets in Comparative and Historical Perspective*. Ithaca, NY: Cornell University Press.

Samuels, R. (2013) *3.11: Disaster and Change in Japan*. 1st ed. Ithaca: Cornell University Press.

Sanden, B. (2004) 'Technology Path Assessment for Sustainable Technology Development.' *Innovation: Management, Policy & Practice* (Corporate Sustainability: Governance, Innovation Strategy, Development & Methods), 6 (2), 316–330.

Sanden, B., and Azar, C. (2005) 'Near-Term Technology Policies for Long-Term Climate Targets – Economy Wide Versus Technology Specific Approaches.' *Energy Policy*, 33 (12), 1557–1576.

SEIA. (2020) *COVID-19 & the U.S. Solar Industry Factsheet*. May. Washington, DC: Solar Energy Industries Association.

Seto, K.C., Davis, S.J., Mitchell, R.B., Stokes, E.C., Unruh, G., and Urge-Vorsatz, D. (2016) 'Carbon Lock-In: Types, Causes, and Policy Implications.' *Annual Review of Environment and Resources*, 41, 425–452.

Sharifi, A., and Yamagata, Y. (2016) 'Principles and Criteria for Assessing Urban Energy Resilience: A Literature Review.' *Renewable and Sustainable Energy Reviews*, 60, 1654–1677.

Shinozuka, M., Chang, S.E., Cheng, T.C., Feng, M., O'Rourke, T.D., Saadeghvaziri, M.A., Dong, X., Jin, X., Wang, Y., and Shi, P. (2004) 'Resilience of Integrated Power and Water Systems.' *Seismic Evaluation and Retrofit of Lifeline Systems*, 65–86.

Sklarew, J.F. (2015) *Shock to the System: How Catastrophic Events and Institutional Relationships Impact Japanese Energy Policymaking, Resilience, and Innovation*. Arlington, VA: George Mason University.

Sklarew, J.F. (2018) 'Power Fluctuations: How Japan's Nuclear Infrastructure Priorities Influence Electric Utilities' Clout.' *Energy Research and Social Science*, 41, 158–167.

Smil, V. (2010) *Energy Transitions: History, Requirements, Prospects*. Santa Barbara: Praeger.

Smil, V. (2016) *Energy Transitions: Global and National Perspectives*. 2nd ed. Santa Barbara: Praeger.

Stefes, C., and Laird, F.N. (2010) 'Creating Path Dependency: The Divergence of German and U.S. Renewable Energy Policy.' *SSRN eLibrary*.

Steinmo, S. (2010) *The Evolution of Modern States: Sweden, Japan, and the United States*. Cambridge: Cambridge University Press.

Streeck, W. (2011) 'Taking Capitalism Seriously: Towards an Institutionalist Approach to Contemporary Political Economy.' *Socio-Economic Review*, 9 (1), 137–167.

Thelen, K. (1999) Historical Institutionalism in Comparative Politics. *Annual Review of Political Science*, 2, 369–404.

Thulasiraman, V., Nandagopal, M.S.G., and Kothakota, A. (2021) 'Need for a Balance Between Short Food Supply Chains and Integrated Food Processing Sectors: COVID-19 Takeaways from India.' *Journal of Food Science and Technology*, 58, 3667–3675.

Trencher, G., Rinscheid, A., Duygan, M., Truong, N., and Asuka, J. (2020) 'Revisiting Carbon Lock-in in Energy Systems: Explaining the Perpetuation of Coal Power in Japan.' *Energy Research & Social Science*, 69, 101770.

Underwood, G., Hill, D., and Lamichhane, S. (2020) 'Earthquakes, Blockades and Energy Crises: A Conceptual Framework for Energy Systems Resilience Applied to Nepal.' *Energy Research & Social Science*, 69, 101609.

Unruh, G. (2000) 'Understanding Carbon Lock-In.' *Energy Policy*, 28 (12), 817–830.

Unruh, G. (2002) 'Escaping Carbon Lock-In.' *Energy Policy*, 30 (4), 317–325.

Van der Vooren, A., and Alkemade, F. (2011) 'Infrastructure Dependent Technologies: Escaping Lock-in and the Role of Policy.' Presentation to the DIME Final Conference, Maastricht, 6 April.

Valentine, S.V., and Sovacool, B. (2010) 'The Socio-Political Economy of Nuclear Power Development in Japan and South Korea.' *Energy Policy*, 38, 7971–7979.

Verbong, G., and Geels, F.W. (2007) 'The Ongoing Energy Transition: Lessons from a Socio-Technical, Multi-Level Analysis of the Dutch Electricity System (1960–2004).' *Energy Policy*, 35, 1025–1037.

Walker, B., Holling, C.S., Carpenter, S., and Kinzig, A. (2003) 'Resilience, Adaptability and Transformability in Social–Ecological Systems.' *Ecology and Society*, 9 (2), 1–9.

Weible, C., and Sabatier, P.A. (2007) 'A Guide to the Advocacy Coalition Framework.' In Miller, G.J., and Sidney, M.S. (eds.), *Handbook of Public Policy Analysis: Theory, Politics and Methods*. London: Routledge, 123–136.

Westrum, R. (1991) *Technologies & Society: The Shaping of People and Things*. Belmont, CA: Wadsworth Pub. Co.

Yarahmadi, M., and Higgins, P. (2012) 'Motivations Towards Environmental Innovation: A Conceptual Framework for Multiparty Cooperation.' *European Journal of Innovation Management*, 15 (4), 400–420.

Yoshimatsu, H. (2014) *Comparing Institution-Building in East Asia: Power Politics, Governance, and Critical Junctures*. Basingstoke: Palgrave Macmillan.

Zedan, S., and Miller, W. (2017) 'Quantifying Stakeholders' Influence on Energy Efficiency of Housing: Development and Application of a Four-Step Methodology.' *Construction Management and Economics*, 36 (7), 375–393.

Zhang, P., and Peeta, S. (2011) 'A Generalized Modeling Framework to Analyze Interdependencies Among Infrastructure Systems.' *Transportation Research Part B Methodological*, 45 (3), 553–579.

3 Oil Shocks

Not So Shocking (1970s–1980s)

"... there was a time ... when after the oil shock, there was a clear shift of energy sources from fossil fuels to nuclear. That was, I think, under a very close relationship with government and industry. They changed the course."

— *Former government official, Ministry of Economy, Trade and Industry (G16, July 2013)*

"... the utilities financially did not have power, so there is no way but to hear the government. They relied on the government and at that time they supposed that government will establish some goal, and utilities and private sector will have to follow the goal."

— *Electric utility executive (I1, July 2013)*

"... the Japanese government has been creating their energy policy as a very serious response to the social changes or the events that happened. So the first one is the oil crisis, so they diversified."

— *Public interest group leader (P2, March 2013)*

Examining Japan's energy policymaking following the 1970s oil crises, we can analyze how the crises and the government's relationships with the electric utilities and the public influenced Japanese energy policy, the policymaking process, and energy system resilience. Interview data, public opinion polls, and government documents reflect a relationship in which policymakers and politicians have clout over and cooperation from the utility industry and public. Despite tensions between the electric utilities and both safety and economic regulators, the 1970s oil shocks did not alter the Japanese government's cooperative relationships with or clout over the electric utilities and the public. Aligned energy system resilience priorities across the utilities, policymakers, and public contributed to this effect. This continued cooperation and government clout enabled the shocks to serve as a focusing event that created a critical juncture for generating dramatic energy policy change in Japan that bolstered energy system resilience without immediate changes to the policymaking process or regulatory structure.

DOI: 10.4324/9781003227588-3

Sudden Shock: The Oil Crises

A vast array of existing literature and government documents describes the origins and global effects of the 1970s oil shocks or oil crises, two episodes of steep oil price rises in the 1970s.[1] After Arab members of the Organization of Petroleum Exporting Countries (OPEC) imposed and lifted an oil embargo against the United States and other nations supporting Israel in 1973–4, the global market price of oil stabilized at a level almost quadruple the pre-crisis price. As Japanese electric utility executive I7 noted, because oil accounted for 75 percent of Japan's primary energy supply, "the price increase of oil had a very big influence on the Japanese economy. So the Japanese economy experienced, for first time after WWII, zero percent GDP growth." Several studies of the first oil crisis' effects on the Japanese economy corroborate this assertion. In fact, Mihut and Daniel's analysis cites slightly negative Japanese economic growth in 1974 (Mihut and Daniel, 2012, 1045). The study also finds that Japan's trade surplus before the crisis, over 5 billion dollars in 1972, plunged into a deficit that peaked at over 6 billion dollars in 1974 (Mihut and Daniel, 2012, 1045). Mihut and Daniel also determine that Japan faced a consumer price increase of over 18 percent, due in part to an exponential increase in electricity prices that affected the manufacturing sector (Mihut and Daniel, 2012, 1044). Economic resilience of Japan's energy system thus became a priority for policymakers, consumers, and utilities.

This impact was not limited to Japan; existing literature portrays similar jolts to the energy systems and economies of other oil-importing nations around the world. However, the policy responses to the oil crises varied by country, and the Japanese government's choices suggest a more complex set of catalysts than just the shock itself.

The oil crises shocked the citizens of oil-importing countries, including Japan. Japanese interviewees who experienced the oil shocks firsthand recalled a new public awareness of the role of oil in their daily lives. I6, who worked at TEPCO at the time, recounted,

> What happened was that there was nothing to buy in the supermarket. No toilet paper. Only from that phenomenon, we, general public, understands, we Japan depend on other countries for energy sources, especially the Middle East. Before that, the general public didn't care about the oil shock and where energy was coming from, and where it changes to electricity. Such kind of knowledge, we don't have any. Only plug in, and we can use it.
>
> (May 2013)

This growing public awareness of the linkage between energy supply and quality of life reflects the oil shocks' generation of a newfound focus on both the economic and social resilience of Japan's energy system.

Interviewees asserted that the second oil crisis in 1978–9 did not alter the Japanese mindset to as great a degree as the 1973 shock. However, it reiterated recognition of the vulnerability associated with oil dependence.

This second shock was precipitated by a decline in Iranian oil production during a revolution in 1978, coupled with a surge in oil demand that some historians and economists believe emerged in part as a hoarding response to the first shock (e.g., see Graefe, 2014). World oil prices more than doubled between 1979 and 1981. Mihut and Daniel assert that this time, Japan's economic growth declined by two percent and did not fall below zero (Mihut and Daniel, 2012, 1047). This improved reaction compared to the first oil crisis response occurred despite continued high levels of Japanese oil imports, according to an analysis by Richard Finn (Finn, 1983, 61).

If the second oil crisis arose partly due to policy responses to the first shock, such as hoarding behavior by oil-importing nations, this linkage represents a pattern repeated in Japanese energy policy over the following four decades. Several interviewees suggested that each policy response to address a shock or other energy system challenge resulted in a new problem. This pattern reflects the diverse aspects of energy system resilience and the complexities associated with balancing them.

We might expect that the 1970s oil crises would serve as a focusing event, spurring a critical juncture in energy policymaking. We would predict that such a shift would involve the Japanese government's efforts to bolster the existing energy system by diversifying oil supply sources, while altering the system by reducing oil dependence through diversification of energy supply alternatives to oil. We also might expect the Japanese government to avoid shifts toward reliance on other imported energy sources, as well as dependence on any one particular energy source. We thus would expect that the Japanese government would pursue a balance of domestically sourced coal and renewables, supplemented by nuclear power. Since the oil crises highlighted the vulnerability associated with imported energy sources, we might expect to see a particular emphasis on nuclear fuel recycling as a key component of nuclear power development, because Japan possesses no indigenous uranium deposits. In the 1970s and 1980s, Japan imported uranium primarily from Australia and Canada.

These same energy security fears would lead to an expectation that Japan would not shift toward imported natural gas as a replacement for oil. We would expect to see these electricity supply changes combined with initiatives to reduce energy consumption through energy efficiency and conservation measures. However, we also would expect difficulty in accomplishing energy efficiency and conservation improvements. These measures should have faced challenges from the public and the electric utilities. The former might have opposed curbing personal energy use, prioritizing social resilience, and the latter would have viewed profit increases as directly related to higher electricity use, reflecting prioritization of economic resilience.

While Japanese energy supply shifts and policy and process changes following the oil crises match some of these expectations, some surprises emerge regarding specific energy supply source shifts. In particular, nuclear power use expanded dramatically, while renewables and coal experienced limited growth. These surprises, as well as accomplishment of some of the expected but challenging goals, lead to examination of stakeholder relationships as a factor influencing the Japanese government's policy and process choices, as well as formation of a critical juncture for energy system changes.

Stakeholder Relationship Changes and Influences

Our analysis of these relationships involves three factors: the effects of the oil shocks on the government's relationships with the electric utilities and the public, institutional features inherent in these relationships, and risk perceptions and priorities of the stakeholder groups. These three factors combine to impact the ways in which each relationship influenced Japanese energy policymaking after the oil shocks.

As we will discover, resilience priorities largely aligned across the three stakeholder groups during the post oil-shocks period, contributing to cooperation and government clout, as well as a later shift toward increasing utility clout. Policymakers' attention to engineering, socio-ecological, and economic resilience overlapped with the public's focus on economic and social resilience. The government's resilience priorities also encompassed the utilities' focus on engineering and economic resilience. These priorities and their intersection with cooperation/ conflict and clout in relationships between the government, utilities, and public influenced shifts in energy supply sources, as well as implementation of energy efficiency and conservation measures.

Unsurprisingly, all interviewees across the government, utility, and public stakeholder groups identified the 1970s oil crises as a major turning point in Japan's energy system, in alignment with existing literature.[2] For examples of scholarly accounts of the oil shocks' impact on Japan, see Sinha, 1974; Morse, 1981; Mihut and Daniel, 2012; Japan Center for Economic Research Middle-Term Economic Forecast Team, 2012. All interviewees also agreed that the shocks did not weaken the strong relationships maintained by bureaucrats and politicians with the electric utilities and the public. In fact, policymakers' relationships with the electric utilities strengthened. Electric utility and government interviewees also suggested that Japanese policymakers in the bureaucracy generally controlled energy policymaking. At the same time, interview data suggests that an ongoing struggle with the electric utilities over economic and safety regulation also added tension to the relationship.

The interviews also yield some surprising nuances regarding the government's relationship with the public and support for policymakers' efforts to change the energy system. While public opinion polls, described later in this chapter, reflect frustration with the government following the oil shocks, NGO and media interviewees explained that the Japanese public trusted the government to implement policies that would protect them from future shocks. Even when these policies involved public sacrifice in the form of energy conservation, the Japanese public complied.

Based on the interview data, Japanese policymakers' cooperation with and clout over the electric utilities and the public after the oil crises enabled the oil shocks to transform energy priorities and policy, while preserving existing policymaking processes. This cooperation also facilitated advancement of nuclear power's share of the electricity supply, while limiting the growth of renewable energy and coal. Variations in resilience priorities contributed to shifts in cooperation and conflict across the three stakeholder groups over the next several decades, as we will observe here and in the next two chapters. We examine each of the relevant relationships to understand how they contributed to these energy system and policy-making outcomes.

Bureaucrats, Politicians, and Electric Utilities

The Japanese government established the electric utility companies as regional monopolies in 1951. In the post-war period leading up to the 1970s oil shocks, bureaucrats in the then MITI and politicians in the ruling Liberal Democratic Party (LDP) sustained cooperative relationships with these electric utilities, according to all electric utility and government interviewees. They collaborated to build a post-war energy system that would promote national security through energy security, jointly focusing on engineering resilience.

Until the 1970s oil crises occurred, the Japanese bureaucrats and politicians wielded clout over the electric utilities in energy policymaking. Electric utility interviewees perceived government clout as due to the utilities' financial insecurity at that time. The utilities felt obligated to cooperate with energy system goals established by the bureaucracy. As electric utility executive I1 noted, the relationship was cooperative because "the utilities financially did not have power, so there is no way but to hear the government. They relied on the government, and at that time they supposed that government will establish some goal, and utilities and private sector will have to follow the goal" (July 2013). Existing work by Samuels, Navarro, and others supports this idea of weak utilities due to financial challenges (Samuels, 1987; Navarro, 1996). The Electricity Business Act, established as the Electric Utility Industry Law in 1964, reinforced government clout by mandating that the electric utilities provide a stable supply of electricity within their service areas. However, the law did not provide the Japanese government with the legal authority to enforce energy supply increases; the government could only ask the electric utilities to construct power plants (Cabinet Secretariat, 1964). This reliance on voluntary compliance with policymakers' resilience priorities also empowered the electric utilities in the energy policymaking process (Sklarew, 2018).

The oil crises, institutional features, and risk perceptions and priorities all contributed to cooperation and clout in Japanese policymakers' relationships with the electric utilities in the 1970s and 1980s. Government and electric utility interviewees' comments suggest that the oil crises deepened the cooperative axis of the government-electric utility relationship. This effect emerged as bureaucrats and utilities worked together on policies to build ecological and economic resilience in the existing energy system by diversifying Japan's oil sources and expanding non-oil supply sources, namely nuclear power and coal. Many interviewees also observed that to reshape an energy system less dependent on fossil fuels, Japanese policymakers needed utility companies' support of and investment in nuclear power. This reliance empowered the electric utilities in the energy policymaking process. As I6, a former electric utility executive, noted of the post-oil shocks era, "METI heavily depends on *Denjiren* [the Federation of Electric Power Companies], and also the Japanese economy heavily depends on the utility companies" (May 2013). Government interviewee G4 cited the aforementioned omission of energy supply increase mandates in the Electric Utilities Industry Law as leverage for government compliance with Japanese utilities' requests for electricity rate increases. Several electric utility and government interviewees described this give-and-take relationship. In his book, Samuels notes that "In 1976, apparently as compensation for earlier cooperation, MITI had approved another 21 percent rate hike for the utilities, bringing Japanese electric rates to the highest levels in the industrialized world" (Samuels, 1987, 163). These examples reflect coordination of policymakers' ecological and economic resilience goals and the utilities' economic resilience priorities.

Informal institutional features like the *amakudari* system and political donations also shaped policymakers' relationships with the electric utilities, as did formal institutional features such as policy advisory committees (*shingikai*). In the *amakudari* system, each utility hired a former high-ranking government official to serve on their boards. The *amakudari* system is well-documented in existing literature, including Chalmers Johnson's work, which examines Japan's energy sector as a case study. Some government and electric utility interviewees highlighted the *amakudari* system as contributing to policymakers' cooperation with the electric utilities until the Fukushima accident occurred. An explanation by G16, a former government official, supports the notion of *amakudari* existence in Japan's energy sector:

> It's a very well adjusted and well managed custom administered by the ministry in consultation with the utilities. If he retires, a new one from ministry comes . . . of course, always the government says no formal [rule], but just the electricity company wants to hire some useful person, something like that, and the company will say the same thing. But if you look at the record of who succeeds who, you can see that was the custom.
>
> (July 2013)

This custom fostered trust, shared interests, and policy coordination between policymakers and the electric utilities' management after the oil crises. It did so by offering policymakers retirement positions within the utilities, as well as input into utilities' energy supply decisions. This tradition also encouraged policymakers to choose post-shock energy policies that would benefit the electric utilities. The features of the *amakudari* system are not unique to Japan. Many other countries' public officials and corporate executives transition between public and private sector roles during their careers, a phenomenon dubbed the "revolving door." For examples from Canada, the United States, Denmark, and Panama, see Yates and

Cardin-Trudeau, 2021; Strickland, 2020; Rasmussen et al., 2021; and Cárdenas and Robles-Rivera, 2020.

The electric utilities also used political donations to increase their influence over politicians following the oil crises. Media interviewee M2 asserted that "relatively the power companies' position went up . . . they were better supporters and lobbyists for the LDP than they had been" before the oil shocks. Observing that "power companies invested much money for nuclear plants in 1970s after oil shocks . . . based on the government's nuclear power policy," the interviewee suggested that this rise in influence resulted from the electric utilities' desire to protect these investments in nuclear plants (March 2013). The electric utilities needed pro-nuclear politicians to perpetuate nuclear power policies that would enable them to recoup their large start-up investments through a long period of low-cost plant operation. The more they funded these politicians, the stronger the electric utilities' clout over them grew.

The policymaking structure itself represents a formal institutional feature that has fostered close cooperation between Japan's bureaucratic policymakers and the electric utilities. Policies are developed on the basis of formal, direct input from advisory committees called *shingikai* or *bukai*. As electric utility industry interviewee I7 summarized, "In Japan, most energy policy, I mean the laws concerning energy policy, are enacted based on the conclusions of *shingikai*" (May 2013). These committees typically include industry representatives as formal members, and electric utility company executives served on energy advisory committee and its subcommittees since the inception of the committee.

Government official G4 confided that from the time of the oil crises, "It seemed to me, still it's not clear who is actually leading the Japanese energy policy" (February 2013). This ambiguity over energy policymaking clout is due in part to institutional features such as the advisory committees, or *shingikai*, which empower industry representatives by enabling their direct, formal input in the policymaking process.

In 1965, the Japanese government established an energy *shingikai*, the General Committee on Energy (*sougou enerugi chousakai*/総合エネルギー調査会), with the mission of discussing long-term energy demand and supply. The 1975 membership list for the advisory, general, and electricity supply subcommittees housed under this committee included TEPCO executives, as well as representatives from *Keidanren*, the Japan Business Federation, comprising Japanese companies, industry associations, and regional economic organizations (Ministry of International Trade and Industry, Government of Japan, 1975, 106–107). The electric utilities were powerful members of Keidanren. As electric utility interviewee I1 summarized,

> Under the LDP, energy policy and government policy was made by the General Committee on Energy. All of the utility companies put their opinions into this committee, and industry, which includes the utilities, also put their opinions in. And they made policy by making all of these views into one policy.
>
> (March 2013)

Former bureaucrat G16 confirmed the importance of this feature in the electric utilities' influence on energy policy:

> I think by international comparison, in Japanese policymaking, especially in energy, influence from industry is very prominent. And in order to emphasize my point, I would like to point out one major factor in Japanese policymaking. Japanese policymaking including in energy, its major direction is normally based on a report from a government panel, called *shingikai*. . . . A great difference from other countries, especially the U.S., is that panel includes as crucial members, the top executives from electricity companies.
>
> (July 2013)

G16 highlighted these electric utility executives' ability to influence the contents of these policy agenda-setting committee reports. This formal cooperation through *shingikai* paved the way for an increase in electric utility clout once policymakers established the goal of more rapid nuclear power expansion following the oil shocks.

In addition to institutional features, alignment of policymakers' and electric utilities' risk perceptions and priorities contributed to cooperation after the oil shocks. Existing studies widely cover the Japanese government's focus on the 3Es – energy security, environmental concerns, and economics – as energy policy priorities that have guided development of Japan's energy system (e.g., Valentine et al., 2011). However, these three categories do not appear to have received equal attention from policymakers throughout the period from the oil shocks through the time of the Fukushima disaster. Government and electric utility interviewees uniformly asserted that the oil crises engendered a heightened focus on energy supply risk and energy security aspects of ecological resilience prevailed across the groups. However, some interviewees believe that energy security was the only priority at the time, while others think that economic resilience emerged as a complementary priority, especially efficiency of power plants and cost of supply sources. Policies to promote nuclear power and rationalize electricity use support this assertion. A few interviewees suggested that the "3Es" all became priorities after the oil shocks, but they provided little evidence of the importance of environmental concerns in Japanese energy policymaking. Official energy policies during the period following the oil shocks also do not support this claim. The primary government document from this period, the MITI advisory committee's 1970s Policies for Energy Stabilization: Choices to Stabilize Supply, recommends energy supply stabilization as the top priority. MITI's policy response includes measures to achieve this goal, and neither document mentions environmental concerns.

Several government and electric utility interviewees partially attributed continuation of cooperative policymaker-electric utility relationships after the oil crises to the fact that these shocks did not involve a domestic technological component, so no distrust arose across these stakeholder groups. On the contrary, the oil shocks engendered a shared perception of external risk. This shared risk perception promoted cooperation across the groups toward energy system change to address the energy security and economic concerns resulting from the shocks.

Bureaucrats' and politicians' cooperative relationships with the electric utilities were strengthened by these groups' shared resilience priorities and mutually reinforcing actions to promote these post-oil shock energy goals, according to all government and electric utility company interviewees. Interviewees' perceptions of mutual priorities are consistent with scholarly accounts by renowned political scientist Chalmers Johnson, Samuels, and newer scholars such as Daniel Aldrich (Samuels, 1987; Johnson, 1978; Aldrich, 2005). Both government and electric utility interviewees referred to the two groups as one, using "we" in describing energy policy priorities. As former government official G21 explained,

> We, the government, and private energy companies including oil companies . . . are going hand in hand to work together on a plan on where we get petroleum and gas. They are always talking about the strategy, or tactics, for getting energy sources. So anyway, so there was zero conflict between government and private companies after the crisis, or around the crisis.
>
> (June 2013)

Electric utility executive I12 similarly voiced the coordination and unified view of the electric utilities and policymakers on expansion of nuclear power use after the oil shocks:

> Before the oil shock, just after World War II, we were using coal and hydro and started to use nuclear power. But after the oil shock, we changed our mind. We have to diversify our sources. So we – the government and Japanese electric power companies – ought to increase nuclear power as a percentage, and natural gas.
>
> (June 2013)

This shared goal of diversification through nuclear power and natural gas expansion facilitated energy policy change and deepened cooperation as policymakers and the electric utilities worked together to achieve it.

Government and electric utility interviewees explained that the two groups needed one another to achieve the shared energy security goal through expansion of nuclear power. The Japanese bureaucrats and politicians crafting energy policy depended on electric utilities' cooperation to diversify away from oil use and develop nuclear power. Concurrently, electric utility companies' investments in nuclear power supported the bureaucrats' and politicians' nuclear power promotion policy. These investments increased the electric utilities' interest in supporting bureaucrats and politicians who would perpetuate the future use of nuclear power and enable them to recoup upfront costs, generating a focus on economic resilience. The interviewees' observations are consistent with scholars' assessments. In an analysis of TEPCO's role in shaping Japan's coal and liquified natural gas (LNG) policies, Roger Gale asserts, "Besides regulating the utilities, MITI also promotes them, especially their nuclear power plant programs. It and the Science and Technology Agency are avowed partisans of nuclear power" (Gale, 1981, 95).

MITI also relied on the electric utilities to invest in electricity infrastructure to support the expanding electricity network (Sklarew, 2018). I6, an electric utility executive during the oil crises, noted that "sometimes when the economy was not so good, at that time, MITI asked for additional investment from utility companies, and the utility companies responded to that" (May 2013). I6 recalled of the period after the oil shocks, "at that time, based on my memory, every year, I think 5 trillion yen for the investment, such big investment by utility companies . . . to extend transmission lines or something like that" (May 2013). He and other government and utility interviewees explained that the rate structure established by MITI enabled the utilities to pay for their investments through rate increases approved by MITI, thus passing the electricity infrastructure investment costs to consumers. This design reflected government and utility prioritization of economic resilience Japan's energy system, with negative implications for its social resilience.

The oil crises thus deepened the bureaucrats' and politicians' cooperation with the electric utilities, while bolstering electric utility clout in energy policymaking. These trends, reinforced by a shared focus on economic resilience, enabled transformation of Japan's energy system and preservation of the existing policymaking process. At the same time, the utilities' infrastructure investments and joint government-utility creation of energy system momentum contributed to future lock-in of Japan's energy system in the coming decades.

Economic Regulators and Electric Utilities

Comments from several government and electric utility interviewees (e.g., I1c and G4) suggest that since the electric utilities' formation in the 1950s, tensions burgeoned over economic regulation and control of the electricity industry. These comments offer evidence to support others' analyses of this relationship. Referenced earlier in this chapter, Richard Samuels' seminal work on the subject has been cited by many subsequent scholarly accounts, and Chalmers Johnson's equally well-known book reflects the electric utilities' resistance to government control (Samuels, 1987; Johnson, 1978). The battle for clout coexisted with the need to cooperate on energy system development, a dichotomous trend reflected in the decades to come.

While the oil crises had little effect on economic regulators' relationship with the electric utilities, institutional features and shared economic resilience priorities did contribute to cooperation and clout in the relationship. As previously mentioned, a struggle over economic control of the electric utilities took place when they were created (see Johnson, 1978; Samuels, 1987). Once this struggle concluded, the economic regulators' relationship with the electric utilities remained cooperative through the decade following the oil crises.

Formal institutional arrangements gave the electric utilities clout over regulators in some ways that also promoted cooperation. First, existing analyses and comments from government and electric utility interviewees indicate that MITI and the electric utilities collaborated on economic regulation during and following the oil crises. As Samuels explains, "regulation is structured largely in collaboration with the regulated companies," such that the electric utilities "serve as the principal architects of the regulatory process rather than as the victims of it" (Samuels, 1989, 636). The electric utility interviewees confirmed this arrangement, citing this jointly crafted regulatory framework as a support structure that enabled the electric utilities to invest in energy infrastructure. As electricity industry executive I6 explained, "I think MITI closely worked together with FEPC on policy related matters, and they prepared for the very comfortable regulation for utility companies' management" (May 2013). MITI's approvals of the electric utilities' 21 percent rate increase in 1976 and 50 percent rate increase in 1979 also reflect cooperation and institutional support for the electric utilities, at the public's expense. Gale and Samuels also cite these examples. These rate increases highlight government and utility focus on economic resilience from the utility perspective, rather than the consumer perspective, with a lack of attention to social resilience of the Japanese energy system.

The institutional structure of MITI itself also empowered the electric utilities. Government and electric utility interviewees observed that MITI's dual responsibility as energy policymaker and regulator allowed the utilities to seek regulations that enabled them to fulfill MITI's energy policy goals. Samuels and Gale depict MITI's regulatory style as protective of electric utility interests. Gale observes that "unlike the domestic oil companies – over which MITI wields considerable legislative and extralegal clout – the ministry is more of an arbiter between the utilities and the contending interests of other industries and the consumer, rather than a regulator" (Gale, 1981, 85–85). Samuels explains that, as a result,

> To the extent that there have been disagreements between MITI, the EPCs, and consumers about consumption of domestic coal, electricity rates, industry structure, and nuclear power development, these disagreements have usually been resolved in a manner congenial to the EPCs, with side payments to industrial consumers.
>
> (Samuels, 1989, 636)

MITI's role as both policymaker and regulator thus contributed to the electric utilities' clout over economic regulators after the oil crises, until economic liberalization coincided with the next set of energy system shocks.

While some government and electric utility interviewees cited economic efficiency and costs of supply sources as priorities catalyzed by the oil crises, they did not suggest that policymakers prioritized electricity liberalization at that time. This situation reflects the bureaucrats' reliance on the utilities to promote economic resilience in Japan's energy system. Although economic regulators and the electric utilities conflicted over control of various aspects of energy, the oil crises encouraged cooperation between the two in order to realize national energy security and economic resilience goals.

Safety Regulators and Electric Utilities

The oil crises themselves did not contribute directly to cooperation or conflict between nuclear safety regulators and the electric utilities. However, electric utility interviewees indicated that policymakers' cooperation with the utilities to expand nuclear power after the oil crises simultaneously pressured and empowered the utilities to de-emphasize safety concerns, exacerbating tension with regulators. Government and electric utility interviewees' comments indicate a worsening of this tension in future decades. We might expect the utilities' ecological and economic resilience focus to include safety as a means of avoiding future shocks and costs associated with recovery. However, upfront costs of system expansion and the recovery of these costs took precedence. This contrasted with safety regulators' focus on ecological and social resilience, with an understandable lack of attention to economic resilience.

Institutional features, risk perceptions, priorities, and resilience framing also strongly influenced cooperation and clout in the relationship. Interview data, existing literature, and government documents indicate that from the inception of Japan's civilian nuclear program shortly after the regional utilities' creation, the structure of the regulatory body, safety regulations, and liability concerns have placed the electric utility companies in conflict with regulators.

Throughout shifts in regulatory authority, government and electric utility interviewees could not recall a time when safety regulators and electric utilities had a cooperative relationship. This tension between regulators and engineers existed alongside close cooperation between policymakers and electric utilities. Government and utility interviewees' comments suggest that this policymaker-utility cooperation more strongly influenced energy policymaking than regulator-engineer conflict from the time of the oil crises until the Fukushima accident.

Institutional features such as the regulatory structure contributed to conflict and the struggle for clout. Until 1978, the Cabinet office-led Atomic Energy Commission (AEC) maintained responsibility for both regulation and promotion of nuclear power in Japan. A Cabinet Office document explains that after a 1974 radiation leak from Japan's first (and last) nuclear-powered ship, the *Mutsu*, the Japanese government redistributed responsibilities for nuclear power promotion and regulation (Cabinet Office, Government of Japan, 2013). The Cabinet Office document explains that in 1978, MITI inherited from the AEC the responsibility for both nuclear power plant promotion and initial regulatory assessments of nuclear power plants. In addition, the Nuclear Safety Commission (NSC), responsible for secondary safety checks, was created as an offshoot of the AEC in 1978.

The AEC's dual role as regulator and promoter of nuclear power until the *Mutsu* accident created a conflict of interest within the AEC and an awkward, close relationship with the electric utilities. Former government official G24 noted that public concern engendered assignment of formal blame for the *Mutsu* accident to the Cabinet Office's Science and Technology Agency (STA), leading to the change in regulatory authority. This transfer of both promotional and regulatory roles to one agency perpetuated the problematic relationship between nuclear safety regulators and electric utilities. MITI's consolidated authority enabled the electric utilities to ask policymakers or politicians involved in energy policy to intervene on their behalf in safety regulation issues, according to several government interviewees. Safety regulators thus viewed the electric utilities as having clout through relationships with politicians and bureaucrats. At the same time, the electric utilities viewed regulators as having clout because they made the regulations.

While only a few interviewees personally recalled interactions between the electric utilities and safety regulators during the 1970s and 1980s, electric utility engineers expressed a general view that government regulators never had enough experience or expertise to effectively regulate nuclear power plants. They cited problematic institutional arrangements that enabled policymakers to serve as regulators. Interviewees with regulatory experience conversely expressed frustration over their perceptions of electric utility engineers' historical disobedience and arrogance. Media revelations of data falsifications by the electric utilities dating from the late 1970s support government and utility interviewees' perceptions of tensions over safety regulations (e.g., *Nuclear Engineering International*, 2002; Shirouzu and Tudor, 2011).

Liability for nuclear accidents posed an additional challenge to the electric utilities' relationship with the Japanese government – both policymakers and regulators. Government interviewee G4 and electric utility interviewee I1 discussed the haggling that took place between the electric utilities and the Ministry of Finance over limited versus unlimited liability for nuclear accident compensation when nuclear power development laws were established in the 1950s. Ultimately, the utilities agreed to accept unlimited liability to preserve public confidence in nuclear power. As G4 explained,

> there was a debate, but the utilities said fine, because we explained to the public that there would be no accident. The utilities said if we publicly oppose the unlimited liability of the nuclear accident, the public may suspect that we think there will be a serious accident. So finally, the utilities accepted no upper limit to liability.
>
> (February 2013)

The electric utilities' acceptance of liability for accidents minimized public perceptions of nuclear risk and promoted public confidence in the Japanese government's ability to manage an energy system shift toward nuclear power and away from oil. These interviewees cited Samuels' account of the conflict between the government and the electric utilities, but they did not mention one key point highlighted by Samuels: the Atomic Power Indemnification Law passed in 1961 required the electric utilities to carry an insurance policy of only five billion yen, and the government became responsible for any amount of damage in excess of it (Samuels, 1987, 240). More than safety regulator versus electric utility tensions, this stipulation reflects the electric utilities' clout over economic regulators during this period, which continued until the reintroduction of the economic liberalization movement in the 1990s.

Government and Public

The oil crises, institutional features, risk perceptions, priorities, and resilience goals yielded conflicting impacts on cooperation and clout in the government's relationship with the public. Public opinion polls reflect dissatisfaction with the Japanese government following the oil crises. As depicted in Table 3.1, a dramatic decline in support for then-Prime Minister Tanaka arose from the rapid land and consumer price increases catalyzed by the first oil shock. Public dissatisfaction continued to rise until a scandal involving financial land price speculation came to light, precipitating Tanaka's resignation.[3]

While the oil crises themselves engendered public dissatisfaction with the government, several institutional features simultaneously contributed to government-public distrust and cooperation, as well as government clout after these shocks occurred. All government, NGO, and media interviewees indicated that the public thought of the government as one entity, with no distinction between bureaucrats, politicians, and regulators. Public trust and distrust were aimed at the government as a whole. The poll data and comments by interviewees across all stakeholder groups suggest that the land speculation and later scandals contributed to public distrust in the Japanese government.[4] And yet, the interview data also indicates that this public frustration, compounded by economic and energy insecurity arising from the oil crises, somehow did not alter the government's paternalistic relationship with the public.

This relationship, a cultural feature that has persisted through numerous crises in many sectors, has enabled the Japanese government to undertake policy changes and protections that might incite a public outcry in nations where this type of government-public relationship does not exist. The Japanese government's paternalistic relationship with the public fostered public trust in the government, coupled with an assumption that the government would take measures to ensure Japan's energy security. Former government interviewee G21 described the

Table 3.1 Public Opinion of Japanese Leadership After the Oil Crises

Month/Year	Cabinet	Support Rate (%)	Opposition Rate (%)
7/1973	Tanaka	25	49
11/1973	Tanaka	22	60
11/1974	Tanaka	12	69
6/1978	Fukuda	24	43
10/1978	Fukuda	28	36
12/1978	Ohira	42	29
3/1979	Ohira	31	30
6/1979	Ohira	33	31

Source: Reprinted from Sklarew, 2015; data from *Asahi Shimbun* public opinion polls, 1973–2011.

Japanese public's view of the government – not the energy industry – as responsible for energy supply: "the last resort for energy supply was regarded as . . . the government. To the eyes of the public, it was not the responsibility of the oil company, but the government's responsibility" (June 2013). The public expected that the government would take the appropriate steps to fix Japan's energy insecurity without public involvement in policymaking, in keeping with the paternalistic government-public relationship. I6, an electric utility executive during the oil crises, recalled, "Japanese energy policy changed from depending on oil, shifting to coal, gas, and nuclear. But the Japanese general public was also not so much concerned about such change. So they didn't know what's going on in the central government" (May 2013). Public trust in the government's energy policymaking ability consequently diminished public involvement in energy policymaking. This public deferral of energy policymaking power and responsibility to the government resulted in a lack of public clout.

In fact, NGO and media interviewees' comments suggested that underlying this public trust in the government was the public's view of the government as superior, and thus better equipped than the public to make energy policy decisions for them. As P2 explained,

> the Japanese government, in consultation with industries, was in charge of creating energy policy without virtually any . . . authorization, dialogue, discussion with the public, because . . . maybe you have heard of the word in Japanese '*okami*' . . . So *okami* is something lower people are using to indicate the upper government, right? So that kind of relationship has been there in Japan for many, many years.
>
> (March 2013)

P2 asserted that because of this view, the public willingly ceded clout to the government in energy policymaking. Japanese energy policymaking, along with policymaking in other sectors, was founded on a model in which the public believed that "the government is a kind of noble and upper people who are smarter, and more knowledgeable, and have more power to change things, and they . . . have the sole responsibility of creating good policies for lower Japanese people." As a result, P2 explained,

> the government had no interest in getting people's opinion, or feedback, because they believed that they are the persons or the organization which have more knowledge and information, and power to create better policies for all Japan. And in return, our people were not interested in getting involved in politics. Because we Japanese people just believed in the government.
>
> (March 2013)

Other government and NGO interviewees echoed this view that the government retained clout in energy policymaking after the oil crises based on public preference for this arrangement.

Public trust and belief in the government's superior decision-making capability enabled the government – with the media's help – to develop public awareness of energy security as a new national priority, fostering public support for the government's focus on ecological resilience. This shared priority further promoted public support for and compliance with the government's energy policy changes after the oil crises. As government official G13 recalled, "Japanese people at that time did understand the need for energy saving and some shift from oil consumption to another form of energy consumption" (June 2013). The Japanese government and public jointly prioritized energy security concerns over other risks, including nuclear safety concerns. G13 asserted that the oil crises' influence overshadowed the impact of nuclear accidents at Three-Mile Island, and later Chernobyl, on public risk perceptions of nuclear power. However, a number of scholars, including Suttmeier, Lesbirel, and Aldrich, have found that public opposition to nuclear power plant siting did arise in the 1970s, but government clout and incentives for cooperation grounded in general public trust overcame this resistance (Suttmeier, 1981; Lesbirel, 1998; Aldrich, 2005). These scholars and others also suggest that the regulatory and policymaking process offered limited opportunities for public influence on energy policymaking (e.g., see Cohen et al., 1995; Aldrich, 2005). NGO interviewees suggested that the general public did not object to this limitation on clout, so the policymaking process continued to constrain public input during the energy system shift after the oil crises.

Shared risk perceptions further contributed to government-public cooperation. Interview data suggests that the public largely viewed the Japanese government's policy responses to the oil crises as logical reactions to the shocks and resulting public needs. For example, P2, the same NGO representative who characterized the public's belief in the government's superiority, also posited that "the Japanese government has been creating their energy policy as a very serious response to the social changes or the events that happened. So the first one is the oil crisis, so they diversified" (March 2013). Belief that the government made logical policy changes in response to the oil crises appears to have deepened public trust in the government's energy policymaking ability. This trust enabled further policy changes that strengthened the energy system shift and contributed to the new system's momentum. The government's energy security framing for the shift to nuclear power also linked the public's interest in social resilience to policymakers' promotion of ecological resilience.

All of these relationship factors and their influences on Japanese energy system change and the energy policymaking process are reflected in Table 3.2. The oil shocks fostered electric utilities' cooperation with and increasing utility clout over all government groups aside from safety regulators. Concurrently, the government maintained cooperation with and clout over the public. These relationships resulted in policy change away from the incumbent energy system, with no change in the policymaking process or electricity market structure. We now take a closer look at these effects.

Table 3.2 Japanese Government's Relationships and Changes to Policy, Process, and Structure After the Oil Crises

Relationship	Change in Cooperation/Conflict	Change in Clout
Bureaucrats-Utilities	Cooperation No change	Bureaucrats > Utilities Change: utilities strengthening
Politicians-Utilities	Cooperation No change	Politicians > Utilities Change: utilities strengthening
Economic Regulators- Utilities	Conflict < Cooperation No change	Regulators < Utilities No change
Safety Regulators- Utilities	Conflict > Cooperation Change: regulatory conflict	Regulators > Utilities No change
Government-Public	Cooperation No change	Government > Public No change

Policy Change	Policymaking Process/Structural Change
Yes, out of incumbent system	No

Source: Reprinted from Sklarew, 2015.

Aftershocks: Electricity Supply and Energy System Changes

The Japanese government's general policy goals following the oil shocks align with our expectations of a critical juncture. However, the specific energy supply source shifts diverge from what we might expect if we did not take into account the relationship changes and influences described earlier. Government-electric utility cooperation, public trust in the government, alignment of priorities for energy security and system resilience, and government clout over the utilities and the public made major energy supply policy change possible after the oil crises, transforming Japan's energy system. No immediate policymaking process changes took place. However, as the electric utilities gained clout from the government's reliance on then to implement the policy changes, eventual policymaking process change codified this relationship shift. This formal institutionalization of the electric utilities' clout later contributed to the government's inability to change energy policy when new shocks to the energy system occurred.

The government's cooperative relationship with the electric utilities and public, government clout, and shared priorities across groups enabled policymakers to collaborate with the electric utilities. This collaboration aimed to bolster resilience of the existing energy system by diversifying oil supply sources and building petroleum stockpiles. At the same time, the government coordinated with the electric utilities and the public to promote a dramatic energy system transformation. Government interviewees linked changes in public priorities, namely heightened sensitivity to energy security concerns, with the government's long-term energy policy shift. Government official G13 explained, "After the oil crisis in the 70s, the public did not anymore trust long-term reliability of such inexpensive oil. And naturally, the government changed its policy so that it may place the greatest priority on saving energy and employment of non-fossil energies such as nuclear and renewables" (June 2013). G13 observed that this priority change and the government policies codifying it after the oil crises shifted Japan's energy system to a path that continued for decades. "The issue of overseas dependence of energy is so crucial in Japan, and basically, since the 70s, the government policy of save energy and employ non-fossil fuel has not much changed." As we will see in this section, Japan's 1970s-1980s electricity supply source data does reflect a shift away from oil, but reliance on coal continued. Increasing dependence on natural gas also accompanied the rise of nuclear power. The emphasis on renewables mentioned by G13 was largely relegated to hydropower, with little attention to other renewable energy sources, such as wind, solar and geothermal. Japanese policymakers' and politicians' cooperation with and clout over the electric utilities and the public impacted the transitions toward and away from these specific electricity supply sources.

Energy System Preservation: Oil Supply Diversification

In the midst of and following the oil crises, the Japanese government developed goals featuring stabilization of oil supplies, diversification of energy supply sources beyond oil, and energy conservation and efficiency. According to several government officials (e.g., G9, G21), the oil crises catalyzed the Japanese government's pursuit of an energy policy focused on securing oil supplies. The government's cooperative relationship with the electric utilities also appears to have played a role in this policy to preserve energy security and oil use.

In 1974, the interim report of the Petroleum Subcommittee of MITI's Advisory Committee for Natural Resources and Energy stated the need for public-private coordination to create a planned 90-day oil stockpile:

> It is needless to say a level of 60-day oil stockpiling should be held; on top of this, the level should be built up to 90 days in a planned manner to develop a reinforced oil stockpiling system through joint efforts of the public and private sectors.
>
> (Petroleum Association of Japan, 2013, 20)

The Japanese government pursued this and other oil supply security policies with electric utilities' and public support. This public support was based on public trust in the government's ability to reestablish energy security after the oil crises.

In 1975, The Ministry of International Trade and Industry's (MITI) Advisory Committee for Energy submitted a report recommending development of a stable energy supply as MITI's top priority (International Atomic Energy Agency, 2004; MITI Advisory Committee for Energy, Government of Japan, 1975). The framing of this goal reflects a focus on engineering, ecological and economic resilience. Based on this report, MITI established five policy pillars: oil dependence reduction; diversification of energy supply alternatives to oil; establishment of stable oil supply through petroleum reserves; exploration and development of oil by Japanese companies; promotion of energy conservation; and promotion of new energy R&D (International Atomic Energy Agency, 2004; MITI Advisory Committee for Energy, Government of Japan, 1975). These goals simultaneously fostered resilience in the existing oil-based energy system, while shifting to a new system comprised of a balance of energy supply sources.

In December 1975, the Japanese government enacted the Petroleum Reserve Law, which established an oil stockpile target; obligated refiners, marketers and importers of petroleum to hold minimum oil stockpiles above the level of their basic obligation volumes; and lowered the basic obligation volume, specifically in the event of an oil supply shortage in Japan (Ministry of International Trade and Industry, Government of Japan, 1975). In 1978, the government-owned Japan Petroleum Development Corporation (JPDC) became the Japan National Oil Corporation (JNOC), when the Japanese government added the function of stockpile operation and strategic petroleum reserves.[5] In 1981, the Japanese government established a system that obligated the private sector to hold a 90-day equivalent oil stockpile.

These measures reflect the Japanese government's efforts to build resilience against future shocks to the existing oil-based energy system. These policies also strengthened MITI's oversight of the electric utilities' oil stockpiling efforts. All of these government initiatives reflect policymakers' and politicians' clout over and cooperation with the electric utilities, as well as an aim to retain public trust.

Energy System Transformation: Diversifying Sources

While working to preserve oil supply security, the Japanese government also undertook a dramatic transformation of the energy system. The oil crises alone did not enable this shift from an oil-dependent electricity supply to a diversified electricity supply portfolio. Policymakers', politicians', and regulators' relationships with the electric utilities and the public contributed to the shifts in Japan's electricity supply. As described, these groups' goals for economic and ecological resilience also shaped these relationships and their influence on energy policy change.

This energy system transformation included policies to reduce Japanese oil consumption. In 1980, the Suzuki Cabinet called for a reduction in the share of imported oil from 75 to 50 percent of Japan's primary energy supply by 1990, supported by imposition of a tariff on petroleum imports (Cabinet Office, Government of Japan, 1980). The tariff revenue financed implementation of the Petroleum Reserve Law, but it also funded R&D on oil alternatives.

The Cabinet approved MITI's proposed 1990 targets for "oil-alternative energy supplies" in the nation's primary energy supply, including increases in nuclear power use from 3.9 to 10.9 percent, coal from 12.9 to 17.7 percent, and natu-ral gas from about 4 percent to 10.2 percent (Cabinet Office, Government of Japan, 1980). According to International Energy Agency (IEA) data, electricity accounted for approximately 30 percent of Japan's energy supply in 1980 (Interna-tional Energy Agency, 2021). A large component of Japan's energy system trans-formation after the oil crises involved reducing the amount of oil used to generate electricity. The Japanese government's cooperation with the electric utilities ena-bled sweeping policy changes that replaced oil use with nuclear power, natural gas, and coal in the electricity sector.

As depicted in Figure 3.1, International Energy Agency figures reveal that oil dropped precipitously from 73 percent of Japan's electricity supply in 1973 to 28.7 percent in 1990 (International Energy Agency, 2021). Concurrently, nuclear power rose from a mere 2 percent to 23.2 percent. Natural gas experi-enced a similar rise from 2 percent to 19.3 percent. Coal use also expanded to a lesser degree from 8 percent to 14.3 percent of the Japanese electricity supply. In the 1970s, hydropower was the only renewable energy source in Japan's electricity mix, a trend that largely continued through 1990. Hydropower's share of Japan's electricity supply actually declined from 15 percent in 1973 to 11 percent in 1990 (International Energy Agency, 2021). The IEA data reflects a 1990 electricity mix that included very small amounts of geothermal power (0.2 percent) and biofuels (0.9 percent).

These shifts in specific fuel sources – and at times, even the policies promot-ing these changes – do not reflect an avoidance of reliance on imported energy sources, despite government framing of Japan's energy transformation as a shift toward energy independence. Japan has no indigenous natural gas or coal. The new policies began to shift Japan's energy system away from oil dependence, but toward reliance on a different energy supply source: nuclear power, with natural

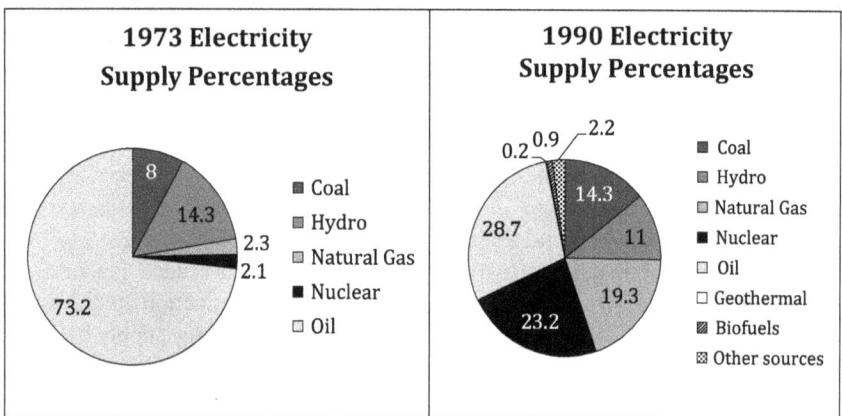

Figure 3.1 Comparison of 1973 Versus 1990 Electricity Supply Fuel Percentages
Source: International Energy Agency, 2021.

gas following closely behind. Japan does not possess any uranium, either, but we will see that measures to address uranium imports are developed alongside other nuclear expansion policies. At the same time, coal and renewables policies were not sustained, and growth of these fuels in Japan's energy supply did not reach the Japanese government's expected targets. We will examine how Japanese government's relationships with the electric utilities and the public impacted the expansion of these sources.

On the demand side, the oil crises also spurred new energy conservation measures. As discussed earlier, these measures could have faced opposition from the public and the electric utilities. We will examine how the government's relationships with the public and the electric utilities played an influential role in the success of the government's conservation and efficiency policies.

Nuclear Powers Up

Nuclear power expansion became the key to Japan's energy system transformation. Given the high start-up costs for nuclear power plants and the negative impacts of the Three-Mile Island and Chernobyl accidents that occurred in 1979 and 1986, respectively, the oil crises alone are unlikely to have propelled this rapid expansion of nuclear power use. The previously described governmental relationships with the electric utilities and the public help to explain this shift. These relationships also shed light on the ways in which policies to promote replacement of oil with nuclear power set the stage for future lock-in of a nuclear-centered energy system.

Nineteen nuclear reactors were operational or under construction when the first oil crisis occurred in 1973. From that time until the 2011 Fukushima accident, the utilities constructed 39 additional nuclear power plants (Sklarew, 2015). For a full list of reactors, their operation stat dates, and status as of 2021, please see Table 5.2 in chapter 5. Nuclear power expanded from 2 percent of Japan's electricity supply in 1973 to 23.2 percent in 1990, according to International Energy Agency data (International Energy Agency, 2021). Since Japan's electricity supply portfolio appears relatively proportionally allocated between nuclear, natural gas, coal, oil, and hydropower during this period, this increase does not yet embody a nuclear-dependent system. However, the large increase in nuclear energy's share reflects the beginnings of such a system, as infrastructure, momentum, and institutional support grew along with nuclear generation capacity.

While the Japanese government's energy supply diversification plan included several types of sources, some government and electric utility interviewees perceived a narrower focus on nuclear power expansion as the key to Japanese energy security. Former electric utility executive I23 observed that "after the oil shock . . . should have had a big impact on energy policy. So, for example, whether or not to do solar . . . in reality, while we're saying diversification, we're saying do nuclear." Government and electric utility interviewees indicated that during and following the oil crises, the Japanese bureaucratic policymakers and politicians coordinated with the electric utilities to escalate plans for increased nuclear power use in the electricity supply. As former government official G16 stated, "there was a time, even under the close relationship, when after the oil shock, there was a clear shift of energy sources from fossil fuels to nuclear. That was, I think, under a very close relationship with government and industry, they changed the course" (July 2013). The official believes that the government did not force this shift on the electric utilities, suggesting that "they cooperated very closely."

Government interviewees indicated that bureaucrats and politicians co-led the policymaking shift to prioritize nuclear power expansion. As government official G18 explained, "Nuclear development is not only driven by bureaucracy, but the politicians of the LDP. That's why the LDP has an institutional memory of favorably regarding nuclear energy" (August 2013). This collaboration between bureaucrats and politicians to pursue nuclear power development and build public acceptance for it predates the oil crises, according to this interviewee and others. Another government official, G21, stated, "Of course, we – I mean the government – started to introduce nuclear power in the 1950s, but the oil shock accelerated the speed of introduction of nuclear power after '73" (June 2013). G21 and other government and electric utility interviewees believe that this earlier cooperation set the stage for the shift toward prioritization of nuclear power after the oil crises.

MITI's clout and the cooperative relationship between MITI bureaucrats and the electric utilities supported this expansion of nuclear power. Government and electric utility interviewees explained that after the oil crises, the government and the electric utilities began to coordinate the national energy policy and the electric utilities' electricity supply plans. In the national energy policy, the government set numerical targets for particular electricity supply sources. The electric utilities developed their 10-year electricity supply plans based on these targets, and MITI approved the plans. Government official G4 highlighted the role of these coordinated policies and plans in promoting public trust in the government's energy policymaking authority and the electric utilities' ability to execute it. The official connected this coordination of official energy policies and electric utilities' supply plans with a series of government incentives for local communities hosting nuclear power plants.

These measures, the most prominent energy policy measures of this era, passed in 1974 and known as the Three Power Source Development Laws (*dengen sanpo*), institutionalized formerly ad hoc compensation to localities to promote siting of nuclear power plants. The Electric Power Resources Development Promotion Tax Law imposed a tax of 85 yen per 1000 kilowatt-hours of power sold by the electric utilities. The Power Resources Development Special Account Law and the Law on Adjustment of Areas Surrounding Generating Plants defined how the tax revenue would be collected and disbursed to localities siting nuclear power plants (Board Audit of Japan, 2001). Analyses by Lesbirel and Aldrich asserted that while the laws provided compensation for nuclear, coal, and hydropower plants, nuclear plant host communities had access to the largest amount of funding (Lesbirel, 1998, 36; Aldrich, 2005, 119). A paper by long-time energy policy scholar and government official Tatsujiro Suzuki confirms this assertion, stating that "nuclear power plants were to be given subsidies twice as high as coal-fired or oil-fired thermal power plants" (Suzuki, 2001, 4). Over time, only nuclear power plants remained eligible for all of the subcategories of grants and subsidies, while those available to hydropower and thermal plants shrank. For more details, see Aldrich (2013, 85). Electric utility interviewee I1 noted that the government eventually phased out thermal and hydropower plant host subsidies, and only communities hosting nuclear plants received funds.

The period following the second oil shock and the Three Mile Island (TMI) accident saw related increases in Japanese government subsidies to localities hosting nuclear plants. An analysis by Richard Suttmeier shows that MITI's grants to localities cooperating with nuclear plant construction increased from 37,514 million yen in FY1979 to 39,974 million yen in FY1980. Grants from the STA rose from 1,405 million yen to 1,440 million yen during the same period. Nuclear power plant safety improvement subsidies and grants from MITI and STA also increased dramatically from FY1979 to 1980. MITI 's grants rose from 360 million yen in FY79 to 1,164 million yen in FY1980, and subsidies increased from 3,345 million yen to 4,440 million yen. STA grants rose from 563 million yen to 1,392 million yen during the same period (Suttmeier, 1981, 115).

These policies further strengthened cooperation between the government and the public, as well as government clout over the public in energy policymaking. While NGO, media, and government interviewees did not recall widespread public opposition to nuclear power expansion, existing work by Suttmeier, Murota and Yano, and Aldrich suggests that the catalyst for the subsidies emerged from local opposition to nuclear plant siting (Suttmeier, 1981; Murota and Yano, 1993; Aldrich, 2008). Between 1973 and 1980, local residents filed administrative lawsuits against siting of six nuclear power plants, including Fukushima unit 2 (Murota and Yano, 1993, 114). This local opposition was overridden by the central government. All of the plants ultimately were constructed and operated until the Fukushima accident. This outcome reflects government clout over the public in energy policy decision-making. Reasons cited for this lack of public clout include insufficient representation of the local majority view in informal negotiations, as well as exclusion of public opinion in formal environmental impact assessments (Aldrich, 2008).

Government and utility company interviewees indicated that the electric utilities exploited this clout in securing public support for nuclear plant siting, framing nuclear power plant construction as a government mandate, rather than a for-profit enterprise.

G4 noted that following government approval of the utilities' electricity supply plans, "it's interesting, because the law says, once it is approved by the government… then *kofukin*, subsidies, will be distributed to local communities. So there was a legal meaning of the utilities' plans" (February 2013). Government approval of the supply plans enabled the electric utilities to secure public approval for nuclear plant siting, "because the utilities also can tell the local communities this is the national government policy approved program, so it's not just for our profit purposes, it is for national energy policy, so please accept this power plant. So the plans and the subsidies are linked." LDP politicians and MITI bureaucrats thus utilized public trust in them to build support for nuclear plants. Aldrich and other scholars examining Japanese public opposition to nuclear plant siting posit that politicians and bureaucrats also made visits to local communities to create a public perception of legitimacy regarding nuclear plant construction (e.g., Aldrich, 2008).

The linkages between national energy policies, electric utilities' supply plans and siting subsidies created momentum in an energy system more focused on nuclear power by deepening electric utilities' and local politicians' vested interests in perpetuating nuclear power operation and expansion. Broad public trust in the government's ability to manage an energy system transition and lack of public clout in concrete energy policy decisions further fostered acceleration of this energy system shift. Economic gains for local communities strengthened government clout and public trust during this period of nuclear power expansion after the oil crises. However, later chapters of this book show that following future shocks resulting in a loss of public trust, the public rejects both economic compensation for hosting nuclear plants and plans for expansion of nuclear power.

The Japanese government's cooperative relationships with the electric utilities and the public also helped to shape a crucial element of Japan's nuclear power policy: nuclear fuel reprocessing. As previously mentioned, the Japanese government initiated nuclear power production policies in the 1950s. They included the nuclear fuel recycling program in the Long-Term Plans for the Research, Development and Use of Nuclear Power established in 1956. Many government and electric utility interviewees suggested that reducing uranium imports served as a key driver behind the nuclear fuel reprocessing plans, reflecting a focus on energy security and ecological resilience. They also noted that reprocessing served as a solution to nuclear waste disposal. Aligning with this second priority, a paper by Tadahiro Katsuta and Tatsujiro Suzuki posits that the Japanese government's commitment to the nuclear fuel cycle emerged from local communities' concerns that spent fuel would remain on reactor sites (Katsuta and Suzuki, 2011). This driver suggests public concerns over the safety and health aspects of social resilience at the local level. As G13 indicated, "the utility companies and government were strongly committed with how to do with spent fuel arising from each site from nuclear power production. Those spent fuels will go somewhere else. Nuclear power production business is ongoing, so how to manage spent fuel is a question. That is a kind of promise" (June 2013). The Japanese government thus assured the electric utilities and localities hosting nuclear power plants that the spent nuclear fuel would not remain on the reactor sites. This pledge propelled the government's nuclear fuel reprocessing program policies, despite economic challenges.

While the reprocessing program's high costs should have constrained its development, G13 intimated, "my understanding was that government decision we had in the 70s and 1980s was not so serious, you know. Just they wanted to continue the program" (June 2013). Rather than balancing energy security and economics in making the decision, as many government and electric utility interviewees suggested was the case, the official cited public trust and acceptance as the reason the government downplayed reprocessing program costs: "For the government, you know, as far as nuclear energy is concerned, you know, it's so socially controversial, and therefore, they just to the public the government wanted to say that nuclear energy is a must because of energy security." This account suggests that the Japanese government focused public attention on nuclear power's contribution to ecological and social resilience, minimizing the economic resilience challenges.

The Japanese public generally accepted the energy security argument for nuclear fuel reprocessing, according to NGO and government interviewees. As a result, G13 suggested, Japan's "nuclear fuel recycling policy . . . has been constantly pursued, with sufficient public support, aiming at reducing imported uranium for strengthening energy independence" (July 2013). In later decades, several bureaucratic policymakers and politicians would raise the question of Japan's fuel cycle economics. Continuation of the program would depend in large part on the role of the central government's relationships with the electric utilities, local governments, and the public. Later chapters of this book will examine continuation of the nuclear fuel recycling program and the evolving economic challenges associated with it.

The government's clout and cooperative relationships with the electric utilities and the public after the oil crises thus enabled nuclear power expansion, defying the high costs of initial investment and fuel reprocessing, as well as safety concerns arising from the Three-Mile Island and Chernobyl accidents.

Natural Gas Expansion

In addition to expanding nuclear power use after the oil crises, the Japanese government also aimed to increase natural gas use in Japan's electricity supply from about 4 percent to 10.2 percent of Japan's primary energy supply by 1990 (Ministry of International Trade and Industry, 1979). Exceeding this goal, Japanese natural gas use in electricity generation rose from 2 percent in 1973 to 19.3 percent in 1990, as stated earlier. After the oil shocks, the Japanese government encouraged the electric utilities to increase LNG use by exempting LNG from the import tariffs imposed on other petroleum products in 1980 (Stewart, 2009, 180).

The electric utilities' LNG expansion plans reflected attention to compliance with environmental standards. TEPCO implemented an ambitious LNG import agenda to meet SOx and NOx pollution standards even before the oil crises occurred (Gale, 1981, 99). From an energy security perspective, LNG also posed an attractive alternative to oil, since the electric utility companies were able to minimize oil imports from the Middle East in favor of natural gas imports from Southeast Asian neighbors such as Indonesia, Malaysia, and Brunei, as well as Australia. LNG also offered less measurable economic advantages over nuclear power. Roger Gale quotes a TEPCO spokesman as confiding during an interview after the second oil crisis, "If we quantify the social costs, the inordinate delays, the remote and extra-large sites, and the ensuing transmission losses with which we have had to contend with nuclear power, then LNG is far less expensive" (Gale, 1981, 100). These advantages suggest that the government and the electric utilities would cooperate to expand natural gas use, and they did. In the 1970s, state-owned JNOC guaranteed loans for projects in Southeast Asia, and MITI provided overseas investment insurance to the electric utilities for their loan guarantees.

However, some economic challenges and energy security concerns also shaped government-utility cooperation on LNG expansion plans. Former government official G21 referenced the high start-up costs for LNG plants. Government and electric utility interviewees also explained that concerns over the energy insecurity associated with fuel imports led the utilities to raise LNG use gradually, importing from a variety of sources.

MITI's cooperative relationship with the electric utilities also played a role in mitigating these concerns and fostering the increase in LNG use. Prior to the oil crises, only TEPCO invested in LNG. TEPCO's leadership on LNG imports, combined with its close relationship with MITI, contributed to development of a regulatory and financial environment conducive to investment in costly LNG infrastructure. The decision to build LNG terminals to supply local electricity consumers protected the electric utilities' and gas companies' regional monopolies, given constraints on moving LNG between regions. This protection encouraged the electric utilities' long-term investment in LNG projects and infrastructure (e.g., see Hayes and Victor, 2006, 327). JNOC and MITI support for the electric utility companies' investments further incentivized expansion of the electric utilities' LNG use. In addition, the Japanese government granted the electric utilities and gas companies access to government-owned roads under which pipelines were constructed. The utilities' gradual, yet dramatic, LNG expansion thus promoted the government's and utilities' shared priorities for ecological and economic resilience.

Government clout and public trust in the government's policy decisions also enabled expansion of LNG use. LNG plant and terminal siting faced little public opposition, according to Gale, who attributes LNG's trumping of nuclear power to this phenomenon in the decade following the oil crises (Gale, 1981, 97). This lack of opposition was accompanied by a related lack of tension between safety regulators and the electric utilities over gas plant and terminal siting. Government cooperation with and clout over the electric utilities and the public thus facilitated the considerable shift toward LNG after the oil crises.

Coal Takes Its Lumps

In addition to spurring nuclear power and natural gas increases, government-public cooperation also incentivized the Japanese government's pursuit of coal use expansion after the oil shocks. The public did not express opposition to coal plant siting, in comparison to concern over nuclear power plants. The oil crises encouraged MITI to alter a previous focus on pollution control toward energy security and diversification away from oil, according to electric utility executive I1 and some analysts of Japanese environmental policy (e.g., Fukasaku, 1995, 1075; Jordan-Korte, 2011, 210). The Japanese government also focused to a lesser degree on the potential of new coal technologies to meet Japanese pollution control standards. While land use, transmission line development, and processing costs posed economic challenges, they resembled problems facing nuclear power. This priority shift toward ecological resilience should have supported expansion of coal, as it did nuclear and natural gas. Policymakers aimed to increase coal use in Japan's primary energy supply from 12.9 to 17.7 percent by 1990 (Ministry of International Trade and Industry, 1979). They fell short of this goal, per the aforementioned rise from 8 percent of Japan's electricity supply in 1973 to 14 percent in 1990. The electric utilities' economic resilience priorities contributed to this shortfall.

While government-electric utility cooperation supported nuclear power expansion and increased LNG use, the electric utilities' disinterest in pursuing coal use stymied the government's plans for coal use expansion following the oil crises. Existing literature and interview data reveal three reasons for the relatively lethargic increase in coal use compared to nuclear and natural gas use expansion: expensive domestic coal procurement, reluctance to import coal, and energy conservation measures' displacement of the need for increased coal use. These factors aligned to define utility reluctance to dramatic coal expansion in the electricity supply, which would have compromised economic resilience.

The first factor hindering utility support for coal expansion, expensive coal procurement, arose from politicians' focus on the coal industry's economic priorities, which diverged from the utilities' focus on economic resilience of the energy system. According to several government interviewees, the domestic coal industry's cooperation with and clout over politicians led to a domestic coal procurement policy. As G21 explained, "about coal, we had a kind of domestic industrial problem. We had a domestic coal industry, and the labor union of the coal industry was very strong and made good ties with the Socialist Party at that time. And the management layer of the coal industry made good friends with the LDP" (June 2013). The interviewee suggested that while the government still retained clout over the electric utilities, the coal industry had clout over the government, enabling the domestic coal procurement policy: "So the political power of the coal industry was very strong, so we could not neglect their demand or request for energy policy." Since domestic coal prices exceeded import prices, the electric utilities lost interest in expanding coal use. This reluctance followed a long effort by MITI to control Japan's domestic coal market (see Samuels, 1987, 101–104).

The second factor, utility reluctance to import coal, aligns with the utilities' focus on economic resilience. Gale's analysis indicates that the electric utilities did not express strong interest in imported coal after the oil crises, due to siting constraints and costly pollution controls, as well as a discomfort regarding pressure from MITI to import coal (Gale, 1981). The Japanese government made efforts to mitigate siting concerns through the same mechanism employed for nuclear power plants, siting subsidies. The 1974 Electric Power Resources Development Promotion Tax that provided subsidies to communities hosting nuclear power plants also funded subsidies to localities hosting coal-fired power plants. Despite the subsidies, coal use did not expand as rapidly as MITI had planned.

Although MITI engaged in coal liquefaction and gasification projects after the oil crises, they terminated these projects a decade later. Government interviewee G9 attributed cancellation of the government's coal liquefaction and gasification projects to the third factor referenced earlier: successful energy conservation measures. According to G9, these measures, discussed later, displaced the need for coal liquefaction and gasification technologies. While this assertion may be partially true, Gale's assessment of electric utility opposition to coal expansion suggests that the electric utilities also may have expressed disinterest in commercializing these technologies, especially after large investments in nuclear power. This rationale aligns with the utilities' focus on economic resilience. G21's observations support this scenario, indicating that "coal was not appealing to the management of electric companies before 1990, when the domestic coal industry was blown out of the water." The electric utilities' growing clout over the government throughout the 1980s enabled them to limit the government's coal expansion plans in exchange for development of nuclear power.

Renewables' Failure to Thrive

We would expect that the emphasis on energy security would have driven more rapid development and use of renewables as indigenous, oil-alternative technologies after the oil crises. However, the government's cooperation with the electric utilities on nuclear power expansion, coupled with mounting electric utility clout, also appears to have stifled renewables growth. Interview data and existing literature suggest that the government's relationships with the electric utilities and the public did play a role in the small increase in renewables following the oil crises. An assessment by the CRIEPI states that development of solar PV, geothermal and hydrogen technologies took place "under close cooperation of industry, government, and academic organizations." The report also notes that the project included coal as a fourth area of research as an alternative to oil (Kimura, 2009, 1). This inclusion of coal indicates energy security and ecological resilience as the drivers for any renewables development, rather than a focus on environmental sustainability.

Per the aforementioned IEA data, hydroelectric power already supplied 14.3 percent of Japan's electricity at the time of the first oil crisis (International Energy Agency, 2021). The drive to diversify and bolster energy security after the oil crises led the Japanese government to create policies and programs to foster development of other renewables, including solar, wind and biomass. However, these policies and programs did not lead to notable increases in renewable energy use. In 1990, hydropower supplied 10.7 percent of Japan's electricity, but replacement by other renewables did not account for or compensate for this decline. Including hydropower, the total renewables share in Japan's electricity production in 1990 amounted to just over 12 percent of Japan's electricity supply.[6] Non-hydroelectric renewables accounted for 1.3 percent, comprised primarily of biofuels, geothermal and waste heat.[7] Government and electric utility documents as well as media analyses widely cite the high cost of renewables as the reason for this slow growth, but this rationale does not fully explain renewables' slow growth. By contrast, despite the high investment costs for nuclear plants, nuclear power's share grew exponentially. Further, the government's incentive programs, described later, should have made renewables more financially appealing.

After the first oil crisis, MITI created the Sunshine Project in 1974 to advance R&D on solar PV, geothermal and hydrogen technologies. After the second oil crisis, the Japanese government increased the budget for this project. Some analyses tout the project as the impetus for expansive growth in Japanese solar PV, but the commercial growth of this technology was not reflected until the 1990s (e.g., see Kimura and Suzuki, 2006).

In 1980, the Japanese government enacted the Law Concerning Promotion of the Development and Introduction of Alternative Energy. This law empowered the MITI Minister to establish and make public supply targets for alternative energy. The law also stipulates that energy users will make efforts to use alternative energy sources. The law defines "alternative" energy sources as alternatives to oil, including renewables. Under the same law, the Japanese government established the New Energy and Industrial Technology Development Organization (NEDO) to promote new energy technology development – including renewables – through R&D that the private sector considered too risky, and through subsidies to private firms developing renewables.[8] However, these projects also made little headway during the post-oil crises period. Some scholars predicted the slow pace of renewables growth in Japan's electricity supply, citing uncertainty regarding the path to commercialization and diffusion. This uncertainty challenged economic resilience, but the same could be said of nuclear power, which expanded rapidly.

Many government and electric utility interviewees suggested that a greater focus on cooperation to promote nuclear expansion dampened interest in renewables growth. G9 explained that MITI officials did not believe that government support for renewables development was necessary: ". . . once we started the renewable projects, photovoltaics and wind and geothermal, the government did not need to support too much, because of having this stable nuclear power supply" (April 2013). Gale's analysis supports this notion that the electric utilities remained uninterested in adding more renewables to their electricity supply portfolios. He observes, "TEPCO . . . has made only a minimal commitment . . . to funding the development of alternative forms of renewable energy" (Gale, 1981, 94). Gale adds that this disinterest expressed by the leading electric utility led other utilities to disavow renewables development, as well. Coupled with this focus on nuclear power as a replacement for oil, the Japanese's government's energy conservation measures further weakened government and utility interest in investing in renewables. G9 summarized this dismissal: "Having so much effort of energy conservation and nuclear, between the two, they think to have this nuclear power supply is good enough for the Japanese economy." This attitude again reflects emphasis on energy security and its implications for ecological and economic resilience.

Japan Saves Itself: Conservation and Efficiency

Existing studies indicate that the oil crises led to the Japanese government's first implementation of supply efficiency and demand conservation measures. In 1978, the Japanese government created the Moonlight Project, which involved MITI-led

R&D on energy efficiency and energy storage technologies, including fuel cells. On the demand side, the Japanese government passed the Act Concerning the Rational Use of Energy in 1979. The measures in the law focused on energy conservation by large users, particularly manufacturers, as well as the housing and transportation industries (Ministry of International Trade and Industry, 1979). While we would expect the electric utilities to oppose conservation and promote greater electricity use, Gale observes that following the oil crises, TEPCO ceased its advertising campaigns encouraging electricity use and implemented a conservation program (Gale, 1981, 94). At the same time, cooperation from Japan's manufacturing industries also proved crucial to this shift.

Public trust in the government's decisions, coupled with the joint shift in the government's and public's priorities toward a focus on energy security, also contributed to broad public compliance with new government mandates on consumers' energy conservation after the oil crises. Several NGO and government interviewees referenced this link between public understanding of government priorities and this compliance. As government official G4 observed, "It's easier actually to mandate reduced energy consumption than to mandate increased energy supply, right?" (February 2013). This view is reflected in the government's positive incentives for energy supply source diversification, in contrast to the imposition of mandatory demand-side restrictions.

As a result of these measures, Japan's already comparatively high energy efficiency improved by three percent per year through 1990 (Japan Center for Economic Research Middle-Term Economic Forecast Team, 2012, 4). Vaclav Smil's analysis of Japan's post-oil crises conservation and efficiency efforts shows that the energy intensities of all major Japanese industries fell by 20 to 50 percent between 1973 and the late 1980s (Smil, 2007, 2). Thus, broad public acceptance of the Japanese government's energy conservation goals and the electric utilities' compliance with them supported a national reduction in energy consumption after the oil crises.

While the Japanese government employed policy changes to pursue energy system transformation from oil dependence to diversification, no energy policymaking process changes occurred as a direct result of the oil crises.

Unshocked: Policy Process and Structural Changes

Like the coordination on dramatic policy change during this period, this preservation of the Japanese energy policymaking process and electricity market structure after the oil crises reflects the government's cooperative relationships with the electric utilities and the public. These groups' generally aligned resilience goals for Japan's energy system contributed to this cooperation.

One process change did take place, but as discussed earlier in this chapter, the Cabinet Office document attributes this shift to the *Mutsu* accident (Cabinet Office, Government of Japan, 2013). While not a result of the externally driven oil crises, the regulatory structure shift does offer an example of Japanese process changes as a response to technological shocks, a pattern repeated after future nuclear accidents in the 1990s and again following the Fukushima disaster.

These energy policy and policymaking process responses to the oil crises offer lessons on energy system lock-in and transition, resilience, and innovation.

Lessons on Lock-In, Resilience, and Innovation

Why did the 1970s oil crises create a critical juncture that elicited dramatic policy and energy system change without policymaking process change, while the Fukushima disaster resulted in the opposite effect? This chapter of Japan's energy system narrative reveals overlap in resilience thinking across policymakers, electric utilities and the public following the oil shocks. This shared focus on ecological and economic resilience enabled cooperation across these groups. Japanese policymakers' cooperative relationships with the electric utilities and the public supported the transition away from an oil-based energy system to growth of an energy system based largely on nuclear power expansion, supported by conservation and efficiency measures to lower electricity demand. Following the Fukushima nuclear disaster more than 30 years later, the government returned to conservation and efficiency measures as a means of promoting resilience while preserving the existing nuclear-based system. Just as they did in the post-oil crisis era, these conservation and efficiency measures mitigated electricity demand, affording the government and utilities more time to plan for nuclear plant restarts and avoid redesigning the energy system to rely on another baseload source.

After the oil crises, the electric utilities cooperated with the government in exchange for economic incentives and increasing clout in the energy policymaking system. The electric utilities' clout over and cooperation with economic regulators further supported this energy system shift. This policy coordination on nuclear power expansion trumped electric utilities' tensions with safety regulators, in contrast to post-Fukushima empowerment of safety regulators to influence the future of nuclear power. Policymakers' clout over and cooperation with the electric utilities following the oil crises enabled an energy policy shift without any policymaking process change.

The government also encouraged public cooperation through economic incentives, such as the local subsidies for nuclear plant host communities. Less tangible factors also shaped this cooperation, as public compliance with the energy system transformation also was grounded in public trust in the government's energy system resilience goals.

These same relationships contributed to difficulties in responding to future shocks to Japan's energy system, especially as the electric utilities gained clout in energy policymaking while continuing the battle with safety regulators. The electric utilities' clout increased in tandem with a deepening of the utilities' interest in perpetuating and expanding nuclear power use to recoup start-up costs and achieve economies of scale, reflecting intensification of a focus on economic resilience. This institutional shift contributed to Japan's movement from oil-based energy system lock-in to diversification, then toward nuclear-based system lock-in. In short, a policy change to exit the incumbent system led to an institutional shift, and this shift catalyzed a policy process change that contributed to new system lock-in in the future.

Japan's energy system transformation after the 1970s oil shocks suggests several lessons for policymakers, regulators, utilities, and consumers. These lessons include attention to each group's resilience focus, as well as implications for cooperation and insights for energy system change in response to shocks. These lessons hold value for many communities across the globe grappling with energy system shocks that range from the immediate – such as earthquakes, tsunami, and politically driven resource shortages – to the gradual, including climate change and pandemics.

The overlap in energy system resilience priorities contributed to cooperation across government, utility and public stakeholders enabled system transformation in Japan. This observation suggests that to foster cooperation on energy system resilience and change, policymakers, regulators, utilities, and consumers should actively define their resilience priorities and consider how they overlap and differ from those of other groups. This strategic, coordinated resilience thinking will empower development of targeted energy policy changes, as well as implementation support from utilities and consumers.

Actively defining resilience goals also enables stakeholders to consider how these goals may affect future energy system change. While building in energy system flexibility and the ability to adapt to future shocks may prove challenging and complex, these features are needed to enable adjustment to maintain system resilience when shocks occur. Japan's narrative after the oil shocks reflects long-term planning, as well as the introduction of conservation and efficiency measures as a tool contributing to this flexibility. At the same time, the Japanese government's and utilities' investments in nuclear power as the primary electricity supply solution to resilience began to limit the system's ability to pivot in response to future shocks.

In the next chapter of Japan's energy system narrative, we will examine continued shifts in resilience thinking, cooperation and clout that shaped policy responses to a series of nuclear accidents and a scandal. We also will observe how these small shocks influenced gradual shifts in these factors.

Notes

1 Michael Ross (2013) offers one scholarly account. The U.S. Department of State's Office of the Historian provides an example of a governmental summary: https://history. state.gov/milestones/1969-1976/oil-embargo.
2 Several interviewees recounted their personal experiences as government officials or utility company executives during the 1970s and early 1980s, while others relied on history imparted to them by their predecessors.
3 For more on the scandal, see, for example, Shinoda, 2000, or Trevor, 2013.
4 Other factors also may have played a role in lowering public support rates for the Japanese government during and after the oil crises. One media interviewee attributed these downturns in public support to rapidly rising consumer prices and financial scandals.

Other potential factors include financial scandals and renewed confidence in new leadership that declined over time.
5　For detailed history, see www.jogmec.go.jp/english/about/about003.html.
6　The total is derived from a 1.4 percent increase from 1990 levels to a 2011 total of 2.8 percent excluding hydropower. Data is extracted from Jones and Kim, 2013, 19.
7　The World Bank Database Indicators site does not have a figure for non-hydroelectric renewables. The IEA's statistics for 1990 indicate that non-hydroelectric renewables accounted for approximately two percent of Japan's electricity. See International Energy Agency, 2021.
8　NEDO's mission resembles the focus of the U.S. Department of Energy's Advanced Research Projects Agency – Energy (ARPA-E), created in 2007 to fund high-risk, high-impact energy technologies not yet ready for private sector investment.

References

Aldrich, D.P. (2005) 'The Limits of Flexible and Adaptive Institutions: The Japanese Government's Role in Nuclear Power Plant Siting Over the Post War Period.' In Lesbirel, S.H., and Shaw, D. (eds.), *Managing Conflict in Facility Siting: An International Comparison*. Northampton, MA: Edward Elgar Publishing.

Aldrich, D.P. (2008) *Site Fights: Divisive Facilities and Civil Society in Japan and the West*. Ithaca, NY: Cornell University Press.

Aldrich, D.P. (2013) 'Revisiting the Limits of Flexible and Adaptive Institutions: The Japanese Government's Role in Nuclear Power Plant Siting Over the Post War Period.' In *Critical Issues in Contemporary Japan*. New York: Routledge, 79–91.

The Asahi Shimbun. (2011) Public Opinion Polls on Cabinet Support 1973–2011. *The Asahi Shimbun*.

Board Audit of Japan. (2001) *2001Audit Inspection Report (Heisei 13 Nendo Kessan Kensa Houkoku)*. https://report.jbaudit.go.jp/org/h13/2001-h13-0630-0.htm.

Cabinet Office, Government of Japan. (1980) 'Supply Goals for Energy Alternatives to Oil. (Sekiyu Daitai Enerugi No Kyoukyuu Mokuhyou/ 石油代替エネルギーの供給目標).' 28 November. www.aec.go.jp/jicst/NC/about/ugoki/geppou/V25/N11/198013V25N11.html.

Cabinet Office, Government of Japan. (2013) 'History of the Atomic Energy Commission (1950s – present). (Genshiryoku Iinkai no Rekishi (1950 Nendai – Genzai/原子力委員会の歴史（1950年だい―現在).' July.

Cabinet Secretariat, Government of Japan. (1964) *Electricity Business Act*. www.cas.go.jp/jp/seisaku/hourei/data/EBA.pdf.

Cárdenas, J., and Robles-Rivera, F. (2020) *Business Elites in Panama: Sources of Power and State Capture*. Geneva: United Nations Research Institute for Social Development. November.

Cohen, L., McCubbins, M., and McCall Rosenbluth, F. (1995) 'He Politics of Nuclear Power in Japan and the United States.' In Cowhey, P.F., and McCubbins, M. (eds.), *Structure and Policy in Japan and the United States*. New York: Cambridge University Press, 177–202.

Finn, R. (1983) *U.S.-Japan Relations: Toward a New Equilibrium*. Piscataway, NJ: Transaction Publishers.

Fukasaku, Y. (1995) 'Energy and Environmental Policy Integration: The Case of Energy Conservation Policies and Technologies in Japan.' *Energy Policy*, 23 (12), 1063–1076.

Gale, R. (1981) 'Tokyo Electric Power Company: Its Role in Shaping Japan's Coal and LNG Policy.' In *The Politics of Japan's Energy Strategy: Resources-Diplomacy-Security*. Berkeley: Institute of East Asian Studies, 85–105.

Graefe, Laurel. (2014) 'Oil Shock of 1978–1979.' www.federalreservehistory.org/Events/DetailView/40.

Hayes, M., and Victor, D. (2006) 'Politics, Markets and the Shift to Gas.' In Victor, D.G., Jaffe, A.M., and Hayes, M. (eds.), *Natural Gas and Geopolitics: From 1970 to 2040*. New York: Cambridge University Press, 319–356.

International Atomic Energy Agency. (2004) Japan. https://www-pub.iaea.org/mtcd/publications/pdf/cnpp2009/countryprofiles/Japan/Japan2004.htm.

International Energy Agency. Japan. www.iea.org/countries/japan.

International Energy Agency. (2021) *Electricity Information 2021 Edition Database Documentation*. http://wds.iea.org/wds/pdf/Ele_documentation.pdf.

Japan Center for Economic Research Middle-Term Economic Forecast Team. (2012) 'Conservation at 70s Levels Could Cut Energy Consumption by 20%.' Topics of the Middle-Term Economic Forecast: Looking to the 70s Oil Crisis for Lessons in Energy-Saving.

Japan Oil, Gas and Metals Corporation. 'History of JOGMEC.' www.jogmec.go.jp/english/about/about003.html.

Johnson, C. (1978) *Japan's Public Policy Companies*. Washington, DC: American Enterprise Institute for Public Policy Research.

Jones, R.S., and Kim, M. (2013) 'Restructuring the Electricity Sector and Promoting Green Growth in Japan.' OECD Economics Department Working Papers, No. 1069. Paris: OECD Publishing.

Jordan-Korte, K. (2011) *Government Promotion of Renewable Energy Technologies: Policy Approaches and Market Development in Germany, the United States, and Japan*. Wiesbaden, Germany: Springer Science and Business Media.

Katsuta, T., and Suzuki, T. (2011) 'Japan's Spent Fuel and Plutonium Management Challenge.' *Energy Policy*, 39 (11), 6827–6841.

Kimura, O. (2009) 'The National Programs for Development of Energy Technologies.' SERC Discussion Paper. SERC09007. Central Research Institute of the Electric Power Industry.

Kimura, O., and Suzuki, T. (2006) '30 Years of Solar Energy Development in Japan: Co-Evolution Process of Technology, Policies, and the Market.' Presentation to the Berlin Conference on the Human Dimensions of Global Environmental Change: "Resource Policies: Effectiveness, Efficiency, and Equity," Berlin, Germany, 17 November.

Lesbirel, S.H. (1998) *NIMBY Politics in Japan: Energy Siting and the Management of Environmental Conflict*. Ithaca, NY: Cornell University Press.

Mihut, M.I., and Daniel, D.L. (2012) 'First Oil Shock Impact on the Japanese Economy.' *Procedia Economics and Finance*, 3, 1042–1048.

Ministry of International Trade and Industry, Government of Japan. (1975) *Sekiyu Bichiku Hou* (石油備蓄法). http://law.e-gov.go.jp/htmldata/S50/S50HO096.html.

Ministry of International Trade and Industry, Government of Japan. (1979) *Interim Report on the Provisional Long-Term Supply and Demand Outlook*. 31 August.

MITI Advisory Committee for Energy, Government of Japan. (1975) *Energy Stabilization Measures*: Government of Japan, *1975–1984*. August.

Morse, R.A. (1981) 'Introduction: Japan's Energy Policies and Options.' In *The Politics of Japan's Energy Strategy: Resources-Diplomacy-Security*. Berkeley, CA: Institute of East Asian Studies, 1–14.

Murota, Y., and Yano, Y. (1993) 'Japan's Policy on Energy and the Environment.' *Annual Review of Energy and the Environment*, 18, 89–135.

Navarro, P. (1996) 'The Japanese Electric Utility Industry.' In Gilbert, R., and Kahn, E. (eds.), *International Comparisons of Electricity Regulation*. New York: Cambridge University Press, 231–276.

Nuclear Engineering International. (2002) 'False Data Disastrous for Japan's Industry.' *Nuclear Engineering International*. 27 September. www.neimagazine.com/news/newsfalse-data-disastrous-for-japan-s-industry.

Petroleum Association of Japan. (2013) *Petroleum Industry in Japan 2013*.

Rasmussen, A., Buhmann-Holmes, N., and Egerod, B.C.K. (2021) 'The Executive Revolving Door: New Dataset on The Career Moves of Former Danish Ministers and Permanent Secretaries.' *Scandinavian Political Studies*, 44 (4), 487–502.

Ross, M. (2013) 'How the 1973 Oil Embargo Saved the Planet: OPEC Gave the Rest of the World a Head Start Against Climate Change.' *Foreign Affairs*, 15 October. https://www.foreignaffairs.com/articles/north-america/2013-10-15/how-1973-oil-embargo-saved-planet

Samuels, R. (1987) *The Business of the Japanese State: Energy Markets in Comparative and Historical Perspective*. Ithaca, NY: Cornell University Press.

Samuels, R. (1989) 'Consuming for Production: Japanese National Security, Nuclear Fuel Procurement, and the Domestic Economy.' *International Organization*, 43 (4), 625–646.

Shinoda, T. (2000) *Leading Japan: The Role of the Prime Minister*. Westport, CT: Praeger Publishers.

Shirouzu, N., and Tudor, A. (2011) 'Crisis Revives Doubts on Regulation.' *The Wall Street Journal*, 15 March. www.wsj.com/articles/SB10001424052748703363904576200533746195522.

Sinha, R.P. (1974) 'Japan and the Oil Crisis.' *The World Today*, 30 (8), 335–344.

Sklarew, J.F. (2015) *Shock to the System: How Catastrophic Events and Institutional Relationships Impact Japanese Energy Policymaking, Resilience, and Innovation*. Arlington, VA: George Mason University.

Sklarew, J.F. (2018) 'Power Fluctuations: How Japan's Nuclear Infrastructure Priorities Influence Electric Utilities' Clout.' *Energy Research and Social Science*, 41, July, 158–167.

Smil, V. (2007) 'Light Behind the Fall: Japan's Electricity Consumption, the Environment, and Economic Growth.' *Japan Focus*, 5 (4). https://apjjf.org/-Vaclav-Smil/2394/article.html

Stewart, D. (2009) 'Japan: The Power of Efficiency.' In *Energy Security Challenges for the 21st Century: A Reference Handbook*. Santa Barbara, CA: Praeger Security International, 176–190.

Strickland, J. (2020) 'The Declining Value of Revolving-Door Lobbyists: Evidence from the American States.' *American Journal of Political Science*, 64 (1), 67–81.

Suttmeier, R. (1981) 'The Japanese Nuclear Power Option: Technological Promise and Social Limitations.' In Morse, R.A. (ed.), *The Politics of Japan's Energy Strategy: Resources-Diplomacy-Security*. Berkeley, CA: Institute of East Asian Studies, 106–133.

Suzuki, T. (2001) *Energy Security and the Role of Nuclear Power in Japan*. Central Research Institute of the Electric Power Industry. http://oldsite.nautilus.org/archives/energy/eaef/Reg_Japan_final.PDF.

Trevor, M. (2013) *Japan – Restless Competitor: The Pursuit of Economic Nationalism*. London: Routledge.

Valentine, S.V., Sovacool, B.K., and Matsuura, M. (2011) 'Empowered? Evaluating Japan's National Energy Strategy Under the DPJ Administration.' *Energy Policy*, 39, 1865–1876.

Yates, S., and Cardin-Trudeau, E. (2021) 'Lobbying "from Within": A New Perspective on the Revolving Door and Regulatory Capture.' *Canadian Public Administration*, 64 (2), 301–319.

4 Nuclear Accidents and Scandal
Shock Absorption (1990s and 2000s)

"Sometimes we asked the utilities to cooperate on nuclear policy, and in order to get that help or cooperation. . . . [W]e somehow had to consider the current situation of the utilities, especially the financial situation of the utilities so that they can introduce more nuclear. So in such a situation, the nuclear accidents gave us some impact on the relations with the utilities. You know, the people asked for a more strict and neutral attitude of the government towards the utilities for the nuclear regulation, and so we have to be very tough with companies."

– Government official (G12, May 2013)

"Staff of NISA or METI feels like nuclear engineers in utilities are too arrogant and won't hear voices from outside. Nuclear engineers in the utilities even said to me that staff in the NISA and NRA do not know so much about nuclear, do not have so much knowledge."

– Government official (G9, April 2013)

"Sometimes, to the general public, the utility company said, this was approved by the government, and that means this is the right thing, and we have to follow, and you, the general public, have to understand it."

– Former electric utility executive (I6, May 2013)

"After the 1990s accidents, the public didn't change their mind. They still trusted the government. It is difficult for me to tell why, because I wrote something, I myself wrote some articles about the risk of nuclear repeatedly, but the response is very rare. So I didn't understand why people trusted the Japanese government so strictly or so strongly."

– Media representative (M2, March 2013)

Beginning approximately two decades after the oil crises, a series of prominent accidents and a data falsification scandal occurred involving nuclear power plants and facilities in Japan. While the accidents and scandal individually did not comprise as dramatic a focusing event as the oil crises, each of these smaller shocks contributed cumulatively to incremental shifts in stakeholder relationships. As

DOI: 10.4324/9781003227588-4

these accidents continued, we would expect that they would create a critical juncture for a shift away from nuclear power promotion policies and a decline in the share of nuclear power in Japan's electricity supply. We also might predict increased regulation of nuclear power.

In fact, Japan's energy policy direction and policymaking process following these shocks continued relatively unchanged, preserving and promoting nuclear power growth. Nuclear energy's share of Japan's electricity supply generally followed an upward trend until the Fukushima Daiichi accident occurred in 2011. Government and electric utility interviewees described the Japanese government's "nuclear power renaissance" initiative after the accidents and scandal. The capstone policy statement of this initiative, the government's 2010 Basic Energy Plan, contains an appendix that called for an increase in nuclear power to at least 50 percent of Japan's electricity supply by 2030 (Ministry of Economy, Trade and Industry, Government of Japan, 2010). Policy process and structural changes after the accidents and scandal appear largely superficial. Changes to safety regulations and authority enhanced the resilience of Japan's existing energy system, reinforcing the role of nuclear power in it.

Scholars of evolutionary institutional change such as Pierson, Mahoney and Thelen might have predicted these outcomes. However, this approach alone also does not completely account for the changes that did occur. The interview data suggests a holistic view that incorporates both shocks and evolutionary influences. The government's cooperative relationships with the electric utilities and the public, coupled with increasing electric utility clout, can help to explain these seemingly paradoxical outcomes. Concurrent trends in electricity liberalization and global climate change policy also created institutional influences that affected these relationships' impact on energy policy and process change. In examining stakeholder relationships that would promote change, we might expect tensions to increase between policymakers and the electric utilities, coupled with a decline in public trust. Instead, interview data, public opinion polls and government documents reflect relationships in which the electric utilities gained increasing clout over time, while tensions with safety regulators worsened. Public trust in the government remained relatively high, though gradually declining. Public clout also remained weak.

Underlying all of these trends, continued alignment of policymakers' and utilities' energy system resilience priorities fueled cooperation and joint messaging to the public promoting trust in these priorities. This combination of factors contributed to a situation in which institutional support for increasing investments in nuclear infrastructure fueled momentum of a nuclear-based system. The series of technological and institutional failures in the 1990s and early 2000s thus did not result in Japanese energy policy directional change, policymaking process change, or impactful regulatory change. The regulatory change that did take place aimed to appease conflict between the government and the public, though the government retained clout.

Multiple Sequential Shocks: 1990s and 2000s Accidents and Scandal

As depicted in Figure 4.1, the series of high-profile accidents at Japanese nuclear power facilities began in 1991 and punctuated every few years throughout the next two decades. The accidents ranged from minor to major and affected both commercial and research facilities.[1]

In February 1991, 55 tons of cooling water leaked into the secondary cooling loop at KEPCO's Mihama pressurized water reactor (PWR) unit 2 after a heat transfer tube in the steam generator broke off due to improper installation. A small amount of radiation was released. No casualties occurred, and the Japanese economy was not affected. In December 1995, 700 kg of molten sodium coolant leaked within the Monju prototype fast breeder reactor (FBR) after a measuring device ruptured. Monju was operated by the Power Reactor and Nuclear Fuel Development Corporation (PNC), a government-funded research and development organization. The reactor had reached criticality for the first time only one year before. No casualties, radiation leakage, or damage to the Japanese economy occurred. However, facility operators attempted to conceal the extent of the accident by falsifying reports, editing a videotape, and issuing a gag order prohibiting employees from revealing the edits (Johnston, 2000).

In March 1997, a fire and explosion at the Tokaimura nuclear fuel processing plant's bitumen waste facility exposed approximately 40 workers to radiation. PNC also managed this facility. No evacuation of residents took place, and the Japanese economy was not affected.

In September 1999, another explosion occurred at Tokaimura's uranium reprocessing facility, operated by Japan Nuclear Fuel Conversion Co. (JCO), a subsidiary of Sumitomo Metal Mining Company. Three employees violated procedure by

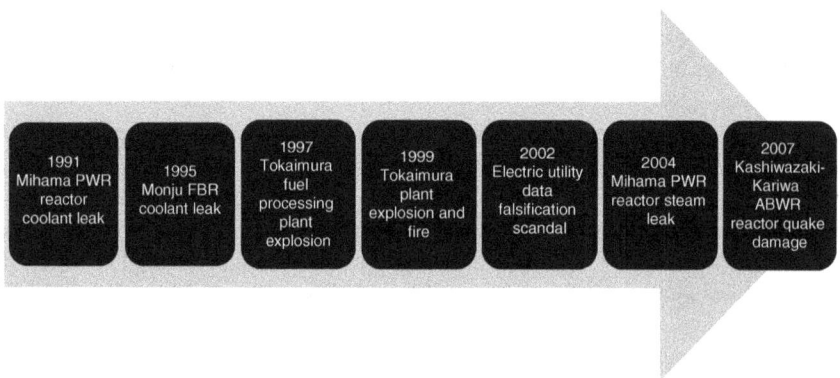

Figure 4.1 Timeline of 1990s and 2000s Accidents

Source: Reprinted from Sklarew, J.F. (2018) 'Power Fluctuations: How Japan's Nuclear Infrastructure Priorities Influence Electric Utilities' Clout.' Energy Research & Social Science, 41 (July), 158–167, 161.

mixing uranium oxide and nitric acid in buckets instead of tanks, then placed seven times the recommended amount of the mixture into a precipitation tank, generating a chain reaction that lasted 20 hours. The radiation killed two of the three workers directly involved in the accident and exposed 66 other workers and emergency responders to excess radiation. An IAEA report released shortly after the Tokaimura criticality accident states that the Ibaraki prefectural government evacuated residents within a radius of 350 meters from the accident site for 48 hours. Officials also advised residents within a 10-km radius to stay indoors for 24 hours and closed schools within the same distance. The governor suspended harvesting of agricultural products for 24 hours. The report notes that monitoring of water supplies and produce took place "to reassure the public." Testing did not detect radiation in water within 10 km of the accident site (International Atomic Energy Agency, 1999, 27).

The IAEA report found that the primary cause of the 1999 accident was "human error and serious breaches of safety principles." The report cites accounts of indirect harm to local industries and businesses, potentially due to mistaken assumptions of radioactive contamination. In addition, the report mentions accounts of public concern regarding the accident's effects on real estate prices and potential links to falling prices of agricultural products (International Atomic Energy Agency, 1999, 33).

In September 2002, a scandal surfaced involving hundreds of counts of TEPCO engineers' falsification of inspection records and reports on integrity of various reactor parts between 1977 and 2001. While not an accident, the scandal represents a similar shock that disrupted Japan's nuclear expansion and disturbed the government's relationships with the electric utilities and the public.

In August 2004, a corroded, ruptured pipe and resulting steam leak at the Mihama-3 reactor resulted in the death of four plant workers and injury to seven others. A Nuclear and Industrial Safety Agency (NISA) report notes that "harmful rumors spread and produced a serious impact on economic activities" (Nuclear and Industrial Safety Agency, Government of Japan, 2005). Kansai Electric Power Company shut down the reactor and restarted it in 2007.

In July 2007, the Chuuetsu earthquake shook the Kashiwazaki-Kariwa Advanced Boiling Water Reactor (ABWR) – the largest nuclear power plant in the world – beyond the parameters of its design. Radioactive water leaked into the Sea of Japan. TEPCO, the operating electric utility, shut down the reactor for 21 months to undertake seismic readiness upgrades. Idling the plant was predicted to impact global oil and gas prices, but a study by the IEEJ found little actual effect (see Murakami et al., 2008). While TEPCO faced financial challenges due to the shutdown, the local and national economy did not. By 2009, four of the reactor's seven units were restarted.

This series of accidents and scandal represents a set of multiple shocks that individually had varying impacts on Japan's energy security and economy. While each of these individual events may not embody a large enough shock to serve as a focusing event that precipitates a critical juncture, we might expect that this series of smaller shocks would gradually erode government cooperation with the utilities and public trust. And yet, collectively, these events resulted in little change to Japan's energy supply profile and policymaking process. No interviewees identified the nuclear accidents and scandal in the 1990s and early 2000s as turning points in Japan's energy system, in alignment with a study by Pickett (Pickett, 2002). However, the accidents and scandal did not occur in a vacuum. They took place in an environment created by stakeholder relationship changes after the oil crises.

Stakeholder Relationship Changes and Influences

The accidents and scandal affected the government's post-oil crises relationships with the electric utilities and the public. Interview and secondary data also reveal that these relationships influenced the accidents and scandal and the policy responses to them. The next several sections highlight the evolving risk perceptions and resilience priorities of these stakeholder groups. They also incorporate the effects of climate change as a new global focus. Combining these factors, we then can develop a holistic view of how they impact the ways in which each relationship influenced Japanese energy policymaking in response to this series of shocks.

The narrative described in this section reflects the influence of continued alignment of ecological and economic resilience priorities across policymakers and electric utilities. During the 1990s and early 2000s, these shared priorities contributed to cooperation and continued increases in utility clout. This coordination was coupled with a gradual shift away from a focus on the safety aspects of engineering resilience. The interview data reveals that as a result of the Monju shutdown, some policymakers began to question the validity of Japan's nuclear fuel recycling policy. This emergence of doubt regarding a key feature of Japan's nuclear program should have deepened pressure for a shift away from nuclear power, but this shift did not occur. Meanwhile, policymakers and the utilities cooperated to retain public trust in the ecological and social resilience of the energy system.

This said, within MITI, which became the METI in a 2001 government overhaul, nuclear policymakers, economic regulators and nuclear regulators developed increasingly divergent economic resilience priorities and views of the role of nuclear power in achieving it. As a result of these shifts in resilience priorities and relationship conflict, MITI's economic regulators initiated liberalization of the electricity sector midway through this period, heightening tension between them and the electric utilities, according to interviewees from both groups. This market restructuring in the short-term focused on enabling large consumer choice of providers, aiming to promote competition among Japan's regional electric utility monopolies. Continued investment in nuclear power expansion encouraged the utilities to place greater emphasis on economic resilience, pressuring METI to slow market liberalization that might compromise it. The next sections examine in more detail how this growing internal governmental rift affected intragovernmental relationships, cooperation and conflict with the utilities, and the pace of this liberalization movement.

Policymakers' and utilities' resilience priorities also contrasted with the engineering resilience goals of safety regulators, increasing tensions between them, policymakers, and the electric utilities. While many critiques of Japan's policy-making structure characterize this relationship as regulatory capture, interviews of safety regulators and electric utility executives and engineers reveal a much more nuanced relationship involving tension and battles for clout that precipitated the accidents and scandal while limiting meaningful regulatory change.

Concurrent with their emerging focus on electricity market liberalization, Japanese policymakers responded to global attention on climate change mitigation policies following the 1997 adoption of the Kyoto Protocol to operationalize the United Nations Framework Convention on Climate Change (UNFCCC).[2] As host of the conference that produced the agreement, Japanese energy policymakers felt pressure to make progress on domestic carbon dioxide emissions reductions. This responsibility also engendered policymakers' cooperation with the utilities and the public on expansion of nuclear power as a non-emitting power source, containing the effects of the shocks and scandal in the face of this broader mandate. Climate change thus provided a social resilience focus that facilitated policymaker-utility cooperation on nuclear power, as well as public support for it.

Shifts in clout across all groups also played an important role in limiting the shocks' impact on energy policymaking and process change. Government and electric utility interviewees generally agreed that the electric utilities wielded increasing clout during the 1990s. Studies by Lesbirel, Aldrich, and others on the government-public relationship describe rising public tension over nuclear plant siting, with little outlet for influence on policies (e.g., Lesbirel, 1998; Aldrich, 2008). NGO and media interviewees' comments support the notion of compromised public clout. However, public opinion polls reflect surprisingly little disapproval of Japanese government leadership after each accident. NGO, media, and government interview data suggests that the government and the electric utilities cooperated to minimize public concern and rebuild trust after each accident, leading to periods of very short-lived distrust embedded in continuation of the paternalistic relationship. In the very early 2000s, the liberalization movement briefly sapped clout from the electric utilities, as regulators showed less interest in the utilities' policy inputs. After several years, ousting of the fuel recycling doubters and many of the regulatory reformers from METI's energy policymaking unit precipitated a return of electric utility clout and cooperation with policymakers.

The interview data thus suggests that overall, electric utilities' tension and battle for clout with safety regulators contributed to the shocks. The data also indicates that the electric utilities' cooperation with energy policymakers, coupled with public trust in the government and little public clout, constrained energy policy and process change after these shocks occurred.

Bureaucrats, Politicians, and Electric Utilities

The accidents and scandal, resilience priorities, institutional influences, and risk perceptions yielded different impacts on the electric utilities' relationships with energy policymakers. While the accidents and scandal had little effect on cooperation between these two groups, resilience priorities and institutional influences had a mixed effect. Economic resilience priorities and stakeholder conflict led policymakers to introduce electricity market liberalization efforts, which injected tension over process change. Concurrently, emerging global attention on climate change mitigation, along with a variety of institutional mechanisms, promoted cooperation on a priority shift. These two trends also produced conflicting effects on the utilities' resilience priorities. Continued investment in nuclear power expansion encouraged the utilities to place greater emphasis on economic resilience, which pressured METI to slow market liberalization that might compromise it. Climate change provided a social resilience focus that facilitated policymaker-utility cooperation on nuclear power, as well as public support for it. At the same time, the potential for heightened public risk perceptions regarding nuclear power required cooperation between electric utilities and policymakers to contain concerns over the potential for a more serious nuclear accident than those that were occurring during this period.

Consistent with existing studies, all energy policymaker and electric utility interviewees agreed that the two groups' cooperative relationship broadly continued through the 1990s and early 2000s, regardless of the accidents. This cooperation aimed to preserve nuclear power expansion, as well as public trust in the government's ability to oversee it and the utilities' ability to execute it. Government interviewee G17 noted that when accidents occurred, especially those involving facilities operated by the electric utilities, the relationship between the electric utilities and METI's Nuclear Energy Policy Planning Division became a bit strained, but it recovered quickly. The Monju accident did not affect policymakers' relationships with the electric utilities at all, since it did not involve utility-operated facilities. In fact, G17 explained that then-MITI and the electric utilities jointly distanced themselves from the government-affiliated operator, PNC. The official said that MITI and the electric utilities cited PNC's lack of intelligent operators as the cause of the accident: "when PNC had the accident, everyone in the electric utilities and METI looked down on them" (July 2013). MITI and the electric utilities thus conveyed a coordinated message that the more capable electric utility engineers would not have suffered such an accident.

Government official G13 indicated a similar response to the 1999 accident at the Tokaimura facility operated by JCO. Since JCO was a private company unaffiliated with the electric utilities, "government and industry dealt with the JCO accident as not connected with the LWR business, but specific for JCO process. This was simply because the industry and government didn't want to have significant impact from the accident." MITI and the electric utilities thus cooperated to preserve public trust in commercial nuclear reactor safety and MITI's ability to manage it.

Policymakers also reacted to public distrust after the accidents by publicly cracking down on the electric utilities. After the 2004 Mihama accident, then-METI Minister Nakagawa announced that "punitive action" against KEPCO might result (Kyodo News, 2004). Still, government interviewees confided that this tough stance coexisted with continued cooperation on nuclear power expansion. As government official G12 explained in May 2013, "Sometimes we asked the utilities to cooperate on nuclear policy, and in order to get that help or cooperation from the utilities, we somehow had to . . . consider the current situation of the utilities, especially the financial situation of the utilities so that they can introduce more nuclear. So in that sense, we have to somehow talk and compromise with the utilities." The official observed that recognizing the utilities' profit goals became more difficult when accidents occurred, leading to costlier regulations: "So in such a situation, the nuclear accidents gave us some impact on the relations with the utilities. You know, the people asked for a more strict and neutral attitude of the government towards the utilities for the nuclear regulation, and so we have to be very tough with companies." Electric utility interviewees also noted this governmental shift toward increased regulation after the accidents, but they generally still viewed the utilities' relationships with policymakers as cooperative. Any policy or regulatory changes policymakers implemented after the accidents thus aimed to rebuild public trust in order to preserve nuclear power's growing role in Japan's energy system. While these changes perpetuated the tension between electric utility engineers and safety regulators, they did not halt cooperation between policymakers and the electric utilities' management, which were removed from the engineer-safety regulator dynamic. Policymaker-utility priorities continued to focus on ecological and economic resilience, in contrast to safety regulators' attention to the safety and structural integrity aspects of engineering resilience.

The 2002 data falsification scandal did force interaction between these two sets of relationships and priorities, however. While the scandal originated in problems between electric utility engineers and safety regulators (discussed later), METI policymakers' relationships with the electric utility management played a role in the timing of the release of information about the falsification. Several government and electric utility interviewees noted that METI knew about the data falsifications for some time before releasing the information to the public. Electric utility interviewee I1 explained that while junior METI officials with close ties to TEPCO did not want to reveal the scandal, one senior METI official made the decision based on his conflict with TEPCO. I1 described a hostile relationship between then-Vice Minister Murata and then President of TEPCO Nobuya Minami. Mr. Murata "who was really opposed to TEPCO's arrogant attitude," decided to release the data falsification to the public. When the scandal became public, Minami and four other senior TEPCO executives resigned. Several electric utility and government interviewees attributed this conflict to METI's electricity market liberalization plans.[3] Some interviewees suggested that the scandal enabled METI to gain clout by increasing public distrust in the electric utilities, which created public support for market liberalization. This said, the utilities' economic resilience priorities continued to drive nuclear power investment. In June 2013, G13 said of the scandal's impact:

> I would say that maybe in the aftermath of that kind of nuclear scandal, the nuclear program in Japan has become more and more sophisticated. That means I don't think we had an impact so that the utility companies failed or abandoned their construction programs of new nuclear plants for instance. Of course some were delayed, but I would say that impact was not so serious.

While the scandal led to the temporary shutdown of all of TEPCO's reactors, it thus did not have a lasting effect on policymakers' cooperation with the electric utilities on nuclear power expansion.

In contrast to this short-lived tension, some policymakers' questioning of the nuclear fuel recycling policy created longer-term conflict between these two groups. Japan Nuclear Fuel Limited began construction of the Rokkasho nuclear fuel reprocessing plant began in 1993. The prolonged shutdown of Monju after the 1995 accident sparked a debate between METI and Diet policymakers regarding whether Japan's fuel reprocessing policy could or should continue. This conflict emerged quietly in the early late 1990s and grew throughout the early 2000s. Monju's Fast Breeder Reactor (FBR) technology was the prototype intended for commercialization that would enable Japan to close the fuel cycle. Underlying this conflict were divergent goals within the frameworks of engineering, ecological and economic resilience. The utilities and some politicians and policymakers viewed nuclear fuel recycling as a solution to nuclear waste challenges to ecological and engineering resilience, as well as an economic resilience contributor that protected nuclear power investments and enabled reuse of imported fuel. Meanwhile, after Monju's shutdown, another group of politicians and policymakers viewed recycling itself as a long-term risk to both ecological and economic resilience.

Monju's shutdown and the challenges that precipitated it led LDP Diet member Taro Kono and several junior METI officials to question the economics and viability of the closed fuel cycle plan. Kono explained that after the Monju accident, "we realized that we have found out that the nuclear fuel cycle is not going anywhere, because . . . there was a Monju accident in 1995, and development of the FBR has stopped, and a lot of people are questioning if we can actually get the FBR for commercial usage, even without the Monju accident. So with the Monju accident, it's kind of hopeless" (March 2013). The Monju accident thus could have served as a focusing event for a shift away from nuclear fuel reprocessing, but Kono's position initially had no supporters and many opposers. Kono asserted that former TEPCO Senior Vice President Tokio Kanoh, an Upper House Diet Member, "was trying to juggernaut all the bills that are good for the power industry." Kanoh had many allies supporting his protection of the electric utilities' investments, aligning with the focus on economic resilience. Kono said that when he began questioning the validity of the fuel cycle without commercial FBRs, Kanoh and other LDP politicians aligned with the electric utilities tried to suppress him:

> I wanted to ask all the questions, and they don't seem to be able to answer my questions. . . . So I asked questions, but the meeting usually adjourned after my questions no one answered. And there was a science minister . . . Matsuda Iwao.[4] . . . He actually came to see me, and he asked, "Why are you making such a noise?"
>
> (March 2013)

These politicians had more influence over other Diet members than Kono did, so they were able to perpetuate nuclear power expansion and the reprocessing program. For example, Kanoh promoted mixed oxide fuel (MOX) use in conventional reactors after Monju's shutdown, since the fast breeder reactor was no longer using the fuel while in hiatus. MOX contains plutonium oxide mixed with uranium oxide, unlike conventional fuel, which is comprised only of uranium oxide. The plutonium in MOX is recovered from used reactor fuel (see World Nuclear Association, 2017). Even when Kono garnered support from several other Diet members in 2004 or 2005, Kanoh and his allies were able to pass legislation promoting use of the Rokkasho nuclear fuel reprocessing plant. In addition to their economic resilience goals, the utilities viewed reprocessing as an engineering resilience feature: Kono explained that the electric utilities sought reprocessing and the pluthermal program as a mechanism for removing spent fuel from their reactor sites.

While Kanoh was passing pro-nuclear legislation, a debate within METI arose over the same issue. Kono worked with several METI officials to calculate the cost of the reprocessing program. As government interviewee G12 explained, "the confusion on the policy of the nuclear fuel cycle was there in the early 2000s. You may have heard a discussion of a so-called bill for 1.9 billion yen. That was some kind of paper . . . that criticized the nuclear fuel cycle policy. Within METI" (May, 2013). According to Kono and several other government interviewees, the report they produced was squelched quickly, and the officials responsible were rotated out of METI's Agency of Natural Resources and Energy (ANRE) during the next personnel shuffle, while Sugiyama was vice minister.

In addition to the fluctuations this issue engendered in cooperation between the electric utilities and policymakers, the ongoing battle between the electric utilities and METI over responsibility for the reprocessing program also signaled an unresolved struggle for clout. One of the officials involved (G17, July 2013) confided that many METI officials also quietly questioned the reprocessing program after Monju was shut down:

> no one seemed to understand or agree on the reason we had to do this reprocessing . . . even METI, when you talked to them, was saying that frankly speaking, it would be better to stop it . . . many METI people were saying that. They were saying that even if we burn fuel at Rokkasho, it doesn't mean anything, so that if possible they want to stop it.

The official also indicated that "even the utility company people, when they spoke frankly – this isn't a rumor – they want to stop it, because it cost so much money." The electric utilities thus expressed both support for reprocessing as a solution to their nuclear waste problem and opposition to the high cost of continuing the program, reflecting a growing internal struggle between engineering and economic resilience priorities.

Some electric utility and government interviewees indicated that the conflict over the reprocessing program stemmed from both sides' belief that the other should shoulder the cost. Electric utility executive I15 (August 2013) summarized the electric utilities' view:

> Many people are against the fuel cycle program as long as industry will be responsible or in charge. But my opinion is that most of the people understand that the fuel cycle is needed. But the big question is why industry should take responsibility. So some people, even management people, sometimes say they want to get out of this program as an industry. I also believe that this so-called back-end fuel cycle should be taken charge by the government, not only because of the economic reason but also the length of the program.

Government interviewees expressed similar sentiments in the reverse, citing the electric utility leadership's initial desire to assume responsibility for the program at its outset.

Despite policymakers' and electric utility executives' hesitation, both groups continued to promote the reprocessing policy as a central element of Japan's nuclear power expansion policy. According to government official G17, this mutual promotion did not originate solely in the desire to continue nuclear power expansion by solving the waste problem. METI and the electric utilities battled over who would back out of the reprocessing program first, suggesting that this conflict emerged from shared economic resilience priorities leading them to the same conclusion. Each side suggested that the other should take the initiative. The electric utilities claimed that they had no right to back out, said the official, because "the utility companies say that the nuclear fuel cycle plan or structure started as a national policy, and we are only following that national policy, so we can't say that we want to quit." METI did not want to end the reprocessing program, either, G17 intimated, because if they did, the electric utilities would demand compensation for the 1.9 trillion yen they had spent on construction of the reprocessing facility. The official added that METI also asserted that the national policy was non-binding, and that the electric utilities pursued reprocessing by choice and could start and end the program voluntarily. Electric utility interviewee I15 corroborated this portrayal of the battle over financial responsibility for reprocessing. The electric utilities and policymakers both wanted to shift responsibility or transition out of the program, but neither could do so because both parties were locked in politically and financially.

Another area of tension arising from the accidents and scandal involved responsibility for public acceptance. Several electric utility and government interviewees asserted that METI and the electric utilities debated over which should convince the public of nuclear power's benefits and safety. As government official G12 explained,

> as for the way to promote nuclear, METI wanted utilities to play more positive role, more important role to persuade the local people and also make the investment. However, always the utilities complained that government should go forward and then persuade people, and show the people that our

nation is determined to promote nuclear. So in that sense, even in the way of the promotion, sometimes the utilities' and METI's position is different.

(May 2013)

Precisely during times when the nuclear-based system faced challenges, the government's sensitivity to public trust led policymakers to distance themselves from nuclear power. Government official G12 observed that "sometimes with that public perception on the accident and other things, METI or the government wanted to be a little bit more neutral stance." This distancing foreshadowed the distancing of policymakers and regulators from the electric utilities after the Fukushima disaster, when regaining public acceptance of nuclear power would hinge on rebuilding of trust in policymakers' and regulators' ability to implement and enforce policies and regulations to protect the public from health and safety risks associated with nuclear technology malfunctions.

The introduction of electricity market liberalization in the late 1990s to early 2000s bolstered public perceptions of the utilities' distancing from policymakers. The reforms focused on introducing two structural changes: supplier competition for high-voltage, large consumers; and accounting separation of the utilities' generation, transmission and distribution assets. These market liberalization measures could have strengthened the transformational ability of the 1990s nuclear accidents and scandal on energy policy and policymaking processes. NGO interviewee Tetsunari Iida observed that in the 1990s, nuclear promotion became challenged by a more market-oriented approach, combined with the fact that nuclear became less popular with the public (March 2013). One government official (G12) asserted that because of market liberalization efforts, "for the first time in history . . . we entered the era of confrontation with the utilities" (May 2013). This conflict posed problems for METI's nuclear power expansion agenda, but only temporarily.

Market liberalization stalled due to prioritization of infrastructure investment's role in system resilience over economic efficiency aspects of resilience. Affirming METI policymakers' internal drive to expand nuclear power, a government official (G12) observed that this commitment required METI's capitulation on market liberalization: "at that time, our policy was to accelerate new construction of the nuclear power plants. That's why we have to think about the market scheme which can facilitate capacity and promote such new construction." METI's nuclear power expansion priority thus bolstered the electric utilities' clout in policymaking.

Government interviewees described how the electric utilities framed market liberalization as a threat to new nuclear plant construction and the reprocessing program. As one government official (G17, July 2013) recalled that "at the final point of electricity industry reform . . . electricity companies strongly insisted that we also have to think about nuclear waste." The electric utilities argued that liberalization would prevent them from recouping spent fuel reprocessing costs through higher electricity prices, as explained in Sklarew (2018), thus threatening economic resilience. Given the emergence of doubts regarding the viability of reprocessing, market liberalization could have provided a further catalyst for shifting away from this program. Instead, the electric utilities' concern contributed to the stoppage of market liberalization. Reflecting strong cooperation with the electric utilities, Diet members noted the linkage between electricity reform and the nuclear waste problem in the liberalization legislation and called for a reform hiatus until the end of 2004 to examine measures for the back end – or waste disposal and reprocessing portions – of the nuclear fuel cycle.

Most interviewees cited electricity market liberalization and global attention to climate change mitigation as concurrent, important influences on energy policymaking during the 1990s and early 2000s. These two trends affected priorities and relationships in contradictory ways, empowering different groups. Contemporaneously with their pursuit of market liberalization, Japanese policymakers announced climate change mitigation goals to address commitments made at the United Nations' Third Conference of Parties, COP-3, in Kyoto in 1997. Policymakers and the electric utilities agreed on nuclear power as the best fuel source to meet these goals. At the same time, some tension existed over whether the government or the electric utilities should take responsibility for promoting public acceptance of nuclear power.

Several interviewees described how METI's focus on nuclear power as the key to meeting these goals conflicted with market liberalization aims, reflecting divergent economic and socio-ecological resilience priorities. Academic interviewee A5 noted that "somehow, there is a tension between the people pushing for deregulation and pushing for the global warming and nuclear. That was some tension in METI" (May 2013). Government official G12 explained that on one hand, market liberalization created tension with the electric utilities and a debate over new nuclear construction. At the same time, because of climate change mitigation priorities, "we had to promote nuclear, anyhow, and in order to promote nuclear, we need a close relationship and cooperation between the industry and METI. So these two things are somehow contradictory" (May 2013). Framing of nuclear power as the key to achieving Japan's climate change mitigation goals thus increased the clout of the electric utilities and pro-nuclear policymakers. Academic interviewee A5 summarized this connection between climate change and nuclear power thus: "From what I understand, the climate change issue was used to defend the current industrial structure" (May 2013). The scholar explained that this connection enabled postponement of market liberalization and further bolstered utility clout: "Rather than deregulation, we should put more emphasis on global warming. It means that we have to use more nuclear, so nuclear requires big investment, so the current utilities should play a more important role. That's the kind of argument, you know." This rationale thus linked the utilities' and policymakers' economic resilience priorities with social resilience concerns prioritized by the public and environmental policymakers.

An institutional shift in the years following the scandal mitigated all of these tensions and shrank the distance between policymakers and the utilities, influencing how the next shocks affected these groups' relationships and energy policy change. Several government and electric utility interviewees observed this dissipation of conflict and a return to cooperation in METI's relationship with the electric utilities between 2004 and 2006. The electric utilities' clout in energy policymaking also rose. Government official G12 observed that "METI very strongly regained confidence in nuclear policy" during this period. G12 attributed this return to cooperation to the efforts of Tadao Yanase, director of METI's Nuclear Policy Division from 2004–2007. The official explained that Yanase "restructured the nuclear policy, and since then, METI very strongly supported, promoted nuclear policy" (May 2013). Yanase cited market liberalization efforts as the source of a "three-way stand-off" between the Japanese government, the electric utilities and plant operators over the responsibility for long-term nuclear energy strategy and investment (Yanase, 2007). This view echoes electric utility interviewees' assertions of market liberalization's negative impact on incentives for electricity grid and plant investments, reflecting the reconvergence of METI's and electric utilities' perspectives on economic resilience during Yanase's tenure as director of the Nuclear Policy Division. Yanase became Prime Minister Abe's administrative aide in 2012. The next chapter will discuss the post-Fukushima implications of this appointment.

Government interviewee G12 noted that during the 2004–2006 period,

> I think METI came back to the very aggressive nuclear policy, and as for the nuclear safety regulation . . . maybe not so strict. . . . Maybe neutral. But not affecting [or] bothering the utilities so much. And as for the market planning, METI was not so aggressive. In that sense, in general, the relation between METI and the utilities was, I think, managed.
>
> (May 2013)

Concurrent with this policy shift, pro-utility, anti-liberalization METI Vice Minister Sugiyama succeeded pro-liberalization Vice Minister Murata. This change in attitude among METI's senior and ANRE officials aligns with the timing of the halt in METI's pursuit of liberalization measures, as well as the departure of the METI officials who questioned Japan's nuclear fuel cycle policy.

This positive shift in METI's relationship with the electric utilities also overlapped with the 2004 Mihama accident and the 2007 Kashiwazaki-Kariwa earthquake-induced problems. These incidents should have hindered METI's nuclear expansion plans, especially because they occurred after the data falsification scandal, and because the 2007 incident revealed the nuclear reactors' vulnerability to earthquakes. Instead, several government and electric utility interviewees asserted that these incidents resulted in intensification of nuclear promotion efforts. Several government and electric utility interviewees highlighted a "nuclear renaissance" initiative, in which METI officials cooperated with the electric utilities to rebuild public support for nuclear power expansion. Government official G9 (April 2013) cited the scandal and the 2004 and 2007 incidents as "the reasons why the ANRE tried to create the so-called nuclear renaissance plan in the year of 2005 or 6 . . . to overcome the problems." The nuclear renaissance embodied a joint effort by METI and the electric utilities to preserve and continue the nuclear power program and rebuild confidence in it. This government-utility focus on the acceptability aspects of social resilience, rather than the effects of disruptions on communities, would later challenge public trust. In addition, the emphasis on preserving and expanding on existing nuclear infrastructure investments reflects continuation of shared economic resilience priorities across the utilities and policymakers.

Formal and informal institutional mechanisms fostering cooperation between the electric utilities and policymakers became increasingly important for shared promotion of nuclear power expansion during this period. For example, a revamping of the government's formal energy policy provided the utilities with more flexibility regarding achievement of electricity supply source targets. Several government interviewees explained that the 2010 Basic Energy Plan did not contain energy supply source targets. These targets appeared in the appendix and were non-binding. This non-binding status differed from the plans of the previous two decades, which were officially linked to the electric utilities' supply plans. Government official G4 described the process as "no longer an official process of 'this is the energy policy, this is the utilities' plan, and then approval of the program'" (February 2013). Because the targets were no longer formally linked to the electric utilities' plans, responsibility for meeting the government's targets became ambiguous. Government interviewee G4 said of the 2010 Basic Energy Plan, "the question, even at that time, was that there was no legal enforcement by the government to ask the utilities to reach some sort of nuclear share. There is no guarantee. So who is responsible for reaching the target of a nuclear share of 50 percent by 2030? It's not clear." This ambiguity over the responsibility for meeting the government targets mirrors the debate over the responsibility for nuclear fuel recycling. The decoupling of utility supply plans and government policies on supply source targets served to reduce tension over these challenges and foster continued cooperation to jointly promote nuclear power development to meet economic and ecological resilience goals.

In addition to market liberalization, global climate change commitments, and electricity supply target policy changes, policymakers' relationships with the electric utilities also responded to informal institutional mechanisms such as the *amakudari* system, university cohort relationships, and political donations. Finally, formal institutions, including subsidies, advisory committees (*shingikai*), and the personnel rotation system, also guided these relationships and the ways in which resilience priorities manifested in energy policy and policymaking process change.

As in the period following the oil crises, the *amakudari* system played a central role as an informal institutional feature contributing to the electric utilities' cooperation with and clout over energy policymakers. Government interviewees' accounts of *amakudari* influence support similar depictions in existing literature (e.g., Aldrich, 2011). As government official G17 explained, "As for the nuclear policy people, some of them . . . work for almost their whole life in the nuclear division. Their predecessors work at the nuclear power plant division at the electricity companies after graduation, after they graduate from METI" (July 2013). In addition to METI officials' retirement to electric utility positions, electric utility executives became Diet members, as Kanoh exemplified. The *amakudari* system built cooperation and electric utility clout and coordinated economic resilience priorities that fostered government policy support for the electric utilities' profits from nuclear power. This policy support included the Basic Act on Energy Policy, which protected nuclear investments, the nuclear renaissance, and halting electricity market liberalization before separation of generation and transmission took place.

Along with *amakudari*, a reverse trend also deepened cooperation between policymakers and the electric utilities, reinforcing shared resilience priorities. *Amaagari* enabled industry executives to hold government posts while retaining roles in industry. The most influential example of *amaagari* during this period occurred when the LDP appointed TEPCO's Kanoh as both chairman of the parliamentary committee overseeing MITI and parliamentary secretary of the Ministry of Education, Science, Sports and Culture. In the 2000–2001 government overhaul, the ministry merged with the Science and Technology Agency to become the Ministry of Education, Culture, Science, Sports and Technology (MEXT).

The *amakudari* and *amaagari* systems complemented another informal set of relationships formed through universities. Government interviewee G17 asserted that graduates from the same universities maintained strong bonds even after they dispersed to government positions and electric utility jobs. G17 offered a former director of the Nuclear Policy Planning Division, as an example: "He graduated from Kyoto University's nuclear department. So because he is from the nuclear engineering department, he had a very good relationship with the nuclear electricity's nuclear power people, and he had a very good relationship with the nuclear power people at the electric utilities." These long-term bonds between government officials and electric utility engineers and executives enabled cooperation and coordination on resilience priorities and nuclear power promotion policies even after the accidents and scandal.

Political donations provided a third informal institutional mechanism that fostered cooperative relations between the electric utilities and policymakers, also affecting energy policymaking priorities and the role of the 3Es. According to G17, "officially, energy policy has three parts. Economy, environment, and energy supply. Officially we think these three, but I think the truth is that political contributions have an extremely strong influence" (July 2013). While these donations did not directly impact relationships between the electric utilities and METI's junior officials, senior officials in Japan's ministries are political appointees. Influential pro-utility Diet members also pressured METI officials to craft policies supportive of the electric utilities. Former government official G21 described a "pressure cycle" in which the electric utilities pressured the LDP, the LDP pressured METI, and METI pressured the electric utilities. Political donations played an important role in the electric utilities' pressure on the LDP. Diet member Kono affirmed that "a lot of politicians have received money from TEPCO, and not only TEPCO, but all the power industries." He also noted the electric utilities' role as influential members of regional business organizations that donated to LDP politicians.

Kono characterized the electric utility-politician relationship as follows: "A lot of LDP politicians try to create good relationships with power companies, because . . . they might give you money, their management will help you in your campaign, and they have a lot of companies that are related to the power company" (March 2013). This perspective reflects the increasing interrelatedness of the nuclear-based system with other systems and sectors, as well as the system's growing momentum. While political donations contributed to the electric utilities' cooperative relationship with and clout over the LDP, government interviewees stated that the electric utilities wielded influence over opposition party Democratic Party of Japan (DPJ) members through donations from the electric utilities' labor unions. However, G17 believes that fewer DPJ members took donations from the electric utilities, while all LDP members except Kono took them. In fact, some DPJ members accepted donations from organizations that fought electric utility influence, such as law associations and local civic associations. G17 suggested that these members supported nuclear power in the absence of accidents. Since the DPJ did not serve as the majority party during the 1990s or early 2000s, anti-utility sentiment among DPJ members during this period had little effect on government policies. Differences between the institutional influences on the LDP and the DPJ became more apparent in the aftermath of the Fukushima disaster, as discussed in the next chapter.

Political donations were linked to formal institutional mechanisms such as subsidies to electric utilities for nuclear power plant construction, as well as the subsidies to local government (*kofukin*) for nuclear plant siting. Kono recalled attending LDP nuclear policy meetings that focused primarily on allocation of these subsidies, rather than on the policy implications of nuclear development. He was surprised to find that most of the meeting attendees were from districts hosting nuclear plants. "The meeting was how to divide the money, the government subsidies, among all the districts where nuclear reactors were being built. So it wasn't really a policy discussion" (March 2013). The siting subsidies propelled Diet-backed policies to promote nuclear power expansion. At the same time, suggested a media interviewee, subsidies for nuclear plant construction were one impetus behind the electric utilities' interest in building more nuclear plants. This institutional support served as an important mechanism to encourage electric utility cooperation with METI's nuclear power expansion goals.

As in the previous period, advisory committees (*shingikai*) also continued to serve as an official vehicle for electric utilities' cooperation with and clout over policymakers. Until the Fukushima accident occurred, electric utility executives served on energy-related advisory committees, including those for electricity supply policy and market reform. One NGO representative who served on several of these committees related:

> I got some secret document . . . during that energy committee I was on . . . At the next committee meeting, a draft report is supposed to be proposed by the secretary, that means bureaucrat. But I got some draft from the electricity industry association's people who dropped it in the Parliament, and

I got a copy, and already the draft was there. It was very detailed negotiations between the secretary of METI and the electricity industry association, text by text, full of red lines and full of inserts and deletions. So the electricity industry and METI are completely in very hard negotiation in between behind the scenes, but the publicly open committee's members had no idea what draft will be shown at the next committee, so those kind of operations were up until 2000. Or even until March 11 [2011], the committee controlled by METI was operated like that.

(P1, March 2013)

This anecdote supports existing studies that broadly characterize *shingikai* as influential bodies that balance stakeholder interests (e.g., Scalise, 2010, 10). It also reveals the extent of electric utility-METI coordination, as well as the struggle for clout.

The Japanese government's personnel rotation system (*jinji idou*) also impacted the electric utilities' cooperation with and clout over METI policymakers. In this system, officials rotate to different ministry offices and divisions every several years. This personnel rotation system enabled pro-nuclear METI officials to return repeatedly to positions of policymaking power. G17 explained that "it isn't necessarily the case that there are that many people deeply involved in nuclear power, so the nuclear people keep coming and going to the same kinds of posts many times" (July 2013). G17 added that because these pro-nuclear officials continually rotated into nuclear-related roles in METI, they "were a little bit isolated from the people at METI who are saying "let's deregulate the electricity sector,'" and they maintained cooperation with the electric utilities even when liberalization was proceeding. This structure enabled nuclear-focused policymakers to continue aligning with the utilities to promote their economic resilience goals involving nuclear investments, while policymakers working on economic regulation and market structure pursued economic resilience goals focused on market efficiency and electricity pricing.

The electric utilities also used *jinji idou* to oust pro-liberalization officials and regain clout over METI policymakers. With the transition within METI from pro-liberalization officials to pro-nuclear, anti-liberalization officials, electric utility supporters within METI regained clout, which also empowered the electric utilities again. Some government interviewees divulged that they had made efforts to resurrect liberalization measures after 2005, but resistance from the electric utilities and their supporters within METI stymied these efforts.

Government, electric utility, and some NGO and media interviewees all suggested that institutional features during the 1990s and 2000s primarily enhanced electric utility clout in the policymaking process. The *amakudari* system, university cohort relationships, and political donations provided the electric utilities with informal channels for influence. The formal institutions – subsidies, advisory committees, and the personnel rotation system – codified official electric utility influence. Iida, the former member of several METI advisory committees, characterized the relationship in this way: "electric utilities have much, much larger political power compared to METI, but they are officially controlled or regulated by METI. So, it was a very stressful relationship with each other." Other interviewees corroborated this view.

In addition to institutional influences, risk perceptions also shaped cooperation between the electric utilities and policymakers. Several government interviewees asserted that LDP and DPJ politicians and METI officials did not believe a serious accident could occur. This assumption colored these groups' actions toward energy system resilience, enabling them to prioritize economic resilience over engineering and ecological resilience.

Existing analyses and this book's interviewees generally agree that until the Fukushima disaster, policymakers and the electric utilities broadly framed energy system risk as energy security and economic risk, and later added environmental risk associated with climate change and air pollutants. Policymakers and the electric utilities did not focus on energy system safety risks, although regulators did. This characterization also reflects resilience priorities focused on certain aspects of socio-ecological resilience and economic resilience, while omitting others.

Former government official G16 attributed this governmental view to electric utility influence: "Before Fukushima . . . ignorance of safety problems was, I think, very prominent in government. So why is a problem and the reason is a problem, and I think that is also, you can say, the influence of industry. Because industry doesn't like to spend much money." This view reflects the complexities of economic resilience priorities, in which infrastructure upgrades are costly, but also necessary for engineering resilience and avoidance of future costs associated with infrastructure failure or damage. G16 indicated that because the electric utilities did not want to invest in safety upgrades, they did not share the risks with government officials, and "also the government itself did not take it seriously enough." Diet member Kono also noted LDP politicians' lack of knowledge regarding nuclear power safety issues. Existing studies support this depiction of the utility companies' awareness of safety risks, but they also suggest that METI's safety regulators had access to safety risk assessments, as well (e.g., Kingston, 2014), as discussed in this chapter's section on safety regulators and utilities.

The 1990s-early 2000s nuclear accidents and scandal thus did not have lasting effects on policymakers' relationships with the electric utilities. However, as we have begun to observe, resilience priorities, institutional influences, and risk perceptions contributed to shifts in cooperation and clout in these relationships during this period.

Economic Regulators and Electric Utilities

While risk perceptions had little impact on economic regulators' relationships with the electric utilities, the accidents and scandal, resilience priorities and institutional influences had a mixed effect. The 1990s accidents occurred concurrently with MITI's pursuit of electricity market reform, with little impact on an already increasingly tense relationship.

The 2002 scandal, however, became a turning point. As government interviewee G9 asserted, "in the middle of 2002 and 3, or maybe 4, the Agency of Energy and Natural Resources . . . needed to handle the falsification scandal. So, you know, all this effort of the deregulation of the utilities stopped. Nobody could do that" (April 2013). Within METI, preservation of nuclear power expansion plans superseded economic efficiency priorities, reflecting the conflict across policymakers' economic resilience priorities.

In addition, informal institutional influences such as *amakudari* and political donations affected economic regulators' relationships with the electric utilities through pro-utility Diet members such as Kanoh. Government interviewees cited the personnel rotation system as an even greater influence on clout and cooperation during this period. Several government interviewees emphasized the significance of rotations of pro-nuclear and pro-liberalization officials in and out of senior METI positions and the Nuclear Policy Planning Division. Former government official G21 described how "many people in the power industry hated Murata and his subordinates" because they were promoting electricity market liberalization, "So industry talked to the LDP to influence the *jinji idou*" to oust pro-liberalization officials within METI, including Murata and his subordinates.

Based on shared economic resilience priorities that yielded these complex policy and personnel shifts, joint utility-policymaker pursuit of nuclear expansion thus continued through this period of accidents and scandal. However, as the story behind the scandal's release demonstrates, electricity market reform introduced short-lived tension in policymakers' relationships with the electric utilities. This tension resurfaced with the resurrection of market liberalization policies after the Fukushima disaster.

In contrast, the accidents and scandal exacerbated tensions between the utilities and safety regulators, but the effects on energy policymaking differ from what we might expect.

Safety Regulators and Electric Utilities

We might predict that the accidents and scandal would create tension between safety regulators and the electric utilities, resulting in stricter regulations. We also might expect that communication between regulators and electric utilities would have included discussion of safety risks, especially during this period of accidents and scandal. Shared risk perceptions would have mitigated tensions and fostered cooperation on maintenance of public trust. Government official G12 suggested that NISA's efforts to tighten regulations after the accidents and scandal did add some tension to METI's relationship with the electric utilities, but this shift alone did not cause many ripples. Most of the interview data indicates that institutional influences, risk perceptions, and resilience priorities played a greater role in the relationship than the accidents and scandal.

Offering one explanation for this phenomenon, existing studies and recent government documents on the relationship frame it as one of regulatory capture. These analyses assert that Japan's regulators and the electric utilities coordinated to craft ineffective regulations and weak enforcement (e.g., Kingston, 2014; Kishimoto, 2017). The Diet's investigation commission's report on the Fukushima accident states that in the decades leading up to the Fukushima disaster, "it became clear that the necessary independence and transparency in the relationship between the operators and the regulatory authorities of the nuclear industry of Japan were lost, a situation best described as "regulatory capture" – a situation that is inconsistent with a safety culture" (The National Diet of Japan Fukushima Nuclear Accident Independent Investigation Commission, 2012, 15). The report also describes a "cozy relationship between the operators, the regulators and academic scholars" (The National Diet of Japan Fukushima Nuclear Accident Independent Investigation Commission, 2012, 43). Comments from electric utility and government interviewees, including former regulators, did reflect informal communication between regulators and the electric utilities, but they also revealed a more nuanced, problematic set of relationships. They confirmed regulatory independence and transparency concerns, but they also provided other details that depict a scenario very different from regulatory capture.

Viewed holistically, the interview data suggests a much more nuanced relationship involving three sets of interactions: electric utility engineers and regulators, electric utility executives and policymakers, and policymakers and regulators. Resilience priorities played a complicated role in these relationships and their effect on energy policy. Government and electric utility interviewees' descriptions of these relationships suggest that the first two sets of relationships operated in relative isolation from one another, while the third both linked and stressed the other two. Thus, lack of effective communication compounded existing transparency and interdependence issues. Based on interviewees' comments, this problematic trifecta that contributed to the 2002 data falsification scandal did not change, even after the Fukushima disaster.

Government interviewee G12 summarized the trade-off between policymakers' cooperative relationship with the electric utilities and the need for stricter safety oversight as follows:

> Sometimes we asked the utilities to cooperate on nuclear policy, and in order to get that help or cooperation from the utilities, we somehow had to consider the current situation of the utilities, especially the financial situation of the utilities so that they can introduce more nuclear. So in that sense, we have to somehow talk and compromise with the utilities. So in such a situation, the nuclear accidents gave us some impact on the relations with the utilities. You know, the people asked for a more strict and neutral attitude of the government towards the utilities for the nuclear regulation, and so we have to be very tough with companies.
>
> (May 2013)

This need for compromise between regulatory oversight and cooperation on nuclear power expansion hints at the tension between policymakers' focus on nuclear power expansion and regulators' need to respond to safety concerns. Once again, economic resilience priorities related to nuclear investment contrasted with engineering resilience priorities focused on safety and infrastructure integrity.

Rather than cooperation indicative of regulatory capture, interviewees' comments revealed strong tension between electric utility engineers and regulators that served as a key factor in regulatory dysfunction during the 1990s and 2000s. Electric utility interviewee I1 suggested that regulatory capture might have described the electric utility-regulator relationship until the 1990s, but the emergence of regulatory challenges created friction, since the regulators did not respond in alignment with utilities' interests as they had done in the past. Engineers and regulators battled for clout over safety regulation revision and compliance. Interviews of electric utility engineers and government officials involved in safety regulation revealed hostility and lack of respect between these groups. A former regulator, G9, summarized: "Between the nuclear engineers in the industry – utilities and vendors – and the staff of the nuclear regulation body in METI, both do not trust one another" (April 2013). Meanwhile, electric utility executives and policymakers cooperated on nuclear expansion and pressured regulators to refrain from enforcement actions or regulatory changes that would constrain nuclear power production. These regulator-electric utility tensions combined with policymaker-utility cooperation to create the chain of events leading to the 2002 scandal.

Several factors fueled the conflict between the utilities and safety regulators during this period: the energy policymaking and nuclear regulatory structure, disrespect and distrust, communication challenges, and divergent risk perceptions. Linked to all of these were differences in these two groups' energy system resilience priorities.

Japan's institutional structure for energy policymaking and nuclear regulation during this period simultaneously contributed to this friction and the perception of regulatory capture. Several government and electric utility interviewees cited NISA's creation within METI in 2001 as an exacerbating factor in the tension between regulators and electric utilities. Government official G13 observed that "NISA was formed as an agency of METI, and it seemed to me that this administrative change to a large extent deteriorated the independence of regulations, because it weakened the commitment of the third administrative party like the Nuclear Safety Commission and MEXT with the nuclear regulations" (July 2013). This lack of regulatory independence from energy policymaking fostered a form of indirect regulatory capture. Electric utility industry representative I9 supported the notion of regulatory capture created by policymakers' pressure on the regulators to support the utilities' views on regulations. He confided,

> Somehow, if NISA makes rules and inspects, then I think the real problem was not identified. And somehow there was not sufficient tension between utilities and regulators. I think we should have such a sound tension. And clearly, I think regulators should listen, but they should make an independent decision after they listen. After they understand what were raised by stakeholders
> (May 2013).

This compromising of regulatory independence, asserted other government interviewees, limited the regulator's authority due to METI policymakers' cooperation with the electric utilities. Interviewed former regulators expressed frustration with pressure from politicians and policymakers that prevented them from addressing violations and tightening regulations. At the same time, they did not respond to the engineers' request to modify regulations to account for degradation of reactor parts over time. ANRE was unaware of the request and did not intervene on behalf of the electric utilities. According to electric utility executive I1, NISA "did not respond to TEPCO's request for many years, many years . . . But TEPCO's issue was that some of the engineers falsified the data" (July 2013). I1 suggested that TEPCO, NISA and METI held informal discussions once policymakers became aware of the data falsification. However, ANRE officials did not want to make the situation public, fearing that it would weaken public trust in nuclear power, the utilities, and regulators.

And yet, news of the scandal did reach the public, as previously discussed. Regulator-engineer tensions culminated in the 2002 announcement of TEPCO's data falsification, based on Murata's hostility toward TEPCO and the actions of a GE whistleblower. TEPCO's case is well described in media accounts and TEPCO presentations (e.g., CNN, 2002; Ashina and Nakata, 2003; Kuroda, 2004). Other electric utilities also falsified data, according to electric utility interviewees, but their cases did not receive much publicity.

Despite what we might expect, the scandal did not lead to revised regulations or a formal change in the regulatory structure. Instead, stricter enforcement of existing regulations complemented superficial separation of regulators from policymakers. I1 stated that as a result of the tension over regulations and the ensuing data falsification and its revelation, "regulation itself did not change at that time. The communication, relationship did change. To get worse." Electric utility interviewee I12 described the regulators' attitude after the scandal as increasingly strict. "I think the government mind changed to "we have to regulate and we have to supervise the power companies more and more'" (June 2013). At the same time, METI proclaimed NISA's independence from policymakers after the scandal. However, former regulator G9 related a telling anecdote from a few years later:

> I made the decision to stop the nuclear power plants due to some troubles two to three times. When I decided, I did not talk to anyone in ANRE. Then, after two or three of my decisions, I was told by the director-general to please meet the ANRE director. When I met him . . . the intent was that I had stopped the plants too many times
>
> (May 2013).

This pressure from ANRE on NISA to continue reactor operations reflects the continuation of policymaker and electric utility clout over safety regulators after the scandal. It also reflects continued tension between policymaker-utility emphasis on economic resilience – in particular, losses associated with plant shutdowns and regulatory compliance – and safety regulator responsibility for engineering resilience. The final report issued by Japan's Nuclear Safety Commission following the 2004 accident at KEPCO's Mihama reactor also reflects this ongoing tension between regulators and plant operators. The report criticizes the electric utility for an attitude of neglect regarding inspections. The report also cites NISA's complaint that KEPCO personnel prioritized efficiency over safety (The Nuclear Safety Commission of Japan, 2005, 4–5).

Lack of respect and trust affected the regulator-utility relationship and these groups' ability to coordinate on energy system resilience. According to government interviewees, safety regulators viewed engineers as condescending and disrespectful of regulatory guidelines. Former regulators complained that electric utility engineers did not respect regulations or the regulators' authority to oversee them. G9 explained that "staff of NISA or METI feel like nuclear engineers in utilities are too arrogant and won't hear voices from outside" (April 2013). Japan's Nuclear Safety Commission (NSC) documentation of NISA's reports supports this depiction. A 2008 NSC document describes NISA's depiction of "repeated malicious conduct of unreported alteration and concealment" by four electric utilities (The Nuclear Safety Commission of Japan, 2008). NISA apparently directed these companies to "revise their operational safety programs for recurrence prevention at their seven power stations, where the cases in evaluation criteria "Level I" had been experienced," citing non-compliance with regulations. Level I describes "cases that impaired, or could have impaired, nuclear safety, by failing to comply with the requirements specified by the Law for the Regulation of Nuclear Source Material, Nuclear Fuel Material and Reactors or the Electricity Utilities Industry Act" (The Nuclear Safety Commission of Japan, 2008).

Former regulators also complained that politicians controlled by electric utility company management and pro-nuclear bureaucrats stifled the regulators' ability to enforce existing regulations or impose new ones. G9 explained that "once NISA finds some issues, it might affect against energy policy, so the head of ANRE can direct them not to do it. That is the concept of NISA" (May 2013). However, I1 described how electric utility engineers and regulators communicated informally at times, without informing ANRE or the utilities' top management. This informal engineer-regulator communication kept problems from reaching the attention of the top management in the electric utilities and METI, preserving cooperation in the latter relationship even as tension escalated in the former.

Electric utility engineers apparently reciprocated the regulators' disdain. In their interviews, electric utility engineers and executives described safety regulators as lacking knowledge of nuclear reactor technology and operation. Former regulator G9 recalled that "nuclear engineers in the utilities even said to me that staff in NISA . . . do not know so much about nuclear, do not have so much knowledge" (April 2013). This concern would reemerge after the Fukushima disaster, during creation of the new, independent nuclear regulatory agency.

Linked to this lack of respect and trust, communication challenges also plagued the relationship between regulators and utilities. The electric utility engineers contended that when they requested changes to regulations they perceived as overly strict or outdated, regulators did not respond. Recognizing the role of communication in coordination on resilience goals, several government and electric utility interviewees cited open communication between regulators and engineers as necessary for an effective regulatory system. I1 conveyed that NISA and the Atomic Energy Commission of Japan (AEC) engaged in informal hearings with the electric utilities. He explained that "from the utilities' point of view, it's very important to obtain information before it was disclosed, because they may have had time to elaborate. From the regulators' point of view, it is better for them to listen to the utilities' idea before it was made official. So there was a benefit on both sides." However, the media and public began to view this coordination as illicit cooperation.

At the heart of these communication challenges lay the fundamental difference in resilience focus between these two groups. The utilities' prioritization of economic resilience drove their concerns about regulatory stringency and reactor outage times. I6 recalled that "during that time, we are majorly focusing on the fact that the Japanese regulatory requirement is too strict. Too much detailed. Preparation of documentation was too detailed" (May 2013). I6 asserted that the electric utilities also felt that the reactor outage times for safety inspections were too long, and they complained that the regulations for plant safety did not account for degradation over time. The utilities were "struggling for discussing with the regulatory body in MITI/METI," but the regulatory agency refused to modify the regulations. A focus on reactor integrity and engineering resilience drove regulators' rejection of the utilities' requested modifications. The lack of communication exacerbated the challenges of these divergent resilience perspectives. Electric utility executive I6 concluded, "That is the basis for the falsification problem, the regulatory system" (May 2013). This disagreement over the stringency of existing regulations created a situation in which the utilities did not feel obligated to comply with the regulations, much less exceed them to create a safety culture.

Risk perceptions also influenced utilities' and regulators' views on system resilience and the role of regulations in achieving it. Government documents and interview data yield four different scenarios, all indicating a problematic electric utility-regulator relationship, as described in my previously published analysis (Sklarew, 2018).

The first scenario suggests shared understanding of risks and a shared focus on economic resilience. Government documents posit that the electric utilities and safety regulators both had knowledge of risks, but they did not apply this knowledge effectively. For example, the Diet's independent commission's report on the Fukushima disaster states:

> Through study groups and other sources, both TEPCO and NISA were aware that if a tsunami higher than that predicted by the Japan Society of Civil Engineers (JSCE) hit the power plant, there was a risk of reactor core damage from a malfunction of seawater pumps. They were also aware that if a tsunami higher than the ground height of the premises hit the nuclear power plant, there was the possibility of a station blackout. They were also aware that no

basis existed for assuming that the probability of such a tsunami hitting the power plant was extremely low.

(The National Diet of Japan Fukushima Nuclear Accident
Independent Investigation Commission, 2012, 2)

Press accounts also cite records indicating that NISA avoided implementing tougher regulations despite awareness of risks, because regulators feared lawsuits over reactor design (The National Diet of Japan Fukushima Nuclear Accident Independent Investigation Commission, 2012, 2). This perspective suggests a scenario of regulatory capture and shared focus on economic resilience, in which safety regulators and the electric utilities cooperated to suppress and ignore risks in crafting and complying with regulations.

In contrast, interviewees' comments suggest three alternative scenarios. In the first of these, risk perceptions and communication challenges combined. Academic interviewee A5 asserted that the electric utilities were aware of safety risks, while regulators were not. He described the electric utilities' efforts to understand nuclear accident risk during the early 2000s, but he cited a communication gap between the electric utilities and NISA. A5 asserted that the findings of academic studies funded by the utilities were "not well communicated to the people working in the nuclear reactor design and safety community. Those were academic experts, but they were sitting in the advisory committee of MEXT, but that kind of discussion was not well communicated to the people in the industry, or the nuclear safety regulation." A5 further suggested that compared to the electric utilities, regulators expressed less interest in risk assessments. "So the industry people were relatively sensitive to the new development, but safety regulation people who should be more sensitive to that kind of development are not so sensitive, actually. That's one of the issues. Especially NISA people." This perspective suggests that regulators and the electric utilities did not communicate or cooperate well, leading to different risk perceptions that affected regulations and compliance with them.

The second of these alternative scenarios identifies this communication gap, but blames the electric utilities for failing to convey risk information. G3 cites the utilities' perceptions of the stringency of regulations as the reason for this communication failure. G3 claims that "METI was not well informed by utilities about nuclear technologies and its risk, because utilities do not want to tell METI the reality or details, because by doing so they just get tougher regulations from METI if they inform the truth. If utilities inform METI, tougher regulations come back. So didn't say anything." This perspective suggests that the utilities' economic resilience priorities, conflict with regulators' engineering resilience focus, and a lack of trust contributed to faulty regulations.

The final alternative scenario involves policymakers as interlocutors. Former regulator G9 asserted that when NISA regulators requested surveys of fault lines, "utility company board members sometimes called director-generals of ANRE or NISA . . . and asked us not to do it. ANRE or director-general of NISA asked us to stop" (May 2013). This depiction of the relationship reflects regulators' interest in and awareness of potential risk, but action to address this risk was stymied by electric utility clout over regulators.

Regardless of their differences, all of these perspectives on risk perceptions indicate regulatory dysfunction. This dysfunction contributed to perpetuation of nuclear power expansion by enabling the electric utilities to avoid investing in safety upgrades and select reactor sites that regulators might have rejected. Along with the accidents and scandal, this regulatory dysfunction should have provoked public distrust in the government's ability to regulate nuclear power. However, other factors averted this result.

Government and Public

The same factors that fostered the conflict between the utilities and safety regulators during this period perpetuated public cooperation with the government. These include trust, communication, risk perceptions, and resilience priorities. While the 1990s and 2000s accidents and scandal may have temporarily sapped public trust in the government, institutional features perpetuated trust and suppressed public clout. These institutional features also mitigated the shocks' effect on public risk perceptions and enabled coordination of government-public resilience priorities.

Interviewees did not have a unified view on the short-term versus long-term impacts of the accidents and scandal on public trust in the government. Some government and NGO interviewees' views supported findings by Aldrich, Lesbirel, and other scholars, which portray waning public trust in the government's ability to manage nuclear power in the 1990s. Iida asserted that "each accident . . . very much shocked the public and also bureaucrats. He argued that the government and electric utilities cooperated to "control the national agenda" for energy policy, despite public perceptions of the seriousness of the accidents and scandal. Government interviewee G13 agreed that the accidents negatively impacted the public's trust in the government's ability to manage nuclear power. Government official G18 also agreed that public trust in the government declined during this period, but he attributed this decline to a series of scandals in a range of sectors, not just energy.[5] At the same time, G18 suggested that "if there is just distrust from the public, that will not create power of change in the society. Some sort of sympathy for anti-nuclear sentiment is coming from inside government and politicians in the ruling party" (August 2013) This perspective indicates that the accidents and scandal did not increase public clout in energy policymaking; the government continued to lead without much public input.

Other government and NGO representatives did not perceive this decline in public trust at all. As shown in Figure 4.1, public opinion polls also reflect little to no change in public support and disapproval of Japanese government leadership after each accident. Several government interviewees suggested that economic priorities more strongly influenced public confidence in the government than energy concerns during this period. The poll data reflects no loss of public trust after the 1991 accident. Prime Minister Murayama resigned shortly after the Monju accident, but not because of it. Rather, he resigned due to blame for Japan's continuing economic recession. The poll data reflects trust in the new Hashimoto government shortly after the accident, a pattern later repeated in Prime Minister Abe's support rate after the Fukushima disaster. Prime Minister Hashimoto's support rate actually rose after the 1997 Tokaimura accident. After the 1999 Tokaimura accident, Prime Minister Obuchi's support rate declined due to a new political coalition. Prime Minister Koizumi's support rate rose dramatically following both revelation of the TEPCO scandal and the 2004 Mihama accident, but press reports and existing studies indicate that the public was focused on foreign policy issues.[6] Prime Minister Abe's support rate also rose after the 2007 Kashiwazaki-Kariwa accident from a historic low caused by a series of financial scandals perpetrated by his Cabinet members.

Media representative M2 summarized the public's relationship with the government during this period of accidents and scandal: "After the 1990s accidents, they didn't change their mind. They still trusted the government." M2 expressed puzzlement over this continued public trust, asserting, "It is difficult for me to tell why, because I wrote something, I myself wrote some articles about the risk of nuclear repeatedly, but the response is very rare. So I didn't understand why people trusted the Japanese government so strictly or so strongly" (*March 2013*). Even some electric utility interviewees commented on the continuity of public trust, confiding that lack of public awareness of the extent of accidents and cover-ups averted the need for change in government policies that would have altered the energy system.

Table 4.1 Public Opinion of Japanese Leadership After 1990s/2000s Accidents and Scandal

Month/Year	Cabinet	Support Rate (%)	Opposition Rate (%)
12/1990	Kaifu	49	32
2/1991	Kaifu	47	34
6/1991	Kaifu	50	32
10/1995	Murayama	35	47
12/1995	Murayama	33	46
1/1996	Hashimoto	61	20
2/1997	Hashimoto	42	37
3/1997	Hashimoto	43	38
4/1997	Hashimoto	44	38
9/1999	Obuchi	51	26
10/1999	Obuchi	46	28
11/1999	Obuchi	41	36
08/2002	Koizumi	43	42
10/2002	Koizumi	65	24
07/2004	Koizumi	36	48
08/2004	Koizumi	39	43
09/2004	Koizumi	45	35
06/2007	Abe	30	49
08/2007	Abe	41	40

Source: Reprinted from Sklarew, 2015; data from *Asahi Shimbun* public opinion polls, 1990–2011.

Interestingly, existing studies find that the accidents affected public trust in nuclear power safety, despite minimal effects on trust in the government. For example, Tsunoda Katsuya's study of public opinion after the 1999 Tokaimura criticality accident found that while trust in nuclear power safety had declined, the accident elicited virtually no increase in public distrust in the government. The study also found a moderate correlation between distrust in the government and trust in nuclear power operation. He attributes this incongruity to the commercial nature of the accident, which he determines could have led to distrust in nuclear power without eliciting distrust in the government (Tsunoda, 2001).

However, government, media, and NGO interviewees provided different explanations for the preservation of public trust in the government after the Tokaimura accident and other accidents preceding it. Communication from the government to the public plays a prominent role in all of these explanations.

The first communication strategy involved distancing of the accidents from commercial power generation and emphasis of minimal impact on the public. Many interviewees' comments suggest that the government and the electric utilities cooperated to instill in the public the impression that the accidents did not involve nuclear power generation, but rather research and development. Media representative M1 observed,

> Monju or Tokai JCO did not a lot to change the policies. It's hard to understand for the general public. And METI's strategy at that time was to accuse STA or PNC severely. And they protected their light water policies. They distinguished between their policies and Monju, which is still in the R&D stage, and it is completely different from the conventional light water reactor. That was the logic of METI at that time.
>
> (March 2013)

Interviewees also posited that the accidents' relatively small impact on the broader population prevented a decline in public trust in the government. Academic interviewee A1 noted that "the 1990s nuclear accidents were serious, for sure, but they never got to the level of the general public is involved. They didn't have anybody being evacuated and relocated, and that sort of thing, right? This accident really happened inside of the compound" (February 2013). A1 explained that although "there is human error and showed some danger," the government was "able to say, well, still nuclear power is safe, because they never had any effect outside of the compound, the big concrete wall, so the public never really got involved." The accidents thus did not affect the general public's trust strongly enough to force the government to change the energy system.

The second communication strategy involved efforts to sustain trust in the central government's ability to ensure nuclear power safety. While the accidents did not diminish public trust enough to warrant changes in nuclear promotion policies or regulations, they did affect local communities' attitudes toward the central government, according to government and NGO interviewees. G4 recalled that due to the accidents, "it was clear the local public no longer trusted what the utilities or the government said. But that happened . . . well before Fukushima" (February 2013). In alignment with analyses by Aldrich, Lesbirel and others, interviewees asserted that this local decline in public trust led to government efforts to reinforce trust at the local level.

The aforementioned conflict between the policymakers and the electric utilities over responsibility for public acceptance arose in part because the electric utilities recognized that public trust in the government could facilitate acceptance of nuclear power more effectively than the electric utilities' promotion. Several electric utility interviewees explained that the utilities leveraged the public's perception of government clout over the utilities. I6 described how the electric utilities used this strategy in nuclear plant siting discussions with local communities: "to the general public, the utility company said, this was approved by the government, and that means this is the right thing, and we have to follow, and you, the general public, have to understand it" (May 2013). This tactic generally worked until the Fukushima disaster occurred.

Public trust in the government also enabled METI to garner public acceptance for nuclear power expansion by voicing support for it as a policy for the good of the nation. Electric utility interviewee I15 relayed that local governments sought this rationale: "It's always been the case, even before the [Fukushima] accident. Any new construction, including Rokkasho, the local government always wants to have the commitment of the central government." The central government continued to overtly support local governments' and electric utilities' nuclear plant siting plans throughout the 1990s and 2000s, despite the accidents and scandal.

This said, some of these efforts worked, and some backfired. For instance, in 1993, PNC created an animated video that PNC officials intended for use by local Japanese government offices to build public confidence in nuclear power. Negative reactions from the U.S. Department of Energy (DOE) and NGOs with whom DOE shared the video resulted in the opposite effect, to PNC officials' surprise.[7] The Japanese public became more distrustful of government involvement in nuclear power promotion. Public relations campaigns and regulatory tweaks after accidents and the scandal aimed to rebuild trust from the public as a whole, but also within plant host communities. For example, government interviewee G13 suggested that regulatory and policy changes after the 1999 Tokaimura accident reflected "more attention to the relationship with the local communities."

A third group of government, NGO and media interviewees identified middle ground between uninterrupted public trust and loss of trust, asserting that public trust declined after each accident but rose again over time. Some interviewees and NGO documents attributed this return of public trust to government efforts to rebuild it. Some of these efforts involved more transparent communication with the public. For example, after the Monju accident, an NGO publication cited a government decision to "make public most of the nuclear policy decision-making meetings of its relevant ministries and agencies." The Citizens' Nuclear Information Center asserted that this decision came "in response to the outcry from the public and NGOs over the government's handling of the accident" (The Citizens'

Nuclear Information Center, 1997). The government also initiated a 1999 Nuclear Power Awareness Campaign to build public trust and encourage public support for nuclear plant construction.

The focus on global climate change also fostered public trust by enabling the government to build a shared environmental priority with the public. Government, electric utility, NGO and media interviewees cited global climate change mitigation as a priority shared by energy policymakers and the public after COP-3. G3 described this link between nuclear power and prioritization of energy security and climate change:

> Nuclear was considered to be self-sufficient energy, so Japan is starting the nuclear fuel cycle options, and that warrants the future energy security of Japan. This argument was strengthened by the climate change discussion after the Kyoto COP meeting. Suddenly, nuclear was also suddenly given a very important role to achieve the targets for CO_2 emission reduction.

Media interviewee M1 asserted that the government conveyed these views to the public after COP-3: "many people are getting awareness of climate change issues. That gave a very good reason for boosting nuclear power for the energy policies" (March 2013). Policymakers framed nuclear power as "a very strong and effective way to reduce our emissions, to replace coal and fossil fuels. And that sounds very much persuasive for the general public and after that, they repeated that kind of theory repeatedly." This social resilience framing deepened public trust in the government. G21 asserted that this shared social resilience priority enabled rapid recovery of public support for nuclear power after the accidents and scandal, since "we had a problem with the policy priority for climate change at that time. So in the face of the public doubt about nuclear power plants, we could promote further the nuclear. The government could, because of climate change." This trajectory continued until the Fukushima disaster, contributing to the nuclear renaissance's successful culmination in the 2010 Strategic Energy Plan.

Several government interviewees added that the public accepted METI's portrayal of nuclear power as an exportable solution to other nations' climate change challenges. G1 summarized this coordinated view as follows:

> I cannot say that Japanese people did not take importance of safety, but the first priority thinking was that energy business is very promising for Japan, and also greenhouse gas emission reduction is very important for Japan. That was the thinking before the Fukushima crisis. Government and public generally thought this direction, and social communities have variety of opinions, but generally they agree.

A perception that the government was implementing nuclear and renewables expansion policies to meet climate change mitigation goals contributed to public trust in the government's energy policymaking. The public did not appear to notice the incongruous rise in coal use throughout this period, which should have raised public doubts about the government's commitment to climate change mitigation.

Informal and formal institutional features also contributed to public trust in the government. The government's paternalistic relationship with the public played the most important informal role in maintaining public trust and minimizing public clout in energy policymaking. Meanwhile, formal institutions such as siting subsidies, town hall hearings, and an ineffective public comment process also promoted trust and suppressed public clout. The paternalistic relationship framed public expectations that the government would act in the public's best interest without a need for public input. G17 related that "before Fukushima, the public had little or no impact" on METI's decisions. Government officials largely assumed they could make better decisions on behalf of the public than average citizens. Government interviewee G18 asserted that while government officials wanted to explain energy policy trade-offs to the public, they believed the public would not understand, highlighting a communication and transparency problem. G7 described an environment in which "the government had the guts to say no to the public." Meanwhile, public trust in the government ceded public clout. NGO leader P2 contended that "many people . . . related that we had so much confidence in the government, because of that trust in government – confidence – the government took control, and they didn't believe they should listen to people. So this is kind of a vicious cycle. Of dependency and more control kind of things" (March 2013). While the accidents and scandal whittled away at public trust and disinterest in policymaking input, the paternalistic relationship enabled rapid recovery of trust after each shock.

As a result of this relationship, policymakers also felt pressure to meet public expectations regarding safety and security. Government official G7 contended that starting in the mid-1990s, "even if we don't have any strong influence from the political side . . . we more and more have the tendency to take into account public opinion." The official asserted that METI policymakers have gradually begun to be concerned about public reactions to their policies, in part due to a decline in METI's clout over the public. NGO and media interviewees did not perceive this accommodation of public views, nor the relative rise in public clout.[8]

Formal institutions also affected public trust and clout in the government's energy policymaking. The aforementioned subsidies to nuclear plant host communities perpetuated cooperation between the local and central governments, encouraging them to cooperate to recover public trust after each shock. At town hall hearings, government officials connected with local citizens to build support for nuclear plant siting.

Formal outlets for public opinion to influence policymaking also constrained public clout. NGO interviewees mentioned the ineffectiveness of the public comment system. P2 asserted that "the government has to have a public hearing period of receiving feedback from the people. But to my knowledge, that kind of public hearing didn't work" (March 2013). P2 explained the ways in which the public comment mechanism yielded minimal public impact on policymaking during the period of accidents and scandal:

> It's kind of just formality. The government has a one-week public hearing website, and nobody knows, and the only feedback they receive is from industries. And if the issue is a very hot issue, for example, global warming – hot issue means different opinions from government, industries and NGOs – then if the government had the public opinion period, they have thousands of emails from industries, the same text. Actually the public hearing or this kind of feedback route between the government and the people didn't exist or did exist but didn't work. That is my opinion.
>
> (March 2013)[9]

The public comment system thus bolstered public trust by appearing to serve as an outlet for public opinion. In reality, it constrained public clout by avoiding the impact of public opinion on energy policymaking.

The overall effect of these institutional influences appears to be continued public trust in the government, albeit with periods of doubt, coupled with constrained public clout, despite some government perceptions of public influence. on energy policy decisions. These institutional features also mitigated the 1990s and 2000s shocks' effects on public risk perceptions and enabled coordination of government-public resilience priorities. The paternalistic relationship led to public trust in the government's assessment of nuclear accident risk, despite the emergence of short-term doubts about nuclear reactor safety after each accident and scandal occurred. At the same time, the public also expected the government to take responsibility for protecting citizens from risk.

The nature of this relationship thus shaped the government's communication of risks to the public. NGO and media interviewees asserted that to preserve this trust, the government avoided informing the public of potential risks, and the general public did not ask for details. Media interviewee M2 suggested that before the Fukushima accident, "I think the lack of education about nuclear energy in Japan is the reason why people didn't pay attention to the risks before. So the traditional way of Japanese governing of people is not to tell them or educate them or tell them the truth about complicated matters. In my opinion, many people in Japan don't know what nuclear power is." According to some government and academic interviewees, the Japanese public's extremely low tolerance of risk led to government suppression of risk communication for fear that local communities would reject nuclear plant siting. As academic interviewee A5 noted, "even though academics were discussing about the necessity for increasing the scope of the severe accident, including the earthquake and tsunami, that kind of discussion was not well incorporated in the regulation also. Partly because of the concern, especially the concern of the regulatory people for the so-called public acceptance issue in the local area." This lack of communication on risks encouraged public perceptions of a safe and resilient energy system.

These relationship factors and their influences on Japanese energy system change and the energy policymaking process during this period of accidents and scandal are reflected in Table 4.2. These shocks contributed to emergence of some

Table 4.2 Changes to Japanese Government's Relationships and Energy Policy, Process, and Structure after 1990s/2000s Accidents and Scandal

Relationship	Change in Cooperation/Conflict	Change in Clout
Bureaucrats-Utilities	Conflict < Cooperation Change: some conflict	Bureaucrats < Utilities Change: utilities stronger
Politicians-Utilities	Conflict < Cooperation Change: some conflict with few politicians	Politicians < Utilities Change: utilities stronger
Economic Regulators-Utilities	Conflict Change: market reform movement	Regulators = Utilities Change: battle for clout
Safety Regulators-Utilities	Conflict Change: regulatory conflict	Regulators = Utilities Change: battle for clout
Government-Public	Conflict < Cooperation Change: periodic public distrust	Government > Public No change

Policy Change
No

Policymaking Process/Structural Change
Yes: safety regulator and market structure change, but not impactful

Source: Reprinted from Sklarew, 2015.

conflict between the electric utilities and some bureaucrats and politicians, complemented by conflict with economic and safety regulators. The utilities' clout over bureaucrats and politicians increased, while the utilities battled regulators for the upper hand. Concurrently, the government maintained clout over the public, despite periods of distrust. These relationships combined with the accidents and scandal to yield no policy change away from the incumbent energy system. Small changes occurred in the structure of safety regulation, and electricity market structure changes were proposed, but with little overall impact on the nuclear-based energy system. The next section examines these effects in more detail.

Shock Absorption: Electricity Supply and Energy System Changes

Japanese energy policy changes after the oil shocks suggest that policymakers would make efforts to shift away from electricity supply sources that threaten energy security or the Japanese economy, redefining a more resilient energy system. Since none of the shocks during this period were large enough to create a critical juncture, we might expect incremental changes to bolster energy system resilience. The energy system trajectory during this period thus would surprise us if we did not consider the aforementioned relationship changes and influences, including divergent resilience priorities. In contrast to the post-oil crises period, when cooperation and alignment of resilience priorities drove transformation, these influences mitigated the impact of the accidents and scandal on energy system change. Without considering this effect, we might expect Japanese policymakers to implement policies to bolster nuclear reactor safety while reducing dependence on nuclear power after each accident. We might envision increased policy emphasis on diversifying sources to include renewable energy and more coal. We would expect more rapid growth in natural gas use, given the advantages of gas over nuclear power presented in the previous chapter, compounded by the nuclear accidents. We also might expect a change in the policymaking process to limit the electric utilities' influence on the energy policymaking process and strengthen the role of safety regulators.

Instead, continued public trust in the government, alignment of priorities, and government clout – the same factors that enabled major energy policy change after the oil crises – contributed to the preservation of Japan's energy system during this period of multiple accidents and scandal. Japan's 1990s-2000s electricity supply source data reflect a continuation in the upward trend in nuclear power use, supported by policy changes to promote this rise. Complementing this trend is a notable absence of renewable energy increases. We also can observe a steady increase in coal use. This development seems rational in response to the accidents, but puzzling in the context of government and electric utility claims of emerging prioritization of global climate change. During this period, we also can see preservation of electric utility clout in the policymaking process and little substantive empowerment of safety regulators. Conflict between the electric utilities and regulators – both economic and safety – underlay both the shocks during this period and the responses to them, compounded by resilience priority differences. The utilities and bureaucrats continued to jointly prioritize nuclear investment and cost recovery as the basis of economic resilience. While economic regulators also focused on economic resilience, they targeted market liberalization and efficiency as the keys to achieving it. Meanwhile, safety regulators' emphasis on engineering and ecological resilience contrasted with all of these values. These divergent resilience priorities helped to shape the trends in nuclear power expansion and supporting policies during this period, as well as market liberalization's start and stall.

While conflict between the government and the public increased, it subsided quickly after each accident, enabling continuation of or a return to increasing nuclear power production as a percentage of the total electricity supply. Fluctuations in public trust also influenced the valleys and peaks in nuclear power's percentage of the electricity supply.

Energy System Preservation: Nuclear Powerhouse

The 1990s and 2000s nuclear accidents and scandal, in combination with electricity market liberalization movement and a decline in oil prices, should have shifted Japan away from nuclear power. Instead, they contributed to the reverse trend. As Figure 4.2: Trends in Electricity Supply Fuel Percentages, 1990–2010 demonstrates, little change occurred in the direction of Japanese energy supply source trends throughout the 1990s and the first decade of the 21st century. Policymakers' and politicians' cooperative relationships with the electric utilities, coupled with efforts to retain or regain public trust, contributed to this continuation of policies

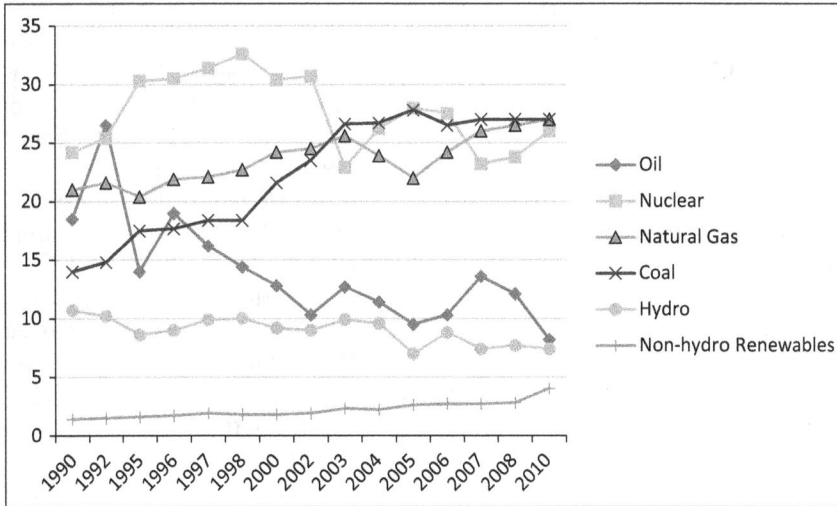

Figure 4.2 Trends in Electricity Supply Fuel Percentages, 1990–2010

Source: Reprinted from Sklarew, 2015; data from International Energy Agency, 2021.

supporting nuclear power expansion. Shared economic resilience priorities framed policymakers' cooperation with the electric utilities, affecting the utilities' relationships with economic and safety regulators, thus influencing the outcomes of market liberalization efforts and nuclear safety regulation. The tension generated by electric utilities' conflict and battle for clout with both economic and safety regulators should have destabilized nuclear power's advancement. However, the relative strength of the electric utilities' relationship with policymakers squelched market liberalization efforts that might have derailed nuclear power expansion, as well as revision or more stringent enforcement of nuclear safety regulations that might have increased the costs of nuclear infrastructure development and maintenance.

Underlying public acceptance of nuclear power expansion was the paternalistic relationship between the government and the public. Public trust in the government's ability to oversee nuclear power should have waned after the accidents and scandal, leading to more stringent regulations and a potential decline in nuclear power use. Government official G13 observed that "that kind of argument was already done, you see, made before Fukushima Daiichi, already in Japan. We had a lot of arguments like that. Once we lose the trust in regulation and once we have such a serious accident, we would not be able to continue to use nuclear energy" (July 2013). Despite this repeated debate, public trust did not decline steeply enough or long enough to seriously challenge the government's nuclear power expansion policy. Even if it had, the lack of public clout generally enabled policymakers to proceed as planned. When a decline in public trust did force regulatory changes or program postponements, such as the delay of FBR commercialization, the government also implemented policies to preserve nuclear expansion policies, including the introduction of the mixed oxide (MOX) fuel program.

After many of the accidents, nuclear power's share of electricity production continued to climb steeply throughout most of the 1990s and 2000s. As seen in Figure 4.2: Trends in Electricity Supply Fuel Percentages, 1990–2010 (International Energy Agency), nuclear power's share grew from 24.2 percent of Japan's electricity supply in 1990 to its peak of 32.6 percent in 1998. It declined slightly in 2000 and again in 2004, after the 1999 Tokaimura accident and 2004 Mihama accident. In both cases, nuclear power quickly returned to an expanding role in electricity production. The only dramatic downward trend occurred in 2002–2003, after news of TEPCO's data falsifications emerged, with the aforementioned utility-regulator conflict and a struggle for clout between policymakers, safety regulators, and utility company engineers and executives as a backdrop. At that time, nuclear power's share of Japan's electricity supply dropped more than 7 percentage points from just over 30 percent to just under 23 percent. TEPCO shut down all 17 of its reactors in 2002, and only five of these were restarted in 2003. By 2005, however, all 17 reactors had restarted with government approval, and the 2002–2003 plummet was followed by a return to an increasing share of electricity supply, even with the Mihama reactor idled for three years after the 2004 accident. As previously discussed, following the scandal, Japanese policymakers and electric utilities collaborated on a nuclear renaissance to preserve nuclear expansion and rebuild public confidence.

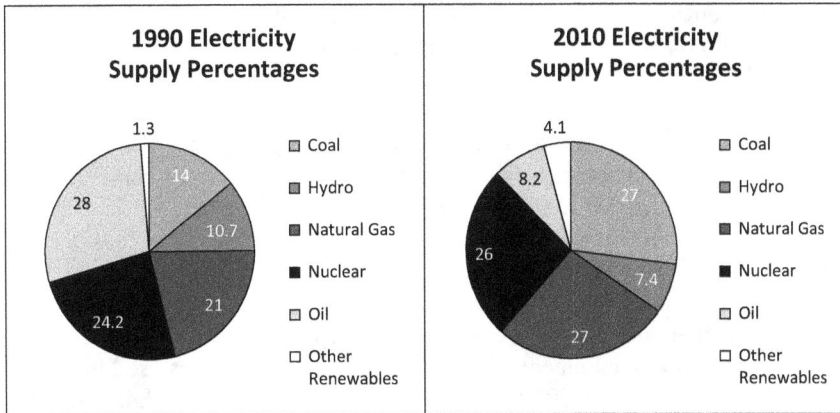

1990 Electricity Supply Percentages	2010 Electricity Supply Percentages

Figure 4.3 Comparison of Electricity Supply Fuel Percentages, 1990–2010

Source: Reprinted from Sklarew, 2015; data from International Energy Agency, 2021.

Following the 2007 Kashiwazaki-Kariwa accident, nuclear energy's share fell again to just over 23 percent, but even with this huge reactor, which supplied approximately 16 percent of Japan's nuclear capacity (8.2 GW), off line for almost two years, nuclear power's share of Japan's electricity supply increased from 2007 to 2010, reaching 26 percent by 2010. Figure 4.3: Comparison of Electricity Supply Fuel Percentages, 1990–2010 reflects these starting and ending ratios.

Supporting this continued nuclear expansion, the Japanese government did not implement any new policies to reduce nuclear power use after any of the accidents. Government and electric utility company interviewees also broadly agreed that none of the accidents in the 1990s or early 2000s garnered enough public attention to warrant a policy shift away from nuclear power. Given that Monju was a prototype reactor, the government had an early opportunity to discontinue plans for this technology and transfer resources to development of a different electricity source after the 1995 accident. As the earlier discussion of the nuclear fuel recycling debate reflects, the Monju accident could have served as a focusing event that discouraged Japanese policymakers from continuing to pursue plans to recycle nuclear fuel. The cooperative relationship between METI and the electric utilities, including their role in advisory committee decisions, helps to explain the puzzling continuation of Japan's nuclear fuel recycling program. In addition, former METI official G3 highlighted the role of energy system momentum and interconnectedness as key factors that explain why the Monju accident did not result in such a technology switch:

> To change the technology paradigm is really difficult, so always the light water reactor with more enrichment, light water reactor spent fuel reprocessing of plutonium, or for the fast reactor or for MOX, or whatever, it was the

paradigm. And all of the technologies were built alongside this paradigm. So even though there is something better, it is very difficult to switch. . . . Monju was not a really serious disaster, just some small accident, so it did not generate this shift.

While Monju was shut down for 15 years, Japanese policymakers implemented measures that preserved Japan's nuclear fuel recycling program plans. In early 1996, the AEC adopted the Advisory Committee on Energy's Nuclear Energy Subcommittee's recommendations for government approval of a "pluthermal" program for MOX utilization and plutonium recycling. Pluthermal refers to utilization of plutonium from spent fuel to create MOX fuel. In 1997, the utilities received Cabinet approval for the pluthermal program. Included in the Commission's policy was a requirement that each of the electric utilities use MOX in at least one LWR by the year 2010. The Cabinet approved the policy shortly thereafter, and the government presented the MOX use plan as part of a long-term FBR development strategy (e.g., see The Citizens' Nuclear Information Center, 1997).

To protect nuclear power after the scandal, especially as the economic regulators' market liberalization plans emerged, the Diet passed the Basic Act on Energy Policy in 2002. This law defined three pillars of Japanese energy policy: energy security, environmental suitability, and utilization of market mechanisms. These pillars appear consistent with Japanese policymakers' post-oil crises goals. At the same time, the law prioritizes the pillars in ways that indirectly favor nuclear power without mentioning it anywhere. It relegated market liberalization to third on the priority list, after energy security and environmental concerns. In particular, the description of the third pillar reflects Diet members' cooperation with the electric utilities:

> With regard to economic structural reforms concerning energy supply and demand such as the liberalization of energy markets, deregulation and other similar measures shall be promoted in a manner such that business operators can fully demonstrate their initiative and such that creativity and the interests of energy consumers are sufficiently secured, while giving due consideration to the policy objectives prescribed in the preceding two Articles [securing of stable supply and environmental suitability].
>
> (Government of Japan, 2002, 2)

This stipulation does not sound unreasonable, given Japanese policymakers' post-oil crises goals. However, the condition that market liberalization measures proceed only if they do not hinder energy supply stability and environmental considerations protects the electric utilities' nuclear power investments. Japanese government officials privately confirmed this interpretation of the legislation during Japanese electricity market liberalization negotiations with the U.S. government at the time.[10] The 2003 Basic Energy Plan built on this 2002 legislation.

As previously mentioned, the electric utilities and pro-utility policymakers later used the personnel rotation system to oust pro-liberalization officials and officials questioning the viability of the nuclear fuel cycle. The officials that replaced them halted regulatory reform measures and implemented policies designed to build public support and perpetuate nuclear power. The accidents and scandal might have impacted the future of nuclear power in Japan's energy mix if electricity market liberalization had proceeded, or if questions about reprocessing arising from the Monju accident had led to policy change instead of an ongoing stand-off between policymakers and the electric utilities over funding and responsibility. Policymakers' cooperation with the electric utilities also constrained meaningful safety regulation, a trend that would contribute to the Fukushima disaster and ultimately challenge the future of the energy system it aimed to protect.

In 2005, the Cabinet approved the Fundamental Principles for Nuclear Energy Policy established by the AEC. These principles cited three main objectives: to "increase the contribution of nuclear energy to the stable supply of energy and to the reduction in carbon dioxide emission" (Kondo, 2005, 2); to "make the share of nuclear power in electricity generation after the year 2030 similar to or greater than the current level of 30–40%" (Kondo, 2005, 3); and to employ reprocessing and commercialize FBRs as part of a strategy for "utilizing nuclear power as a long-term and major method of power generation" (Kondo, 2005, 6). Referencing this framework, the Japanese government's 2006 Nuclear Energy National Plan and 2007 Strategic Energy Plan embed attention to safety concerns in a broader context of continued promotion of nuclear energy and the nuclear fuel cycle. The plans frame nuclear energy as a primary power source contributing to a stable energy supply and global warming mitigation goals (Yanase, 2007). The Nuclear Energy National Plan contains five guidelines for nuclear energy policy:

I. Establish a firm national strategy and policy framework that does not waver over time.
II. For individual policy measures and time frames, maintain a "strategic flexibility" to adjust to global realities and technology trends.
III. Break down the three-way standoff among government, electric power utilities, and plant makers, to achieve true communication and a shared vision among players. The government must take the first step by indicating the overall direction.
IV. Place importance on policy measures of individual regions along the lines of national strategy.
V. Ensure policy stability by basing strategy decisions on open and even-handed discussions (Ministry of Economy, Trade and Industry, Government of Japan, 2006).

This codified commitment to nuclear power expansion thus acknowledges the rising conflict across policymakers, regulators and utilities, urging coordination of priorities centered on this nuclear development.

As previously discussed, during this period, global climate change helped to galvanize public trust in the government and promote support for these policy elements of the nuclear renaissance in the years following the scandal and subsequent accidents. Prime Minister Hatoyama's 2009 announcement of a CO_2 emissions reduction target of 25 percent below 1990 levels by 2020 propelled METI's nuclear expansion goals beyond even the electric utilities' expectations, according to at least one government interviewee.[11] This ambitious target set the stage for the 2010 revision of Japan's Strategic Energy Plan. The plan contains an appendix that includes the goal of nuclear power generation equal to 50 percent of Japan's electricity supply by 2030. Specific measures call for construction of 9 new nuclear plants by 2020 and more than 14 new plants by 2030.

This target reflected institutional support and system momentum reflective of nuclear lock-in. Some government interviewees saw this target as a sign that policymakers had surpassed the utilities in expectations of nuclear power's role in Japan's energy system resilience. Government official G12 confided that the 50 percent target "was too aggressive. Even the utilities felt so. So in the late 2000s . . . METI was beyond the utilities for the promotion of nuclear, I think" (May 2013). Some government interviewees perceived that the climate change target left policymakers little choice when considering options to achieve economic and social resilience. Government official G7 suggested that the bold emissions reduction target dictated a steep increase in nuclear power use because "we cannot really use the coal-fired plants, and we would rely more and more on nuclear and renewable energy. But needless to say, we need time to have the good portion of new renewable energy, so we should rely on nuclear power" (March 2013). Nuclear power expansion policies thus proceeded throughout the 1990s and early 2000s, partly in spite of the accidents and scandal, and partly due to enhanced government efforts to maintain public as a result of them.

Oil's Downward Slide

As expected based on the Japanese government's commitment to bolster energy security by reducing oil use, oil's share in Japan's electricity supply generally continued its downward trend despite the series of nuclear accidents and low oil prices. As seen in Figure 4.2, oil's share of Japan's electricity supply declined relatively steadily from 1997 through 2010. It spiked three times – to 26.5 percent in 1992, again to 19 percent in 1996, and in 2007 to 13.6 percent, but dropped steeply again afterwards each time. The 1997 increase was due to TEPCO's replacement of idled nuclear plants with oil and gas-fired plants after the Kashiwazaki-Kariwa accident. As shown in Figure 4.3, in 2010, oil accounted for only 8.2 percent of Japan's electricity supply. After 1997, climate change commitments further incentivized oil use reduction. Maintaining cooperation begun after the oil crises, policymakers and the electric utilities thus coordinated to continue reducing oil's role in Japan's electricity supply, reflecting shared economic and ecological resilience priorities.

Natural Gas Hike

Also as expected, the share of natural gas continued to rise slowly but steadily from 21 percent in 1990 to 27 percent in 2010, as seen in Figure 4.3. The slight decline in 2003–2005 shown in Figure 4.3 coincides with increased nuclear and coal use. Without insight into the effects of government-utility relationships and resilience priorities, we might have expected more rapid natural gas growth, given the advantages of gas over nuclear power presented in the previous chapter, compounded by the Mihama accident. Policymakers and the electric utilities cooperated to continue increased use of natural gas, but the steeper rise in nuclear power and the plethora of policies in support of it reflect coordination to prioritize the latter over the former.

Without considering the role of relationships and resilience priorities, we also might have expected natural gas use to rise more rapidly than coal, given the government's emphasis on climate change mitigation beginning in the late 1990s. The comparatively steeper rise in coal use during this period of emphasis on climate change mitigation reflects policymakers' cooperation with electric utility prioritization of economic resilience focused on cheap electricity sources, especially as electricity market liberalization progressed.

King Coal

Despite the government's professed prioritization of climate change mitigation and environmental goals over market liberalization and efficiency, the share of coal rose in Japan's electricity supply rose quietly and steadily throughout the first decade of the 21st century. As just noted, coal use grew more rapidly than natural gas during this period, rising from 14 percent of Japan's electricity supply in 1990 to 26 or 27 percent by 2003 and remaining there through 2010, as seen in Figure 4.2. Former government official G21 pointed out this apparent inconsistency with the Japanese government's climate change goals. Noting that coal replaced nuclear power during the reactor shutdowns after the 2002 scandal, he stated:

> in place of nuclear, coal had been promoted, to the extent that the Japanese government is worried about whether we can achieve the target of the Kyoto Protocol. So coal is the worst thing for climate change, right? So the second purpose of energy policy, which is economy, and the third purpose, which is environment . . . started to conflict with each other.
>
> (June 2013)

As in the rise of nuclear power, policymakers' and politicians' cooperative relationships with the electric utilities, as well as resilience priorities, played a role in this coal growth in Japan's electricity supply. The interview data reveals that these two groups' actual prioritization of energy security, economics and environmental issues differs from official rhetoric. While global climate change emerged as an official priority reflective of social resilience, influence from electricity market liberalization, which encouraged the electric utilities to opt for the cheapest fuel sources, boosted coal use. NGO leader Iida noted the link between this trend and market liberalization, asserting that "climate change is a more central topic, but the real effort of combating climate change was rather poor because at the same time, coal power was strongly promoted since the early 90s because of more pressure on cheaper electricity" (March 2013). The electric utilities particularly sought to reduce costs as market liberalization proceeded, observed Iida. "A more competitive electricity market converted into cheaper electricity pressures. So it is more aggressive deployment of coal power since 1990. It extremely increased carbon emissions in the Japanese energy sector . . . in spite of the effort to promote nuclear." Several government and NGO interviewees suggested this rationale, which benefited both the electric utilities and large users. M1 asserted, "Economics is the champion. That's one of the reasons that we depend heavily on cheap coal plants, coal fired plants." This same prioritization of economic resilience limited the utilities' interest in developing renewables while investing so heavily in nuclear power. Economic resilience thus remained a shared top priority for the utilities and policymakers.

Renewables' Nonrenewal

The renewable energy figures reflect very small increases after each nuclear accident, despite a growing array of policy measures to advance renewables, particularly after COP-3. Per Figure 4.2, hydropower hovered at around ten percent of Japan's electricity supply from 1990 through 2005, when it dropped to about seven percent and remained there through 2010. Other renewables (biofuels, waste, and geothermal) represented less than two percent of Japan's electricity supply until 2003. Solar PV and wind power were too small to count until the year 2000, when they totaled 0.04 percent combined. Non-hydro renewables accounted for four percent of Japan's electricity supply in 2010. This chapter's discussion of the government's relationship with the electric utilities and their shared economic resilience priorities sheds light on this continued trend of slow renewables growth.

As stated earlier, economic priorities stifled utility interest in renewables investments. At the same time, policymakers favored nuclear power investments over renewables investments. G17 noted, "I think before the Fukushima accident, most of METI's people are for nuclear energy rather than new energy" (July 2013). The government's nuclear R&D investments reflected this prioritization of nuclear technology development over funding for renewables research. An IEA report on Japan's 1990s renewable energy programs notes that Japan's renewable energy RD&D comprised only three percent of total energy-related RD&D, adding a parenthetical that "most of Japan's energy RD&D funding is funding for nuclear power research" (International Energy Agency, 2012).

This said, motivated by the desire to further reduce oil use, METI and NEDO did introduce several policies to advance renewables during the early 1990s. However, none of these measures catalyzed significant renewables growth. In 1993, the "New Sunshine Program" integrated the Sunshine Project, the Moonlight Project, and an RD&D system focused on environmental technologies. The first phase of the program aimed to develop PV technology that could produce electricity at a cost competitive with conventional electricity rates by 2000. In

1994, the Japanese government implemented a subsidy program for individual households and owners and developers of housing complexes installing new PV systems. The subsidy covered half of the cost of PV modules, equipment, distribution lines and installation work from 1994 to 1996, and one-third of the cost from 1997 to 1999.

According to government documents and existing studies, an array of measures implemented after 1996 also supported the Japanese government's goals of reducing oil use, while responding to commitments made at COP-3 in Kyoto in 1997 (e.g., see Häder et al., 2005; Ohira, 2005; Agency for Natural Resources and Energy, Ministry of Economy, Trade and Industry, 2009). These measures, passed during and after the time of COP-3 in Kyoto, should have led to more dramatic increases in renewables use. That year, METI enacted the Law on Promoting New Energy (New Energy Law) to accelerate the introduction of renewables. Other measures to increase renewables uptake ranged from local promotion subsidies and incentives for private firms' renewables investment to specific support for PV system introduction. In 2001, the Japanese government revised its Long-Term Energy Policy, emphasizing promotion of energy efficiency and conservation measures, additional introduction of renewable energy, and fuel switching (International Energy Agency, 2015).

In keeping with the economic resilience priorities shared by policymakers and the utilities, the 2003 Basic Energy Plan focused on nuclear power rather than renewable energy. The same year, the Japanese government introduced a renewable energy portfolio standard (RPS), with a national target of 12.2 TWh from renewable sources by 2010, equivalent to 1.35 percent of Japan's electricity supply (Government of Japan, 2015). The RPS focused on wind, PV, geothermal heat, hydropower (less than 1,000 KW) and biomass. In 2007, the government increased the target to 16 TWh, or 1.63 percent of total electricity supply, by 2014. The amount of renewable energy generation the RPS obligated for each electricity provider was equal to the provider's supply volume from the previous year multiplied by the usage target rate (the national target rate divided by the national electricity volume), multiplied by an "adjustment rate." This adjustment rate accounted for "voltage variation that necessarily accompanies the installation of new energy generation facilities" (Government of Japan, 2015). The RPS allowed electricity suppliers to meet their obligations via generation, purchases of renewable electricity from other suppliers, or purchases of tradable "new energy certificates," Japan's version of renewable energy credits. Japan's RPS aimed at a very low target for renewables increases, especially given the government's climate change mitigation goals. The cooperative relationship between the electric utilities and METI suggests that this low target intentionally enabled the electric utilities to meet or slightly exceed it without significant renewables increases. This phenomenon is not unique to Japan. My prior research finds that a number of U.S. states also selected low targets for renewable portfolio standards based on input from local electric utility companies (see Sklarew, 2009).

Resilience priorities framed this cooperation. Electric utility interviewee I11 suggested that the need to recoup nuclear investments quelled the utilities' interest in investing in expensive renewables. Electric utility industry interviewee I6 offered a related reason: the RPS failed due to a lack of cost-effective resources in Japan. Both rationales reflect prioritization of economic resilience over social resilience. Electric utility interviewee I1 suggested that engineering resilience priorities also played a role, citing utilities' concerns over technical problems with stability of the grid and renewable energy technologies.

The interview data reveals that these resilience priorities, coupled with the electric utilities' rising clout, prevented renewable energy from making headway in Japan's electricity share, even after the 1990s and 2000s accidents and scandal. Former government official G21 asserted, "The political power of electric companies was extremely too big . . . it was very difficult for them [the government] to make a big introduction of renewable energy, because, even under the RPS, because they [the utilities] had political power." Several media and government interviewees noted the influence of the electric utilities on the RPS parameters. Media interviewee M1 explained that "in Japan, the electric utilities decide, basically the utilities decide the RPS. Actually they dominate the data, and they dominate the information on the grid, so they can decide how much energy they can get from renewables. It was very tricky, the political decision on RPS system." M1 went on to describe how policymakers initiated the RPS as a way to stymie discussion of a feed-in tariff.

The feed-in tariff movement, which began shortly after announcement of the Kyoto Protocol commitments, was supported by a coalition of politicians and the citizens' groups. According to M1, "the utilities and METI didn't like that idea, and instead they introduced RPS system to kill that bill." M1 asserted that policymakers' and electric utilities' desire to control and limit renewables entry into the market drove cooperation to implement an RPS, in which "the utilities and bureaucrats dominate the system," instead of an FIT, in which "the market dominates the supply of renewables." This decision reflected not only electric utilities' clout over policymakers but also the public's lack of clout. The RPS shelved the publicly supported FIT until after the Fukushima accident occurred. This chain of events also reflects the utilities' and policymakers' continued focus on economic resilience over social resilience.

The 2010 revision of the Strategic Energy Plan appendix called for an increase in renewable energy to 20 percent of Japan's electricity supply by 2030. To accomplish this goal, the plan lists several general measures, including expansion of the planned feed-in tariff and increased financial incentives. While the electric utilities had no interest in renewables increases, interviewee G12 indicated that the economic regulators attempted to encourage them to allow renewables and energy efficiency technologies to enter the market in order to revitalize Japan's manufacturing sector. "I explained to the utilities . . . if Japan successfully introduces renewable energy, maybe Japanese manufacturers can export this. So utilities can be the incubator for these industries" (May 2013). This reasoning also did not lead to immediate increases in renewables. Energy efficiency technologies, on the other hand, did interest the utilities.

Saving Up: Conservation and Energy Efficiency

Following the adoption of the Kyoto Protocol, the Japanese government introduced several energy efficiency incentives during the 1990s-early 2000s, thus
promoting social resilience through contributions to GHG emissions reductions.
These measures targeted manufacturing of energy efficient products, serving as
innovation catalysts welcomed by the utilities. These positive incentives strengthened the role of energy efficiency and conservation in demand-side management,
which also contributed to ecological resilience when nuclear reactor shutdowns
reduced supply.

In 1998, MITI introduced the Top Runner Program. The program focused
on three criteria: "(1) products involving large domestic shipments; (2) products that consume a substantial amount of energy in the use phase; (3) products with considerable room to improve energy efficiency" (Kimura, 2010). To
engage manufacturers and the utilities in a collaborative manner, the program
established mandatory efficiency standards, but they applied an annual weighted
average of a company's products as for compliance. The program also set the
standards based on the most efficient products on the market at the time. The
program initially comprised nine product categories, including several products
influencing peak electricity demand: room air conditioners, fluorescent light-
ing, television sets, copying machines, and computers. By 2009, the program
expanded to include 21 categories, adding products such as water heaters, vend-
ing machines and electric transformers. For an evaluation of the Top Runner
program, see Osamu Kimura, 2010.

To further spur innovation, the government also offered and R&D subsidies to
manufacturers and utilities for development of high-performance heat pumps and
other efficient technologies. Similar incentives appeared following the Fukushima
disaster, when utility companies innovated on energy efficient products aimed at
reducing consumer electricity demand while their nuclear power plants were shut
down. The utilities also sought to develop new products attractive to overseas
markets in the aftermath of the Fukushima disaster, reflecting G12's logic from
the early 2000s.

Several revisions of the 1979 Act Concerning the Rational Use of Energy
(Energy Efficiency Act), described in Chapter 3, took place during the 1990s and
early 2000s. These revisions focused on manufacturing and residential efficiency
improvements that would contribute to meeting Kyoto Protocol goals. As previously mentioned, the 2001 Long-Term Energy Policy also highlighted energy
efficiency and conservation measures alongside nuclear power promotion as the
primary means of achieving CO_2 emissions reductions. The same year, to appeal
to consumers, the government also began to produce guidebooks on conservation
and efficiency for factories and homes.

While the 1990s-early 2000s saw a continuation of energy supply trends initiated in the previous post-oil crisis period, we might have expected policy process
changes to strengthen safety regulatory authority and diminish electric utilities'

clout in the policymaking process. However, little meaningful policy process change took place.

Shock Prevention: Policy Process and Structural Changes

Policymakers' and politicians' cooperative relationships with the electric utilities, as well as increasing utility clout, perpetuated a policymaking process in which the electric utilities played a direct role. The electric utilities' conflict with regulators contributed to the accidents and scandal, with little effect on energy system change. Public input in the policy process remained minimal due to the paternalistic relationship with the government and other institutional features.

Just as the accidents and scandal did not result in shifts away from nuclear promotion policies, no impactful safety regulatory changes occurred. The government did implement several incremental safety regulations within the existing system, and these changes sustained and deepened its momentum. These changes included revision of regulatory guidelines for reviewing seismic considerations in reactor design and location. For more detailed information on regulatory changes during this period, see Kishimoto (2017). Interviewees agreed that these changes did not result in a revision of nuclear safety culture, nor did they force a shift away from nuclear power by raising the costs of compliance. This stasis reflects continued prioritization of economic resilience over ecological and engineering resilience. At the same time, these modifications, as well as several institutional changes and support mechanisms, aimed to rebuild public trust in nuclear power and the Japanese government's ability to oversee it. Some of these changes reflect expected tightening of safety regulations and increased regulatory authority. However, continued tensions between regulators and engineers, in conjunction with cooperation between electric utility executives and policymakers, led to repeated accidents and data falsifications that reveal the inadequacy (whether intended or unintended) of these reforms.

In the first of these, after the 1997 Tokaimura explosion, PNC was recreated as the Japan Nuclear Cycle Development Institute (JNC) in 1998. The functions of JNC did not differ dramatically from the functions of PNC. One academic recalled receiving a holiday card from a JNC friend whose message noted that only the organization's name had changed, a view corroborated by my own conversations with officials at JNC and STA after announcement of the reorganization. After the 1999 criticality accident at Tokaimura, the Japanese government decided to merge JNC with the Japan Atomic Energy Research Institute (JAERI) to form a new entity housed under the Ministry of Education, Culture, Sports, Science & Technology (MEXT). The resulting organization, the Japan Atomic Energy Agency (JAEA), was established in 2005 by the Japan Atomic Energy Agency Act of 2005.

Safety regulator changes also resulted from the 1999 accident, when the NSC received a personnel increase, and a transfer of its Secretariat to the Prime Minister's Office elevated its stature in 2000. The Japanese government also established the Act on Special Measures Concerning Nuclear Emergency Preparedness. The interim report by the Cabinet Office's Investigation Committee on the Accident at the Fukushima Nuclear Power Stations of TEPCO describes the Act's mandates as presenting "the obligations of a nuclear operator to prevent a nuclear disaster" and providing for "the declaration of a nuclear emergency situation, the establishment of a Nuclear Emergency Response Headquarters, the implementation of emergency response measures, and other countermeasures" (Investigation Committee on the Accident at the Fukushima Nuclear Power Stations of Tokyo Electric Power Company, 2011, 55). This Act did not limit nuclear power expansion, and the same Cabinet Office report faults TEPCO for violating the first of these provisions in the years leading up to the Fukushima Daiichi accident.

Most interviewees and government documents attribute the ensuing 2001 creation of the Nuclear Industrial Safety Agency (NISA), housed within METI, to then-Prime Minister Koizumi's broad government reorganization agenda. However, two interviewees (G12 and I6) hinted at a connection between the 1999 accident and creation of NISA. Based on the relationships between the electric utilities, policymakers, politicians, and this new safety regulator, this process change did impact energy policymaking and safety regulations following the accidents that occurred after NISA's inception. Under the same reorganization, the NSC's Secretariat moved to the Cabinet Office. The 1999 accident also prompted measures to codify NSC oversight of NISA. An NSC document describes a "newly established Subsequent Regulation Review [that] aims to observe adequacy of regulatory activities of NISA at each stage after issuing establishment licenses" (The Nuclear Safety Commission of Japan, 2001). These reviews empowered the NSC to supervise and audit NISA's regulatory oversight of reactor construction, operation and decommissioning. In October 2003, the Japanese government created the Japan Nuclear Energy Safety Organization (JNES), endowed with a staff of 460, to provide technical support to NISA's 300 regulators. This increased oversight, staffing and expertise should have curbed future data falsifications and safety violations, but it did not. These continuing problems arose from NISA's tense relationships with policymakers, politicians and the electric utilities, combined with the electric utilities' cooperative relationships with policymakers and politicians. Underlying these conflicts was a continued discrepancy between regulators' focus on engineering resilience and the utilities focus on economic resilience.

No regulatory changes occurred after the 2004 accident at the Mihama nuclear plant. NISA ordered KEPCO and six other electric utilities to review their inspection records of cooling pipes (CBC News, 2004). The government did establish the Nuclear Safety Public Relations and Training Division within NISA in response to the 2002 scandal, with little effect on the regulations themselves, or their enforcement. Instead, policymakers' cooperation with the electric utilities inhibited real change toward tougher regulations. At the same time, tensions between the electric utilities and safety regulators led to non-compliance with existing regulations and failure to revise them to meet the electric utilities' expectations for realistic guidelines. Local officials and NISA approved the Mihama reactor's restart in 2007, following KEPCO's "safety culture improvements," which a NISA report cites as "face-to-face discussions between the management and workers at sites to improve the safety culture," "reinforcement of personnel working at power plants," and review of all periodic inspection processes" The Nuclear and Industrial Safety Agency, Government of Japan, 2005). No government-led regulatory changes accompanied these measures developed by the electric utility.

In 2005, then-Chairman of the AEC Shunsuke Kondo cited the Policy Planning Advisory Council's concern over renewal of public trust as a foundation of the Framework for Nuclear Energy. He noted the advisory council's recognition of "the need for the recovery of the public confidence in both the plant operators' safety management and the effectiveness of regulators activities for the assurance of nuclear safety." Kondo highlighted first among the Framework's short-term actions "activities for maintaining the public confidence in the safety management of existing nuclear power plants and related facilities" (Kondo, 2005, 4). Some government interviewees confided that the real aim of the nuclear renaissance was public confidence-building. Explaining this goal, G9 intimated that "the falsification scandal by TEPCO and the [nuclear accident] problem in Kansai caused the loss of reliability by the public to the nuclear power operations. At that time, the ANRE needed to create, you know, a plan of the future, how to do nuclear technology and nuclear power plants" (April 2013). All of these measures in response to the accidents and scandal, combined with institutional influences, prevented public distrust from sustaining enough momentum to pressure the government to alter the energy system.

After the 2007 Kashiwazaki-Kariwa accident, METI established a committee to investigate the impact of the earthquake and identify necessary measures for the government and electric utilities to "ensure" nuclear plant safety. This focus on "ensuring" safety reflects the Japanese government's sensitivity to the public's zero tolerance for risk. NISA, The NSC, TEPCO and the IAEA collaborated on a safety report released in September 2007. In May 2008, TEPCO adopted increased earthquake resistance standards. NISA and the NSC reviewed and approved these standards. While we would expect revised standards, the development and framing of these standards emerged from safety regulators' tense relationships with the electric utilities and the government's need to bolster public trust.

During the same period of accidents and scandal, momentum behind electricity market liberalization grew, then waned. According to some government, electric utility, and academic interviewees, the accidents and scandal impacted both the rise and fall of liberalization efforts. While market liberalization seems an unlikely fix for accidents and scandals, the previously described effect of these incidents on policymakers' relationships with the electric utilities helps to explain the connection. The same relationships also influenced the halt of METI's liberalization efforts before introduction of any measures that would have affected the electric utilities, such as unbundling of transmission and generation. G12 observed of the first decade of the 21st century, "now that the Japanese nuclear people regained their power, I think that later in this decade, our main policy project was to facilitate nuclear, and so that's why in the fourth [regulatory] reform, that was very gradual" (May 2013).

Some government interviewees cited electric utility clout over and cooperation with policymakers as the reason for the demise of regulatory reform prior to the Fukushima disaster.

Interviewees' depictions of policymakers' and electric utilities' cooperation on expansion of nuclear power and tension over electricity market liberalization are consistent with my experience as a U.S. Department of Commerce official working on Japanese electricity deregulation during this period. Diet member Kanoh crafted and secured passage of the capstone 2002 Basic Energy Law that prioritized the 3Es in a particular order: energy security and environmental concerns took precedence over economics, with the latter defined as economic efficiency. This framing suggested that energy security and environmental considerations would receive priority over market liberalization in Japan's energy system policymaking. At that time, some METI officials confided that the law was intended to stall regulatory reform measures that would have threatened continued expansion of nuclear power and the electric utilities' profits from existing nuclear plants. The timing of this legislation aligns with the ousting of Minami and the ensuing arrival of anti-liberalization officials to senior METI posts.

Several government interviewees suggested that the 2004 and 2007 accidents incurred a further shift away from market liberalization by siphoning clout from regulatory reformers and shifting METI's focus toward safety reforms to preserve nuclear power. Other government interviewees highlighted these accidents' role in spurring the nuclear renaissance, precipitating a decline in economic regulators' clout during this period.

Several government interviewees, as well as documents from the government and NGOs, raised the issue of transparency in energy policy decision-making. The interviewees suggested that changes did occur after the accidents and scandal, but they also voiced concern that these changes were either insufficient or aimed at an inappropriately defined concept of transparency. They felt that the changes did not foster necessary open communication between regulators and the electric utilities, or between the government and the public. The Citizens' Nuclear Information Center cited a "commitment from the government to make public most of the nuclear policy decision-making meetings of its relevant ministries and agencies" after the Monju accident (The Citizens' Nuclear Information Center, 1997). This transparency commitment arose due to public distrust in the government over the government's handling of the accident. Minutes of advisory committee meetings became publicly available, but this change sent policymakers' coordination with the electric utilities under the table. G13 offered the example of the Japan Nuclear Technology Institute (JANTI), established by the electric utilities after the scandal. JANTI aimed to facilitate knowledge sharing between the electric utilities, the government and academia. G18 asserted that this inclusion of participants from multiple stakeholder groups limited the information the electric utilities were willing to share. A 2004 NSC document states that the legal framework for safety regulations was "tuned to recover nuclear safety confidence" with the initiation of Subsequent Regulation Reviews after the 1999 Tokaimura accident (The Nuclear

Safety Commission of Japan, 2004, 1). One of the main objectives the document cites is transparency of regulatory processes. However, subsequent accidents and revelations of falsified data reflect the inadequacy of these reviews in promoting transparency.

Just as Japan's energy policy and policymaking process responses to the oil crises provided lessons, changes and stasis during 1990s and early 2000s also offer insights on energy system lock-in and transition, resilience, and innovation.

Lessons on Lock-In and Resilience

In the 1990s-2000s, Japanese policymakers and utilities could have applied the lessons that the oil shocks provided on energy system transformation and cooperation to promote resilience. Instead, Japan's energy system moved toward lock-in and accompanying challenges to system resilience. Unlike the oil crises, the series of technological and institutional failures that occurred during the 1990s and early 2000s did not combine to create a critical juncture that catalyzed changes to Japan's energy policy direction. They also did not yield significant policymaking process change or impactful regulatory change. Instead, the policies that emerged during this period helped the existing energy system to gain momentum and move closer to energy policy lock-in. This chapter of Japan's energy system narrative has shown how resilience priorities contributed to the factors that shaped this path.

Japan's energy system during this period reflected rapid infrastructure development, institutional support, momentum, and mitigation of uncertainty and financial risk. As Japan's nuclear infrastructure grew to accommodate ecological and economic resilience priorities shared by many policymakers and the electric utilities, the utilities became increasingly focused on recouping the investment costs of this infrastructure by perpetuating its use. This focus encouraged both the utilities and policymakers to emphasize economic resilience over ecological resilience as a network of nuclear-related industries grew around this infrastructure, reflecting energy system lock-in.

The government's relationships with the electric utilities and the public contributed to this trend, providing institutional support. The electric utilities continually increased clout over and sustained cooperation with policymakers. Relationships between the electric utility companies, politicians and METI pushed out officials questioning the economic or ecological resilience of nuclear power, strengthening the relationship between METI and the electric utilities and further perpetuating nuclear power development. The electricity market liberalization movement that emerged concurrent to the accidents and scandal challenged nuclear power's dominance, but the same cooperative relationships quashed this effort. At the same time, the emergence of global climate change as a priority supported nuclear power lock-in and built momentum through the nuclear renaissance, while acting as a rationale for postponing market liberalization.

Meanwhile, tensions and the battle for clout between the electric utilities and safety regulators worsened throughout the period. Lack of risk communication across the utilities, policymakers, and the public perpetuated acceptance of the nuclear-based energy system, but it also set in motion the future shattering of public trust in the government when the Fukushima disaster revealed risks to socio-ecological and economic resilience. This problem, combined with the continued regulator-electric utility conflict that fueled the accidents and scandal, later would challenge nuclear power expansion.

Public trust in the government remained relatively high during this period, though declining slowly over time. Public clout also remained constrained. Only a major catastrophe seemed likely to dramatically alter this government-public relationship and incite a broad-based public call for energy system and process change heard by policymakers.

Just as Japan's energy system transformation after the oil crises provided lessons, this movement toward energy system lock-in offers insights for policymakers, regulators, utilities and consumers. These lessons include stakeholders' resilience focus considerations, accompanying communication and transparency challenges, the role of regulators and regulation, and implications for cooperation. Japan's trajectory also offers insights on the effects of these factors on all aspects of system resilience – ecological, economic, and social – and how they relate to one another.

The nuclear accidents and scandal that occurred in the 1990s and 2000s should have encouraged regulators and utilities to focus on engineering and ecological resilience, with economic resilience as complementary context for realistic solutions to regulatory mismatches with utilities' abilities and infrastructure realities. Instead, increasing focus on economic resilience over engineering and economic resilience hindered the ability of utilities and policymakers to embed safety culture in the growth of nuclear power and respond effectively and in cost-effective ways to future shocks. This conflict over resilience priorities thus threatened all three types of resilience. It also posed potential threats to social resilience, since the system disruptions and the accidents' health and safety implications increasingly affected communities, culminating in the Fukushima disaster described in the next chapter. Differences within economic resilience priorities further exacerbated these challenges, as utilities and policymakers focused on infrastructure investments, while economic regulators focused on market efficiency and electricity rates.

The Japanese government's approach to conservation and efficiency policies, as well as the electric utilities' responses to this approach, also serve as a positive example of how various perceptions of economic resilience can yield different results. Japanese policymakers and utilities shared the view that conservation and efficiency measures could support nuclear power investments by reducing electricity demand during times when nuclear reactors were offline, especially during periods of uncertain outage duration, such as after the 1990s-2000s accidents. This view of conservation and efficiency as demand-side tools to support electricity supply enables these measures and technologies to contribute to socio-economic resilience of energy systems.

In contrast, utility companies in some other nations perceive conservation and efficiency as threats to infrastructure investment recovery through revenue from electricity supply provision. This view separates social resilience from economic resilience, requiring prioritization of one over the other. Recent movements toward performance-based regulation and ratemaking are changing this dynamic, decoupling electricity rates from infrastructure expenditures, instead linking revenue to performance goals that better reflect energy system resilience. Viewing conservation and efficiency as tools to accomplish both ecological and economic resilience priorities can enable utilities and policymakers to collaborate on achieving both types of resilience as energy systems develop, mature, and adapt.

Japan's lessons on resilience priorities connect to insights on communication and transparency between energy system stakeholders. Japan's narrative from the 1990s and 2000s demonstrates that communication and transparency challenges affecting safety regulators, utilities, and policymakers contributed to the accidents and scandal. These challenges also inhibited regulatory responses that could have strengthened safety features and contributed to all forms of system resilience. Communication with the public aimed to preserve trust, but a complementary lack of transparency intended to shield the public from concern resulted in false expectations of safety and resilience. Government and utility sensitivity to the public's zero tolerance for risk contributed to these trends, disabling communal development of necessary measures and effective communication strategies to promote a resilient system. Finding ways to communicate risk realistically and effectively across stakeholder groups would contribute to design and enforcement of regulatory frameworks that foster all aspects of system resilience.

Japan's nuclear fuel cycle debate during this period also reflects communication and transparency challenges. When questions arose regarding how the nuclear fuel cycle would affect Japan's energy system's economic or ecological/engineering resilience, suppression of these questions and removal of those who asked them did not improve resilience. Difficult questions require development of solutions to address economic and safety risks, promote system resilience, and address lock-in challenges.

Policymakers, regulators and utilities face the difficult task of finding a balance of transparency and communication that enables cooperation to promote an energy system's long-term ecological, economic and social resilience. Transparency and effective communication also can define this cooperation in ways that prevent the reality and appearance of regulatory capture. In Japan's case, communication patterns between utilities, regulators, and policymakers created both conflict and an outward impression of capture. Both harmed Japan's energy system resilience. Transparent communication frameworks can enable stakeholder input needed for effective, realistic regulations to promote system resilience. Such frameworks also can distinguish between this input and the type of influence that constrains regulations in ways that harm system resilience.

In addition to highlighting the need for transparent communication, Japan's regulatory challenges during the 1990s to early 2000s also offer lessons for the role of regulators and regulation as drivers of system resilience. Regulations and the regulators who design and enforce them serve as tools for achieving energy system resilience, as well as shapers of risks to this resilience. As we observed in Japan's case during this period, the relationship between regulators and utilities influences whether and how these regulators and regulations help or hinder system resilience and mitigate or exacerbate risk.

Japan's regulatory structure contributed to the challenges regulators faced in designing and enforcing regulations. Housing the regulators within Japan's energy policymaking organization created a lack of independence that led to creation of tougher regulations in order to gain public trust. Government interviewee G3 explained:

> This lack of independence of the regulatory commission created this kind of mindset that regulation should be tougher. If the safety agency was independent, outside of METI, they would not have to make tougher regulations, because this kind of scientific, legal decision of safety has been enough to convince the public because it is decided by an independent body. Because they were within the promotional agency of METI, they had to be excessive.
>
> (February 2013)

However, this same structure enabled pressure from policymakers to accommodate the utilities' priorities, resulting in conflict and insufficient enforcement of these regulations. This imposition of tougher regulations also exacerbated transparency and communication challenges, as the utilities withheld information on risks to avoid even more stringent regulations in this period leading up to the Fukushima disaster. G3 observed, "TEPCO did not want to tell the truth or details or necessary steps for safer operation of nuclear power to METI, which would have meant much tougher, more detailed regulations." From Japan's situation, we can observe the benefits of structurally separating regulators from policymakers. We also can recognize the value of stakeholder cooperation on resilience goals and shared recognition of the role of regulation in achieving them.

The relationships between Japan's safety regulators and the utilities after each accident and during the scandal reveal a focus on regulatory compliance, rather than system resilience and risk. Interviewee G3 depicted Japan's nuclear safety culture as "just culture of obedience to the details of the regulations and standards." G3 explained that the relationship between the utilities, regulators and policymakers defined this view of safety culture: "utilities' emotion or perception that whatever METI says, we will deploy or introduce, and that will mean safety, and this created the view that this will strengthen the mindset of safety culture in Japan. Actually, they could have done more, but obedience to the existing level of regulations was the mental setting of safety culture in Japan." This focus on compliance, rather than a focus on the resilience and risk reduction goals underlying the regulations, contributed to the accidents and scandal, as well as the responses to them. We can learn from this aspect of Japan's narrative that framing of shared priorities for risk and resilience across stakeholder groups can promote effective regulations and goals that move beyond mere compliance.

Complementing this focus on compliance, Japan's safety regulators were encouraged to view their roles as supporting continuity of operations. While this priority features as a prominent aspect of engineering, economic and social resilience, placing minimization of operational disruptions above long-term safety and infrastructure integrity considerations weakens all of these types of resilience. This challenge is not unique to Japan. Accounts of the 2010 BP Deepwater Horizon oil spill observe a similar situation. For example, Norse and Amos describe how regulators overseeing oil and gas drilling perceived their role as "facilitating (or at least not impeding) operations of private companies . . . even in deep waters where there was inadequate capacity to deal with a major accident" (Norse and Amos, 2010). Shifting the focus to long-term engineering, ecological, economic and social resilience will foster more effective safety regulations to achieve it. This reframing also will redirect regulatory attention to protection of the public and system infrastructure.

Realistic, effective regulations thus require resilience thinking shared across stakeholders, input without undue influence, and resilience goals that frame compliance, rather than considering compliance as the goal in itself. Such regulations will be achievable by the utilities, but they also will maintain focus on safety and integrity as features of engineering, ecological, economic and social resilience. To enable development of a safety culture that transcends compliance and focuses on system resilience, regulatory environments need to account for and address aging of infrastructure, as well as advances in existing technologies. Keeping regulatory pace with infrastructure and technology changes is a formidable task, but failure to do so challenges both energy innovation and effective regulation, contributing to conflict between regulators and regulated.

Synthesizing these challenges to Japan's resilience priorities, transparency and communication, and regulation during the 1990s to early 2000s offers some general insights on stakeholder cooperation to achieve energy system resilience goals. Japan's energy system trajectory and the roles of relationships in shaping it reveal that the electric utilities can serve as collaborators or antagonists in energy policymaking and regulation. In contrast to the period following the oil crises, when Japanese utilities and policymakers collaborated to achieve energy system transformation and strengthen system resilience, the 1990s to early 2000s saw a shift toward utility-regulator antagonism, as well as utility-policymaker tension spurred by liability and cost concerns. This shift suggests a question for energy system stakeholders everywhere: Can policymakers, regulators and electric utilities find a relationship balance that best supports resilient systems? Japan's experiences teach us that collaboration to promote energy system resilience – engineering, ecological, economic, and social – and mitigate the challenges of system lock-in must achieve this balance of transparency, risk awareness, responsibility, and realism. We can consider this goal as we examine the final narrative chapter that describes how the Fukushima nuclear disaster combined with relationships and resilience priorities to influence energy system change and resilience.

Notes

1   Some existing literature references several accidents – at the Sendai reactor in 1991, the Fukui reactor in 1991, and the Fukushima reactor in 1993 – not included here for two

reasons. First, interviewees did not mention them, and second, much of the existing literature and many of the publicized lists of nuclear incidents do not include them, either.

2 For more background on the Kyoto Protocol, see United Nations Framework Convention on Climate Change's "What Is the Kyoto Protocol?" at https://unfccc.int/kyoto_protocol.

3 Electric utility interviewee I1 and three government interviewees (G16, G21, and G23) linked the handling of the scandal and the aforementioned conflict between TEPCO President Minami and METI Vice Minister Murata to METI's electricity market liberalization efforts, but with contradictory views. I1 said of METI, "at that time, they were discussing how they are going to liberalize the market. And they didn't like the way of TEPCO, and not only TEPCO, but all of the nine utilities, ten utilities way to respond to METI's idea. So Mr. Murata decided to make [the scandal] public." This account suggests that METI's economic reformers used the scandal to build momentum for liberalization by drawing negative attention to the electric utilities. Few studies describe the scandal, but some press accounts also depict Murata as pro-liberalization (e.g., Fukushima News Online, 2011). In contrast, all three government interviewees suggested that TEPCO President Minami alone voiced some resignation regarding METI's liberalization plans, while other utility executives opposed any further liberalization measures. The government interviewees' version thus suggests the possibility that while METI's regulatory reformers used the scandal to malign TEPCO, METI supporters of the electric utilities and nuclear power may have exploited the scandal to oust Minami. The government interviewees' account further suggests that METI policymakers did so in order to eliminate the sole electric utility voice less opposed to regulatory reform measures that would have weakened momentum on nuclear power expansion. At the same time, announcing the scandal created the impression of distance between METI and the electric utilities. Thus, as previously discussed, although METI reformers employed the news of the scandal to garner support for market liberalization, the same scandal ultimately suppressed METI's liberalization efforts in order to allow the utilities to recover trust and continue nuclear infrastructure expansion. Divergent economic resilience priorities underlay this complicated set of interactions.

4 Iwao served as METI Vice Minister in 2001 and Minister for Science and Technology in 2005.

5 Examples of other scandals include financial scandals such as the Recruit scandal and medical scandals such as the HIV blood transfusion scandal.

6 Existing literature and press reports cite Koizumi's efforts to resolve the case of Japanese citizens abducted by North Koreans as the source of his popularity in 2002. For example, see Kim Sung Chull et al., 2012, 84.

7 From the book author's personal observations while employed in the PNC Washington office in 1993.

8 The Japanese ban of imported beef in 2004–2005 due to mad cow disease concerns represents another shock that reflects the paternalistic relationship. The book author's personal observations while a Mike Mansfield Fellow revealed that the Ministry of Foreign Affairs (MOFA) feared public backlash against lifting of the ban. A public hearing on the issue mostly consisted of government explanations, rather than a quest for public input. Consumers in attendance demanded that the government do a better job of protecting citizens, without demanding public involvement in the policymaking process.

9 This view is corroborated by the book author's personal observations during participation in discussions between U.S. and Japanese government officials during the Cross-Sectoral Regulatory Reform Working Group negotiations in 2000–2003.

10 Author's personal conversations during participation in bilateral U.S.-Japan electricity market liberalization negotiations, 2002.

11 Hatoyama's surprising announcement came in the context of DPJ efforts to wrest control of policy issues from the bureaucrats.

References

Agency for Natural Resources and Energy, Ministry of Economy, Trade and Industry. (2009) 'Recent Developments in New and Renewable Energy Policy & Measures in Japan.' Presentation to the Asia-Pacific Partnership on Clean Development and Climate, April.

Aldrich, D.P. (2008) *Site Fights: Divisive Facilities and Civil Society in Japan and the West.* Ithaca, NY: Cornell University Press.

Aldrich, D.P. (2011) 'Future Fission: Why Japan Won't Abandon Nuclear Power.' *Global Asia*, 6 (2), 62–67.

The Asahi Shimbun. (2011) Public Opinion Polls on Cabinet Support 1973–2011. *The Asahi Shimbun.*

Ashina, S., and Nakata, T. (2003) 'Assessing the Impacts of Shutdown of TEPCO's n\ Nuclear Reactors on CO_2 Emission in the Japan's Electricity Sector.' In Conference Proceedings: Integrating the Energy Markets in North America: Issues & Problems, Terms & Conditions. International Association for Energy Economics.

CBC News. (2004) 'Japanese Nuclear Operator to Shut 11 Plants.' 13 August. www.cbc.ca/news/world/japanese-nuclear-operator-to-shut-11-plants-1.516801.

Chull, K.S., Jain, P., and Lam, P.E. (2012) 'Japan's Strategic Response to North Korea: Activistic Security Policy, Eroding Pacifism.' In *Japan's Strategic Challenges in a Changing Regional Environment.* Singapore: World Scientific, 73–95.

The Citizens' Nuclear Information Center. (1997) *An Update on the Japanese Government's MOX Utilization Policy.* Tokyo: The Citizens' Nuclear Information Center.

CNN. (2002) 'Heavy Fallout from Japan Nuclear Scandal.' *CNN.com/Business.* 2 September. http://edition.cnn.com/2002/BUSINESS/asia/09/02/japan.tepco/.

FukushimaNewsOnline. (2011) 'Japan | Government Considering Plan to Dismantle TEPCO.' 16 April. https://fukushimanewsresearch.wordpress.com/2011/04/16/japan-government-considering-plan-to-dismantle-tepco-2/.

Government of Japan. (2002) *Basic Act on Energy Policy* (Act No. 71 of June 14 of 2002).

Government of Japan. (2015) 'Outline of the RPS System.' www.rps.go.jp/RPS/new-contents/top/toplink-english.html

Häder, D.P., Hemmersbach, R., and Lebert, M. (2005) *The Law of Energy for Sustainable Development.* Cambridge: Cambridge University Press.

International Atomic Energy Agency. (1999) *Report on the Preliminary Fact Finding Mission Following the Accident at the Nuclear Fuel Processing Facility in Tokaimura Japan.* Vienna: International Atomic Energy Agency.

International Energy Agency. (2012) 'New Sunshine Programme.' www.iea.org/policies?country=Japan&page=4

International Energy Agency. (2015) 'Policies Database.' www.iea.org/policies?country=Japan&page=4

International Energy Agency. (2021) 'Electricity Information 2021 Edition Database Documentation.' http://wds.iea.org/wds/pdf/Ele_documentation.pdf.

Investigation Committee on the Accident at the Fukushima Nuclear Power Stations of Tokyo Electric Power Company. (2011) *Interim Report on the Accident at Fukushima Nuclear Power Stations of Tokyo Electric Power Company.* Tokyo: Secretariat of the Investigation Committee on the Accident at the Fukushima Nuclear Power Stations of Tokyo Electric Power Company.

Johnston, E. (2000) 'Monju Touts Safety Campaign in Restart Bid.' *The Japan Times.* 8 December.

Kimura, O. (2010) 'Japanese Top Runner Approach for Energy Efficiency Standards.' SERC Discussion Paper: SERC09035. Socio-Economic RESEARCH Center, Central Research Institute of Electric Power Industry.

Kingston, J. (2014) 'Mismanaging Risk and the Fukushima Crisis.' In Bacon, P., and Hobson, C. (eds.), *Human Security and Japan's Triple Disaster: Responding to the 2011 Earthquake, Tsunami and Fukushima Nuclear Crisis*. London: Routledge, 9–58.

Kishimoto, A. (2017) 'Public Attitudes and Institutional Changes in Japan Following Nuclear Accidents.' In Balleisen, E., Bennear, L., Krawiec, K.D., and Wiener, J.B. (eds.), *Policy Shock: Recalibrating Risk and Regulation after Oil Spills, Nuclear Accidents and Financial Crises*. Cambridge: Cambridge University Press, 269–304.

Kondo, S. (2005) 'The Framework for Nuclear Energy Policy in Japan.' Japan Atomic Energy Commission Speech. 19 October.

Kuroda, H. (2004) 'Lesson Learned from TEPCO Nuclear Power Scandal.' Presentation to the 2004 Pacific Basin Nuclear Conference. 25 March.

Kyodo News. (2004) 'Official Calls Mihama, Japan, Nuclear Plant Accident a "Manmade Disaster".' 12 August. www.highbeam.com/doc/1G1-120776682.html.

Lesbirel, S.H. (1998) *NIMBY Politics in Japan: Energy Siting and the Management of Environmental Conflict*. Ithaca, NY: Cornell University Press.

Ministry of Economy, Trade and Industry, Government of Japan. (2006) *Main Points and Policy Package in 'Japan's Nuclear Energy National Plan'* (Report by METI's Nuclear Energy Subcommittee).

Ministry of Economy, Trade and Industry, Government of Japan. (2010) *The Strategic Energy Plan of Japan* (Revised 2010).

Murakami, T., Watanabe, M., Sato, S., and Shida, K. (2008) *Impacts on International Energy Markets of Unplanned Shutdown of Kashiwazaki-Kariwa Nuclear Power Station*. Tokyo: Institute of Energy Economics Japan.

The National Diet of Japan Fukushima Nuclear Accident Independent Investigation Commission. (2012) *The Official Report of The Fukushima Nuclear Accident Independent Investigation Commission*. Tokyo: The National Diet of Japan.

Norse, E.A., and Amos, J. (2010) 'Impacts, Perception, and Policy Implications of the BP/Deepwater Horizon Oil and Gas Disaster.' *Environmental Law Reporter*, 40 (11), 11058–11073.

Nuclear and Industrial Safety Agency, Government of Japan. (2005) 'Summary of the Final Report on the Secondary System Pipe Rupture at Unit 3.' Mihama Nuclear Power Plant (NPP), Kansai Electric Power Co., Inc. (KEPCO).

The Nuclear Safety Commission of Japan. (2001) *Convention on Nuclear Safety National Report of Japan for Second Review Meeting*. Tokyo: Government of Japan.

The Nuclear Safety Commission of Japan. (2004) 'Revision of "Implementation Guidance of 'Subsequent Regulation Reviews' of the Regulatory Agency's Programs".' NSC Decision No. 2004-D11.

The Nuclear Safety Commission of Japan. (2005) 'Final Report on the Secondary Piping Rupture Accident of Unit 3.' Mihama Nuclear Power Station, The Kansai Electric Power Company, Inc.

The Nuclear Safety Commission of Japan. (2008) 'Results of the "Subsequent Regulation Reviews" Concerning the Examination of the Revision of the Operational Safety Programs upon Direction (Summary).' NSC Decision No. 2008-D7.

Ohira, T. (2005) 'Trends and Prospects for Japan-China Technical Assistance in Energy and the Environment – From the Viewpoint of Global Environmental Problems and Energy Security.' *Science & Technology Trends Quarterly Review*, 69–82.

Pickett, S. (2002) 'Japan's Nuclear Energy Policy: From Firm Commitment to Difficult Dilemma Addressing Growing Stocks of Plutonium, Program Delays, Domestic Opposition and International Pressure.' *Energy Policy*, 30 (15), 1337–1355.

Scalise, P. (2010) 'Rethinking Hatoyama's Energy Policy.' *The Oriental Economist*, May 10.

Sklarew, J.F. (2009) 'Power Houses: The Politics Behind Birth and Deaths of the Federal Renewable Energy Portfolio Standard.' Unpublished manuscript.

Sklarew, J.F. (2015) *Shock to the System: How Catastrophic Events and Institutional Relationships Impact Japanese Energy Policymaking, Resilience, and Innovation*. Arlington, VA: George Mason University.

Sklarew, J.F. (2018) 'Power Fluctuations: How Japan's Nuclear Infrastructure Priorities Influence Electric Utilities' Clout.' *Energy Research & Social Science*, 41, July, 158–167.

Tsunoda, K. (2001) 'Public Response to the Tokai Nuclear Accident.' *Risk Analysis*, 21 (6), 1039–1046.

United Nations Framework Convention on Climate Change. 'What Is the Kyoto Protocol?' https://unfccc.int/kyoto_protocol.

World Nuclear Association. (2017) 'Mixed Oxide (MOX) Fuel.' https://world-nuclear.org/information-library/nuclear-fuel-cycle/fuel-recycling/mixed-oxide-fuel-mox.aspx.

Yanase, T. (2007) 'Challenges and Strategies for Nuclear Energy Policy in Japan.' *Nuclear News*, December, 56–59.

5 The Fukushima Accident

Shock to the System or Not? (2011–2022)

"The LDP and METI and the utilities want to keep the nuclear policy, and nuclear policy doesn't have popularity among the people. Nuclear is more important for these three than keeping the current market structure. These three have some kind of implicit consensus that we should further proceed on deregulation. Otherwise, we cannot have trust from the people. And then, with such regulatory reform efforts, maybe the LDP and METI or government can say we have a very confrontational stance toward the utilities, and the utilities also can say we are very strongly led by, or forced by deregulation. And so, with such a structure, now the three can proceed with nuclear policy."

– Government official (G12, August 2013)

"The problem that mainly exists is that the government cannot clearly support these issues in public. Because of the politics. When they talk to industry, they say we support nuclear restarts, and in the future, they support new builds, and also fuel cycle. To the industry, but they cannot say that to the public, and they are saying that to the local government, sometimes, but it depends. They are comfortable to make a policy, but implementation of the policy should be done by the industry."

– Electric utility industry executive (I15, August 2013)

". . . you need cooperation from industry to radically expand the role of renewables. And I think still, it is a very solid, determined position of Japanese utilities not to expand renewables. So there is every effort by them to deemphasize the importance or feasibility of renewable energy. And also they have many reasons to claim it is the utilities network that can, that should manage the new world of renewable energy. So unless the utilities industry is a kind of positive or more welcoming stance, in general, you cannot expect the new, really meaningful progress toward renewable energy."

– Government official (G16, July 2013)

". . . after Fukushima, many people lost confidence in governmental power to create policies, and many people started to want their control back, so to speak. So we have something to say to the government, and the government should listen to us. That is a very big movement after Fukushima among people."

– NGO representative (P2, March 2013)

DOI: 10.4324/9781003227588-5

Until March 11, 2011, momentum was building in Japan for a vast expansion of nuclear power and the energy system it supported. Buoyed by the nuclear renaissance, policymakers, the electric utilities and the public appeared to agree on nuclear power as a solution to socio-ecological and economic resilience. Then-Prime Minister Hatoyama's 2009 call for a reduction in CO_2 levels of 25 percent below 1990 levels fueled this forward momentum, supported by the ruling and opposition parties at the time, the DPJ and LDP. This institutional support from politicians was coupled with support from policymakers in the bureaucracy. Investment in transmission grid infrastructure and new plant construction bolstered these plans for nuclear power expansion. A broad consensus across policymakers, the electric utilities and the public supported the 2010 Strategic Energy Plan's call for nuclear expansion to 50 percent of Japan's electricity supply by 2030. A nuclear-dependent path seemed locked in, despite conflicting resilience priorities, transparency and communication complications, and regulatory challenges.

We would expect that the Fukushima Daiichi nuclear disaster that began on March 11, 2011, would shock Japan's energy system, as well as the policymaking processes supporting it. The disaster seems to embody the focusing event described by Kingdon, accompanied by the institutional changes depicted by historical institutionalists.

And yet, a decade later, official policies represent incremental changes to Japan's energy system, rather than dramatic transformation. While 9 of Japan's 54 nuclear reactors have returned to operation as of the end of 2021, post-disaster policy revisions have shifted from a zero-nuclear goal to an assumed eventual return to use of nuclear power as a primary baseload fuel, complemented by renewables, coal, and natural gas. The 2021 Strategic Energy Plan includes a higher 2030 target for renewables than in the past, accompanied by planned reductions in fossil fuel powered plants. The plan includes the same target for nuclear power that appears in previous post-Fukushima plans, with expectations of reactor restarts and nuclear fuel cycle program advancement. This direction reflects a gradual transition from the pre-Fukushima era, focusing on changes within the existing system rather than a complete transformation. Building on the analyses of the previous two periods, examining the government's relationships with the electric utilities and the public after the Fukushima disaster, these groups' resilience priorities, and their risk perceptions illuminates this puzzle and offers lessons for energy system resilience.

Major Shock: The Fukushima Daiichi Accident

The March 2011 accident at TEPCO's Fukushima Daiichi nuclear power plant and its aftermath have revealed engineering, socio-ecological and economic resilience challenges. The engineering aspects have been reported widely, as the accident received worldwide news coverage. Countless articles have described how a 15-meter high tsunami flooded the plant on March 11, 2011. The Diet's Fukushima Nuclear Accident Independent Investigation Commission report describes how the flooding "totally destroyed the emergency diesel generators, the seawater cooling pumps, the electric wiring system and the DC power supply for Units 1, 2 and 4, resulting in loss of all power" (National Diet of Japan Fukushima Nuclear Accident Independent Investigation Commission, 2012, 12). This loss of power prevented timely cooling of the reactors, and obstructed roads prevented delivery of external water supplies and repairs to the electricity system. Attempts to cool the reactor cores using external water supplies resulted in creation of steam pressure that led to hydrogen explosions and release of airborne radiation. TEPCO also released tens of thousands of tons of radioactive seawater from the plant into the Pacific Ocean.

When the accident occurred, since the country's eastern and western power grids were split between 50 and 60 hertz frequencies, the utilities in the west were able to use converters to transfer only 1 GW of power to the stricken east side. To compound this challenge of transferring power to areas in need after the events of March 11, because each electric utility's grid was developed to be self-sufficient, the network of transmission lines within each service area far exceeds the interconnections between them (Asia Pacific Energy Research Centre, 2004). This set of challenges revealed a combination of engineering and social resilience weaknesses in Japan's energy system.

The social resilience aspects of the accident include health implications. The Fukushima Daiichi accident was assigned the same ranking as the Chernobyl accident, a level 7 – severe – on the INES scale. Although the accident exposed 167 plant workers to more than 100 millisieverts of radiation, no casualties occurred as a direct result of the accident. The direct health impacts on the surrounding population remain inconclusive, though concerns regarding long-term effects of radiation exposure continue. However, the accident had less direct, widespread individual, regional and national impacts on citizens' health. According to the Diet's Investigation Commission report, "[a]pproximately 150,000 people were evacuated in response to the accident. It is estimated that as much as 1,800 square kilometers of land in Fukushima Prefecture has now been contaminated by a cumulative radiation dose of 5 millisieverts or higher per year" (National Diet of Japan Fukushima Nuclear Accident Independent Investigation Commission, 2012, 19). Japan's Reconstruction Agency, created to manage recovery from the triple disaster, reported that by November 2021, the peak number of evacuees due to the nuclear accident, earthquake and tsunami combined totaled over 470,000, with 39,000 still displaced (Reconstruction Agency, 2021).

The disaster has also challenged economic resilience of Japan's energy system. The economic impact of the Fukushima nuclear accident is intertwined with that of the tsunami and earthquake that caused it. This said, an academic report from 2012 estimates compensation to residents and decontamination efforts alone at $105 billion (Oshima and Yokemoto, 2012). In 2016, the Japanese government released a total cost estimate of $202.5 billion, with Fukushima reactor decommissioning costs predicted to comprise around $73 billion of this total (Yamaguchi, 2019). As of December 2020, TEPCO had spent approximately $13 billion on decommissioning (Jiji Press, 2021). In addition, land, agricultural, and water contamination, increased fossil fuel imports, and the initial rolling blackouts precipitated by the nuclear accident have added billions of dollars in lost revenue and additional costs.

In addition to the natural and technological aspects of the accident, the human contributions to the disaster received broad coverage nationally and globally. Official assessments and media reports criticized relationships between TEPCO and government safety regulators for failing to implement and enforce effective preventive measures, reflecting the previous chapter's discussion of challenges to engineering and ecological resilience. The Diet's Investigation Commission report finds that "The TEPCO Fukushima Nuclear Power Plant accident was the result of collusion between the government, the regulators and TEPCO, and the lack of governance by said parties" (National Diet of Japan Fukushima Nuclear Accident Independent Investigation Commission, 2012, 16). The report and media coverage also condemned emergency, communications, and investigative responses by TEPCO, safety regulators and policymakers. The Diet report further finds that "The government, the regulators, TEPCO management, and the Kantei [Prime Minister's Office] lacked the preparation and the mindset to efficiently operate an emergency response to an accident of this scope. None, therefore, were effective in preventing or limiting the consequential damage" (National Diet of Japan Fukushima Nuclear Accident Independent Investigation Commission, 2012, 18). The report and media coverage cite these problems as the reason for further troubles with communication to and evacuation of citizens.

Due to the accident, all 54 of Japan's nuclear reactors were shut down by September 2013. TEPCO permanently shuttered Fukushima Daiichi units one, two, three, four, five, and six. As a result of this loss of nuclear baseload generating capacity, Japanese imports of fossil fuels increased steeply, contributing to Japan's trade deficit and raising electricity prices. Based on safety and economic considerations we will examine later in this chapter, the utilities have slated 18 additional reactors for decommissioning.

We might expect that an accident of this magnitude would lead to a significant reduction of nuclear power's role in Japan's energy system. Widespread criticism of the relationship between the Japanese government and TEPCO as a contributing factor to the lack of preparation for and mismanagement of the accident should have compounded this effect. In this chapter, we analyze how resilience priorities and risk perceptions have affected policymaker-regulator-utility relationships and energy policy and policymaking process responses to the Fukushima disaster.

Stakeholder Relationship Changes and Influences

The 2011 Fukushima nuclear accident occurred in an environment shaped by the electric utilities' cooperation with policymakers and conflict with regulators. Government-public trust and balances of cooperation and clout also played a role. As in the previous periods of shocks, these groups' resilience priorities, the relationships' institutional features, and risk perceptions both contributed to the disaster and were affected by it. The interview and secondary data reflect these linkages and highlight ways in which these factors have affected the shock's effects on energy policymaking.

In previous periods, shocks competed or combined with resilience priorities, institutional features, and risk perceptions to affect the government's relationships with the electric utilities and the public. The Fukushima disaster altered all of these factors. It has intensified differences between regulators' focus on engineering resilience and the utilities' economic resilience priorities, while highlighting overlap in economic resilience priorities of policymakers and utilities. The accident and its aftermath, couched in the broader challenges of the tsunami and earthquake, has raised public awareness of social resilience challenges, including electricity access, health and environmental concerns. The utilities and policymakers initially grappled with supply risks facing social resilience. The disaster additionally has elevated awareness of safety risk considerations as a necessary element of all forms of energy system resilience.

Like the oil shocks, the Fukushima disaster has dramatically altered risk perceptions regarding stability of supply source choices for Japan's energy system. In contrast, the disaster also drew attention to safety risks. The public's perception of energy system risk has become particularly heightened, accompanied by a decline in public trust in the government's ability to manage such risks. This shift has encouraged government and utility acknowledgment of safety risks and elevated safety regulator clout.

Despite their effects on risk perceptions, neither the oil crises nor the 1990s and 2000s accidents and scandal significantly changed existing relationships or institutional features. In contrast to these previous shocks, the Fukushima disaster initially altered both. The accident shattered the tenuous public trust that had fluctuated during the previous string of accidents and scandal. In response, policymakers and the electric utilities distanced themselves from one another to prevent further erosion of trust. Paradoxically, shocks such as the Fukushima disaster, earthquake and tsunami require cooperation to promote recovery and resilience. Removal of the safety regulator from METI, the energy policymaking entity, has contributed to system resilience, while also challenging it as regulators and the utilities have struggled to define a relationship that balances independence and cooperation.

Examination of the government's relationships with the electric utilities and the public during the decade following the Fukushima disaster reveals that some of these relationship changes have begun to reverse, and these relationships are slowly reverting to their previous state over time. This trend particularly applies to policymakers' relationships with the electric utilities and the public. Regulators' relationships with the electric utilities have changed dramatically in some ways after the disaster and remain the same in others. These developments reflect these groups' application of some of the lessons that have emerged from the disaster, and they also reveal some remaining challenges and opportunities for changes to support future energy system resilience.

Bureaucrats, Politicians, and Utilities

Existing studies of the Fukushima disaster's impact on relationships largely assert that policymakers' relationships with the electric utilities have not changed. The electric utilities' ties to the LDP and METI remain strong, and the utilities still wield considerable clout behind closed doors (e.g., DeWit et al., 2012; Kingston, 2013; Vivoda, 2016). Few, if any, studies posit that the Fukushima disaster collapsed cooperation and extinguished electric utility clout.

The interview data reveals a reality that falls in between, and one that is changing as time passes, a trend consistent with the effects of the disaster on resilience priorities, institutional influences, and risk perceptions. Many government and electric utility interviewees asserted that the Fukushima disaster forced change in the electric utilities' cooperative relationships with METI bureaucrats and politicians, along with a loss of electric utility clout. Other interviewees confided that they believe the relationship has not changed much since March 11. A third group suggested that the disaster initially injected conflict into the relationship, but as time has passed, and the LDP has resumed political leadership, cooperation is returning, along with a subtle increase in electric utility clout. Policy and process evidence substantiates this last view. In particular, interviewees identifying the return of cooperation cited its reflection in 2014–2015 policies supporting a significant role for nuclear power, as well as METI's resumption of advisory council leadership. The 2018 revision of Japan's Strategic Energy Plan also retained nuclear power as a baseload electricity generation source. The 2021 version of the Strategic Energy Plan does not mention expansion of nuclear power use, but it does include continuation of nuclear power as a baseload source, as well as continuation of plans for nuclear fuel recycling.

A number of government and electric utility interviewees indicated a dramatic change in the policymaker-electric utility relationship. Comparing cooperation prior to the Fukushima disaster to the situation since March 11, they highlighted distancing of the two groups and loss of electric utility clout over policymakers and energy policy decisions. In May 2013, electric utility interviewee I7 asserted that there was "currently almost no relationship between the government and electric power companies." I7 offered institutional changes as examples, citing the utilities' inability to offer opinions to the newly formed independent nuclear regulator, discussed later in this chapter, regarding reactor restarts. I7 also emphasized the utilities' removal from METI's energy advisory committees, while noting that "under the LDP administration, electric power companies have the opportunity to say their opinions at the government committees." Another electric utility interviewee, I10, clarified in July 2013 that "we can consult with METI, but now they never say confidential information to us. Now we can talk with METI, but not so much as before Fukushima." Electric utility interviewee I5 stated a similar view of distance between the electric utilities and policymakers, noting intensification of the conflict over responsibility for the nuclear fuel cycle. These institutional changes reflect attention to public perceptions, but they do not necessarily indicate divisions in policymakers' and utilities' resilience priorities.

Both the utilities and policymakers have continued to direct their attention to economic resilience priorities. The electric utilities – in particular, TEPCO – suffered infrastructure and economic investment losses from the Fukushima disaster. Recovery of these losses and liability for damages heightened the utilities' focus on economic resilience. With the government purchase of a percentage of TEPCO's assets and liability, policymakers thus assumed a portion of this economic burden, further elevating economic resilience as a priority.

At the same time, the need to provide electricity to consumers in the absence of nuclear power catalyzed a complementary prioritization of ecological and social resilience by both the utilities and policymakers. Over time, as natural gas and coal have replaced the offline nuclear reactors to provide a stable electricity supply, economic priorities have overtaken ecological resilience once again.

The utilities and policymakers have concentrated on restarting the existing nuclear reactors. In this context, the utilities have focused on calculating the tradeoffs associated with the revenue these restarts will provide versus the costs of infrastructure upgrades to comply with new safety regulations, especially for older reactors that face license expiration in the coming decade or two. These new regulations have bolstered engineering resilience, while concurrently challenging the utilities' and policymakers' short- and mid-term economic resilience goals. In the long-term, reactors that comply with the new safety regulations may avoid future costs of damage from averted accidents and the ability to respond to effectively to natural disasters and other shocks. For both the utilities and policymakers, the Fukushima disaster thus amplified the role of safety considerations in all forms of resilience.

While priorities may have remained aligned, some interviewees who say the relationship has changed attribute it to public awareness and distrust of the close relationship revealed by the Fukushima accident. The bureaucracy and politicians are responding to public criticism of the electric utilities and their relationship with the government. This response has included resurrection of electricity market liberalization. G12 explained that

> after the earthquake, I think things changed very drastically . . . every politician had to change their attitude toward electricity companies. So I think, still, many politicians and government, especially under the LDP, people want to keep the nuclear policy, while, as for the market reform, somehow they have to push market reform to show the people that they are doing something against the will of the electricity companies. So I think after the earthquake, of course the political strength, the political influence of the electricity companies very drastically dropped, and at the same time, the politicians' attitude toward the electricity companies changed.
>
> (August 2013)

Interviewees like G12 assert that the electric utilities have lost clout over policymakers because public clout has risen, forcing the government to demonstrate at least the appearance of a rift. Some government interviewees suggested that the public's loss of confidence in the electric utilities has forced the politicians to criticize them. This criticism has relatively strengthened policymakers' clout over the utilities. G18 described this scenario specifically for TEPCO: "the electricity industry, TEPCO lost public confidence, and politicians have to criticize TEPCO. So the power balance for METI changed. Both lost to some extent confidence from the public, but the degree lost is more for TEPCO. The government has a better position compared to electric utilities" (August 2013).

The Fukushima disaster weakened the electric utilities' collective bargaining power with the government in several other ways. Some electric utility interviewees cited the loss of TEPCO's leadership as the reason for the utilities' diminished access to and leverage over METI. After the March 11 disaster, the government partially nationalized TEPCO, formerly Japan's most influential electric utility. KEPCO's ascension to the leadership role in FEPC compounded this problem, since KEPCO lacks TEPCO's government connections and diplomacy skills, according to several interviewees. I1 summarized the problems facing the electric utilities: "the question is now raised if Kansai can be a leader of the ten utilities or not, where the interests, the stakes are so different from company to company . . . currently Kansai is the leader of the electricity industry, and historically, they do not have good access to METI. And historically they are not accustomed to being a leader. And also they are in a very unique position to have a priority on nuclear power" (July 2013). I1 predicted that "if the utilities are not in agreement, they do not present some unified request." These challenges may signal the end of the electric utilities' unified front on nuclear power promotion and the future of Japanese energy policy, according to I1 and other electric utility interviewees. This breach in cooperation among the utilities has implications for broader collaboration with policymakers and regulators on energy system resilience, as individual utilities focus on their disparate economic resilience goals, rather than overall system resilience.

As highlighted in previous chapters, the electric utilities' relationship with METI is not monolithic, and resilience priority overlap and divergence have contributed to cooperation and conflict with METI's divisions. Even before the Fukushima disaster, some offices within METI, including those focused on regulatory reform or renewables introduction, had contentious interactions with the electric utilities, while METI's nuclear policy office maintained a strong relationship. Government and electric utility interviewees' comments regarding the various METI offices suggest that the Fukushima disaster further diversified METI's relationship with the electric utilities, as METI created new offices specifically to address the disaster and renewables promotion. The disaster also initially shifted clout from utility supporters within METI to factions interested in diminishing electric utility clout in energy policymaking.

While resilience priorities have remained relatively aligned, government and electric utility interviewees' comments suggest that the Fukushima disaster has altered some institutional features in ways that have compromised cooperation and clout in the electric utilities' relationship with energy policymakers. However, some of these changes have begun to reverse, suggesting that shifts in cooperation and clout may do the same. Other institutional changes have fostered continued cooperation. Informal institutions include government legitimization of utilities' nuclear power plans and political donations. Formal institutions include advisory councils, processes for public input, and the nuclear safety regulatory structure.

As mentioned in the previous chapter, the electric utilities historically solicited government endorsement to garner public trust in their nuclear power expansion activities. Government and electric utility interviewees indicated that after the Fukushima disaster, the utilities have sought even more government approval. Government official G11 explained that the electric utilities "use the government to get the trust from the public. They are doing that, I think, more since the earthquake, since they lost public trust" (June 2013). Since the government has felt public pressure to maintain distance from the utilities, few clear statements of government support for the utilities have emerged. This ambiguity has led to conflict and a struggle for clout between policymakers and the electric utilities.

The Fukushima disaster also has challenged the electric utilities' ability to continue large political donations to both the LDP and the DPJ. With their nuclear reactors shut down, the electric utilities have no profits to allocate for this relationship-building. Electric utility and government interviewees said that without these donations, electric utility clout over these politicians has waned, as has cooperation. As electric utility industry interviewee I7 explained, "now, electric power companies have much financial difficulties, so for politicians, it's not so interesting to have a very close relationship with the industry. And also in this sense, politicians and electric power companies don't have such a close relationship currently and also perhaps in the future." Thus, newly elected politicians, even in the LDP, have felt less obligated to pressure METI or otherwise support the electric utilities' interest in continuing nuclear power and stopping market liberalization. In March 2013, Diet member Kono observed that "there are more LDP politicians who just don't listen to power companies now. They have a more independent view." However, he said that these politicians represent a minority when compared to pro-utility politicians. He also predicted that the electric utilities would find ways to build relationships with these new politicians in order to gain support for nuclear power and stall market liberalization. Both of Kono's observations appear valid. In 2019, then-Environment Minister Shinjiro Koizumi proposed eliminating nuclear power from Japan's electricity mix. At his first press conference, Koizumi said of Japan's nuclear reactors, "I would like to study how we will scrap them, not how to retain them" (Reuters Staff, 2019b). In a reversal in 2021, newly appointed Environment Minister Tsuyoshi Yamaguchi and METI Minister Koichi Hagiuda indicated support for nuclear power as a necessary element of Japan's decarbonization strategy. Yamaguchi also expressed willingness to listen to the electric utilities' views. At the same time, Hagiuda disavowed plans to resurrect expansion of nuclear power beyond existing reactors, stating, "We do not envisage projects to build nuclear reactors or replace old ones with new ones" (The Asahi Shimbun, 2021). Hagiuda affirmed adherence to Japan's Sixth Strategic Energy Plan, released in 2021, which includes "stable use of nuclear power" without mention of expansion (Agency for Natural Resources and Energy,

Ministry of Economy, Trade and Industry, 2021). In 2022, the geopolitical shock of Russia's invasion of Ukraine and related effects on oil and gas supplies and prices advanced some LDP Diet members' calls for nuclear reactor restarts. One such lawmaker, Itsunori Onodera, told the press in March 2022 that "If you could obtain the understanding of the people after having verified safety, speeding up inspections and then speeding up the restarts, that's definitely a choice" (Kelly and Lies, 2022).

This plan to maintain nuclear power without replacing existing plants or adding new ones holds implications for Japan's future electricity supply mix, since the existing plants' licenses will expire by the 2060s. This conundrum and the continued construction of the Rokkasho reprocessing and MOX fuel fabrication facilities suggest a long-term plan based on the return of public trust. Plans for new nuclear power plant infrastructure – involving new nuclear technologies – may remain on hold until policymakers see a sufficient return of public trust in both nuclear power and the Japanese government's ability to oversee it. This longer-term plan to public confidence through current regulation of operating plants relies on reactor restarts. This scenario aligns with government-utility priorities for economic resilience based on recouping existing infrastructure investments while assessing the potential to recover future investments. A second possibility, less likely possibility, is that policymakers and utilities have revised their economic resilience goals based on long-term public opposition and expensive safety requirements that hinder new construction, making a gradual transition away from nuclear power more cost-effective than new investment.

The clout of electric utilities and METI pro-utility supporters has fluctuated with the priorities of each post-Fukushima Cabinet. After the Fukushima accident, the DPJ government changed several policymaking institutions to shift clout away from the electric utilities and sever cooperation with them to rebuild public trust in government policymaking. First, they cut METI out of the energy policymaking process, forming the Cabinet-level Energy and Environment Committee to handle decision-making on Japan's energy mix. The Kan Administration also revamped the energy policy advisory committee, renamed the Fundamental Energy Issues Subcommittee, and ousted the electric utilities from it. I7 said that the electric utilities "had a big influence on the decision of the committee, now the public believes, so therefore the government [removed them]."

The advisory committee reorganizations also empowered the public during the DPJ's leadership. Several antinuclear NGO leaders became members of the new Fundamental Energy and Environmental Issues Subcommittee. These changes caused both the electric utilities and their METI supporters to lose clout. As mentioned previously, the DPJ had distanced itself from the bureaucracy, and this move crippled the government's ability to address the accident in a coordinated manner. Subsequent changes undertaken by the DPJ preserved this separation of politicians from bureaucrats, including formation of a committee that superseded METI's authority. Government official G4 explained that the DPJ "set up a so-called Energy and Environment Council above METI and MOE. So they wanted to take political leadership in making energy policy decisions. And they did not want to let METI or bureaucrats or Atomic Energy Commission bureaucrats make a decision. They wanted to make a decision by themselves" (February 2013).

However, when the LDP's Abe administration assumed power in 2012, government and electric utility interviewees largely perceived a return to pre-Fukushima relationships between policymakers and the electric utilities, as well as a reversion to pre-3/11 relationships. Prime Minister Abe appointed former METI nuclear renaissance architect Yanase, introduced in the previous chapter, as his administrative aide. METI assumed advisory committee leadership again, and the electric utilities were granted observer status at committee meetings. Most of the antinuclear members were ousted, including NGO leader Iida. Government and electric utility interviewees' views on the actual clout of the utilities in the advisory committees is mixed. Some say that the electric utilities still play an influential role in the committees, voicing their opinions freely. Others argue that the utilities have no veto power and are only able to express their opinions publicly in committee meetings, limiting their ability to voice their true opinions. The utilities also hold observer status in new subcommittees formed toward the end of Abe's time as prime minister, discussed later in this chapter. This formal observer status has not changed during the Suga and Kishida Cabinets. Former Prime Minister Abe has become even more outwardly supportive of nuclear power during the Kishida Cabinet, asserting its necessity to meet decarbonization goals and urging construction of new plants that meet higher safety standards.

While removal of the safety regulatory function from METI has negatively affected the utilities' clout over safety regulators, this change has enabled less conflict and greater cooperation between METI and the electric utilities. METI no longer must balance nuclear promotion with regulatory responsibilities, so the agency is free to openly support nuclear power promotion. Government official G12 captured this new freedom as follows:

> As for nuclear, we can stand on the industry's side or nuclear promotion side more freely. You know, when we have the regulatory authority, we had to somehow . . . we had to contain ourselves, because we are regulators. But now that we are not regulators, we somehow freely can say things from the viewpoint of the energy policy.
>
> (August 2013)

This change contributes to preservation of the incumbent system, since it enables policymakers and electric utilities to continue to work together. At the same time, the transfer of Japan's nuclear regulatory agency out of METI to the Ministry of Environment increased MOE's clout over the electric utilities, while deepening conflict. Government interviewee G2 asserted that "the responsibility for nuclear oversight was foisted on MOE, so there is a lot of resentment and anti-nuclear sentiment." In addition, the electric utilities initially turned to coal use to replace nuclear power, seeking MOE's agreement to expedite environmental impact assessments for coal plants. This request added tension to the relationship, since it conflicts with MOE's climate change mitigation mission. It also reflects the utilities' focus on economic resilience, in contrast to the MOE's social resilience priorities. We examine the policy effects of this priority divergence later in this chapter.

All of these institutional changes have yielded a mixed effect on policymaker-utility cooperation and clout. Challenges to cooperation on previously shared risk perceptions have further complicated cooperation.

The Fukushima disaster elevated safety risk on the government's priority list, according to most government and electric utility interviewees, as well as existing studies (e.g., Vivoda, 2012). This emergence of nuclear safety risks as a priority has challenged policymakers' and electric utilities' shared focus on nuclear power as a solution to risks to the 3Es discussed in the previous chapter: energy security, economics and environmental concerns. The Fukushima disaster further revealed linkages between these safety risks and risks to each of the 3Es: nuclear reactor shutdowns, accident damage costs, land and water contamination, and health implications. A slow return of nuclear power has resulted from these risks' effects on public support for a return of nuclear power as a baseload electricity source, as well as the pace of operators' compliance with new regulatory measures to mitigate the risks.

The emergence of safety risk has not eliminated METI's and the electric utilities' support of nuclear power to achieve the 3Es, but public opposition continues to challenge open admission of this priority. At the same time, the economic implications of safety risks have compounded the differences between economic resilience goals of policymakers, electric utilities, and economic regulators.

Economic Regulators and Electric Utilities

Resilience priorities, institutional influences and risk perceptions all influenced economic regulators' relationships with the electric utilities following the Fukushima disaster. Government and electric utility interviewees generally agreed that the disaster empowered economic regulators and weakened the electric utilities' clout. My 2018 study finds that this relatively weakened utility influence enabled resurrection of electricity market liberalization after the disaster. In that prior study, some interviewees cited the shutdown of Japan's nuclear reactors as a catalyst for delinking infrastructure investment priorities and electricity market reform. These two factors – the decline in utility clout and disconnection of divergent economic resilience priorities – merged to force the electric utilities to seek compromise rather than elimination of liberalization (Sklarew, 2018, 164–165). Complementing this trend, some government interviewees asserted, the electric utilities' continued prioritization of nuclear power infrastructure preservation promoted a willingness to compromise on market liberalization in exchange for government support for continued nuclear power use. Meanwhile, METI's economic regulators considered full electricity market competition and unbundling of generation, transmission and distribution as higher priorities than before the Fukushima disaster.

Interviewees also suggested that this movement on regulatory reform after the disaster revived conflict between the two groups. At the same time, the shock's revelation of the opaqueness of policymaking improved transparency, driving METI's Office of Electricity and Gas Market Reform to share more information with the electric utilities than in the past. Electric utility interviewee I19 noted that the officials in charge of market liberalization "tried to do everything openly. So when you visit the website of METI, all the information is listed. I'm very surprised" (May 2014).

As market liberalization plans proceeded, outsiders criticized the housing of METI's economic regulator inside ANRE, positing the need for an independent regulator to ensure fair competition and grid access. METI's 2013 market liberalization legislation included creation of a regulator outside of ANRE by 2020, and at that time, G16 noted, "I think in terms of economic regulation, there has not been great change. The regulator is inside METI and still doesn't have kind of independent support even now" (July 2013). This view suggests that the economic regulators may not have wielded enough clout to choose a market structure design opposed by the electric utilities.

As discussed in more detail later in this chapter, in 2015, the Electricity Market Surveillance Commission was created. The commission's mission was expanded in 2016, accompanied by a name change to the Electricity and Gas Market Surveillance Commission (EGC). The commission's website states its function as follows: "The EGC conducts appropriate monitoring of the electricity, gas and heat power market and enforces strict regulations to ensure neutrality of electricity and gas networks." Still housed under METI, but separate from ANRE, the commission consists of a chairman and four commissioners from academic institutions and private firms.

The disaster affected depiction of risks associated with market liberalization. As discussed previously, prior to the disaster, the electric utilities were able to frame risks and uncertainty of market liberalization as a threat to economic and energy security. After the disaster, Japan was already in an unstable economic and energy security situation. The electric utilities posited that market liberalization would worsen these risks by discouraging investment in infrastructure and introducing electricity supply instability. I21 predicted that

> after the deregulation starts, there is no guarantee for the utilities to collect investment to their facilities, especially for the generation assets. So far, utilities can invest in nuclear and fossil power plants under regulation, because they can collect investments from the electricity fee from the customers, but after deregulation, they cannot. As a result, nobody will be able to invest in huge investment like nuclear or big fossil power plants. So that would cause a shortage of electric supply.
>
> (May 2014)

In contrast, METI's reformers defined liberalization as a solution to these risks. They asserted that competition would promote economic gain through efficiency and lower electricity prices, as well as local employment. G10 explained that "pressure from [manufacturing] companies to reduce the cost of energy was one motivation to pursue deregulation." G10 also noted that renewables "are one big tool to promote [the local] economy" by providing new job opportunities. Existing analyses of electricity market liberalization are split on whether full deregulation and unbundling help or harm an economy. For a balanced view, see Michael Pollitt (2012). METI reformers also asserted that liberalization would foster energy security by diversifying suppliers. Existing studies on this topic present mixed views that suggest that reform and market design determine whether liberalization bolsters or compromises energy security (e.g., Gnansounou, 2010). Diet member Kono dismissed the electric utilities' portrayal of liberalization as a threat to energy security as "total nonsense."

Differences in economic resilience priorities and risk perceptions thus have fueled post-disaster conflict between economic regulators and the utilities. The utilities' divergence from safety regulators' views on resilience and risk have emerged even more vividly since the Fukushima disaster, with implications for clout and cooperation.

Safety Regulators and Electric Utilities

While the Fukushima disaster deepened preexisting safety regulator-utility resilience priority differences and risk perceptions, institutional changes have highlighted these disparities and dramatically impacted the relationship between these two groups. The disaster markedly altered the dynamic between the electric utilities and nuclear safety regulators by granting the regulatory agency independence from METI. The Diet Investigation Commission and many academic studies recommended this shift (e.g., Aoki and Rothwell, 2013). Creation of the Nuclear Regulation Authority (NRA) as an independent regulatory body has freed the agency from policymakers' pressure to accommodate electric utility interests. Government official G13 asserted that "when we had NISA, that belonged to METI, and METI is the policymaker. And so policymaker METI can control, to some extent, NISA's ideas. Used to control, used to be able to control. But now, they cannot do it" (July 2013). Government interviewee G9 also described how the NRA has more clout over the electric utilities than NISA did, because the electric utilities are now required to respond to all of the NRA's requests for information in order to continue operations:

> Before, if we have some doubt or questions we could not ask [the utilities] to stop, but now, the NRA can ask them to stop if they cannot answer every question. [The utilities] could ask us to show them all the data, the reason why you have some doubt. They could ask us to explain all your doubts. But now it changed, and we can ask them all the questions.
>
> (May 2013)

These changes have resolved the former clout battle in favor of the regulator. G9 explained that this new clout is coupled with continued conflict. Many of the NRA staff are former NISA officials who are happy to be free of utility and METI influence. "My feeling is that two-thirds or three-fourths of NRA officials hate utility people and they do not trust them at all. Before also." However, the ruling party selects the commissioners, and those selected under the DPJ can be replaced by commissioners chosen by the LDP. Changes in the NRA's composition thus can affect the relationship between the NRA, politicians, METI and the utilities. Nuclear regulatory agencies in other nations face similar shifts, as new commissioners are appointed by the party in power. For example, in the United States, the president appoints Nuclear Regulatory Commissioners who are confirmed by the U.S. Senate for five-year terms. In Japan's case, the LDP did appoint two new commissioners in 2014, replacing an official critical of Japan's nuclear safety practices with an official with research funding ties to the utilities and the nuclear industry. While NRA composition has influenced relationships with the utilities and public trust, several features have aimed at rebuilding this trust and improving Japan's energy system engineering and socio-ecological resilience. However, these features, including rules on no-return employment and meeting transparency, have yielded mixed effects.

The no return rule for NRA staff aims to enhance the NRA's independence by breaking the personnel rotation tradition. However, it has a mixed effect on the NRA's ability to function as an effective, independent regulator. On the one hand, G17 indicated that NRA staff do not fear retribution for their decisions, since they cannot return to METI. But the no return rule hinders staffing, because bureaucrats who want to return to their home agencies refuse to transfer to the NRA, shrinking the pool of knowledgeable regulators. Compounding NRA's staffing problems, nuclear power opponents accuse potential NRA candidates with a background in nuclear power of ties to the "nuclear village," arguing that they will bias regulations in favor of the electric utilities. This staffing problem has contributed to continuation of some aspects of the previous tension between NISA and the utilities, indicated government and electric utility interviewees. For several years after the disaster, the electric utilities criticized the NRA's lack of nuclear reactor knowledge. In May 2014, I20 asserted that "one big problem is that NRA commissioner and staff have little experience with [nuclear reactor] operation. It is a big problem." In 2014, JNES, the technical agency described in chapter 4, merged with the NRA to address this problem by boosting the NRA's staffing and expertise. This change has reduced conflict between the NRA and the electric utilities, who trust JNES' knowledge. At the same time, skeptics argue that JNES has strong ties to the electric utilities. And yet, the utilities have continued to criticize the NRA, which weakens the regulator's credibility, say some government interviewees. "We established the NRA as an independent body, but still it seems to me that the utilities try to blame the NRA. I advised them not to do it," said G9.

Electric utility and some government interviewees also criticized the NRA for excessive independence, resulting in isolation from the electric utilities and the rest of the government. New transparency requirements aimed at building public trust compounded this isolation effect. Under the new measures, all meetings between NRA officials and anyone outside the NRA must be recorded and made publicly available if longer than five minutes. According to energy industry executives, this requirement initially discouraged NRA officials from engaging in any contact with utility and nuclear facility operators. Chapter 6 discusses the resilience implications of this isolation effect in more detail.

The NRA's isolation, electric utility interviewees assert, could again lead to unrealistic regulations if the NRA is uninformed by any electric utility perspectives. I22 offered the example of a new regulation requiring all cables in the reactors to be fire resistant. "There is a lot of cable, long, long cables that extend more than five hundred, six hundred miles in total. And the new regulation requires that the cable should be non-flammable, fire-resistant. So the newer plants are using those non-flammable cables, but old plants don't. And it's almost impossible [to replace them], because those cables are going everywhere inside the plant." The utilities are expected to provide data for the NRA to use in crafting regulations, but electric utility interviewees asserted that NRA staff did not communicate at all with utility engineers for the first year or so, after an NRA commissioner was publicly condemned for meeting with electric utility executives shortly after creation of the new agency.

Discussions between the NRA and the electric utilities on the regulations began after the NRA had formulated and released them. Now, the electric utilities can meet with the NRA, but only publicly. The transparency rule has made candid discussions difficult, since the electric utilities do not want to be publicly perceived as saying that they cannot comply with the regulations or implying that their facilities are unsafe. A few electric utility interviewees supported the concept of more open interactions with regulators, but they emphasized that transparency should include regular exchanges to allow development of viable regulations.

The electric utilities' questioning of regulators' qualifications and the concern over potentially unrealistic guidelines echo a setting that contributed to the Fukushima disaster and other accidents and scandals in the past. The electric utilities did not respect the regulators, and they believed they could not comply with overly severe regulations, so they did not report non-compliance.

The new transparency regulations have increased the NRA's clout. Interviewees say that the utilities, politicians, and METI policymakers and utilities are able to pressure the NRA, for fear that the public will learn about it. G9 explained that "now the utilities are asking politicians, members of the LDP to give political pressure on the NRA. But once politicians make some action to the NRA, they make a record, so politicians cannot call NRA to ask for change" (May 2013).

Some government and electric utility interviewees offered evidence that the isolation argument is aimed at enabling METI and the electric utilities to regain clout over the safety regulator. They say that METI has been trying to find a way to reassert influence on nuclear regulation. In July 2013, I1 said that the former

NISA officials in the NRA "didn't want to listen to METI at all. So even METI officials do not have a meeting with NRA officials. Because of that, METI didn't like NRA. So they wanted to establish a NISA-like organization within METI with the support from the utilities." I1c confided that "They may say this is an agenda of energy policy, but the reality is that they just lost the power for regulating nuclear power."

In addition to developing new regulations for reactor design, operation and maintenance, as well as processes for approving reactor restarts, the NRA has applied these responsibilities to alter the utilities' approach to safety culture and risk. Highlighting the role of transparency and communication in engineering resilience, in August 2021, the NRA halted the restart screening of Japan Atomic Power Company's (JAPC's) Tsuruga unit 2 reactor. JAPC is jointly owned by six Japanese electric utilities. In the midst of an ongoing debate over seismic risks to the plant, the decision emerged from the NRA's 2020 discovery of JAPC's data modifications regarding fault line location and activity, which received wide media coverage. The data alteration prompted a screening hiatus at that time, resumption based on additional data from JAPC, and the second halt in 2021 following an interim report criticizing JAPC's data management. These actions hamper the utilities' economic resilience in the short term, but they promote long-term economic, engineering and socio-ecological resilience through improvement of safety practices aimed at reactor safety, integrity and longevity.

Beyond the external challenges the electric utilities face in interacting with the NRA, they also face an internal challenge to rebuilding clout. The disaster and ensuing challenge to the return of nuclear power in Japan's energy mix revealed a split in the utilities' priorities that has divided and weakened their negotiating power with the NRA. KEPCO, as well as Kyushu and Shikoku, have more nuclear facilities than the other electric utilities. As the electric utility with the largest share of nuclear power, KEPCO has the largest stake in nuclear reactor restarts. Additionally, the utilities don't even agree on priorities within nuclear power. Since KEPCO's reactors are all PWRs, the utility has promoted restarts of this reactor type over BWRS. Electric utility interviewee I18 complained that "Kansai Electric would like to say our nuclear is always safe because we only have PWRs. Fukushima Daiichi is a BWR, and we don't have any concern such as Fukushima. Any utilities who have a BWR complain about Kansai Electric's stance" (May 2014). This tactic has pitted KEPCO against TEPCO and the other three utilities on Japan's eastern side, all of which have only BWRs. Electric utility interviewee I19 explained that, as a result, "it's very difficult to coordinate. Each company has to survive. So if we cooperate with each other, some company has to give up some request, but it's very difficult." This internal conflict based on economic resilience priorities threatens ecological resilience, as it hinders utility cooperation with regulators to define effective, realistic regulations for all types of reactors, as well as cooperation with policymakers to develop more resilient reactor designs.

Overall, the NRA's independence from METI and the utilities has enabled safety regulators' focus on new regulations for engineering resilience without consideration of economic resilience. When informed by utility data that enables realistic regulations, this new dynamic opens the opportunity for improved eco-logical resilience as utilities choose to shut plants down in order to meet economic resilience goals when the cost of compliance with new regulations is too high to recover before plant licenses expire.

These decisions facing the utilities also reflect the role of risk perceptions and uncertainty in the regulator-utility relationship, as well as implications of these for system resilience. Economic risk and uncertainty frames the utilities' resilience considerations in the post-Fukushima era. Plant operators' long-term cost recovery plans depend on uncertain license renewal, while they must make short-term investment decisions that balance the costs of upgrades and regulatory compliance. For example, the NRA identified insufficient fire prevention measures for cables in plants constructed before 1975. In May 2014, electric utility interviewee I22 explained that the electric utilities had negotiated for the ability to coat the existing cables with flame-retardant paint, rather than replacing them. Asserting that the paint would not prevent the cables beneath it from melting, the NRA did not approve this more cost-effective but less comprehensive option. The regulator did allow KEPCO to wrap fireproof sheets around some of the cables in two of its Takahama units. The company replaced the remaining 1300 kilometers of cable with fire-resistant cable. While the NRA granted 20-year license extensions for the two units, several electric utilities opted to decommission older plants when faced with the high costs of such cable replacement and other required upgrades, given the uncertainty of recovering these expenses during the remaining years of plant operation.

While they hold divergent views on the details and levels of safety risk for various aspects of nuclear power, both the NRA and the electric utilities are focused on the steps necessary to determine eligibility for reactor restarts. However, as mentioned previously, friction between the two groups has contributed to public distrust, impairing the NRA's ability to build public confidence that will enable reactor restarts.

Government and Public

While conducting the research for this study in 2013, I sat at my dining room table in Tokyo with the mother of one of my daughter's friends. The mother explained that she had taken her daughter to Fukuoka for two years after the Fukushima accident. When asked why, she responded, "Because of the radiation exposure. We were told that it would be safer to leave Tokyo." I asked her who had given this guidance. The government? "Of course not," she scoffed. "The government would never tell us something like that." Then who? She retorted, "I read it on the Internet." This anecdote, which reflects the sentiments and actions of many Japanese citizens, reveals the lack of public trust in the government following the Fukushima nuclear disaster. A decade after the disaster, this trust has not yet returned. Acute awareness of social resilience implications of Japan's energy policies and regulations, coupled with institutional factors and risk perceptions, has influenced this distrust.

The results of deliberative polling, a mechanism described in this chapter's policy process and structural change section, conducted in August 2012 also revealed this high level of public distrust in the government. The report on Japan's deliberative polling found that "participants came in with extremely low levels of trust for all the information sources available to them. On first contact only 6.4 percent trusted information from the government" (Sone, 2012a, 4). The only group the public trusted less was the electric power industry. Increasing participants' knowledge of nuclear power did not improve trust in the government. The report concluded that "these levels of distrust are remarkable and speak to the traumatic nature of the disaster" (Sone, 2012a, 5). Provision of information on nuclear power to the polling participants also did not improve their trust in it as an electricity supply source. Almost 50 percent of participants voted to eliminate nuclear power by 2030. A much smaller 15 percent of participants voted for a 15 percent nuclear share by 2030, and only 13 percent supported a 25 percent nuclear share (Sone, 2012b). This public interest in an energy system transformation to promote socio-ecological resilience challenged the government's economic resilience priorities.

All government and public representative interviewees agreed that the Fukushima disaster shattered public trust in the government's ability to manage not only nuclear power but the energy policymaking process and crafting of energy policies in the public's best interest. Existing studies on public opinion after the Fukushima disaster supports this view and maintains that trust had not yet returned several years later (e.g., Aldrich, 2013; Suzuki, 2018). Media and NGO interviewees asserted that public trust in the government has remained relatively low since the Fukushima disaster. Media interviewee M1 asserted, "After the Fukushima event, the impact was huge. They lost their credibility. I don't think they regained, no, still, I think their credibility is together with politicians and bureaucrats, very low" (March 2013). Media interviewee M2 suggested that public trust might return slowly over time. "Of course, people less trust the bureaucrats after Fukushima than before, but you know, I would say again that Japanese people are very forgetful. So I don't know if distrust will continue for a long time or not" (March 2013).

The popularity of the Abe Cabinet from 2012 until non-nuclear scandals emerged in 2017 did not reflect trust in the government's ability to regulate nuclear power. Almost two years after the disaster, a January 2014 poll by Fuji Television found that 52 percent of 1,000 respondents said they supported the Abe Cabinet, but 60 percent of them said they opposed restarting any of Japan's nuclear reactors (Iwata, 2014). Two years later, a 2016 Asahi Shimbun poll found that 57 percent of respondents opposed reactor restarts even under the revised, stricter safety regulations, reflecting distrust in the government's ability to regulate nuclear power and protect the public from safety risks. In addition, 73 percent supported a nuclear phaseout, and 14 percent wanted this action immediately (Suzuki, 2017). A 2017 poll by the Japan Atomic Energy Relations Organization (JAERO) found that in October 2016, only 1.8 percent of 1,200 respondents believed in the safety of nuclear reactors certified by the NRA as compliant with the NRA's new regulations (JAERO, 2018). The same percentage supported expansion of nuclear power. Only 8.3 percent supported maintaining pre-Fukushima levels of nuclear power, while 16.9 percent favored a complete and immediate phaseout, and 4.5 percent wanted a gradual phaseout. While these figures have fluctuated slightly, support for nuclear expansion has not risen higher than 2.2 percent, and support for returning to pre-Fukushima levels has remained below 9.5 percent. During this four-year period, support for a gradual phaseout of nuclear power also remained at around 48 to 49 percent (JAERO, 2020).

JAERO's poll results on reactor restarts also reflect continued diminished public trust in the new regulations and regulator. As Figure 5.1 shows, in the 2017 poll, 14.3 percent accepted approval of reactor restarts that meet the new safety standards, while 20.5 percent did not agree. JAERO's October 2018 poll saw a slight increase in respondents to 17.9 percent who would accept restart approval for compliant reactors, while 15.8 percent disagreed (JAERO, 2018). In the 2019 poll, 17.6 percent accepted compliant reactor restart approval, and 14.5 percent did not (JAERO, 2019). While the figures remain low, these results seem to demonstrate very slight improvement in public trust in the NRA and new regulations, which may be coupled with media coverage of the NRA's enforcement of these regulations. The 2020 poll also shows a decline in both reactor restart approval acceptance and refusal, with 16.5 percent agreeing, 11.8 percent rejecting approval, and a larger percentage uncertain of their preference. This timing aligns with the aforementioned media reports on JAPC's seismic data modification. As Figure 5.2 reflects, respondents who believe that Japan's earthquake response and disaster prevention measures were sufficient to enable restarts remained below seven percent in all four polls. These results reveal the need for regulators and

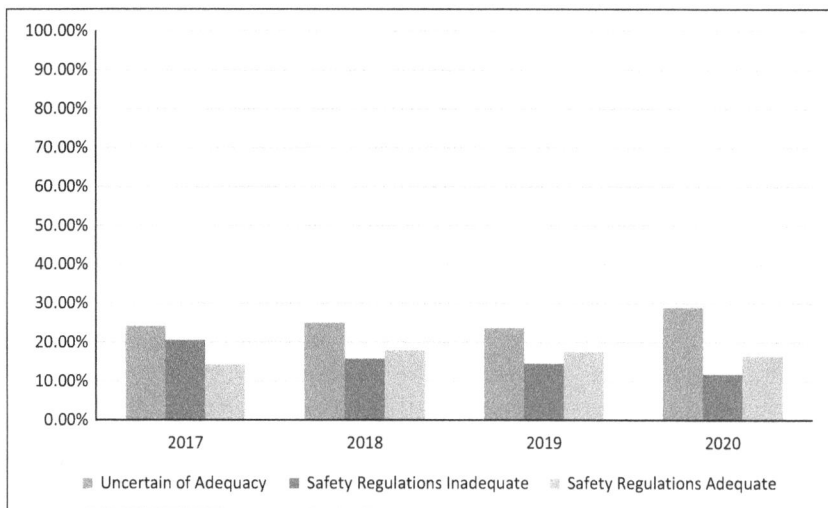

Figure 5.1 Public Acceptance of Safety Regulation Adequacy for Reactor Restarts

Source: Data from Japan Atomic Energy Relations Organization polls 2017–2020.

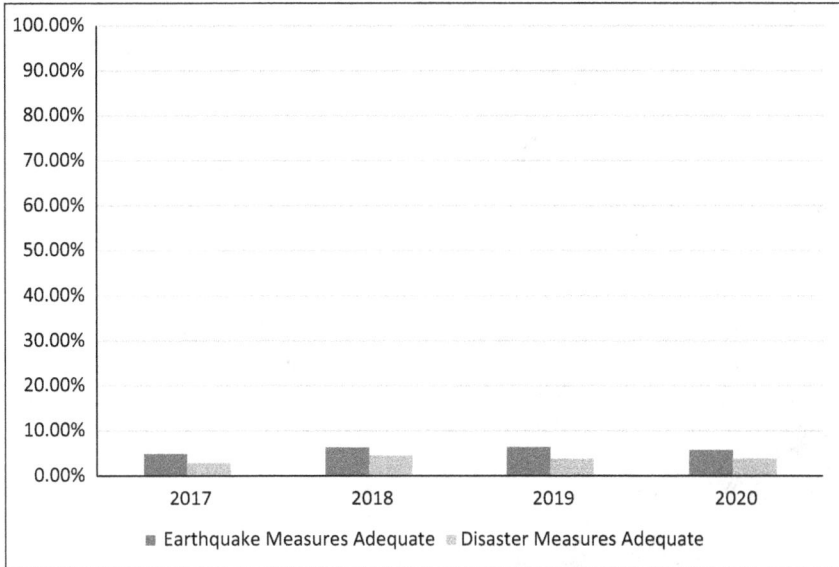

Figure 5.2 Public Acceptance of Earthquake and Disaster Response Adequacy for Reactor Restarts

Source: Data from Japan Atomic Energy Relations Organization polls 2017–2020.

policymakers' continued rebuilding of public trust in their ability to design, implement and enforce a framework for social resilience in Japan's energy system.

Public distrust in the new regulations' ability to ensure nuclear safety has led to local court injunctions against reactor restarts. In April 2015, the NRA approved restarts of two reactors at the Takahama nuclear power plant in Fukui prefecture, operated by KEPCO. However, the Fukui District Court approved an injunction filed by local residents against the restarts. The court criticized NRA standards as too lax, asserting that meeting the standards does not guarantee safety. Kagoshima residents filed a similar injunction against the restart of two NRA-approved reactor restarts at the Sendai power plant, but the district court rejected it.

A post-Abe Cabinet poll conducted by NHK in November and December 2020 found that 50 percent of 2,311 national respondents supported reduction of nuclear power use, and 17 percent supported its elimination from the electricity supply (NHK, 2021; NHK Broadcasting Culture Research Institute, 2021). Only three percent supported increasing nuclear power use, and 29 percent supported maintaining the existing pre-disaster level. Opinions on resuming existing nuclear plant operations split a bit more evenly, with 39 percent opposed, 16 percent in support, and 44 percent expressing neutrality (NHK, 2021; NHK Broadcasting Culture Research Institute, 2021). Reflecting the connection to public concern over nuclear safety risk, the poll also found that 61 percent of respondents believed nuclear power cannot be used safely, while 37 percent believed it can. Of the respondents who believed nuclear power could be used safely, 37 percent supported nuclear power reduction or elimination, and 86 percent of those who did not believe in safe nuclear power use supported reduction or elimination (NHK, 2021; NHK Broadcasting Culture Research Institute, 2021).

A decade after the disaster, Japanese citizens' trust in the government as a whole, as well as trust in political parties and the Diet, largely has not recovered. In 2019, prior to the effects of the COVID-19 pandemic, The Genron NPO conducted a public opinion poll of 1,000 constituents that included questions on trust in the national government, political parties and the Diet. The poll found that 53 percent of respondents had little to no trust in the national government, 67.6 percent had little to no trust in political parties, and 60.4 percent had little to no trust in the Diet (The Genron NPO, 2019). Diet member Kono's transparent communication with the public has contributed to his popularity among voters; he has 2.4 million Twitter followers.

The COVID-19 pandemic affected the results of subsequent media polls conducted in 2020 and 2021, as measures to address the pandemic and promote national and individual economic stability became the top public priorities affecting approval ratings. An October 2021 Asahi Shimbun poll found that 74 percent of respondents collectively chose these issues as the most crucial, while 4 percent of respondents identified nuclear power and energy as the top issue (The Asahi Shimbun, 2021). These results suggest that public attention has shifted away from nuclear safety and energy system resilience concerns, but when the topic of nuclear power arises, public awareness of risks drives opposition.

Collectively, the interview and poll data thus reveal that the Fukushima disaster raised public awareness of risks to social resilience of Japan's energy system. This new awareness, combined with the paternalistic government-public relationship discussed in previous chapters, as well as extremely low public tolerance for risk, to influence public acceptance of nuclear power and trust in government oversight of it. The public perception that the government was both partly responsible for and unresponsive to the accident led to distrust in government policies and the policymaking process after the shock. P2 summarized the shift in the public's view of the roles of public and government in energy policymaking:

> An increasing number of people are now believing that they have to voice their opinions, they have to think and make choices by themselves, while in the past, they just let the government decide. But now people believe that we have to get involved in the policymaking for energy, because energy is so important for our lives, as well.
>
> (March 2013)

M2 faults the paternalistic relationship for the government's failure to effectively convey risk to the public prior to the disaster.

I think . . . the lack of education about nuclear energy in Japan is the reason why people didn't pay attention to the risks before. So the traditional way of Japanese governing people is not to tell them or educate them or tell them the truth about complicated matters. In my opinion, many people in Japan don't know what nuclear power is.

(March 2013)

The Fukushima disaster's sudden highlighting of the existence of safety risk contributed to public distrust in government policymaking and communication.

The Fukushima disaster also has highlighted a more fundamental issue associated with risk perceptions and the paternalistic relationship. As discussed in the previous chapter, government interviewees' comments indicate that the government has avoided conveying safety risks because the public expects zero risk.[1] Before the Fukushima accident, this zero risk tolerance also extended to energy security, embodied in intolerance for power outages, no matter how short. The communication of zero safety risk and zero energy security risk in order to meet public expectations resulted in public distrust when the Fukushima accident revealed the existence of both risks.

The risks revealed by the Fukushima accident have altered the public's energy priorities. Since the disaster, say NGO and media interviewees, the public has prioritized safety risk over all three of the Es. The deliberative polling results reflect this shift. P3 explained that the polling results showed that "Among 3Es plus S, S is first. S can explain almost everything. Safety influenced almost every choice. But in the deliberative polling results, S is overwhelming." Media interviewee M1 summarized: "The public, now they are very keen for the risks regarding nuclear accidents. Safety" (March 2013). While this focus on safety to the exclusion of other priorities seems to be waning five to ten years after the disaster, JAERO's 2017–2020 polls reflect continued public prioritization of nuclear plant safety. While more than half of the respondents in each poll identified global warming as a concern, between 25 and 40 percent also identified nuclear safety and nuclear facility risk as concerns, per Figure 5.3. In contrast, less than ten percent identified comparative costs of different power generation sources as a concern (JAERO, 2020). In the 2018 poll, 12.4 percent identified energy import costs as a concern; this category was not included in the polls from other years (JAERO, 2018). Respondents were permitted to choose multiple categories. An NHK poll conducted in late 2021 offered four categories for top priorities and found that of 2,311 national respondents, 31 percent identified global warming as the most important consideration for electricity generation, and the same percentage chose stable and adequate electricity supply. Of the remaining respondents, 22 percent identified safe power generation as most important, and 14 percent chose cheap electricity prices (NHK, 2021). A comparison with previous NHK polls also shows a steady decline in safety prioritization since 2011, coupled with increases in focus on global warming and electricity prices. Since respondents could choose only one answer, the NHK poll results may minimize the number of respondents who might have chosen one or more other answers as equal or slightly lesser priorities.

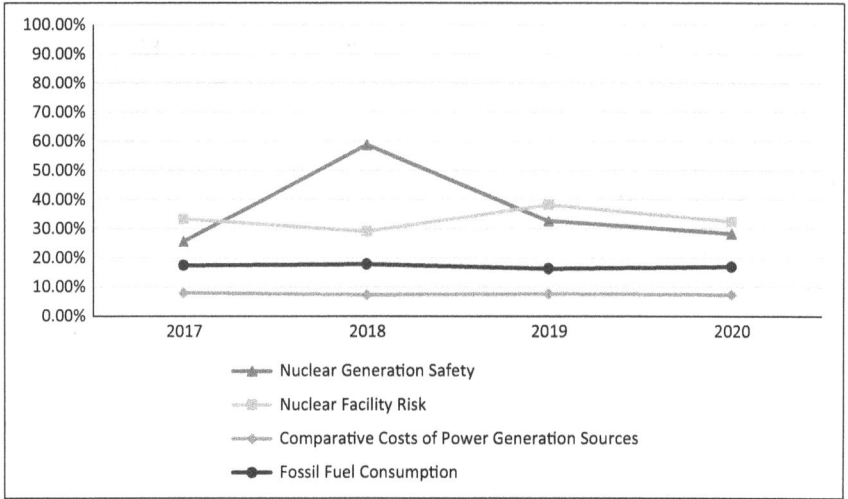

Figure 5.3 Japanese Public's Energy Concerns 2017–2020
Source: Data from Japan Atomic Energy Relations Organization polls 2017–2020.

Meanwhile, policymakers have continued to focus on energy security and economic resilience priorities and ways to incorporate safety into these. Media interviewee M1 (March 2013) observed, "The government, METI, I think among the 3Es, economics, energy security and environment, always, in Japanese energy policy, it's always economics comes first." Some Japanese government officials have framed energy risks as a trade-off between energy security risk and safety risk. Diet member Kono asserts that this is a false dichotomy aimed at convincing the public that nuclear power's energy security benefits outweigh the safety risks. This framing of risk trade-offs complicates cooperation to achieve socio-ecological resilience, which encompasses both energy security and safety.

Some government and NGO interviewees also indicated that the public no longer trusts the government's characterization of environmental risk. The Fukushima disaster alerted the public to nuclear waste disposal challenges and environmental implications of accident risks, such as water and soil contamination and radiation exposure. The 2018–2020 JAERO polls reflect public concern regarding these challenges, with 37 to 38 percent of respondents identifying waste disposal as a concern. The percentage of respondents identifying radiation as a concern remains substantial but has dropped from over 45 percent to just under 35 percent during this period. The aforementioned NHK poll found that 89 percent of respondents were somewhat to very concerned about nuclear waste (NHK Broadcasting Culture Research Institute, 2021). This group was split almost equally regarding whether the level of nuclear power should be maintained or reduced, suggesting that resolving the nuclear waste disposal challenge will be vital to future public support for nuclear power generation.

In April 2021, the Cabinet announced a decision to discharge contaminated water from the Fukushima accident into the ocean (Prime Minister's Office of Japan, 2021). The treated water contains high levels of tritium. The Japanese government also announced creation of an Inter-Ministerial Council for Contaminated Water, Treated Water and Decommissioning Issues to implement the plan, and the IAEA agreed to review the plan's consistency with international safety standards and oversee its implementation (IAEA, 2022). However, the Japanese public's continued distrust in the government and doubt over transparency of information following the Fukushima disaster have contributed to distrust of this solution and concern that the government is hiding potential environmental effects. The previously mentioned NHK poll found that 52 percent of respondents somewhat or completely opposed dumping the contaminated water from the Fukushima accident into the ocean, and 18 percent somewhat or completely supported the decision. The percentages of respondents that were undecided on these two issues – 44 percent and 30 percent respectively – open the possibility that more effective communication on these risks can encourage cooperation on solutions to them.

Interviewees asserted that the distrust catalyzed by the Fukushima disaster encouraged the public to seek more clout in energy policymaking, as well as greater transparency of the energy policymaking process. P2 explained, "After Fukushima, many people lost confidence in governmental power to create policies, and many people started to want their control back, so to speak. So we have something to say to the government, and the government should listen to us. That is a very big movement after Fukushima among people" (March 2013). Citizens utilized an informal institution to voice distrust in the government and its energy policies. Demonstrations by over 20,000 people took place outside of government buildings frequently in the year after the disaster, shrinking in volume and frequency since then. Interviewees say that these demonstrations have had little direct influence on post-Fukushima energy policies and policymaking processes. In addition, the aforementioned ousting of antinuclear members from the energy advisory committee under the Abe Cabinet also signaled a potential decline in public clout in formal policymaking processes under the LDP. M1 described this change:

> The LDP wants to decide energy policy in a conventional way. They set up some committees, and some of the anti-nuke opinion leaders were rejected. The conventional decision-making process will come back at the LDP meeting. That makes it much, much harder for the public to intervene, to say something about energy policies.
>
> (March 2013)

This said, government official G7 suggested that this decline in public trust did lead to an increase in public clout. The official indicated that "public trust in the Japanese government is kind of eroded, so the Japanese government is listening more to the public opinion" (March 2013). Interviewee G4 recognized the need for the government to respond to this public distrust: "I think Fukushima has changed universally the public perception of how government behaves on nuclear energy policy. That's for sure. So the public will demand reform, definitely. And utilities have to be liberalized, and energy policymaking should be changed" (March 2013).

Distrust in the government's risk communications has affected public views on electricity market liberalization. Since the late 1990s, some policymakers have cited public concern over electricity price risk as a reason for avoiding market liberalization and promoting continued nuclear reactor use. And yet, JAERO polls reflect declining public concern over electricity prices from 2018–2020, which dovetails with a 2019–2020 rise in public belief that a nuclear phaseout will not raise electricity prices (JAERO, 2020). These trends suggest a further disconnect between government and public risk perceptions and economic resilience priorities.

Public distrust in the government's communication of energy system risks also has reduced the effectiveness of a previously used government mechanism for nuclear infrastructure siting. Since the Fukushima disaster, one town in Fukushima prefecture has shunned subsidies for nuclear plant construction. The government has revised the subsidies to enable municipalities awaiting restarts to continue to receive the funds. A few months after the Fukushima disaster, Minami-soma chose to end construction of Tohoku Electric Power Company's Namie-Odaka plant, rejecting the subsidies that would come once the plant started operation. As evidenced by Minami-soma's rejection of nuclear plant construction, some localities have begun to prioritize perceptions of safety risk and local socio-ecological resilience over the subsidies' contributions to economic resilience.

Several government officials asserted that institutions must change permanently in order to regain public trust. As one such policy reformer, G4 contended, "My personal feeling is that the relationship should change given the Fukushima accident." The official clarified that "we need a change in the governance of the nuclear energy policymaking process. We should have more public participation. We should have more transparency. We need to do everything we can do to regain public trust. That's what I personally believe we should do" (February 2013).

The DPJ initiated a series of formal institutional changes intended to rebuild public trust after the disaster and respond to public demand for a role in energy policymaking. These changes, which include use of the aforementioned deliberative polling and revamping of the energy policy advisory committee, are described later in this chapter's discussion of policy process and structural changes. Resurrection of market liberalization also has aimed to rebuild public trust in the government's oversight of the utilities, nuclear power use, and electricity supply resilience. The LDP government has reversed some of the DPJ's institutional changes, while the public continues to distrust the effectiveness or intent of others. Overall, institutional changes have aimed at building public trust in government policymaking, but public perceptions of the genuineness of these changes affect their success.

Public reactions to institutional changes also depend on alignment of public and governmental risk perceptions and priorities.

Some convergence of government and public priorities has been emerging over the 10 years since the Fukushima disaster. Renewable energy increasingly has drawn support from the public and many policymakers, offering the opportunity for cooperation to achieve both groups' ecological and social resilience priorities. As discussed in the previous chapters, nuclear power became a galvanizing solution to achieve government, utility and public resilience priorities after the oil crises. The Fukushima disaster has elicited citizens' recognition of renewable energy sources as alternatives or supplements to nuclear power and fossil fuels to meet ecological and social resilience goals. In March 2013, NGO leader P1 asserted that "the vast majority . . . supports renewable energy because of replacing nuclear and because of more national independence and because of local independence or energy by our own [means]." The 2020 JAERO polls found that approximately 75 percent of respondents supported solar energy use, falling slightly since 2015. Around 63–65 percent have supported wind power use, and around 53–56 percent have supported hydropower use. About 40–45 percent have supported geothermal use. Biomass support has risen from around 26 percent to over 33 percent. Support for waste use to generate power generally has hovered around 24–25 percent. In the next section, we will see whether this support has translated into policies to develop these electricity supply sources.

While this public support for increased renewables uses conflicted with government priorities for reactor restarts and increased coal use for several years after the disaster, two factors have moved the government and the public closer to collaboration on priorities and the role of renewables in achieving them. Japan's CO_2 emissions reduction commitments and the slow return of nuclear power since the Fukushima disaster have combined to promote gradually increasing government support for renewable energy expansion as a complement to nuclear power in achieving ecological and social resilience priorities. The government's 2021 announcement of an increased renewables target, discussed in the next section, suggests such a shift. Policymakers, the public and the utilities have approached the economic resilience implications of renewables differently. Policymakers and utilities have focused on technology and infrastructure costs, while indicating to the public that these costs and economic incentives might translate to electricity price hikes. The next section examines some of these economic incentives.

Overall, the Fukushima disaster and the related relationship and priority shifts examined thus far in this chapter have catalyzed some changes to Japanese energy policies, as well as regulatory and market structure modifications. These relationship changes and policy effects are depicted in Table 5.1: Changes to Government Relationships and Energy Policy, Process, and Structure after the Fukushima Accident. Energy policy changes to promote resilience following the Fukushima disaster have been influenced by the disaster's initial fracturing of the government's relationships with the electric utilities and the public, followed by a return of policymaker-electric utility cooperation and a slower restoration of public trust in the government. As discussed in previous chapters, policymakers' relationships with the electric utilities and public largely were not in conflict before March 11, 2011. The Fukushima disaster generated conflict in each of the two relationships, and METI also has faced difficulties in balancing these relationships' contradictory demands. The electric utilities want METI to play a role in restoring public trust in the utilities and nuclear power. On the other hand, the public wants METI to keep its distance from the utilities. This public pressure on the government to maintain a more detached relationship with the utilities is coupled with public demand for a policy shift away from nuclear power. At the same time, the electric utilities are struggling to keep nuclear power and maintain strong ties to the government. In May 2013, I7 explained, "Japanese people don't have any good impression toward electric power companies currently. So the politicians don't want to have a close relationship with electric power companies." The electric utility industry executive said that at the same time, politicians want to support nuclear restarts for economic and energy security reasons. "So in this sense, politicians have a common way of thinking with electric power companies." This continued alignment of politicians' and utilities' resilience priorities, coupled with public pressure for distance between these two groups, has yielded mixed policy results.

The Fukushima disaster also has created friction among the electric utilities. Without TEPCO's leadership, the companies are pursuing disparate strategies and priorities on reactor restarts. Thus, they no longer present a unified front seeking preservation of the incumbent energy system, and their individual economic resilience goals have influenced the electricity supply mix through their independent decisions on nuclear plant restarts and decommissioning, renewables, and fossil fuel use.

Some government and NGO interviewees highlighted the role of the Fukushima disaster in raising public awareness of energy system choices. Some of these interviewees observed that this new awareness has encouraged the government to make changes to the energy system. Government official G1 asserted, "Until the Fukushima crisis happened, Japanese public did not feel the need for any change, so the government could not make any change and did not think there needed to be any change. Crisis allowed people to realize that there could be a different way, allows new innovation." Meanwhile, a loss of public trust in the government's management of energy policy has led to public demand for a greater voice in energy policy decisions.

The disaster also has empowered energy system reformers who previously received little attention. Like the backlash that emerged from Exxon's failure to rapidly address and define the Exxon-Valdez oil spill, TEPCO's belated, disjointed efforts to explain the Fukushima Daiichi nuclear disaster have empowered policy entrepreneurs.[2] Diet member Kono, whose efforts to redirect Japan's energy system over the past few decades, has gained a stronger voice in the media, the Diet, and the public arena. After the accident, Kono spearheaded a committee to reform Japan's energy policy. He also played a role in drafting of Japan's renewables feed-in tariff (FIT), discussed later in this section. Kono's calls for a solution to the

Table 5.1 Changes to Government Relationships and Energy Policy, Process, and Structure after the Fukushima Accident

Relationship	Change in Cooperation/Conflict	Change in Clout
Bureaucrats-Utilities	Conflict < Cooperation Change: initial conflict, then cooperation return	Bureaucrats > Utilities Change: bureaucrats stronger
Politicians-Utilities	Conflict > Cooperation Change: move toward conflict	Politicians > Utilities Change: politicians stronger
Economic Regulators-Utilities	Conflict No change	Regulators > Utilities Change: politicians stronger
Safety Regulators-Utilities	Conflict No change	Regulators > Utilities Change: regulators stronger
Government-Public	Conflict > Cooperation Change: greater public distrust	Government > Public Change: public stronger, then weaker

Policy Change	**Policymaking Process/Structural Change**
Yes, but incremental	Yes: safety regulator and market structure change, with mixed long-term impact

Source: Reprinted from Sklarew, 2015.

nuclear waste problem, the fuel cycle debate, and opportunities for public input in policies on electricity grid access have raised these socio-ecological challenges to the forefront, linking their resolution to a return of public trust in government management of Japan's energy system.

Shocked?: Electricity Supply and Energy System Changes

The government's choices for energy system change following the Fukushima disaster contrast with policies implemented after the oil crises, when the government opted to shift away from an oil-based energy system in order to promote economic and ecological resilience. This time, the focus on revitalizing the existing nuclear-based system has led to incremental changes within the existing system to promote economic and engineering resilience. The effects on social resilience have varied, dependent in part on alignment or divergence of local and national priorities.

The Fukushima disaster and the relationship changes it caused thus have shaped a mixed effect on energy system transformation and resilience. All 54 of Japan's nuclear reactors were shut down in 2011. However, as depicted in Figure 5.4: Comparison of Electricity Supply Fuel Percentages 2010–2012 (International Energy Agency), nuclear power accounted for 1.5 percent of Japan's electricity supply in 2012, since two reactors operated temporarily that year. Kansai Electric Power Company shut down Oi units 3 and 4 in September 2013. Efficiency and conservation efforts dramatically reduced electricity demand, easing the stress on a supply compromised by the absence of nuclear power. To make up for the nuclear supply shortfall, policies and overseas gas and oil development project financing supported a turn toward fossil fuels, with a return to oil use, as well as a dramatic increase in the use of natural gas and a slight rise in coal use. After a relatively steady two-decade decline, oil use rose from 6.7 percent in 2010 to 17.5 percent

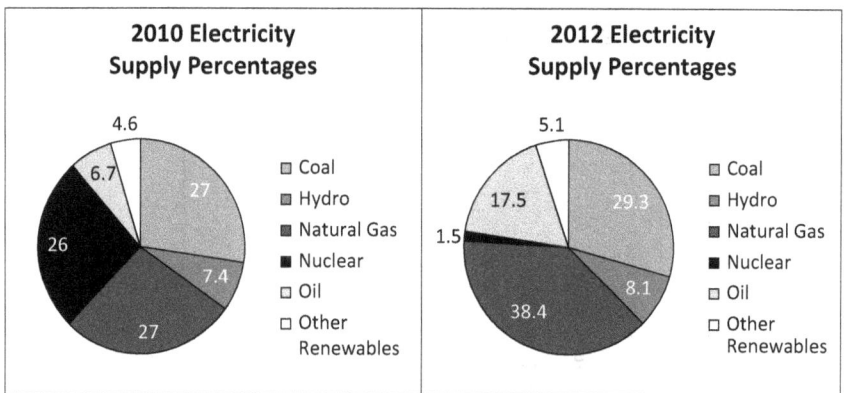

Figure 5.4 Comparison of Electricity Supply Fuel Percentages 2010–2012

Source: Reprinted from Sklarew, 2015; data from International Energy Agency, 2021a.

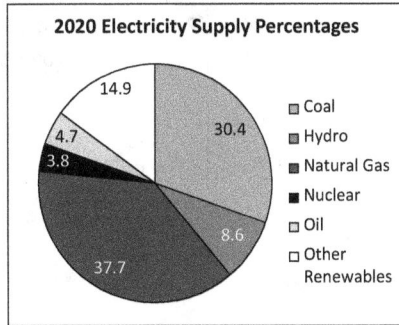

Figure 5.5 Electricity Supply Fuel Percentages 2020
Source: Data from International Energy Agency, 2021a.

of Japan's 2012 electricity supply. Natural gas increased from 27 percent in 2010 to a whopping 38.4 percent of supply in 2012. By contrast, coal grew slightly from 27 percent to 29.3 percent. Hydropower remained unchanged at 8.1 percent from 2010 to 2012. Non-hydro renewable energy rose minimally from 4.6 percent of Japan's 2010 electricity supply to 5.1 percent in 2012.[3]

As depicted in Figure 5.5: Electricity Supply Fuel Percentages 2020 (International Energy Agency), with nine reactors back online, nuclear power accounted for 3.8 percent of Japan's electricity supply. Oil use dropped back down to 4.7 percent. Natural gas use remained high, at 37.7 percent of supply. Coal use increased further by 2020, reaching 30.4 percent of Japan's electricity mix. Hydropower use rose very slightly to 8.6 percent between 2012 and 2020. Non-hydro renewables use rose to almost 15 percent of Japan's electricity supply, with solar PV accounting for a bit more than half of this amount, 7.6 percent of Japan's total electricity supply, as shown in Figure 5.6: Non-Hydro Renewables Sources in 2020 Electricity Supply (International Energy Agency). Biofuels accounted for 2.2 percent of Japan's electricity supply, waste incineration for 2.2 percent, wind for 0.84 percent, and geothermal for 0.28 percent. Other sources – which IEA defines as "generation from chemical heat and other sources" – accounted for 1.8 percent. The next sections describe these trends in greater detail.

As time has passed since March 2011, new and revised policies have supported these electricity supply source changes, with relationships and resilience priorities as a backdrop. Several longer-term policy changes have emerged, as well as policymaking process and structural changes. Some of these process and structural changes, including climate change commitments and electricity market liberalization, examined later in this chapter, are impacting further policy changes that affect Japan's electricity supply mix. As we will see, some of these changes have bolstered Japan's energy system resilience by improving engineering and social resilience aspects of existing nuclear and coal-fired power generation. Other

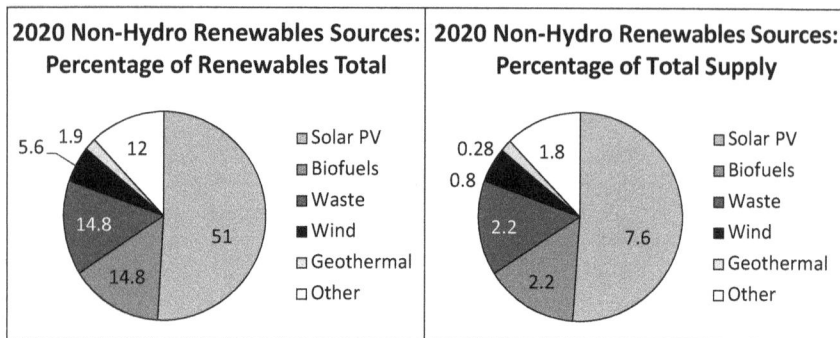

2020 Non-Hydro Renewables Sources: Percentage of Renewables Total	2020 Non-Hydro Renewables Sources: Percentage of Total Supply

Figure 5.6 Non-Hydro Renewables Sources in 2020 Electricity Supply

Source: Data from International Energy Agency, 2021a.

changes have shifted Japan's energy system toward transformation to build socio-ecological resilience. Economic resilience remains both a driver and a challenge to these shifts.

Energy System Flux: Nuclear Nixed or Not?

As mentioned, nuclear power represented 26 percent of Japan's electricity supply in 2010, per Figure 5.4. Following the 2011 Fukushima nuclear disaster, the Japanese government declared reconsideration of the 2010 Strategic Energy Plan, including revision of the planned increase in nuclear power to 50 percent of Japan's electricity supply by 2030, depicted in Figure 5.7: 2030 Electricity Supply Percentage Targets in 2010 (Ministry of Economy, Trade and Industry). As discussed, nuclear power's share dropped precipitously to 1.5 percent in 2012, and remained at zero from 2013 to 2015. And yet, the majority of interviewees suggested that many policymakers and the electric utilities still support nuclear power's continued major role in Japan's energy system. Resilience priorities serve as drivers for this ongoing support, and they also have influenced the policy outcomes.

Resilience priorities and relationship clout have driven both incremental and transformative changes, as well as stasis in some aspects of Japan's energy system since the Fukushima disaster. The Japanese government has made largely incremental changes to the role and implementation of nuclear power, accompanied by transformative safety regulation changes. While they have modified the pre-Fukushima target for a huge increase in nuclear power's share of electricity supply, the shift away from nuclear power as a baseload electricity source has not been codified in any policies produced since the disaster. In fact, the 2014, 2018 and 2021 Strategic Energy Plans specifically state that nuclear power remains an important baseload source for long-term energy supply stability.

**2030 Electricity Supply
Percentage Targets in 2010**

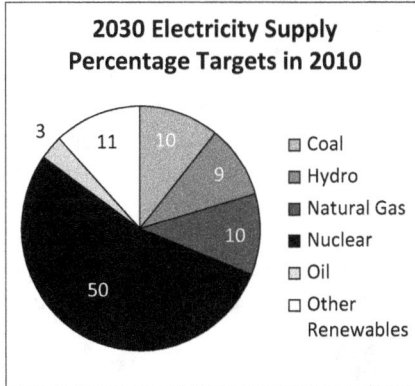

Pie chart values: 3, 11, 10, 9, 10, 50

Legend:
- Coal
- Hydro
- Natural Gas
- Nuclear
- Oil
- Other Renewables

Figure 5.7 2030 Electricity Supply Percentage Targets in 2010

Source: Data from Ministry of Economy, Trade and Industry, 2010.

However, the Fukushima disaster has created several institutional roadblocks to nuclear power expansion. First, some changes to policymakers' relationships with the electric utilities have challenged nuclear power's central role in Japan's energy system. New LDP politicians are less likely to support nuclear power. Government interviewee G21 explained that

> the new LDP Diet members did not depend on utility companies or utility unions or nuclear issues, so they didn't get votes or money from utilities for this election. So many new LDP members . . . don't want to be involved in nuclear issues, or they don't want to be seen by the public as nuclear promoters.

> (August 2013)

This comment highlights a second complication facing policymakers' overt promotion of nuclear power. Policymakers fear that outright support of nuclear power's return could foil attempts to rebuild public trust in government-led policymaking. G12 intimated that

> maybe METI's position is that we want to promote nuclear, but at the same time, we somehow have the face of the neutral people or face to the people which are opposing to nuclear. So from the viewpoint of the utilities, they have been complaining that METI is somehow not so aggressive. But from the viewpoint of the people who are opposing nuclear, still they see that METI is very close to the utilities.

> (May 2013)

Electric utility interviewees have expressed frustration with the government's lack of publicly voiced support for nuclear power. I15 said that while the electric utilities understand the government's need to build public trust, Japan's nuclear program cannot proceed without some signs of government support:

> The problem that mainly exists is that the government cannot clearly support these issues in public. Because of the politics. When they talk to industry, they say we support nuclear restarts, and in the future, they support new builds, and also fuel cycle. To the industry, but they cannot say that to the public, and they are saying that to the local government, sometimes, but it depends. They are comfortable to make a policy, but implementation of the policy should be done by the industry.
>
> (August 2013)

I15 noted that central government support and assurances of safety are necessary to convince local governments to accept restarts and new construction. Several government interviewees suggested that policymakers are awaiting the return of public trust before openly pursuing a pro-nuclear policy. We see these conflicting pressures on the Japanese government embodied in the Strategic Energy Plans in 2014, 2018, and 2021.

These policies on the direction of Japan's future energy system reflect an effort to reconcile public opinion on nuclear power with the utilities' resilience goals and the role of reactor restarts and nuclear power expansion in achieving them. The 2014 Strategic Energy Plan serves as the most prominent example. The Japanese government withdrew the original Strategic Energy Plan released in January 2014 after receiving 19,000 public comments reflecting opposition to the plan's inclusion of nuclear power as the key to electricity supply-demand stabilization. The plan released a few months later still contained language describing nuclear power as an "important baseload power source," but the revised version also included language on reducing nuclear power dependence. These contradictory statements on the future of nuclear power aimed to promote public trust by acquiescing to public demand for a decline in nuclear power use, while simultaneously signaling support for the utilities' investments and economic resilience goals through resumption of nuclear power. One section of the plan states that "Japan will minimize its dependency on nuclear power. Needless to say, that is the starting point for rebuilding Japan's energy policy" (Government of Japan, 2014b, 5). This stated aim of reducing nuclear dependency responds to the public demand for movement away from nuclear power. It also reflects the reality of the electric utilities' decommissioning plans, based on some older reactors' inability to comply with NRA guidelines. The report later caveats this nuclear reduction goal by adding that nuclear energy use "will be lowered to the extent possible . . . taking Japan's energy constraints into consideration, from the viewpoint of stable energy supply, cost reduction, global warming and maintaining nuclear technologies and human resources" (Government of Japan, 2014b, 24). This later section characterizes nuclear power as an "important baseload power source "to meet energy security, economic costs and efficiency and environmental goals (Government of Japan, 2014b, 24). The emphasis on nuclear power as an important baseload fuel signals to the electric utilities that the government supports continued use of nuclear power. Several electric utility interviewees explained that their firms sought this signal as a guide for their future investment plans. The assertion that the government will reduce nuclear dependency "to the extent possible" allowed both the government and the electric utilities the flexibility to determine what is possible. During my time as a negotiator on Japanese electricity market liberalization, METI officials often inserted this term to allow for flexibility, or even future disregard for the terms of an agreement.

These two sections of the report may seem incongruous, but they aimed to appeal separately to the public and the utilities. As G16 observed,

> I think that METI has been in a very fragile, uncertain position, pushed by one side and pushed another side. And it seems to have been just spending time to react to many pressures. But I think finally under DPJ the political pressure finally got METI to conclude the phasing out of nuclear power. But . . . because it is not a kind of wholehearted commitment of the bureaucracy . . . after LDP came back to power, the bureaucracy again pushed for another direction.
>
> (July 2013)

The Japanese government's delayed release of specific electricity supply source targets also reflects this challenge. The 2014 plan notably lacked an appendix, which in previous plans contained specific electricity supply source targets. Recognizing that any mention of a nuclear target would draw public criticism, policymakers chose to avoid targets completely by eliminating the appendix, said government interviewees. The 2014 plan's text lists all energy supply sources as important, while referencing nuclear safety concerns, fossil fuel import risks, the technical challenges associated with renewables, and the environmental problems with coal. After months of debate, METI's Fundamental Issues Subcommittee on Energy and Environment announced targets for specific fuel sources at the end of April 2015. As seen in Figure 5.8: 2030 Electricity Supply Percentage Targets in 2015 (Ministry of Economy, Trade and Industry), the 2030 targets announced in 2015 included 20 to 22 percent nuclear power, 3 percent oil, 27 percent natural gas, 26 percent coal, and 22 to 24 percent renewables. The nuclear target, while dramatically reduced from the 50 percent selected in 2010, still allowed for a share close to pre-Fukushima levels.

In addition to the Strategic Energy Plan language signaling the future return of nuclear power, the Japanese government implemented other measures to support the utilities' economic resilience goals. Coupled with the nuclear power target introduced in 2015, ANRE revised the Electricity Business Act's accounting provisions to enable the utilities to calculate decommissioning costs in 10-year increments. This revision mitigates the utilities' financial risks, facilitating decommissioning plans for older plants (World Nuclear Association, 2021).

2030 Electricity Supply Percentage Targets in 2015

□ Coal	
▨ Hydro	
▨ Natural Gas	
■ Nuclear	
□ Oil	
□ Other Renewables	

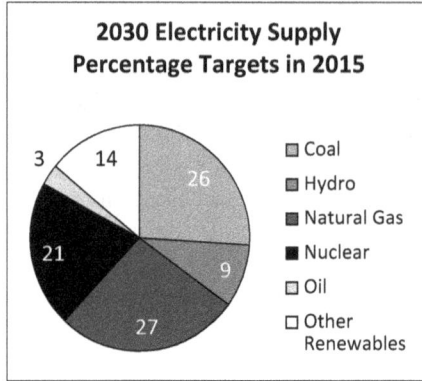

Figure 5.8 2030 Electricity Supply Percentage Targets in 2015
Source: Data from Government of Japan, 2014b.

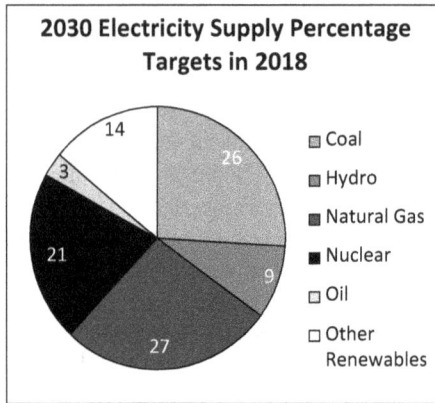

2030 Electricity Supply Percentage Targets in 2018

▨ Coal	
▨ Hydro	
■ Natural Gas	
■ Nuclear	
□ Oil	
□ Other Renewables	

Figure 5.9 2030 Electricity Supply Percentage Targets in 2018
Source: Data from Government of Japan, 2018.

The 2030 electricity supply source targets from 2018, shown in Figure 5.9: 2030 Electricity Supply Percentage Targets in 2018 (Ministry of Economy, Trade and Industry), reflect no change from the 2015 targets. The 2030 nuclear target from 2021, depicted in Figure 5.10: 2030 Electricity Supply Percentage Targets in 2021, remains unchanged from prior targets, despite modified targets for other sources, as discussed in the next sections. The 20 to 22 percent nuclear target reflects policymakers' focus on economic resilience, as well as antinuclear policymakers' prioritization of the climate change aspects of social resilience. Energy industry interviewees confided that in the post-disaster debate within the advisory

2030 Electricity Supply Percentage Targets in 2021

Coal — 19
Hydro — 11
Natural Gas — 27
Nuclear — 21
Oil — 2
Other Renewables — 27
Hydrogen & Ammonia — 1

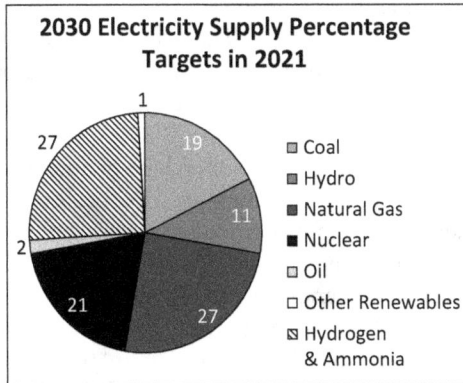

Figure 5.10 2030 Electricity Supply Percentage Targets in 2021
Source: Data from Government of Japan, 2021.

committee responsible for the proposed targets, even antinuclear committee members suggested a nuclear power target of 15 to 20 percent, while nuclear supporters proposed a 20–25 percent target.

Nuclear power remains listed as an important baseload source in the 5th Strategic Energy Plan, announced in 2018, and the 6th Plan, announced in 2021 (Government of Japan, 2018, 2021). Both plans use the same language to highlight the same reasons for retention of nuclear power. All of these reasons reflect economic and socio-ecological resilience priorities that overlap with the previously described 3Es factors that supported nuclear power use prior to the Fukushima disaster. The primary economic resilience factor described in both plans is nuclear plants' low and relatively stable operating costs. While this factor appeals to utility companies, it does not necessarily translate to lower electricity prices, the public's primary economic concern. The socio-ecological resilience factors listed as support for nuclear power as a baseload source in both plans include several energy security considerations. The plans describe nuclear power's role in offsetting the large amounts of fuel imports with a "semi-domestic," stable, efficient energy source. The semi-domestic nature implies the Japanese government's plans to recycle imported uranium domestically for long-term reuse. Both plans also highlight environmental benefits of nuclear power as a low-carbon and non-emitting electricity supply source.

These priorities also resonate with some of JAERO's 2017–2020 public opinion poll results described earlier in this chapter, which showed high public concern regarding global climate change. However, the 2018 poll reflected little public interest in greenhouse gas emissions reduction goals (13 percent), and almost no interest in comparative CO_2 emissions rates from different electricity generation sources (5.5 percent) (JAERO, 2018). This discrepancy in priorities indicates a potential disconnect between government prioritization of nuclear power as a climate change solution and public perceptions of this linkage between nuclear power and climate change mitigation. These two categories – greenhouse gas reduction goals and comparative supply sources' CO_2 emissions rates – do not appear in subsequent polls, complicating a comparison of this public opinion context for the 2021 plan.

The two plans also emphasize that continued use of nuclear power relies on the premise of safety. The 2018 plan acknowledges the need for the government to prioritize safety under any circumstances and dedicate all effort necessary to eliminate public concern. This statement suggests an underlying challenge regarding the Japanese public's zero tolerance for risk. To mitigate this challenge, the 2018 plan describes trust in the NRA's expert judgment and acceptance of the need to conform to NRA regulations that the plan depicts as "the strictest level of regulatory standards in the world" (Government of Japan, 2018). With this context, the 2018 plan text asks for local community and national public understanding and cooperation for reactors restarts.

The 2018 plan also addresses safety in the broader context of public risk perceptions and regulatory compliance. The plan acknowledges that in the case of nuclear power, the "'myth of safety' created the impression that if the criteria and requirements set by GOJ and business operators were satisfied, there would be no risk, requiring no further consideration of it" (Government of Japan, 2018, 113). Recognizing this problem's implications for creation and destruction of public trust, the plan identifies this "myth of safety" as a "major obstacle to the effort to expand opportunities for all levels of the society to deepen their understanding of the energy circumstances" (Government of Japan, 2018, 113). Echoing several government and academic interviewees' comments on the challenges of addressing the Japanese public's zero risk tolerance, the plan highlights the need to provide information on risks to the public, emphasizing that "such information make clear that risks always exist" (Government of Japan, 2018, 113). This movement toward transparency, risk communication, and relationship reframing offers lessons applicable to all energy technologies and all aspects of the energy system. The end of this chapter illuminates these lessons in greater detail.

Aligning with the public demand for a reduction in nuclear power use, the 2018 plan asserts a reduction "to the extent possible" based on energy conservation, renewable energy introduction, and thermal plant efficiency (Government of Japan, 2018). This language does not commit to a specific level of reduction, and its linkage of such reduction to advancement of renewables suggests the importance of incentives to promote renewables implementation. In 2019, nuclear power retained its position as the largest energy sector recipient of public spending, at 36 percent of total Japanese government spending on energy (International Energy Agency, 2021b, 112). The 2021 plan uses similar language to link conditional nuclear power reductions to expansion of renewable energy use, citing both renewables and nuclear power as elements of Japan's carbon neutrality and emissions reduction goals.

The 2021 plan recognizes that public trust in nuclear power has not yet returned and acknowledges the need to respond to issues regarding spent nuclear fuel, the nuclear fuel cycle, final disposal of nuclear waste, and decommissioning of nuclear plants. The 2020 and 2021 JAERO polls reflect moderate public concern regarding some of these specific issues, with around 20–23 percent concerned about spent fuel storage, and 37–38 percent concerned about waste disposal (JAERO, 2020, 2021). Through their electricity supply source targets and policy language, the 2018 and 2021 Strategic Energy Plans thus reflect policymakers' efforts to balance the utilities' economic resilience goals with the public's concerns regarding nuclear safety risks and environmental risks to social resilience.

As previously mentioned, the NRA's formation as a new regulatory agency comprises a key element of the Japanese government's strategy for addressing these risks and regaining public trust. This chapter's section on safety regulation changes discusses in more detail the NRA features designed to foster this trust. Additionally, the NRA's activities directly have impacted Japan's future nuclear power supply in positive and negative ways.

The NRA has advanced nuclear power's return to Japan's electricity mix by implementing new safety regulations that build engineering resilience of nuclear infrastructure. The NRA also has implemented related regulations that improve social resilience, such as development of evacuation plans and other emergency response measures for future nuclear accidents. The utilities' compliance with these new regulations has enabled reactor restarts to begin. The NRA's effectiveness at promoting engineering and social resilience will affect the electric utilities' long-term planning for nuclear power to achieve their economic and socio-ecological resilience goals. G4 identified this effect, asserting that the creation of the NRA will impact not only nuclear plant safety, "but also the business strategy of the utility companies." Whether creation of the NRA leads to reinforcement of nuclear power's role in the existing system or fosters a dramatic shift away from nuclear-generated electricity depends on three factors.

First, the NRA's pace and rate of approvals for nuclear reactor restarts and approval of plants under construction already has influenced some utilities' plans for nuclear plant restarts, relicensing, decommissioning and construction. These decisions have reflected the utilities' economic resilience goals. NRA restart and construction approvals will continue to shape the utilities' decisions based on these goals, thus affecting related electricity supply source ratios. As of the end of 2021, ten nuclear units have resumed operation, per Table 5.2: Status of Japan's Post-Disaster Nuclear Reactors as of December 2021. The first two approved reactor restarts for Kyushu's Sendai units 1 and 2 commenced in 2015. Eight additional reactors restarted between 2015 and 2021, raising the share of nuclear power in Japan's electricity supply back up to the previously noted 3.8 percent in 2020. These include Shikoku's Ikata unit 3, KEPCO's Takahama units 3 and 4, KEPCO's Ohi units 3 and 4, Kyushu's Genkai units 3 and 4, and KEPCO's Mihama unit 3. The NRA has approved seven more units for restart, and the regulator is vetting applications for restarts of 9 more units and the start of two new

Table 5.2 Status of Japan's Post-Disaster Nuclear Reactors as of December 2021

Plant	Operator	Operation Start	Status	Date
Fukushima Daiichi 1	TEPCO	1971	Decommissioning begun	3/2011
Fukushima Daiichi 2	TEPCO	1974	Decommissioning begun	3/2011
Fukushima Daiichi 3*	TEPCO	1976	Decommissioning begun	3/2011
Fukushima Daiichi 4	TEPCO	1978	Decommissioning begun	3/2011
Fukushima Daiichi 5	TEPCO	1978	Decommissioning decision	12/2013
Fukushima Daiichi 6	TEPCO	1979	Decommissioning decision	12/2013
Fukushima Daini 1	TEPCO	1982	Decommissioning decision	7/2019
Fukushima Daini 2	TEPCO	1984	Decommissioning decision	7/2019
Fukushima Daini 3	TEPCO	1985	Decommissioning decision	7/2019
Fukushima Daini 4	TEPCO	1987	Decommissioning decision	7/2019
Genkai 1	Kyushu	1975	Decommissioning begun	2017
Genkai 2	Kyushu	1981	Decommissioning decision	2/2019
Genkai 3*	Kyushu	1994	Restarted	3/2018
Genkai 4	Kyushu	1997	Restarted	6/2018
Hamaoka 3	Chubu	1987	NRA restart review	6/2015
Hamaoka 4*	Chubu	1993	NRA restart review	2/2014
Hamaoka-5	Chubu	2005	Not yet applied for restart	
Higashidori 1	Tohoku	2005	NRA restart review	6/2014
Ikata 1	Shikoku	1977	Decommissioning begun	2019
Ikata 2	Shikoku	1982	Decommission plan approved	10/2020
Ikata 3*	Shikoku	1994	Restarted	8/2016
Kashiwazaki-Kariwa 1	TEPCO	1985	Not yet applied for restart	
Kashiwazaki-Kariwa 2	TEPCO	1990	Not yet applied for restart	
Kashiwazaki-Kariwa 3*	TEPCO	1993	Not yet applied for restart	
Kashiwazaki-Kariwa 4	TEPCO	1994	Not yet applied for restart	
Kashiwazaki-Kariwa 5	TEPCO	1990	Not yet applied for restart	
Kashiwazaki-Kariwa 6	TEPCO	1996	Restart approved	12/2017
Kashiwazaki-Kariwa 7	TEPCO	1997	Restart approved	12/2017

Plant	Operator	Operation Start	Status	Date
Mihama 1	KEPCO	1970	Decommissioning begun	4/2017
Mihama 2	KEPCO	1972	Decommissioning begun	4/2017
Mihama 3	KEPCO	1976	Restarted	6/2021
Ohi 1**	KEPCO	1979	Decommissioning begun	12/2019
Ohi 2**	KEPCO	1979	Decommissioning begun	12/2019
Ohi 3	KEPCO	1991	Restarted	3/2018
Ohi 4	KEPCO	1993	Restarted	3/2018
Oma**	EPDC/ J-Power	N/A	Under construction/ NRA start review	12/2014
Onagawa 1	Tohoku	1984	Decommissioning begun	8/2019
Onagawa 2	Tohoku	1995	Restart approved	2/2020
Onagawa 3*	Tohoku	2002	Not yet applied for restart	
Sendai 1	Kyushu	1984	Restarted	8/2015
Sendai 2	Kyushu	1984	Restarted	10/2015
Shika 1**	Hokuriku	1993	Not yet applied for restart	
Shika 2	Hokuriku	2006	NRA restart review	8/2014
Shimane 1	Chugoku	1974	Decommissioning begun	4/2017
Shimane 2*	Chugoku	1989	Restart approved	9/2021
Shimane 3	Chugoku	N/A	Under construction/ NRA start review	8/2018
Takahama 1	KEPCO	1974	Restart approved	4/2016
Takahama 2	KEPCO	1975	Restart approved	4/2016
Takahama 3*	KEPCO	1985	Restarted	1/2016
Takahama 4*	KEPCO	1985	Restarted	1/2016
Tokai 2**	JAPC	1978	Restart approved	9/2018
Tomari 1	Hokkaido	1989	NRA restart review	7/2013
Tomari 2	Hokkaido	1991	NRA restart review	7/2013
Tomari 3*	Hokkaido	2009	NRA restart review	7/2013
Tsuruga 1	JAPC	1970	Decommissioning begun	4/2017
Tsuruga 2**	JAPC	1987	NRA restart review	11/2015

Source: Data from World Nuclear Association, 2021; Japan Nuclear Safety Institute, 2021; International Atomic Energy Agency, 2021.

* Reactors approved to use MOX fuel
** Additional reactors included in FEPC's future plans for MOX fuel use

units, Chugoku's Shimane 3 and EPDC/J-Power's Oma plant (Nuclear Regulation Authority, 2021).

The second factor guiding the NRA's effect on the future of nuclear power involves how the NRA's new guidelines shape the electric utilities' responses to relevant required changes to existing reactors and future reactor design. These responses reflect the utilities' perceptions of NRA influence on achievement of their economic resilience priorities.

The third factor involves how public trust in the NRA's guidelines and decisions will influence public support for reactor restarts and new construction, which can help or hinder the utilities' plans. The NRA's regulations and their enforcement aim to rebuild public trust in nuclear power and the Japanese government's ability to prevent and manage related risks. Government interviewees indicated that energy policymakers believe that regaining public trust will facilitate restarts of reactors approved by the NRA. G16 explained that "the NRA is trying to . . . create trust. And if the public sees that it is doing its job well, then public acceptance of nuclear power will be increased" (July 2013).

The NRA issued new nuclear reactor safety guidelines in June 2013. These standards address perceived vulnerabilities based on the Fukushima accident, including sea wall construction, filters for radiation removal, fire protection, secondary control rooms, and fault lines. For further details on these standards, see Kishimoto (2017). The electric utilities must implement the new standards for existing reactors and new construction. The new guidelines also allow a one-time 20-year extension for plants that have or surpassed reached their 40-year lifetime. After issuing the new guidelines, the NRA began reviewing applications for nuclear reactor restarts.

However, in creating the NRA as a tool to rebuild trust, the Japanese government may have set it up to fail, endangering the return of nuclear power. As previously mentioned, government interviewees indicated that the government felt obligated to convey that nuclear power held zero risk, since the public would not have agreed to nuclear power expansion if associated with any risk. The NRA represents a vehicle to restore trust in nuclear power and the government's ability to manage safety risks, but if this trust is based on the belief that the NRA can guarantee zero risk, it will collapse when another accident occurs. Actions at the local level indicate that some communities already fear the NRA's inability to guarantee zero risk, challenging reactor restarts.

In 2015, Fukui District Court rejected local citizens' application for an injunction to prevent restarts of KEPCO's Takahama nuclear power plant units 3 and 4. The NRA had approved the restarts, and the injunction request reflects continued public distrust in the new regulatory agency's ability to manage safety risks. In 2016, the nearby Otsu District Court rejected restarts of the same two units. While the Osaka High Court lifted the injunction in 2017, the district court's criticism of the NRA standards as inadequate to guarantee safety reflects public distrust of the NRA's regulations. Shikoku's Ikata 3 unit also has faced several injunctions imposed by the Hiroshima High Court, which led to a temporary shutdown in 2017–2018 and another in 2020–2021. In both cases, local residents and the court questioned the NRA's assessment of safety risks associated with nearby Mt. Aso's volcanic eruption potential.

In addition to revealing continued distrust, these public rejections of restart approvals also demonstrate growing public clout in energy policy decisions at the local level. Minami-soma's town and city councils' refusal to continue with Tohoku Electric's planned construction of the Namie-Odaka plant represents another example. Some policymakers' statements recognize this shift. For instance, in an October 2021 media interview, METI Minister Hagiuda announced, "We will work to restart Japan's nuclear reactors with a focus on safety and with the understanding of local communities" (Nikkei staff writers, 2021).

The electric utilities' criticism of the NRA has further weakened the regulator's credibility, deepening public distrust in the new regulations. If the electric utilities undermine public confidence in the regulator, they challenge their own ability to continue nuclear power use.

The electric utilities' criticism of the NRA stems in part from frustration over the previously described agency's isolation from utility input on regulations.

Given the electric utilities' focus on economic resilience, the NRA's new regulations also have catalyzed retirement of many older plants that would be costly to upgrade to meet the new standards. As Table 5.3 reflects, as of the end of 2021, eight electric utilities have commenced decommissioning of 13 reactors in addition to the mandated decommissioning of the six Fukushima Daiichi units. These reactors include KEPCO's Mihama units 1 and 2, Japan Atomic Power Company's (JAPC) Tsuruga unit 1, Kyushu's Genkai units 1 and 2, Chugoku's Shimane unit 1, JAPC's Tokai, Chubu's Hamaoka units 1 and 2, Shikoku's Ikata unit 1, KEPCO's Ohi units 1 and 2, and Tohoku's Onagawa unit 1. The NRA began reviewing Shikoku's decommissioning plan for Ikata unit 2 in March 2020. TEPCO's four Fukushima Daini units also are slated for decommissioning.

Several electric utility interviewees indicated that the NRA regulations also may deter new plant construction. Interviewee I11 noted that "of course, the utility company wants to continue construction, but the new rule is 'always safe'" (June 2013). As a result, said interviewee I12, "brand new projects will be difficult in Japan. I don't think new nuclear plant activity will start." EPDC/J-Power's construction of one new reactor, the aforementioned Oma plant, has continued, though NRA reviews of safety upgrades have delayed completion. Oma's planned 1383 MWe is half the output of decommissioned Fukushima Daiichi units 1–4. As mentioned earlier, Chugoku Electric also plans to complete Shimane Unit 3, which is almost the same size as Oma.

Government-utility conflict and cooperation, NRA regulations, public distrust and resilience priorities have influenced the future of Japan's nuclear fuel cycle program, as well. The previously discussed government-electric utility conflict over fuel cycle responsibility sheds light on the puzzling discussion of fuel reprocessing program advancement in the context of limited reactor operations. Energy industry executive I15 explained that if the Rokkasho nuclear fuel reprocessing facility does not start operating soon, the nuclear plants will need to remain off, since the spent fuel sites are filling up. The Fukushima disaster also intensified the battle between the government and the electric utilities over responsibility for the nuclear fuel cycle. I15 asserted, "If METI pushes industry to start up Rokkasho too much, they fear industry may say then the government should take responsibility for the back end of fuel cycle" (August 2013). At the same time, government interviewee G6 confided that some electric utilities secretly continue to hope for the end of the fuel cycle. I15 did not dispute this claim, but offered a caveat. "Of course, there will be some opponents, even in industry, but in general, we understand that we need the fuel cycle in any case." The utilities and some policymakers view reprocessing as a key piece of Japan's strategy for economic and social resilience.

This said, the NRA's new regulations also have affected construction of Rokkasho's reprocessing and MOX fuel fabrication facilities, simultaneously benefiting engineering and long-term economic resilience while also challenging short-term economic and social resilience. The NRA's role in resurrecting public trust has required the regulator to proceed with caution in approving the Rokkasho nuclear fuel reprocessing facility. Repeated revisions of construction plans for Japan's Rokkasho nuclear fuel reprocessing facility in response to the NRA's review have delayed its completion significantly. Regulatory rigor promotes safety and design resilience to physical shocks, protecting against damage costs. At the same time, the delays and requirements have extended the timeframe for investments in construction, as well as the time period for on-site storage of nuclear waste. In 2020, the NRA approved the Rokkasho facility as compliant with safety standards, and as of the end of 2021, the regulator is reviewing the plant's design and construction plans. JNFL aims to complete the reprocessing facility by September 2022; however, at a January 2022 press conference, NRA Chairman Fuketa characterized this completion date as "extremely ambitious" (Nuclear Regulation Authority, 2022).

Co-located with the Rokkasho reprocessing facility, the MOX fuel fabrication facility commenced construction in late 2010, shortly before the Fukushima disaster occurred. It has faced similar delays. This facility also passed the NRA's safety review in 2020 and is undergoing the regulator's design and construction plan review. JNFL expects completion in 2024, two years after the reprocessing plant's planned completion. The reprocessing plant will remove spent nuclear fuel from storage at reactor sites, serving the dual purpose of preparing the fuel for reuse in reactors and contributing to resolution of the utilities' challenge of high-level nuclear waste storage and disposal.

This said, some U.S. government officials have voiced concerns that reprocessed fuel will pose a proliferation threat without the domestic fabrication plant to complete the plutonium conversion process to reactor fuel. In July 2018, the Japan Atomic Energy Commission (JAEC) issued the "Basic Principles on Japan's Utilization of Plutonium," which commits to reducing Japan's plutonium stockpile and supports the role of the MOX fuel fabrication facility, in conjunction with the reprocessing plant and MOX use in nuclear power plants, in doing so (Japan Atomic Energy Commission, 2018).

The termination of FBR Monju has intensified policymakers' and utilities' focus on MOX use in commercial reactors to reduce the spent fuel stored at their sites. Following a series of regulatory violations during Monju's sporadic operation since the 1995 accident, the Japanese government announced the decision to decommission the prototype reactor in 2016. This decision elicited initial opposition from the governor of Fukui Prefecture, the host of the Monju site. He expressed concern over economic resilience challenges through lost jobs and subsidies, as well as social resilience concerns regarding the fate of existing spent nuclear fuel stored at plants in the prefecture. He ultimately agreed to the decommissioning in 2017, and NRA approved the JAEA's decommissioning plan in 2018.

Additional decommissioning of some of the reactors planned for MOX use and the delay in reactor restarts have complicated the utilities' options. In February 2021, FEPC revised the utilities' pre-2011 plan for MOX use in 16–18 reactors by 2015, announcing a lengthened and reduced goal of 12 reactors using MOX fuel by 2030 (Federation of Electric Power Companies of Japan, 2021). As Table 5.3 indicates, as of the end of 2021, four of the ten reactors originally approved for MOX use have restarted. Of the rest, one is a Fukushima Daiichi unit, one is approved for restart, two are undergoing NRA restart review, and two have not applied for restart review. Of the reactors FEPC identified for MOX use by 2030, which include these nine operable reactors, two of them – KEPCO's Ohi units 1 and 2 – have begun decommissioning. The additional reactors identified include one approved for restart, one under NRA review, one that has not yet applied for restart, and one under construction. The plan also includes the possibility of a TEPCO reactor restart but does not name a specific unit.

The 2021 Strategic Energy Plan contains several pages dedicated to the fuel cycle, including a reference to the aforementioned utilities' plan to implement pluthermal in at least 12 nuclear reactors by 2030. Much of the plan's language on the fuel cycle is adapted from FEPC's December 2020 statement on the pluthermal program (The Federation of Electric Power Companies of Japan, 2020). Reflecting utility and government priorities for economic resilience, as well spent fuel solutions to promote social resilience, the 2021 plan links nuclear waste disposal and the fuel cycle policy. It describes spent fuel reprocessing and use of MOX fuel as an effective use of resources and a means of reducing the volume of high-level radioactive waste. The text also solicits public cooperation, several times mentioning efforts to secure understanding and approval from local municipalities and the international community for fuel reprocessing and the pluthermal program. The reference to the international community suggests a response to the aforementioned proliferation concerns expressed by U.S. officials, substantiated by the plan's recognition of the effects of Rokkasho completion delays and Monju decommissioning, as well as a commitment to reducing plutonium stockpiles and avoiding stockpiling of plutonium not planned for use in reactor fuel. The plan also describes planned efforts on R&D to establish reprocessing and disposal technologies for used MOX fuel by the latter half of the 2030s.

The 2021 plan asserts that the knowledge and technology acquired from Monju research, operation and decommissioning will be applied to future R&D on FBR technology. This adaptation of existing technology based on acquired knowledge and lessons from accidents can align with ecological resilience. Inclusion of FBR R&D in the plan signals an intent to continue further incremental changes to retain nuclear power in Japan's energy mix, aligning with economic resilience priorities based on prior investment.

Oil's Temporary Rise

Government and utility risk perceptions, as well as economic and socio-ecological resilience priorities, have continued to influence oil use in Japan's electricity mix. After a steep decline since the 1970s oil crises, oil partially replaced nuclear power after the Fukushima nuclear disaster. As seen in Figure 5.4, oil use rose from 6.7 percent in 2010 to 17.5 percent of Japan's 2012 electricity supply. The 2014 Strategic Energy Plan characterizes oil as a "peaking power source, whose power output can respond quickly and flexibly to the situation of electricity demand in spite of high cost" (Government of Japan, 2014b, 21). The plan describes oil as politically risky, but useful as an alternative in emergencies.

Based on this perception of oil's geopolitical risks, the temporary increase in oil use as a replacement for nuclear power was short-lived. The government's three percent target for oil's role in electricity supply announced in April 2015 reflected continuation of the pre-Fukushima suppression of oil use, as seen in Figure 5.8. Both the 2015 and 2018 plans designate oil as a "peaking power source" that remains important (Government of Japan, 2018). Figure 5.5 shows that oil accounted for 4.7 percent of Japan's electricity supply in 2020. As Figures 5.9 and 5.10 show, the 2018 and 2021 plans include a three percent 2030 target for oil use. In the context of electricity production, the 2021 plan acknowledges Japan's declining trend in oil use for power production, while anticipating that oil will retain a role as an adaptable fuel source that can be used in emergency situations when substitute fuels are unavailable. This characterization, as well as the plans' discussion of diversification of oil supplies to minimize supply risk, reflects the government's and utilities' socio-ecological resilience goals.

Natural Gas Powers Up

Economic resilience priorities and risk perceptions also have framed the role of natural gas in Japan's electricity mix since the Fukushima disaster. As previously mentioned, the shutdown of all nuclear reactors after the disaster led to a massive natural gas increase. The percentage of natural gas in Japan's electricity supply rocketed from 27 percent in 2010 to 38.4 percent in 2012, per Figure 5.4. And yet, the 2014 and 2018 Strategic Energy Plans classify natural gas not as a base-load source, but as an "intermediate power source" (Government of Japan, 2014b, 25, 2018, 20). This characterization reflects policymakers' expectation, shared by the electric utilities, that nuclear power would reclaim a percentage of the electricity supply currently produced by natural gas since the disaster. G7 high-lighted this expectation: "Frankly speaking, from the energy policy side, ambiguity about nuclear energy is really a big problem. So right now natural gas is supporting our energy supply, but apparently, there is a big risk . . . supply risk. And also we have price risk" (March 2013). This view reflects policymakers' and electric utili-ties' mutual focus on energy security and economic resilience risks associated with longer-term natural gas use. The 2014 plan cites the low emissions and flexibility of natural gas in responding to electricity demand, but it also cautioned against overdependence due to price fluctuations, aligning with policymakers' and utili-ties' economic resilience goals. The 27 percent 2030 target announced in 2015, a large jump from the 10 percent target announced in 2010, also reflects these goals. Describing natural gas as the lowest carbon emitting fossil fuel, with supply stabilized due to U.S. shale gas availability, the 2018 plan includes a return to 2010 levels with a 27 percent natural gas target by 2030, as shown in Figure 5.9. How-ever, in 2020, per Figure 5.5, natural gas still accounted for 37.7 percent of Japan's electricity supply. The 2021 plan contains the same target, as seen in Figure 5.10, as well as similar explanations of benefits, while adding a description of opportuni-ties for natural gas to support renewable power generation and employ hydrogen co-firing. The 2021 plan also highlights the need for supply source diversification to mitigate price instability, reflecting policymakers' and utilities' economic resil-ience focus.

Coal's Shifting Role

Economic and social resilience priorities have framed Japan's post-Fukushima coal use trajectory. Despite the Japanese government's decarbonization commitments, the Fukushima accident promoted continued cooperation between METI and the electric utilities on coal use, with the need to fill the nuclear generation gap as a catalyst. The disaster's removal of nuclear generation from the mix also forced MOE officials to reluctantly provide institutional support for coal use expansion. However, decarbonization commitments have urged replacement of older, inef-ficient coal plants, while new plant construction continue, with applications for Japan's planned hydrogen economy, as described in the next section.

Coal use increased slightly from 27 percent in 2010 to 29.1 percent in 2012, as Figure 5.4 shows. However, the 2014 Strategic Energy Plan states that coal "is now being re-evaluated as an important base-load power supply because it involves the lowest geopolitical risk and has the lowest price per unit of heat energy among fossil fuels" (Government of Japan, 2014b, 25). The 2014 Strategic Energy Plan's reference to reevaluation of coal as an "important baseload source" reflects the electric utilities' economic resilience goals, enabling them to invest in cheap electricity sources, especially in the context of price competition emerging from market liberalization. G2 noted the manufacturing sector's influence on the government's and electric utilities' promotion of coal use: "METI is increasing coal power because industry wants that." A METI document explains that this policy shift aims to "create an environment that facilitates smooth investment by private enterprises in highly efficient thermal power generation" (Government of Japan, 2014a).

Paving the way for this coal expansion policy was MOE's 2013 agreement to expedite environmental impact assessments for coal plants, shortening them from three years to one year. Electric utility interviewee I21 explained that "actually, before the Fukushima accident, utility companies were not allowed to build coal power plants, but after the Fukushima accident, I think the Environment Ministry has to approve for the utilities new coal power building" (May 2014). MOE also agreed to expedite environmental impact assessments for coal plants. I21 suggested that the electric utilities pushed for this change. "I think FEPC was giving some pressure to change the rule to the Environment Ministry."

MOE's cooperation with the electric utilities to promote coal use also strengthened due to a shift in public priorities after the Fukushima disaster. As the JAERO polls indicated, public pressure to stabilize electricity rates rose, then waned as climate change concerns became more pressing. Government interviewee G7 said that "after March 11, there is a strong request from the public that we should stabilize the rates of the power sector as much as possible, we should avoid the rise of the rates as much as possible" (March 2013). G7 explained that "without nuclear power, coal-fired power plants are one strong option. But there is little future sense of building power plants because of the assessment process, so that's why they have a discussion."

At the end of 2014, the electric utilities, gas companies, and large manufacturers announced plans for a major coal plant expansion, with 28 new plants expected to generate power by 2027. The government's 2015 coal target aimed for 26 percent of Japan's electricity supply by 2030. Beginning in 2017, the utilities began to cancel some of this planned construction, but as of 2019, 21 new plants are still planned by 2030 (Reuters Staff, 2019a). In the 2018 Strategic Energy Plan, coal remains listed as a "base-load power source" due to 24-hour operation stability and low cost, reflecting economic resilience goals. Acknowledging the social resilience challenges of greenhouse gas emissions and aligning with the planned new construction, the plan states the goals of inefficient plan phaseouts coupled with promotion of "conversion to high efficiency and next-generation coal thermal power generation" (Government of Japan, 2018, 24). The 2018 plan contains a continued 2030 coal target of 26 percent (Government of Japan, 2018).

The 2021 Strategic Energy Plan reflects a compromise between the utilities' economic resilience priorities and MOE's social resilience focus, particularly emissions reductions. The plan includes continued reliance on coal, describing thermal power as an important electricity source that supported electricity supply resilience and stability following the Fukushima disaster. However, aligning with the Suga Cabinet's April 2021 announcement of a 46 percent emissions reduction target below 2013 levels by 2030, the plan couples this continued coal use with decarbonization technologies such as carbon capture, utilization and storage (CCUS), as well as plans to shut down inefficient plants gradually. The 2021 plan's significantly reduced 2030 coal target of 19 percent, as seen in Figure 5.10, also embodies this compromise, emerging from the utilities' planned shutdowns of inefficient plants and the aforementioned canceled new construction.

Hydrogen and Ammonia Fire Up

In 2017, Japan's newly formed Ministerial Council on Renewable Energy, Hydrogen and Related Issues released Japan's Basic Hydrogen Strategy (Ministerial Council on Renewable Energy, Hydrogen and Related Issues, 2018). The strategy's joint focus on decarbonizing the power sector and reducing fuel procurement and supply costs reflects socio-ecological and economic resilience goals. In keeping with these goals, the 2021 Strategic Energy Plan introduces electricity production from hydrogen and ammonia as decarbonizing sources. The 2030 target of one percent, shown in Figure 5.10, carves out a small piece of Japan's electricity supply for these sources, and the plan identifies and pledges to address the cost challenges affecting economic resilience. The Japanese government's hydrogen production strategy bridges the thermal and renewable sectors in both hydrogen production and power generation. The 2021 plan proposes hydrogen sourced through imports, as well as "green" hydrogen from renewables electrolysis and "purple" hydrogen produced from high-temperature gas-cooled nuclear reactors. The latter is a type of nuclear reactor, and Japan's prototype in Ibaraki Prefecture, operated by the JAEA, received the NRA's restart approval and resumed operation in 2021. Regarding power generation from hydrogen and ammonia, the 2021 plan introduces a target of 30 percent hydrogen co-firing in gas-fired power generation or hydrogen-fired generation, as well as 20 percent ammonia co-firing in coal-fired power generation (Government of Japan, 2021, 77).

Renewables Newly Able or Not?

The Fukushima disaster catalyzed some growth of renewables through 2021, but policymakers' and utilities' economic resilience priorities and relationships constrained it. Some of the initial policy changes reflect efforts to boost renewables, but subsequent policy revisions curbed the transformative effects, until the 2021 Strategic Plan's release. This policy fluctuation reflects METI's position of balancing between the utilities' economic resilience priorities and the public's social resilience needs. Statements by policymakers also signal this balance. METI Minister Hagiuda's aforementioned comments supporting nuclear reactor restarts were coupled with a commitment to renewables expansion: "We will give top priority to the promotion of renewables and introduce them as much as possible" (The Asahi Shimbun, 2021).

The Fukushima disaster initially did not increase the electric utilities' interest in using renewables, climate change commitments' required replacement of inefficient coal plants notwithstanding. When asked about the future of renewables in 2013, electric utility interviewee I6 rolled his eyes. "This . . . investment is a very, very small amount. Less than one percent. In Japan, about nine to ten percent is renewables. Of that, most is hydro, but some of the small hydro is one of the investment areas, maybe." Sixteen confided that the rest of the renewables investment is intended as a perfunctory nod to government efforts to demonstrate renewables progress to the public. "The other is only to show how we do our best to introduce renewable power. Like wind power and solar system." I12 had an equally pessimistic view: "The DPJ insists renewable energy can assist the power source, but it's a very long way."

Government and electric utility interviewees presented divergent reasons for electric utility opposition to renewables. Electric utility engineers and pro-nuclear politicians and bureaucrats cited complicated technological issues that challenge grid and supply stability, including voltage and frequency fluctuation and rotor angle stability. Pro-renewables politicians and bureaucrats accused them of fabricating these problems to preserve market share and avoid having to purchase renewables that would jeopardize profits from low-cost operation of their existing power plants. The utilities' reluctance likely involves both sets of priorities, which affect engineering and economic resilience.

At the same time, the Fukushima disaster has prevented the electric utilities from overtly saying that they do not support renewables growth, for fear of appearing to oppose national energy security and environmental goals. In August 2013, government interviewee G21 explained, "It is very awkward or embarrassing for the utilities now. They can't say we are opposed to introduction of renewable energy." At the same time, government interviewee G16 argued that without real cooperation from the electric utilities, renewables entry remains difficult.

> [Y]ou need cooperation from industry to radically expand the role of renewables. And I think still, it is a very solid, determined position of Japanese utilities not to expand renewables. So there is every effort by them to deemphasize the importance or feasibility of renewable energy. And also they have many reasons to claim . . . it is the utilities network that can, that should manage the new world of renewable energy. So unless the utilities industry is a kind of positive or more welcoming stance, in general, you cannot expect the new, really meaningful progress toward renewable energy.
>
> (July 2013)

This situation has empowered pro-renewables officials in METI to move forward with renewable energy promotion policies. Concurrently, METI officials opposed to renewables expansion have undertaken policies to limit it. This dichotomy has resulted in conflicting policies that incentivize new entrants while limiting their access to the transmission grid.

The year after the disaster saw little growth in renewables. Renewable energy's share of Japan's electricity supply increased from 12.6 percent of Japan's 2010 electricity supply to just over 13 percent in 2012, as seen in Figure 5.4. Hydropower's share did not account for any of the increase, remaining steady at 8.1 percent from 2010 to 2012. Non-hydro renewables sources increased from 4.6 percent of Japan's 2010 electricity supply to 5.1 percent in 2012. Biofuels and waste accounted for most of this increase. Solar PV almost doubled, but it still accounted for only 0.67 percent by 2012 (International Energy Agency, 2021a).

Government statements and policies two years after the Fukushima disaster appeared geared toward a large renewables increase to replace nuclear power.

The most prominent measure was a feed-in tariff (FIT) introduced in 2012 under the Act concerning the Procurement of Renewable Electric Energy by Operators of Electric Utilities, heralded by the media as an important step toward building a robust renewables market in Japan, as well as a policy tool to reduce nuclear dependence (e.g., Ayoub and Naka, 2012). Media interviewee M1 asserted that the FIT "may not happen, if we don't have any Fukushima event (March 2013). And after the Fukushima event is a huge incentive to have a FIT system." The tariff covers solar, wind, geothermal, biomass, non-pumped hydropower and methane. METI's rates for each source from 2012 to 2021 are reflected in Figure 5.11: Japanese Feed-In Tariff Rates 2012–2021. As the figure shows, the tariffs for methane, wind greater than 20 KW, unused wood biomass less than 2 MW, small hydro less than 1 MW, wood waste, and waste biomass all remained relatively stable. The tariff for geothermal greater than 15 MW increased in 2015 and remained at this higher rate. Conversely, the tariff for solar installations greater than 10 KW has been set to decline steadily through the period.

As Japan's FIT catalyzed an influx of solar investments, the share of renewables more than doubled by 2020. Per Figure 5.5, hydropower's percentage rose very slightly, accounting for 8.6 percent of electricity supply in 2020. Non-hydro renewables almost tripled, accounting for 14.9 percent. As Figure 5.6 shows, solar PV accounted for slightly more than half of this amount, or 7.6 percent of Japan's

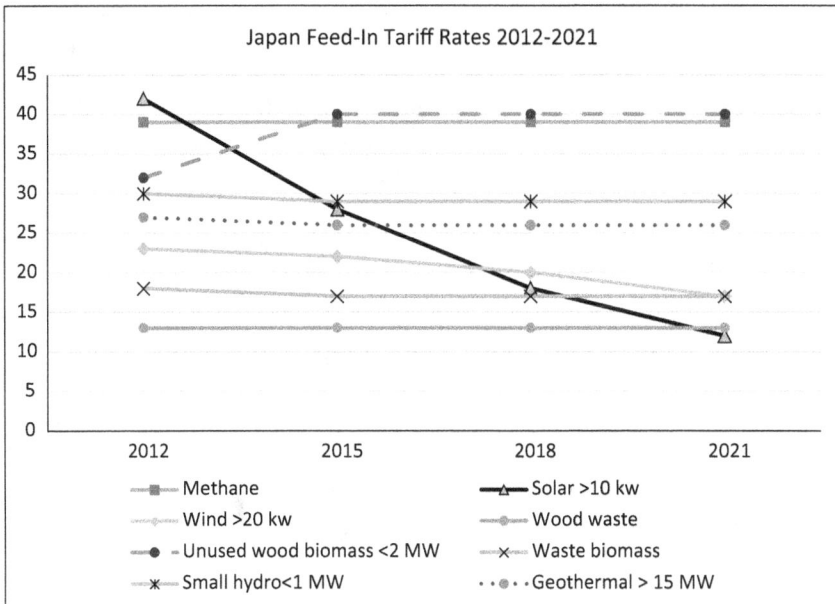

Figure 5.11 2030 Japanese Feed-In Tariff Rates 2012–2021

Source: Data from Agency for Natural Resources and Energy, 2015; Agency for Natural Resources and Energy, 2020; Ministry of Economy, Trade and Industry, 2021.

total electricity supply. Biofuels and waste each accounted for 2.2. percent of supply (14.8 percent of the renewables total), and wind accounted for 0.8 percent (5.6 percent of renewables). Despite a higher FIT rate than that offered for wind, geothermal accounted for 0.28 percent of Japan's electricity supply (1.9 percent of renewables). These trends reflect the economic resilience priorities of policymakers, the utilities, and some local businesses affected by siting. They also reflect the influence of additional policies that supported or counteracted the FIT's effects.

Following introduction of the FIT, ensuing policy changes have sent mixed messages regarding renewables promotion. These inconsistent policy changes reflect economic and ecological resilience concerns. The FIT generated a huge influx of solar projects, and the electric utilities asserted that the grid could not support them. Electric utility interviewees also asserted that passing through the high tariffs to consumers' electric bills would deepen public distrust, since the government did not inform the public of these future increases. I21 said, "We can collect additional fees through the electric bill, so actually, we don't have any impact from the FIT, but electric fee is going to get higher, so I think that's a problem, and that isn't fair for the customers as well" (May 2014). Citing economic resilience concerns of this pass-through of tariff costs to consumers, excessive market entry, and reduced equipment costs, policymakers responded with steady price reductions for solar and wind tariffs. They also approved a measure to limit renewables access to the grid, based on utility predictions of instability and oversupply.

However, NGO leaders asserted that METI's solar FIT reduction was based on grid calculations that included the return of many nuclear plants to operational status. Electric utility interviewees' comments on renewables corroborate this perception that policymakers' cooperation with the electric utilities was driving the direction of the FIT. METI's "calculations for the new rules are based on the premise that all of Japan's nuclear reactors, including those that are 40 years old, will be in operation. The result is nuclear power accounting for between 50 and 60 percent of the supply at Hokkaido Electric and Kyushu Electric during minimum load demand times, and the reduction of available renewable energy," the Japan Renewable Energy Foundation, said in a report released just after METI's announcement (Johnston, 2015).

These same NGOs highlighted restrictions on grid access that reflected the electric utilities' cooperation with METI to keep new entrants out of the market. NGO leader Iida argued that the inability to guarantee grid access through an independent third-party operator would cause the FIT to fail. Iida asserted that the market liberalization reforms do not include creation of a truly independent operator. Iida and M2 also posited that unbundling of generation from transmission can prevent the electric utilities from passing on high prices from the FIT to consumers. Asserting that "the utilities know this very well," M2 said that the government supported the electric utilities' economic resilience goals by implementing unbundling too late to stop electricity price hikes that could cause public opposition to the FIT. A decade after the Fukushima disaster, decarbonization commitments have combined with the slow return of nuclear power to promote changes to the FIT system, described later in this section.

The 2014 Strategic Energy Plan highlights renewables as a promising option for future energy supply. And yet, the 22 to 24 percent renewables target announced in 2015 and repeated in 2018 is only slightly higher than the 20 percent target included in the 2010 Strategic Energy Plan, as seen in Figure 5.8. Coupled with the 2030 coal and natural gas targets announced in 2015, the renewables targets reveal a focus on inexpensive coal and gas as interim solutions to Japan's electricity supply while awaiting nuclear reactors restarts. The 2030 renewables targets announced in 2015 and 2018 thus reflect the electric utilities' cooperative relationships with policymakers, as well as these groups' economic resilience priorities. Both the 2014 and 2018 Strategic Energy Plans emphasize the energy security benefits and challenges, as well as the economic difficulties associated with renewables. The low 2015 and 2018 targets for 2030 reflected limited expectations for electric utility adoption of renewables and new entrants' grid access. An unreleased study commissioned by MOE found that a 30 percent share of renewables by 2030 is feasible, according to Diet member Kono. Kono said that the electric utilities convinced METI to downplay this potential (Iwata, 2015). The 2021 Strategic Energy Plan's inclusion of a 36–38 percent target for renewables reflects policymakers' acknowledgment of the ability of renewables to fulfill a higher percentage of Japan's electricity mix than previously recognized.

The 2014 plan's language and the 2015 breakdown of individual renewable energy sources' 2030 targets and supply categories are equally contradictory. The government's relationships with the electric utilities and the public can help to explain these inconsistent policy signals. The plan's discussion of renewables responds to increased public demand for renewables after the Fukushima disaster. At the same time, the utilities' and policymakers' economic priorities for nuclear investment recovery shaped the plan's classifications and targets for each source. The plan classifies solar power, a major target of the FIT, as an "emergency power source" (Government of Japan, 2014b, 22), coupled with a 2030 target of seven percent announced in 2015. Hydropower, listed in the plan as a baseload energy source, was assigned a target of around nine percent of Japan's electricity supply by 2030, about two percent higher than the ratio before March 11. The plan lists pumped hydropower as a peak power source. Geothermal, which the plan also considers a baseload power source, had a measly one percent target for 2030. Biomass, with a target of around 4 percent, is not even assigned a category in the 2014 Strategic Energy Plan. Wind power, the other major FIT beneficiary, is referenced in the plan, also is not assigned a specific role in Japan's energy mix, along with a 1.5 percent 2030 target.

These targets present an inconsistent message in the context of Japan's FIT. Government interviewees explained some of the priorities driving this policy ambiguity. Diet member Kono asserted that at first, "METI was trying to introduce not a comprehensive FIT. Their original plan was really weird. It was even counterproductive." This unhelpful design suggests electric utility cooperation with METI to limit its effect. Kono said that passage of the FIT was supported in part by renewables advocates, joined by politicians who simply wanted to oust Kan. "I think even within DPJ, they were going to vote against Prime Minister Kan, and there was a vote of no confidence in the parliament. Kan said he will step down if he could accomplish three things . . . one of them was the FIT." Government interviewees suggested that Kan's determination to introduce the FIT was based on his anger toward the electric utilities for the Fukushima disaster. Kono said that the DPJ's FIT was based on METI's incomplete plan, but "it came to the LDP, and those power industry friendly politicians were not able to sit in front. That was the atmosphere back then, so we actually rewrote the bill so that a complete FIT would go through." Because of the Fukushima disaster, politicians could not appear to be overtly representing the electric utilities' interests. The high solar tariff "was a byproduct of political infighting."

Local institutional support for or opposition to renewables also has affected individual renewable sources. Ohira (2017) attributes the slow growth of renewables to a lack of linkages between them and local economies. The historical community ties formed by the nuclear industry via local subsidies was not replicated for renewables siting, and the FIT does not form such connections. The electric utilities' influence over local governments' decisions on renewables also has slowed market entry. New renewables players have been battling at the local level with the utilities over claims that introduction of renewables will destabilize the grid. Softbank megasolar is an example of an influential stakeholder who helped to resurrect the electricity market deregulation movement, only to be pushed back out of the market by the electric utilities' ability to persuade the local government that renewables instability could jeopardize energy security. Electric utility interviewee I1 confided that Softbank abandoned their megasolar plans "because of opposition from Hokkaido Electric Power and Tohoku Electric Power Company." And yet, the high FIT rate and local interest have generated solar projects across the nation.

Following the 2014 Strategic Energy Plan's release, economic resilience considerations suppressed onshore wind power development despite the high wind power tariff. Little investment emerged due to high installation costs for small-scale turbines.

The sudden interest in biomass, evidenced in an increased FIT and a four percent 2030 target announced in 2015, reflects electric utility cooperation with METI, but it also reveals the influence of policymakers from the Ministry of Agriculture, Forestry and Fisheries (MAFF) and the Ministry of Land, Infrastructure and Transport (MLIT). The wood and construction industries have pushed for biomass support, which also appeals to local governments and local voters, according to interviewees G2 and I6.

In contrast, geothermal growth suffers from opposition from MOE and local spa owners. While METI and the electric utilities agree that geothermal could serve as a baseload energy source, political obstacles to siting have continued to relegate it to a one percent target by 2030. The FIT for small-scale geothermal has remained high – 40 yen per kWh – and the FIT for large-scale geothermal has remained at 26 yen per kWh. Despite these incentives, government and electric utility interviewees have predicted small, slow growth due to MOE's concerns regarding drilling in national parks, as well as spa owners' opposition to drilling near their facilities. The latter's opposition, according to some interviewees, emerges from two types of concerns. The first is that geothermal will deplete the hot springs' water, thus compromising their ability to maintain their facilities and depriving them of revenue. The second concern is that geothermal drilling will reveal that some hot springs' water sources have already disappeared, and that these originally natural springs are now enhanced with additives and artificial heat. The 2021 Strategic Energy Plan does include plans for a review of existing regulations under the Natural Parks Act, Hot Springs Act and Forest Act to facilitate expansion of geothermal, with consideration of the concerns expressed by hot spring operators (Government of Japan, 2021, 62).

The 2018 Strategic Energy Plan highlights the utilities' economic resilience concerns as the main factors influencing the government's decision to modify the FIT structure:

> The large amount of renewable energy that was introduced by using the subsidies under the FIT system amplifies electricity price fluctuations, and also lowers price levels by the amount of policy support that is received. This inhibits the recovery of investment in other electricity sources that would otherwise be selected by the market
>
> (Government of Japan, 2018, 126).

The 2018 plan introduces auctions for renewables to promote lower costs through price competition. The proposed changes also reflect the government's efforts to address economic and social resilience challenges resulting from the high FIT rates, including the utilities' passing through of FIT costs to consumers. Coupled with these measures, the 2018 plan commits the Japanese government to fully opening the transmission system, a step included in the government's electricity market liberalization plans. In 2019, renewables accounted for 11 percent of the Japanese government's energy budget, primarily focused on wind power (International Energy Agency, 2021b, 112). This contrasts with the aforementioned higher allocation for nuclear power, reflecting continued focus on revitalization of the latter.

The 2021 plan reiterates the 2018 plan's economic resilience points, including the concern regarding return on investment in electricity supply sources not covered under the FIT or the new feed-in premium (FIP) system discussed later. The 2021 plan also notes the need to make renewables cost-competitive with fossil fuels for electricity generation. These economic concerns align with the socio-ecological resilience goals expressed in the plan, which include replacement of inefficient coal plants with renewables, as depicted in Figure 5.10. Providing further support for socio-ecological resilience, the 2021 plan indicates that rules will be reviewed to allow renewables preferential access to transmission lines, displacing coal.

The 2018 and 2021 plans describe the ecological and engineering challenges associated with an influx of unbuilt renewables projects. The high FIT rates attracted developers that did not complete their renewables projects, leading to grid capacity reserved for these unbuilt projects. The Act to Partially Amend the Electricity Business Act and Other Acts in Order to Establish a Resilient and Sustainable Electricity Supply System, enacted by the Diet in 2020 for implementation in 2022, aims to address the economic resilience challenge of FIT cost pass-through to consumers, as well as this socio-ecological resilience challenge of reserved, unused grid capacity (Kobayashi et al., 2021). To mitigate costs to utilities and passing through of these costs to consumers, the Act shifts Japan's incentive structure from an FIT to an FIP. Projects already approved for the FIT will not transition to the new system. Under the FIP structure, developers receive a subsidy to cover the difference between the designated FIP price they pay for renewables and the market price.

To address the ecological resilience risks of grid capacity constraints imposed by unfinished FIT projects, the Act's provisions include cancellation of FIT approval for projects that do not commence commercial operations by a certain date. The cancellation provisions differ for each renewable energy source. The Nullification Rule includes cancellation timelines based on achievement of specific progress milestones, including transmission operators' acceptance of an interconnection construction commencement application (ICCA), environmental impact assessments, and construction plan notices (Kawamura and Wakabayashi, 2021a).

Relationships and resilience priorities have continued to shape the targets for specific renewable resources in Japan's electricity supply. The 2021 plan's increased renewables target includes a significant increase in non-hydro renewables to 27 percent from the 2018 target of 14 percent. The Japanese government has prioritized solar power over other non-hydro renewables, building on booming solar investment since implementation of the FIT. As Figure 5.12 shows, solar accounts for much of the planned increase, at 14–16 percent of total electricity supply. This target represents a doubling from solar's 2020 levels. Aligned with the government's general increase in renewables, this focus reflects economic resilience priorities, as well as socio-ecological resilience priorities tied to solar's ability to promote the government's decarbonization goals. The 2021 plan includes enhancement of solar installation safety through technical standards and accident reporting, bolstering engineering resilience and socio-ecological resilience. The plan also aims to employ "positive zoning" to address local concerns regarding erosion connected with solar farms located on slopes.

The plan likewise aims to use positive zoning for onshore wind development, while also accelerating offshore wind development. To encourage the latter and address opposition from local fishery industry organizations, the Japanese government implemented the 2018 Act on Promoting the Utilization of Sea Areas for the Development of Marine Renewable Energy Power Generation Facilities, which introduced offshore wind planning, siting and regulatory frameworks (Ministry of Economy, Trade and Industry, 2019a). Despite Japan's geographical viability for onshore wind power, economic resilience priorities have hampered widespread deployment, in comparison to interest in less expensive solar power. Per Figure 5.12, wind and biomass each account for five percent by 2030 in the 2021 plan. While the wind power target represents a significant increase from 2020 levels, the overall target remains relatively low.

Per the previous discussion of biomass interest from the private sector and MAFF, the plan also supports biomass development. It emphasizes economic resilience priorities such as cost-effectiveness, while also recognizing the need for sustainable biomass production that does not threaten food or forest resilience. The 2021 plan specifically describes plans for woody biomass expansion, and it also references biomass derived from waste.

Against the backdrop of the aforementioned hot springs industry opposition to geothermal, as described, the plan mentions a review of relevant regulations to determine siting. Geothermal is listed again as a baseload electricity source. However, the minimal one percent 2030 target remains unchanged, per Figure 5.12.

The 2021 plan also builds on the 2014 and 2018 plans' discussion of battery storage as an important feature of socio-ecological resilience. Despite this recognition of the role of energy storage in electricity supply stability, Japan's policies did not include a strategic framework for enabling battery storage deployment until 2021. The 2021 Strategic Plan paves the way for such a framework, focusing on energy storage system cost reductions, regulatory clarifications, storage aggregation to improve efficiency of supply-demand balancing, and use of storage to prevent curtailment of renewable energy power generation. In its fiscal year 2021 supplementary budget, the Japanese government included subsidies for battery storage systems. A legislative change to the Electricity Business Act in 2022 will require electric utilities to allow grid access for operators of energy storage systems (Ebuchi, 2022).

To support the decarbonization transition away from inefficient coal plants and the reduction in natural gas use without even greater adoption of renewables, the 2021 Strategic Energy Plan also includes a prominent role for conservation and efficiency.

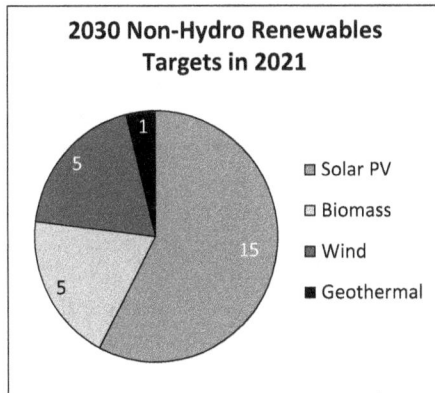

Figure 5.12 2030 Non-Hydro Renewables Targets in 2021

Source: Data from Government of Japan, 2021.

Saved Again: Conservation and Efficiency

Reminiscent of the post-oil crises, the Japanese government utilized demand-side conservation and efficiency measures to lower electricity consumption immediately following the Fukushima disaster, compensating for the electricity supply gap caused by the absence of nuclear power generation. For two weeks after the disaster, the Japanese government mandated a series of rolling blackouts in TEPCO's service area. The government also implemented an energy saving campaign (*setsuden*) to avoid planned blackouts. METI invoked article 27 of the Electricity Business Act, which enables the government to mandate reduced electricity use to avoid blackouts. The 2011 application of the article required users of over 500 kW to restrict their electricity use by 15 percent below 2010 levels in areas serviced by TEPCO and Tohoku Electric Power during the summer months. These utilities were identified based on the customers most affected by the March 11 triple disaster. The Fukushima accident affected TEPCO's service area, and the Tohoku service area was the epicenter of the earthquake and tsunami. Smaller users in these and other service areas were asked to implement voluntary energy saving protocols. Government requests for conservation by all users in all service areas in subsequent winters and summers ranged from 1.5 to 7 percent below 2010 levels (Electricity Supply-Demand Review Committee, Energy and Environment Council, Ministry of Economy, Trade and Industry, Government of Japan, 2012). In 2013, the Diet passed the Amended Energy Conservation Act. The revised act includes expanded categories for building materials, implemented in December 2013, and measures to address peak electricity demand, implemented in April 2014. Building efficiency improvement measures included expansions of the Top Runner program initiated in 1998 to spur competition and innovation in energy-efficient products, as described in Chapter 4. For a detailed overview of all energy conservation measures implemented in 2011 and 2012, see Hidemasa Nishiyama (2013).

The utilities recognized the opportunity to promote their own economic resilience goals, as well as those of the public, through energy efficient technology development and sales, as consumers responded to the government's energy conservation requirements. Electric utility interviewees indicated that the utilities engaged innovation on design and manufacturing of energy efficient heat pumps. Providing more energy efficient products to consumers also promoted socio-ecological resilience by lowering household electricity demand, promoting supply stability while the nuclear reactors' generating capacity remained largely offline.

In support of this goal of reducing energy demand, METI also began promoting construction Zero Energy Housing (ZEH) after the Fukushima disaster. METI included heat insulation, high-efficiency equipment, and solar PV in the components supporting ZEHs. This inclusion of solar PV enabled community-level advancement of renewables adoption, even as the renewable energy targets in total electricity supply remained unchanged. Providing time-limited subsidies for construction, coupled with creation of a ZEH standard, METI aimed to ensure that ZEHs would comprise more than half of all newly constructed homes by 2020 (Energy Efficiency and Conservation Division, ANRE, METI, 2015).

Government policies also have continued to include conservation and efficiency as important support mechanisms for Japan's electricity supply targets. The 1979 Act on the Rational Use of Energy underwent several sets of further revisions during the post-disaster period, including incentives for building construction and consumer energy savings. The 2013 revision focused on housing and buildings, adding building materials to the Top Runner Program. The same revision also modified the evaluation and ratings system for consumers' peak use of electricity from the grid, adding credit for storage batteries, energy management systems, and on-site power generation (International Energy Agency, 2017). The 2016 revision added incentives for using waste heat to promote energy efficiency. This revision was complemented by the Act on the Improvement of Energy Consumption Performance of Buildings, implemented the same year, which targeted large-scale non-residential building compliance with energy efficiency standards, as well as incentives for energy efficiency and conservation improvements for all buildings (Ministry of Land, Infrastructure and Transport, 2016). After nuclear power, energy efficiency received the second largest portion of the Japanese government's energy budget in 2019, 25 percent of the total (International Energy Agency, 2021b, 112). As a result of these various policies, the electric utilities have secured the minimum three percent electricity supply reserve margins in all service areas since 2011.

Despite the similar measures taken by the government after the oil crises and the Fukushima disaster, the reactions from consumers differed during these two periods. Following the oil crises, the public trusted the government's decision to promote energy conservation for the good of the nation. In contrast, after the Fukushima disaster, consumers complied out of necessity, not cooperation with the government. Manufacturers complained about the conservation measures, and consumers blamed the government and the electric utilities for the need to conserve. To address this conflict, the Japanese government has shifted the framing on conservation and efficiency and removed some of the short-term conservation mandates.

While the 2014 Strategic Energy Plan emphasized a continued focus on energy conservation and efficiency as a means of reducing total energy consumption in the absence of nuclear power, the 2018 and 2021 Strategic Energy Plans frame decarbonization as a driving force behind this emphasis on conservation and efficiency. This framing links public interest in social resilience with the utilities' economic resilience goals, as the latter lose supply and the associated revenue from retiring inefficient coal plants.

Policymakers' recognition of the conflict with consumers over continued conservation requirements led METI's Electricity and Gas Basic Subcommittee to decide against requiring public conservation measures during the summer of 2019. However, METI couched this decision in a longer-term request for continued public cooperation on "energy-saving efforts and energy conservation at a reasonable pace as usual in past years" (Ministry of Economy, Trade and Industry, 2019c).

Both the 2018 and 2021 plan focus on local production and local consumption to build energy resilience. The 2018 plan identifies this locally produced energy as "mainly thermal," while the 2021 plan includes measures to include renewables.

Both plans include goals for zero energy buildings, highlighting the need for advancement and coordinated implementation of renewables and energy efficient technologies. The 2021 plan promotes R&D and introduction of energy efficient technologies through new "Energy Efficient Technological Strategies."

As discussed, these incremental energy policy shifts have occurred in the context of policy process and structural changes prompted by the Fukushima disaster, relationship shifts, resilience priorities, and pressure to meet decarbonization commitments.

Somewhat Shocked: Policy Process and Structural Changes

The Japanese government's policy process and structural changes after the Fukushima nuclear disaster have included changes to the formal policymaking process, safety regulation, and economic regulation. Incorporating new transparency measures, these changes aimed to rebuild public trust and respond to public demand for a role in energy policymaking. The government also implemented new technical measures and mechanisms focused on disaster response, not described in detail in this book, but outlined in the *Report of Japanese Government to IAEA Ministerial Conference on Nuclear Safety – Accident at TEPCO's Fukushima Nuclear Power Stations*, transmitted in September 2011 (Nuclear Emergency Response Headquarters, 2011). Public perceptions of the genuineness of all of these changes affect their success in rebuilding trust and promoting system resilience, as does alignment of public and governmental risk perceptions and resilience priorities.

Formal Policymaking Process Changes

The first policymaking process change involves the composition and focus of energy policy advisory groups. As mentioned earlier in this chapter, to regain public trust in the energy policymaking process and the advisory committees' decisions, the DPJ removed the electric utilities from formal membership in the government's energy policy advisory committees. The DPJ also made the committee meetings open to the public and available on the internet. As also previously mentioned, the utilities continue to attend committee meetings as observers. They are permitted to voice their opinions, though they have no veto power. Government interviewee G7 explained that

> the policymaking process has changed . . . after the earthquake, those industry representatives were not included in the advisory council. So we, as an advisory council, called them observers so they had chances to make their comments, but finally, they don't have any power to veto the report of the advisory council. So I think that's a difference . . . especially after the earthquake, there is big criticism toward the power sector, the power companies, and that might be one reason to exclude them from the policy formulating process.
>
> (March 2013)

This compromise reflects the government's efforts to balance two conflicting goals: the need to recover public trust in policymaking, and METI's continued cooperation with the utilities. It also reflects a recognition that some level of utility input is needed for realistic policy development to achieve socio-ecological and economic resilience goals for Japan's energy system.

In addition to the membership change, METI also formed several new advisory subcommittees to address energy system reform aimed at meeting emissions reduction goals. In 2019, toward the end of the Abe Cabinet's leadership, METI formed the Subcommittee on System Reform for Renewable Energy as Main Power Source, the Subcommittee for Sustainable Power Systems, and the Subcommittee on Electricity Resilience towards a Decarbonized Society. The first two subcommittees emerged from concerns regarding engineering resilience risks from natural disasters and geopolitical factors, as well as socio-ecological goals related to decarbonization (METI, 2019d). The third subcommittee also aims to address engineering and socio-ecological resilience risks, with an additional focus on economic risk. This subcommittee aims to enhance electricity infrastructure resilience and supply stability, as well as minimize uncertainty regarding infrastructure investment recovery (METI, 2019b).

These advisory group composition changes and additions may yield long-term effects on Japan's electricity supply source ratios, infrastructure development and access, and system resilience, though these effects will depend on each committee's membership. Other policymaking process changes have proved short-lived, with short-term effects on Japan's energy policies and energy system resilience.

The deliberative polling referenced earlier in this chapter represents one such temporary change. To restore public trust by enabling public involvement in Japanese energy policymaking after the Fukushima disaster, the DPJ for the first time employed deliberative polling to determine the future of nuclear power in Japan's energy mix. This exercise focused on Japan's 2030 nuclear power's electricity supply percentage. Deliberative polling is a policymaking technique in which a random, representative sample is polled on an issue. The participants then engage in a two-day discussion of the issue with experts from all sides, supported by balanced briefing materials. After the session, the participants take the same poll. The Kan Administration used the deliberative polling results to determine that nuclear power should be reduced to zero by 2030. For more information on the polling results, see Yasunori Sone (2012a). However, interviewees indicated that the DPJ did not know what to do with the deliberative polling results, so no formal policy path to reduce or eliminate nuclear energy use emerged. Public interest group interviewee P2 expressed mixed feelings about the DPJ's efforts to empower the public through deliberative polling.

> I think the DPJ was trying to listen to people's voices, but their mistake, to my understanding, is that they didn't have a goal or the process before going into that period. So they just go to the people, and listen to them, but actually, they didn't know what to do with so many opinions. Actually, they didn't

know how to reflect these opinions in their policies. So actually, they just discarded those opinions. So in that sense, they also didn't change in that respect.

(March 2013)

The DPJ may have intended to build public trust through empowerment, but their efforts did not result in increased public clout. When the LDP assumed leadership, the use of deliberative polling ended.

While the DPJ offered the public increased clout in energy policymaking through changes to formal institutions, the LDP has tried to rebuild trust in government policymaking without public input. Interviewees noted that the LDP would not use the DPJ's deliberative polling results, nor would the Abe administration conduct a new polling exercise. While the LDP-led administrations have made energy policies such as the Strategic Energy Plans available for public comment, the procedure for reviewing such comments appears designed for minimal impact. For example, METI held a public comment period for proposed reform that would protect electric utilities' transmission lines from renewables entrants. On the day of the public comment deadline, METI announced that the agency would begin work on the reform four days later, after a three-day holiday weekend. Diet member Kono criticized this timeline as disregarding any comments received (Kono, 9 January, 2015). Many interviewees suggested that the LDP's focus on relationships with the electric utilities led to this reversion to an energy policy-making process without public input. This reversion could elevate the utilities' economic resilience priorities over public social resilience priorities, unless these goals converge due to decarbonization commitments and ongoing reduction of renewables infrastructure costs. Changes in safety regulation also have impacted the utilities' economic resilience framing.

Safety Regulation Changes

As discussed earlier in this chapter, the Fukushima disaster severely damaged public trust in the existing safety regulator's ability to regulate the nuclear industry. Government interviewees indicated that to reestablish this trust while enhancing energy system resilience, the Japanese government created the NRA as a new, nuclear safety regulator independent from METI in September 2012. One of many interviewees to note this trust-building as NRA's mission, G13 confirmed that the new NRA's "first priority they are trying to make is to rebuild the regulatory body's trust" (June 2013). The NRA's new safety regulations for nuclear facilities also aim to bolster energy system resilience while rebuilding public trust. These regulations, available on the NRA's website, include new safety standards for nuclear power plants, as well as regulatory requirements to protect against structural damage from severe accidents, earthquakes, and tsunamis (Nuclear Regulation Authority, 2013).

The complications regarding hiring of qualified, yet neutral, NRA staff have challenged the return of public trust, even after the merge of JNES with the NRA.

Public trust in the genuineness of the NRA's intentions to promote safety has grown slowly in the decade since the Fukushima disaster. Most government, NGO, media and academic interviewees suggested that regaining public trust in the nuclear safety regulator will take more time, given the media's coverage of the previous regulator's role in the Fukushima accident. In addition, trust hinges on the afore-mentioned discrepancy between the public's zero risk tolerance and the presence of risk even in a strictly regulated environment. This situation creates pressure on the NRA to guarantee zero risk if the Japanese government and the utilities cannot successfully alter public risk tolerance through transparent communication of risks. To address this challenge, the Japanese government incorporated probabilistic risk assessment (PRA) in revising its approach to safety regulations (Nuclear Emergency Response Headquarters, 2011). The U.S. NRC defines PRA as a mechanism to "estimate risk by computing real numbers to determine what can go wrong, how likely is it, and what are its consequences" (Nuclear Regulatory Commission, 2020). Several government and energy industry interviewees also mentioned the need to explain PRA to the public as an alternative to zero risk tolerance.

The NRA's independence from METI aims to promote public trust by removing bias from policymakers aligned with nuclear power expansion. Housed within MOE, the NRA aims to demonstrate this independence through two design features. First, the NRA's office is located in a different part of Tokyo than all other government offices. The NRA's new home under MOE does suggest the potential for influence to shift from METI to this ministry, which historically housed critics of nuclear power due to nuclear waste and other environmental concerns. However, MOE's tone has shifted depending on the minister, as evidenced by the previously described attitudes of Suga Cabinet Environment Minister Koizumi, who asserted his aim of decommissioning existing nuclear plants, and his successor in the Kishida Cabinet, Environment Minister Yamaguchi, who has not taken this stance. The second measure to promote NRA independence involves legislation stipulating that staff cannot return to their home agencies after serving in the NRA. This delinking of NRA staff from future obligations to METI or other agencies weakens these agencies' potential influence. However, this condition has yielded a new challenge, as government officials have expressed reluctance to leave their home agencies with no opportunity to return.

Policymakers' and electric utilities' mutual aim of continued nuclear power use also has driven this creation of the NRA as an independent safety agency. Separation of regulators from policymakers aims to eliminate the conflict of interest between nuclear policy and safety regulation. Government interviewees indicated that by doing so, the government aims to rebuild public confidence in regulators' clout over the electric utilities and the government's ability to manage nuclear power policy. As evidenced by the aforementioned local injunctions against restarts, the NRA's activities have received a mixed public response, with public opposition to some reactor restart decisions and support for others reflecting ambiguous trust in the new regulator.

Economic Regulation Changes

Public trust restoration also has played a key role in economic regulation changes following the Fukushima disaster. A number of government and electric utility interviewees cited this driver. Electric utility interviewee I22 explained that

> after the nuclear accident, almost all utilities are blamed for the lack of safety of nuclear. So utilities lost trust from the public. So public people think they want to choose utility companies. So METI also has to be sensitive to the public opinion, so METI thinks they have to change the structure of the utility companies, the electric utility industry structure, to get approval from the public.
>
> (May 2014)

Market liberalization under the Abe Cabinet surprised observers of Japanese energy policy, as well as several interviewees. They expected the LDP's cooperation with the electric utilities on nuclear power and preservation of electric utility profits to stymie regulatory reform, as it did before the Fukushima accident. In the early 2000s, the data falsification scandal and accidents shifted attention away from market liberalization, halting structural change. Conversely, the Fukushima disaster appears to have enabled resumption of market liberalization efforts, promoting change.

The disaster injected conflict between the electric utilities and policymakers – at least publicly, enabling the return of the market liberalization movement. Some government and electric utility interviewees suggested that the Fukushima disaster's boosting of METI's pro-reformers' clout over the electric utilities also allowed resurrection of market liberalization. Electric utility interviewee I1 said that "after 2011, METI has become strong again. The electric utility companies' power became relatively weakened. In reality, METI's power was relatively strengthened. In that power relationship, METI, who was considering market liberalization, took advantage of the Fukushima Daiichi accident." Some interviewees linked this increase in METI's pro-reformers' clout to the elimination of TEPCO's influence, though others said that TEPCO was less opposed to market liberalization than some of the other electric utilities.

The disaster strengthened reformers' clout, while leaving cooperation between the electric utilities and their LDP supporters untouched. G16 observed, "So even at this time, when METI tried to propose legislation for further liberalization, the LDP's energy group tried to moderate or weaken the substance. Finally, it was passed. LDP finally endorsed the Cabinet proposal for new legislation" (July 2013). This balance of cooperation and clout thus enabled passage of liberalization measures, but LDP influence weakened these measures' potential impact on energy system change. Several interviewees offered the example of delayed, legal unbundling, rather than rapid, operational unbundling.

In 2013, the Diet passed three measures proposed by the Abe Cabinet. Included in Prime Minister Abe's third arrow of Abenomics reforms, the three liberalization pillars include coordination between the electric utilities' nine grids; small retail and household electricity market competition; and vertical unbundling, or separation of generation, transmission and distribution. Grid coordination measures involve establishment of an Organization for Cross-regional Coordination of Transmission Operators to coordinate supply-demand balance and order generators to reinforce interconnections in supply emergencies (Electricity Market Reform Office, Agency for Energy and Natural Resources, Ministry of Economy, Trade and Industry, Government of Japan, 2013). The government implemented the first measure in 2015, the second in 2016, and the third in 2020. While the first measure appears a sensible response to the grid isolation risks exposed by the Fukushima disaster, the others may at first glance seem an unlikely result of a nuclear accident.

My 2018 study found that government and electric utility interviewees' comments yielded six possible motivations for LDP and METI pursuit of market liberalization measures after 3/11 (Sklarew, 2018). All six of these drivers involve government efforts to rebuild public trust, and all emerge from the government's need to balance relationships with the utilities and the public. Two of these motives support the electric utilities' economic resilience goals, while the other four build public trust by challenging the electric utilities.

The first motive for market liberalization is a trade-off for nuclear restarts, as suggested by some interviewees. By appearing to diminish utility clout in policymaking, market liberalization paves the way for nuclear power's return by convincing the public that the government has clout over the electric utilities. G12 explained:

> The LDP and METI and the utilities want to keep the nuclear policy, and . . . I would say, nuclear policy doesn't have popularity among the people. And then, nuclear is more important for these three [groups] than keeping the current market structure. So in that sense, these three have some kind of implicit consensus that we should further proceed on deregulation. Otherwise, we cannot have the confidence, or we can't have trust from the people. And then, of course, with such regulatory reform efforts, maybe the LDP and METI or government can say we have . . . a very confrontational stance . . . toward the utilities, and the utilities also can say . . . we are very strongly led by, or forced by deregulation. And so, with such a structure, now the three can proceed with nuclear policy.
>
> (August 2013)

This renewed trust would support NRA approvals of reactor restarts, as well as METI and utility plans for the long-term role of nuclear power in Japan's electricity supply mix.

The second market liberalization motive that supports the utilities' economic resilience is connected to the fuel cycle. By introducing price competition, liberalization helps to justify the electric utilities' request for government assistance with nuclear fuel cycle investment costs, according to interviewee G12. Since taxpayers' money would fund the fuel cycle if the government takes over, this shift requires public trust in the government's decision-making.

The other four market liberalization motives promote public trust by potentially limiting the electric utilities' influence on energy policymaking and challenging their economic resilience goals. Electric utility interviewees described the first of these motives, positing that policymakers' pursuit of market liberalization aims to build METI's clout over the electric utilities in order to gain public trust. Some electric utility interviewees went a step beyond enhancement of METI's clout, asserting that liberalization intends to punish the electric utilities for the Fukushima disaster and past scandals. They asserted that the government is responding to the public's desire to see the electric utilities suffer for creating the Fukushima disaster. I18 contended, "My personal opinion and my feeling is deregulation is some kind of punishment to our organization. We should be punished because utilities and electric industry had the Fukushima nuclear disaster to all the Japanese people, so the Japanese government should punish."

Diet member Kono and some NGO leaders think that the market liberalization plan aimed only at the impression of punishment, while actually designed for minimal impact. NGO leader Iida asserted that

> the original intention by the Cabinet is obviously kind of fake. The LDP pretends they are more revolutionary, or more progressive, looks like. But in reality, that is a very slow step of electricity market reform. And actually nothing to be promised . . . if the government or the LDP Abe administration seriously considers unbundling or electricity market reform, TEPCO must be the first. But they never discuss about that. So that is another evidence that this electricity market reform is something like just drawing big pictures on the wall, but nothing to do with reality.

The design of the unbundling scheme seems to support this impression. METI chose to implement legal unbundling, rather than operational unbundling. Legal unbundling separates generation from transmission and distribution, but the electric utilities control a holding company that houses the separate firms handling these operations. This design results in little change in utility clout and continued utility control of the electricity grid.

The second of the four motives that constrain the utilities links market liberalization with renewables expansion. Some government interviewees suggested that unbundling is necessary to open grid access to new entrants in order to foster renewables increases. They believe that the FIT cannot effectively accomplish renewables growth without it. G10 asserted that "this deregulation debate is for expanding renewables. The most important thing is for the grid system to be much more independent from the utility companies. The grid is infrastructure, so everyone should use it" (April 2013). G10 and others say that unbundling is needed to enable new entrants access to the transmission grid. "New entrants are suspicious, so they think the utilities will do unfair treatment to new entrants. For renewables, heightening openness of the grid is very important." Electric utility interviewees argued that unbundling limits interest in investing in expansion of transmission networks needed to add a large amount of renewables. In August 2013, I16 contended that "the government's goal is to increase renewables to around 25 percent by 2030, they are saying. I think they will have to add a fair amount of electricity supply lines for the stability of transmission and distribution areas, but if we liberalize, I think investment in that will be extremely difficult." The 2021 Strategic Energy Plan's 2030 increased renewables target of 36–38 percent, imposed after unbundling has already taken place, would increase the need for grid investment. Addressing the utilities' investment concerns, in 2018, METI introduced plans for a new generation charge to be imposed on power producers to pay for grid upgrades to support renewables. This charge, based on capacity factor, adversely affects renewables power producers, since renewables traditionally have lower capacity factors than thermal plants such as coal, nuclear, and gas. For more details on the effects of capacity factor on power producers, see Kawamura and Wakabayashi (2021b). METI aims to implement the new charge by 2023.

In 2015, the Organization for Cross-Regional Coordination of Transmission Operators (OCCTO) was created as an independent non-governmental agency. OCCTO's responsibilities include securing stable supply through a plan for a cross-regional network (Organization for Cross-Regional Coordination of Transmission Operators, 2021), as well as managing a "switching support system" that facilitates switching of transmission network use agreements between retail electricity providers and transmission and distribution operators. OCCTO also maintains responsibility for promotion of fair and equitable use of transmission and distribution facilities. However, OCCTO's grid access guidelines appear to have prioritized use of the existing grid, with an assumption of curtailment in cases of excess capacity, thus challenging renewables expansion and ecological resilience. OCCTO serves as the mediator for electricity supplier disputes regarding transmission and distribution system access. With the 2020 implementation of the Act for Establishing Energy Supply Resilience, OCCTO also assumed responsibility for FIT grant subsidies and FIP grant premiums. The Act also promotes distributed generation as a means of bolstering engineering resilience at the local level.

As previously discussed, the 2016 establishment of the Electricity and Gas Market Surveillance Commission (EGC) provides a mechanism for identifying market violations, but the EGC has no independent authority to enforce actions to address such violations by market participants. In addition, as an agency within METI, the EGC is subject to the previously described *jinji idou* personnel rotation system, which creates the potential for influence from other departments within METI. This said, the 2018 Strategic Energy Plan includes a commitment to "thoroughly open up the existing transmission system" (Government of Japan, 2018, 122).

The third and final motives that negatively influence the electric utilities' economic resilience involve overall market efficiency, electricity rate reductions and consumer choice. According to government and electric utility interviewees, unbundling and competition will enable the Japanese government to focus on transmission line access, while lowering prices and enabling consumers to choose their providers. Energy industry interviewee I18 presented this argument as follows:

> Just after the Fukushima accident, many public opinion groups or consumers' entities say utilities should change to be more and more efficient, and the Japanese government thinks, 'oh, unbundling is very good to change utilities' organization to be more efficient.' . . . [T]he Japanese government can focus on the regulation of only wire business. And they can more strictly check the wire business efficiency.
>
> (May 2014)

These motives reflect economic resilience challenges for utilities, while also framing economic and social resilience benefits for consumers. They hold particular salience after the Fukushima accident raised prices and highlighted the lack of choice. Several electric utility interviewees agreed that liberalization is METI's response to the public's demand to choose their electricity providers after the Fukushima disaster. I21 expressed this view:

> I think that after the nuclear accident, almost all utilities are blamed for the lack of safety of nuclear. So utilities lost trust from the public. So public people think they want to choose utility companies. So METI also has to be sensitive to the public opinion, so METI thinks they have to change the structure of the utility companies, the electric utility industry structure, to get approval from the public, to get consensus of the public.
>
> (May 2014)

METI's efforts to rebuild public trust thus underlie the price reduction and consumer choice rationale for market liberalization, as well. As of January 2022, over 23.85 million retail customers have applied to switch their electricity provider (Organization for Cross-Regional Coordination of Transmission Operators, 2022). However, public trust in the government and utilities has remained elusive, per the JAERO polls described earlier in this chapter.

All six of these motives aim to build public trust in the Japanese government's ability to manage the utilities and the electricity system; they also allow the government to preserve nuclear infrastructure, regardless of whether they appear to challenge it. G12 and other interviewees suggested that the government has designed Japan's electricity market liberalization in a way that does not harm nuclear power, a priority shared by policymakers and the electric utilities. Some government interviewees asserted that the electric utilities consider preservation of nuclear power their top priority, so they are willing to compromise on market liberalization. These policymakers' and utilities' priorities reflect a set of trade-offs that promote these groups' economic resilience goals, but they could compromise socio-ecological resilience if the market design hinders renewables expansion.

Transparency Changes

Following the Fukushima disaster, government recognition of the role of transparency in restoring public trust has driven some of the changes to Japan's energy policymaking process and regulation. Several of the structural changes described in this chapter include transparency features intended to bolster public trust in governmental oversight and the energy policymaking process. The restrictions on private meetings between the NRA and the utilities offer an example. Policy documents such as the Strategic Energy Plans also highlight the need for greater transparency in energy policymaking, but they do not contain specific measures to accomplish this goal. In addition, some actions have hindered public input into the policymaking process. These mixed effects on policymaking transparency and input suggest a need for revision of the framing of transparency goals and definitions as applied to policymaking, as discussed at the end of this chapter.

One example of ambiguous transparency improvement begins with the 2014 Strategic Energy Plan revision, which includes a section on government communication regarding energy policy. The focus is on communication of accurate, timely information to the public. The plan also cites "two-way communication," with the goal of promoting "dialogue with all levels of the society in order to increase transparency over the energy policy planning process and obtain public trust in the policy." At odds with this statement is the lack of consideration of public comments on energy-related policies such as the transmission grid access limitation ordinance mentioned earlier in this chapter.

The 2018 and 2021 Strategic Energy Plans also include statements on transparency, linking it to public trust and reaffirming the need for two-way communication. The 2018 plan asserts that in making decisions on energy choices, the Government of Japan needs to "disclose relevant information and ensure thorough transparency," but the plan does not define what is "relevant" (Government of Japan, 2018, 112). It does include some specific areas of transparency focus, stating that the government "will maximize the openness of the policymaking process through advisory councils, meeting of experts and the like and enhance their transparency (Government of Japan, 2018, 114). The plan also notes the need for "dialogue-based policy planning implementation processes," and it includes a general description of a new mechanism to incorporate municipalities, business operators and non-profits in discussions on energy policy (Government of Japan, 2018, 114). The example offered describes "utilizing local energy councils under collaboration between the relevant government agencies and municipalities across Japan and building platforms concerning local coexistence in line with local circumstances to engage in communication concerning nuclear power" (Government of Japan, 2018, 114). The plan does not explain how such a mechanism will operate, nor how it differs from the existing advisory committees and study groups that include the same sets of stakeholder groups identified in the plan.

The 2021 Strategic Energy Plan notes the connection between transparency of the energy policymaking process and trust in energy policies. The plan announces increased transparency and opening of advisory groups' and expert groups' policy planning process "to the greatest extent" (Government of Japan, 2021, 128). This language suggests that full transparency in these groups may not always result.

These policy changes reflect the Japanese government's recognition of the need for transparency that extends beyond the results of the policymaking process to include the process itself. This said, the government's measures to promote transparent communication between policymakers, regulators, utilities, and consumers do not yet appear to have restored public trust in the energy policymaking process and nuclear power regulation. In addition to promoting public trust, transparency in Japan's energy policymaking process, regulation, energy system development, and response to shocks can provide crucial support for economic, socio-ecological and engineering resilience.

Lessons on Lock-In and Resilience

The Fukushima disaster embodied a shock commensurate with the 1970s oil crises, and it could have generated a similar critical juncture that initiated energy system transformation. However, the energy system lock-in created in the previous decades challenged dramatic changes to build resilience. The Fukushima disaster, resilience priorities, and relationships have yielded a mixed effect on the traits that foster energy system lock-in: infrastructure, interrelatedness and complexity, institutional support, momentum and risk and uncertainty. In addition, public distrust in policymakers, regulators and utilities further constrained the government's ability to enact changes beyond measures to improve policymaking process transparency. To rebuild trust, the government has employed structural changes in regulation and the policymaking process, while concurrently relying on time to heal distrust as the memory of the accident fades.

The Fukushima disaster has highlighted the ecological and engineering resilience challenges facing Japan's energy system, as well as opportunities to build holistic system resilience. Regulatory adjustments following the accident have enhanced engineering resilience. At the same time, economic resilience priorities linked to infrastructure investment have hindered ecological resilience by slowing a shift away from reliance on nuclear power toward a balance with other sources, including a variety of renewables. As discussed earlier in this chapter, measures supportive of renewables have appeared alongside measures countering expansion of their deployment. The 2021 Strategic Energy Plan's planned increase in renewables to replace inefficient coal plants demonstrates movement toward energy policies to improve ecological as well as social resilience. This transition can offer lessons for other fossil fuel-dependent communities and nations.

The disaster also challenged social resilience through loss of electricity access, both directly through elimination of the Fukushima reactors, and indirectly through the government-imposed blackouts to compensate for the nationwide shutdown of all nuclear reactors. Echoing the post-oil crises period, conservation and efficiency have played a role in bolstering all forms of resilience during a time of constrained electricity resources. As discussed, in the post-3/11 period, conservation and efficiency measures have supported social and economic resilience by limiting demand in the absence of nuclear supply. These measures also can bolster socio-ecological and economic resilience by promoting decarbonization goals through demand reduction as inefficient coal plants cease electricity generation.

The Fukushima disaster also has jeopardized the economic resilience of Japan's energy system. Unexpected costs of clean-up, compensation, and decommissioning pose new burdens on utilities and the Japanese government. From the public perspective, the disaster imposed costs in the form of electricity price hikes and local, negative effects on livelihoods and housing. At the same time, policymakers' and utilities' economic resilience priorities have supported incremental, internal energy system changes rather than movement away from the incumbent system.

Several infrastructure challenges have encouraged this incremental energy system change, rather than divestment of nuclear power, after the triple disaster. All of these challenges connect to economic resilience priorities. In the first set of challenges, policymaker-electric utility cooperation on cost recovery of existing infrastructure and hesitance to invest in new infrastructure has slowed energy system change. Policymakers, the electric utilities, and local government officials have voiced concern regarding recouping of prior investments in nuclear plants and fuel cycle facilities. The electric utilities say they will optimize the lifetimes of newer plants if the NRA approves resumption of their operations. At the same time, the policymaker-utility struggle over nuclear fuel cycle infrastructure cost and responsibility has continued. In addition, policymakers and the electric utilities have warned against the high costs of transmission line expansion to accommodate a major shift to renewable energy, leading to measures that impose costs on renewables producers and consumers. Further, cooperation with policymakers has enabled the electric utilities to continue control of existing shared infrastructure. Even after legal unbundling of generation and transmission takes place, new entrants have faced challenges to accessing the grid.

The second set of challenges involves costs associated with infrastructure that is no longer needed as the energy system changes. Clean-up efforts have highlighted the difficulties associated with infrastructure end-of-life, including nuclear reactor decommissioning and spent fuel disposal. These challenges will face the utilities' future retirement of nuclear and coal plants, affecting economic and social resilience. Interrelatedness of subsystems within Japan's energy system compound these difficulties. G18 observed, "Even if today, we commit to stop any nuclear power plant activities right now, we have to still cope with the waste from nuclear power plants. Period. And we have to dispose of those by using recycling of nuclear power fuel at Rokkasho plant in Aomori prefecture. But stop nuclear activity means that simultaneously we stop nuclear fuel recycling program." Local officials in Aomori Prefecture fear that cancellation of the nuclear fuel cycle will mean that the prefecture indefinitely will need to house the spent fuel that Rokkasho would have reprocessed. They periodically seek the central Japanese government's confirmation that Aomori will not serve as the final disposal site of high radioactive waste, reflecting social resilience concerns. Aomori officials support the siting of the reprocessing facility based on a cooperative relationship with the central government, as well as local employment that bolsters the prefecture's economic resilience.

The Fukushima disaster also demonstrated the interrelatedness of Japan's energy system with many other sectors. In particular, say government and electric utility interviewees, the manufacturing sector has lobbied heavily to restart the nuclear reactors to lower electricity prices and end conservation measures. The disaster also has challenged Japan's food and water sectors, discussed in more detail in the next chapter. However, linkages between IT and energy systems have enabled IT companies such as NTT to offer bundled IT and electricity services to consumers, lowering their electricity rates, bolstering economic resilience.

Institutional support, another key factor in promoting or breaking energy system lock-in, has faced mixed impacts from the Fukushima disaster. Policy support for a return to the incumbent nuclear-based system is hampered by the government's inability to actively promote nuclear power until public trust returns. If the creation of the NRA rebuilds public trust, reactors approved for restart can restore nuclear power's prominent role in Japan's energy mix. At the same time, the absence of explicit policy support has hindered the utilities' ability to make long-term investment decisions.

Policy frameworks that include decarbonization goals concurrently have affected the future of incumbent coal, replacing a portion of it with renewables. While we have observed some replacement of conflicting policy measures hindering renewables deployment, the electric utilities' cooperation with policymakers and economic regulators has perpetuated grid access difficulties for new market entrants supplying renewables. Grid access regulations and enforcement of them, as well as the effects of changes to the FIT and introduction of the FIP, will shape the role of renewables' contributions to economic and socio-ecological resilience.

The Fukushima disaster has interrupted the incumbent energy system's momentum built through infrastructure investment, interrelated elements and institutional support. Risk and uncertainty have further influenced system momentum. The Fukushima disaster has altered all groups' risk perceptions regarding a nuclear-based energy system, affecting views of economic, social and engineering risk. New considerations of safety risk have joined the traditional three Es concerns in shaping these perceptions. Institutional changes resulting from the disaster also have injected further uncertainty that affects the electric utilities' investment decisions. The electric utilities' redefined risk focus involves all forms of resilience, comprising financial uncertainty in a liberalized market with stricter nuclear safety standards, decarbonization goals, and public distrust.

These shifts in lock-in features, resilience priorities, and relationships after the Fukushima disaster offer lessons that build on previous chapters' insights from the post-oil shocks energy system transformation and increasing lock-in during the 1990s and 2000s. As in the previous periods, these lessons for policymakers, regulators, utilities and consumers include stakeholders' resilience focus considerations, accompanying communication and transparency challenges, the role of regulators and regulation, and implications for cooperation. This final phase of Japan's trajectory also provides insights on these factors' influences on ecological, economic and social resilience, as well as connections across these aspects of holistic energy system resilience.

Unlike the accidents and scandal in the previous period, the Fukushima disaster induced a new focus on safety as a component of engineering and socio-ecological resilience. At the same time, some policymakers and the electric utilities appear to view fulfilling this safety requirement of engineering and socio-ecological resilience as a threat to economic resilience. This perceived threat emerges from a focus on the costs of compliance with new safety regulations, as well as the potential for stranded assets when the cost of compliance outweighs the anticipated return on investment in it. The TEPCO leadership and other electric utility executives have suggested that the utilities prioritize budget and schedule over safety because they believe they cannot accomplish economic resilience and safety goals simultaneously. However, the Fukushima disaster has encouraged them to reframe energy operations in ways that optimize safety, time and cost. Safety investments also can be viewed as supporting the economic resilience priorities of policymakers and the utilities. Measures to bolster safety can avoid future disaster mitigation, liability, and compensation costs, as well as infrastructure damage costs. Further, they can prolong the life of energy infrastructure, enabling longer returns on safety investments. This reframing of economic resilience needs to be placed in the broader context of problematic delinking of compliance and resilience. When infrastructure operators view regulatory compliance as the goal, compliance costs frame economic resilience. This framing misses the link between regulatory compliance and all forms of energy system resilience. When the regulations are instead viewed as tools to achieve such resilience, and compliance as a means of achieving it, economic costs can be redefined. This reframing can include incentives, such as performance-based regulation, to enable energy infrastructure operators to move beyond mere regulatory compliance toward true economic and socio-ecological resilience.

In addition to safety, the Fukushima disaster highlighted the need for modifications of existing electricity supply resources to best balance various stakeholders' energy security, environmental concerns, and economic considerations, striving to achieve all forms of energy system resilience.

This holistic resilience includes system adaptability to promote supply diversity and enable shifts toward new electricity supply resources when existing sources face resilience challenges. Additionally, as mentioned in each empirical chapter, policy and regulatory frameworks for energy storage, as well as conservation and efficiency measures, can mitigate short-term supply risks and contribute to supply stability in long-term supply plans, while promoting socio-ecological resilience goals such as decarbonization.

The Fukushima disaster has combined with other factors driving shifts in Japan's energy supply sources, including decarbonization commitments. Climate change and decarbonization goals can serve as a unifying focus for cooperation across policymakers, the utilities and the public to advance socio-ecological resilience.

Again, integrating these goals with economic resilience priorities can foster such collaboration. This integration includes recognition of the costs of climate change-related natural disaster and weather-induced power outages and energy infrastructure damage.

At the local level, the Fukushima disaster demonstrated the need to shift toward more distributed, community-based solutions to energy system resilience. In the 2018 and 2021 Strategic Energy Plans and other policies, the Japanese government has begun to include opportunities for local microgrids to enhance all forms of resilience. To support these opportunities, clear definitions of the roles of various renewables in economic resilience can enable development of policy and regulatory frameworks that foster economic resilience from renewables. Community-based energy planning could foster local-level cooperation across all stakeholders, enabling the utilities and local governments to build consensus with communities on achievable electricity mixes that promote local socio-ecological and economic resilience.

Local opposition to energy infrastructure siting remains an obstacle for all energy supply sources. In Japan, social resilience concerns have challenged nuclear power, but also wind and solar facilities. In the case of large power plants, such as traditional nuclear, coal and natural gas reactors, not-in-my-backyard syndrome (NIMBY) encourages utilities to build multiple reactors on the same site, which can lead to cascading disasters if an accident or natural disaster occurs, as evidenced by the Fukushima disaster. Local community support for infrastructure siting can emerge from trust in safety protocols, social resilience considerations, and communication and transparency.

Building trust through transparency and more effective communication faces several cultural challenges. First, the Japanese public's zero risk tolerance can exacerbate distrust in energy technologies when any risk is communicated. When accidents or environmental damage occur, this zero risk tolerance creates distrust in regulators and facility operators. To avoid negative reactions, policymakers and energy facility operators have downplayed risks and postponed or avoided communication of accidents and damage. As in the case of the 1990s-2000s accidents and scandal, and to an even greater extent after the Fukushima disaster, this lack of communication and transparency has deepened distrust in the technology, as well as operation and regulatory oversight of it. This problem of safety myth creation, highlighted in Japan's 2018 Strategic Energy Plan, offers lessons for all technologies and all components of energy systems. Without asking the public to accept a particular level of risk, policymakers, regulators, and energy facility operators need to communicate risks clearly and seek public understanding of known risks. Regulations and enforcement should strive to prevent risk to the greatest extent possible, but they also must include measures to address situations when these risks are realized. Risks of all technologies, including renewables, need to be communicated. Erosion from solar panels installed on slopes provides an example. Effective communication can enable innovation to address such technology risks and promote all forms of resilience.

According to government officials and utility executives, a second, related challenge is the tendency of policymakers and engineers to secure as much information as possible, including solutions, prior to reporting a problem to the public. This tendency contributed to the Fukushima disaster and its aftermath. To rebuild public trust, the Japanese utilities' leadership has begun to instruct employees to report problems immediately and acknowledge when causes and solutions are not yet known. This form of transparency has proven difficult in places around the globe. And yet, it is necessary in order to create realistic expectations of technological risks and collaboration to prevent and mitigate them.

Rebuilding trust in nuclear power and its oversight requires demonstration of effective regulations and safe nuclear reactor operation. However, these conditions face several challenges. First, Japan's case has demonstrated that public distrust can lead to suspicion regarding the effectiveness of new regulations, regardless of their actual effectiveness. Second, the government's transparent communication has included reporting of continued utility violations of these regulations, deepening public distrust in safe reactor operation and signaling that cultural change within the utilities has not yet caught up with the change in regulatory culture. The NRA's annual reports document continued data falsifications from 2015 to 2021 (e.g., Nuclear Regulation Authority, 2019). Third, the technologies used in older reactors do not employ the same safety features as newer reactors. Updated technologies require effective enforcement of appropriate regulatory frameworks that account for such changes. This hurdle reflects a broader difficulty facing regulatory frameworks: keeping pace with new technologies for resource extraction and use, especially those deployed rapidly to solve an existing energy system resilience challenge. Fourth, ambiguity regarding institutional support challenges the utilities' long-term investment plans. In Japan's case, without construction of new nuclear plants, the existing nuclear reactor fleet will reach license expiration by the 2060s. Achieving a resilient energy system requires such long-term planning, but also flexibility to adjust to new realities regarding risks, enabling collaboration on measures to mitigate them.

The fifth challenge links these trust, communication and regulatory framework difficulties. As discussed earlier in this chapter, regulators' relationships with infrastructure operators face the complex problem of balancing information exchanges and perspectives without engaging in regulatory capture or the appearance of it. The lines dividing regulatory capture from cooperation and regulator independence from isolation are not easily defined, but the results determine whether regulatory frameworks promote or diminish energy system resilience. With the aforementioned framing of regulation as a resilience tool, capture becomes less useful to the regulated entities, replaced by cooperation toward all forms of resilience.

Japan's trajectory from the 1970s oil crises through the post-Fukushima disaster period thus offers a variety of lessons for policymakers at national to local levels, regulators, energy industries, and consumers. In the final chapter, we will examine these lessons' further implications for energy system resilience and change, as well as innovation.

Notes

1 This zero risk tolerance extends to all areas. Government interviewees noted the ban on imported beef due to public perceptions of risks associated with mad cow disease. See Sklarew, 2008.
2 For more on the impact of Exxon-Valdez, see Birkland, 1997.
3 Many media sources and Japanese government documents state that renewables accounted for less than two percent of Japan's electricity supply prior to the Fukushima accident. These sources also state that renewables use accounted for only two percent of Japan's electricity supply in 2012. For consistency, and because these sources do not cite the original data sources for these numbers, IEA numbers are used for all fuel types in the analyses of Japan's electricity supply from 2010–2020. The IEA numbers reflect a higher percentage of non-hydro renewables for both 2010 and 2012. Biofuels, which are included in the IEA's data, may account for this difference.

References

Agency for Natural Resources and Energy, Ministry of Economy, Trade and Industry, Government of Japan. (2015) 'Settlement of FY2015 Purchase Prices and FY2015 Surcharge Rates under the Feed-In Tariff Scheme for Renewable Energy.' www.meti.go.jp/english/press/2015/0319_01.html.

Agency for Natural Resources and Energy, Ministry of Economy, Trade and Industry, Government of Japan. (2020) 'Current Conditions of Domestic and International Renewable Energy and This Year's Procurement Price Calculation Committee's Proposal (国内外の再生可能エネルギーの現状と 今年度の調達価格等算定委員会の論点案).' 10 September. www.meti.go.jp/shingikai/santeii/pdf/061_01_00.pdf.

Agency for Natural Resources and Energy, Ministry of Economy, Trade and Industry, Government of Japan. (2021) 'Outline of Strategic Energy Plan.' October.

Aldrich, D.P. (2013) 'Rethinking Civil Society – State Relations in Japan after the Fukushima Accident.' *Polity*, 45, 249–264.

Aoki, M., and Rothwell, G. (2013) 'A Comparative Institutional Analysis of the Fukushima Nuclear Disaster: Lessons and Policy Implications.' *Energy Policy*, 53 (February), 240–247.

The Asahi Shimbun. (2021) 'Nuclear hawks under Kishida Threaten Suga's Renewables Push.' *The Asahi Shimbun.* 14 October. https://www.asahi.com/ajw/articles/14460623

Asia Pacific Energy Research Centre. (2004) *Electric Power Grid Interconnections in the APEC Region.* Japan: Asia Pacific Energy Research Centre, Institute of Energy Economics.

Ayoub, N., and Naka, Y. (2012) 'Governmental Intervention Approaches to Promote Renewable Energies – Special Emphasis on Japanese Feed-In Tariff.' *Energy Policy*, 43 (C), 191–201.

Birkland, T.A. (1997) *After Disaster: Agenda Setting, Public Policy, and Focusing Events.* Washington, DC: Georgetown University Press.

DeWit, A., Iida, T., and Kaneko., M. (2012) 'Fukushima and the Political Economy of Power Policy in Japan.' In Kingston, J. (ed.), *Natural Disaster and Nuclear Crisis in Japan – Response and Recovery After Japan's 3/11.* London: Routledge.

Ebuchi, T. (2022) 'Japan to Require Utilities to Open Grids to Energy Storage Options. *Nikkei Asia.* 27 January.' https://ieefa.org/japan-to-require-utilities-to-open-grids-to-energy-storage-options/.

Electricity and Gas Market Surveillance Commission. 'About EGC.' www.emsc.meti.go.jp/english/committee/.

Electricity Market Reform Office, Agency for Energy and Natural Resources, Ministry of Economy, Trade and Industry, Government of Japan. (2013) *Electricity Market Reform in Japan*. Tokyo: Ministry of Economy, Trade and Industry.

Electricity Supply-Demand Review Committee, Energy and Environment Council, Ministry of Economy, Trade and Industry, Government of Japan. (2012) *Electricity Supply-Demand Measures This Winter*. Tokyo: Ministry of Economy, Trade and Industry.

Energy Efficiency and Conservation Division, Agency for Natural Resources and Energy, Ministry of Economy, Trade and Industry. (2015) *Definition of ZEH and Future Measures Proposed by the ZEH Roadmap Examination Committee*. December. Tokyo: Ministry of Economy, Trade and Industry.

The Federation of Electric Power Companies of Japan. (2020) 'The New Pluthermal Program.' 17 December. www.fepc.or.jp/english/news/message/__icsFiles/afieldfile/2020/12/17/press_e_20201217.pdf.

The Genron NPO. (2019) 'Trust in Japanese Democratic System, Public Opinion Poll.' www.genron-npo.net/en/opinion_polls/archives/5496.html.

Gnansounou, E. (2010) 'Measuring Energy Security Vulnerability.' In Sovacool, B. (ed.), *The Routledge Handbook of Energy Security*. London: Routledge, 396–413.

Government of Japan. (2014a) '"Abenomics" Is Progressing!' The Latest Progress and Achievements in the First Year of the Abe Administration.

Government of Japan. (2014b) *Fourth Strategic Energy Plan* （エネルギー基本計画、平成26年4月）. 26 April.

Government of Japan. (2018) *Fifth Strategic Energy Plan* （エネルギー基本計画、平成３０年７月）. 30 July.

Government of Japan. (2021) *Sixth Strategic Energy Plan* （エネルギー基本計画、令和３年１０月）. October.

International Atomic Energy Agency. (2021) 'International Nuclear Information Safety System.' www.iaea.org/resources/databases/inis.

International Atomic Energy Agency. (2022) 'IAEA Experts Make Headway in Reviewing Safety of Plan to Discharge Treated Water from Fukushima Site.' 18 February.

International Energy Agency. (2017) 'Act on the Rational Use of Energy (Energy Efficiency Act).' 5 November. www.iea.org/policies/573-act-on-the-rational-use-of-energy-energy-efficiency-act.

International Energy Agency. (2021a) 'Electricity Information 2021 Edition Database Documentation.' http://wds.iea.org/wds/pdf/Ele_documentation.pdf

International Energy Agency. (2021b) *Japan 2021 Energy Policy Review*. Paris: International Energy Agency.

Iwata, M. (2014) 'As Nuclear Concerns Rise, Japan Delays Energy Plan.' *WSJ Blogs – Japan Real Time*. 14 January. http://blogs.wsj.com/japanrealtime/2014/01/14/as-nuclear-concerns-rise-japan-delays-energy-plan/.

Iwata, M. (2015) 'Lawmaker Uses Leaked Document to Argue for Renewable Energy.' *WSJ Blogs – Japan Real Time. The Wall Street Journal Japan*. 12 March. http://blogs.wsj.com/japanrealtime/2015/03/12/lawmaker-uses-leaked-document-to-argue-for-renewable-energy/.

Japan Atomic Energy Commission. (2018) *Basic Principles on Japan's Utilization of Plutonium*. July.

Japan Atomic Energy Relations Organization. (2017) '2017 Public Opinion Poll Regarding Nuclear Power.' www.jaero.or.jp/data/01jigyou/pdf/tyousakenkyu29/section4.pdf.

Japan Atomic Energy Relations Organization. (2018) '2018 Public Opinion Poll Regarding Nuclear Power.' www.jaero.or.jp/data/01jigyou/pdf/tyousakenkyu30/r2018.pdf.

Japan Atomic Energy Relations Organization. (2019) '2019 Public Opinion Poll Regarding Nuclear Power.' www.jaero.or.jp/data/01jigyou/pdf/tyousakenkyu2019/r2019.pdf.

Japan Atomic Energy Relations Organization. (2020) '2020 Public Opinion Poll Regarding Nuclear Power.' www.jaero.or.jp/data/01jigyou/pdf/tyousakenkyu2020/results_2020.pdf.

Japan Atomic Energy Relations Organization. (2021) '2021 Public Opinion Poll Regarding Nuclear Power.' https://www.jaero.or.jp/data/01jigyou/pdf/tyousakenkyu2021/results_2021.pdf

Japan Nuclear Safety Institute. (2021) 'Licensing Status for the Japanese Nuclear Facilities.' 15 September. www.genanshin.jp/english/facility/map/index.html.

The Jiji Press. (2021) '10 Years On: Fukushima N-Plant Decommissioning Costs Over 1.4 T. Yen.' *Nippon.com.* 9 March. www.nippon.com/en/news/yjj2021030600388/.

Johnston, E. (2015) 'Nuclear Motive Suspected in Feed-in Tariff Reforms.' *The Japan Times Online.* 2 January. www.japantimes.co.jp/news/2015/01/02/national/nuclear-motive-suspected-in-feed-in-tariff-reforms/.

Kawamura, G., and Wakabayashi, M. (2021a) 'Japan Renewable Alert 51.' Orrick, Herrington & Sutcliffe, LLP. 14 January. www.jdsupra.com/legalnews/japan-renewable-alert-51-7084493/.

Kawamura, G., and Wakabayashi, M. (2021b) 'Japan Renewable Alert 53.' Orrick, Herrington & Sutcliffe, LLP. 23 April. www.jdsupra.com/legalnews/japan-renewable-alert-53-8476960/.

Kelly, T., and Lies, E. (2022) 'Nuclear Reactor Restarts Could Be "Best Option" for Japan to Ride Out Energy Shortages – Senior Ruling Party Lawmaker.' *Reuters.* 7 March. www.reuters.com/article/ukraine-crisis-japan-reactors/nuclear-reactor-restarts-could-be-best-option-for-japan-to-ride-out-energy-shortages-senior-ruling-party-lawmaker-idUSL2N2VB06B.

Kingston, J. (2013) 'Japan's Nuclear Village: Power and Resilience.' In Kingston, J. (ed.), *Critical Issues in Contemporary Japan.* London: Routledge, 107–119.

Kishimoto, A. (2017) 'Public Attitudes and Institutional Changes in Japan Following Nuclear Accidents.' In Balleisen, E., Bennear, L., Krawiec, K.D., and Wiener, J.B. (eds.), *Policy Shock: Recalibrating Risk and Regulation after Oil Spills, Nuclear Accidents and Financial Crises.* Cambridge: Cambridge University Press, 269–304.

Kobayashi, T., Okatani, S., Murakami, Y., and Noma, H. (2021) *Alternative Energy & Power 2021: Japan.* Chambers & Partners. 20 July. https://practiceguides.chambers.com/practice-guides/alternative-energy-power-2021/japan/trends-and-developments.

Kono, T. (2015) 'Dead Letter Public Comment.' E-Newsletter *Gomame No Hagijiri* (ごまめの歯ぎしり), 9 January.

Ministerial Council on Renewable Energy, Hydrogen and Related Issues, Government of Japan. (2018) *The Basic Hydrogen Strategy.* 26 December. Tokyo: Cabinet Office, Government of Japan.

Ministry of Economy, Trade and Industry, Government of Japan. (2010) *The Strategic Energy Plan of Japan* (Revised 2010).

Ministry of Economy, Trade and Industry, Government of Japan. (2019a) *Cabinet Orders concerning the Act of Promoting Utilization of Sea Areas in Development of Power Generation*

Facilities Using Maritime Renewable Energy Resources Approved. 15 March. Tokyo: Ministry of Economy, Trade and Industry, Government of Japan.

Ministry of Economy, Trade and Industry, Government of Japan. (2019b) 'METI to Launch Subcommittee on Electricity Resilience Towards a Decarbonized Society.' 14 February. www.meti.go.jp/english/press/2019/0214_002.html.

Ministry of Economy, Trade and Industry, Government of Japan. (2019c) *Results Compiled for the Electricity Supply and Demand for the Winter of FY2018 as well as Outlook and Measures for Electricity Supply and Demand for the Summer of FY2019.* 26 April. Tokyo: Ministry of Economy, Trade and Industry, Government of Japan.

Ministry of Economy, Trade and Industry, Government of Japan. (2019d) 'Two Bodies Inaugurated: Subcommittee on System Reform for Renewable Energy as Main Power Source and Subcommittee for Sustainable Power Systems.' 27 August. www.meti.go.jp/english/press/2019/0827_004.html.

Ministry of Economy, Trade and Industry, Government of Japan. (2021) '2021 Purchase Prices for the FIT System Were Decided.' (FIT制度における2021年度の買取価格・賦課金単価等を決定しました). 24 March. www.meti.go.jp/press/2020/03/20210324004/20210324004.html.

Ministry of Land, Infrastructure and Transport. (2016) *Overview of the Act on the Improvement of Energy Performance Consumption of Buildings.* April. Tokyo: Ministry of Land, Infrastructure and Transport, Government of Japan.

The National Diet of Japan Fukushima Nuclear Accident Independent Investigation Commission. (2012) *The Official Report of The Fukushima Nuclear Accident Independent Investigation Commission.* Tokyo: The National Diet of Japan.

NHK. (2021) 'What Should Be Done with Domestic Nuclear Power Generation from Now On: Survey 10 Years after the Nuclear Power Generation Accident' (国内原発を今後どうすべき：原発事故１０年世論調査). NHK. 2 March. www.nhk.or.jp/politics/articles/lastweek/54794.html.

NHK Broadcasting Culture Research Institute. (2021) *People's Attitudes Found in a Public Opinion Survey a Decade After the Disaster* (世論調査に見る震災10年の人々の意識). NHK. 1 July. www.nhk.or.jp/bunken/research/yoron/pdf/20210701_8.pdf.

Nikkei Staff Writers. (2021) 'Nuclear Power Crucial to Japan's Net-Zero Goal: Industry Minister.' *NikkeiAsia.* 6 October. https://asia.nikkei.com/Business/Energy/Nuclear-power-crucial-to-Japan-s-net-zero-goal-industry-minister.

Nishiyama, H. (2013) 'Japan's Policy on Energy Conservation.' International Affairs Office, Energy Conservation and Renewable Energy Department. Agency for Natural Resources and Energy, Ministry of Economy, Trade and Industry, Government of Japan.

Nuclear Emergency Response Headquarters, Government of Japan. (2011) *Report of Japanese Government to IAEA Ministerial Conference on Nuclear Safety – Accident at TEPCO's Fukushima Nuclear Power Stations.* 15 September. Tokyo: Nuclear Emergency Response Headquarters, Government of Japan.

Nuclear Regulation Authority, Government of Japan. (2013) 'New Regulatory Requirements.' 3 April. www.nsr.go.jp/english/regulatory/index.html.

Nuclear Regulation Authority, Government of Japan. (2019) *FY 2019 Annual Report.*

Nuclear Regulation Authority, Government of Japan. (2021) 'Individual Power Reactor Information' (発電所別情報). www.nsr.go.jp/Selection/hatudensho_betu_index.html.

Nuclear Regulation Authority, Government of Japan. (2022) 'Nuclear Regulation Authority Press Conference Transcript.' 19 January. www.nsr.go.jp/data/000379021.pdf.

Nuclear Regulatory Commission. (2020) 'Probabilistic Risk Assessment.' www.nrc.gov/about-nrc/regulatory/risk-informed/pra.html.

Ohira, Y. (2017) 'Renewable Energy Policies and Economic Revitalization in Fukushima: Issues and Prospects.' In Yamakawa, M., and Yamamoto, D. (eds.), *Rebuilding Fukushima*. London: Routledge, 148–163.

Organization for Cross-Regional Coordination of Transmission Operators. (2021) 'Role of OCCTO in the Electricity System Reform.' 1 June. www.occto.or.jp/en/about_occto/about_occto.html.

Organization for Cross-Regional Coordination of Transmission Operators. (2022) 'Regarding Usage Situation for Switching Support System.' (スイッチング支援システムの利用状況について). 9 February. www.occto.or.jp/system/riyoujoukyou/files/20220209_swsys_riyoujyoukyou.pdf.

Oshima, K., and Yokemoto, M. (2012) *Damage of the Fukushima Nuclear Accident and Compensation*. Tokyo: Otsuki Shoten.

Pollitt, M. (2012) 'The Role of Policy in Energy Transitions: Lessons from the Liberalisation Era.' *Energy Policy*, 50 (C), 128–137.

Prime Minister's Office of Japan. (2021) 'Inter-Ministerial Council for Contaminated Water, Treated Water and Decommissioning Issues, Government of Japan.' 13 April. https://japan.kantei.go.jp/99_suga/actions/202104/_00012.html.

Reconstruction Agency, Government of Japan. (2021) 'Great East Japan Earthquake.' www.reconstruction.go.jp/english/topics/GEJE/.

Reuters Staff. (2019a) 'FACTBOX-Japan's Construction Plans for New Coal-Fired Power Stations.' *Reuters*. 15 August. www.reuters.com/article/japan-coal-plant/factbox-japans-construction-plans-for-new-coal-fired-power-stations-idUKL4N1FM1T4

Reuters Staff. (2019b) 'New Environment Minister Says Japan Should Stop Using Nuclear Power.' *Reuters*. 11 September. www.reuters.com/article/us-japan-nuclear-koizumi/new-environment-minister-says-japan-should-stop-using-nuclear-power-idUSKCN1VX01E

Sklarew, J.F. (2008) 'The Role of 'Anshin' in U.S.-Japan Relations.' In *U.S.-Japan Relations as Portrayed by a Hundred People: Japan Commerce Association of Washington, DC 20th Anniversary Issue*. Washington, DC: Japan Commerce Association of Washington, DC, Inc, 119–121.

Sklarew, J.F. (2015) *Shock to the System: How Catastrophic Events and Institutional Relationships Impact Japanese Energy Policymaking, Resilience, and Innovation*. Arlington, VA: George Mason University.

Sklarew, J.F. (2018) 'Power Fluctuations: How Japan's Nuclear Infrastructure Priorities Influence Electric Utilities' Clout.' *Energy Research & Social Science*, 41, 158–167.

Sone, Y. (2012a) *Executive Summary: The National Deliberative Poll in Japan, August 4–5, 2012 on Energy and Environmental Policy Options*. Tokyo: Keio University.

Sone, Y. (2012b) *National Japan Deliberative Poll, August 2012 Report: Initial Results, Attitude Change T1-T3*. Tokyo: Keio University.

Suzuki, T. (2017) 'Six Years After Fukushima, Much of Japan Has Lost Faith in Nuclear Power.' *The Conversation*. 9 March. https://theconversation.com/six-years-after-fukushima-much-of-japan-has-lost-faith-in-nuclear-power-73042.

Suzuki, T. (2018) 'Updating from Lessons Learnt from Fukushima.' In Maiani, L., Abousahl, S., and Plastino, W. (eds.), *International Cooperation for Enhancing Nuclear Safety, Security, Safeguards and Non-Proliferation – 60 Years of IAEA and EURATOM*. Springer Proceedings in Physics, vol 206. Berlin, Heidelberg: Springer.

Vivoda, V. (2012) 'Japan's Energy Security Predicament Post Fukushima.' *Energy Policy*, 46, 135–143.

Vivoda, V. (2016) *Energy Security in Japan: Challenges After Fukushima.* London: Routledge.

World Nuclear Association. (2021) 'Nuclear Power in Japan.' https://world-nuclear.org/information-library/country-profiles/countries-g-n/japan-nuclear-power.aspx.

Yamaguchi, M. (2019) 'Japan Revises Fukushima Cleanup Plan, Delays Key Steps.' *AP News*. 27 December.

6 Conclusions

Lessons for Resilience

Japan's energy policymaking trajectory offers compelling lessons on how shocks, stakeholder relationships, resilience priorities, and risk perceptions combine to shape and transform energy systems and their resilience. Japan's narrative also offers related insights on how these factors influence stakeholder cooperation and conflict that can enable or hinder innovation to promote all forms of resilience: engineering, ecological, economic and social.

Other Important Actors and Factors for Energy System Resilience

Two additional sets of actors and related factors contribute significantly to this cooperation and conflict, also influencing energy system resilience. In particular, the interview data illuminated intergovernmental relationships and the roles of the manufacturing sector and media in Japan's energy system trajectory and implications for all forms of resilience.

The interview data for this book confirms repeatedly that intragovernmental relationships are intertwined with government relationships with the public and the energy sector. Government interviewees emphasized the role of relationships between METI's energy-related offices, between METI and MOE, and between the central government and local governments in energy policymaking. The NRA's relationships with METI and MOE also would offer useful insights. In particular, interviewees highlighted tensions between these groups that grew as their missions blurred or conflicted due to shocks, shifts in risk perceptions and resilience priorities, and institutional changes. This tension challenged cooperation on advancing energy system resilience, providing additional lessons for other cases in which diverse government actors influence energy policies and regulations. While this book touches briefly on these relationships, a more detailed analysis is needed. Assessing the changes in these relationships during the three periods analyzed in this book and merging them with the book's findings will provide an even more holistic perspective on Japan's energy system trajectory, enabling further lessons for other places.

The interview data also reflects the importance of the manufacturing sector's relationships with the government and the electric utilities, as well as the media's

DOI: 10.4324/9781003227588-6

relationships with the government and the public. These two groups of stakeholders, their relationships with other stakeholders, and their resilience priorities and risk perceptions also influence energy system resilience.

The interview data confirms that the government's relationship with the manufacturing sector wields considerable impact in Japan's energy policymaking. As mentioned in chapter three, existing studies suggest that the manufacturing sector typically competes or coordinates with, but does not trump, the electric utilities for influence over energy policymaking. However, as large electricity users, these companies have relationships with the government and the electricity utilities that influence energy policies through pressure on the government to lower electricity prices. Other national governments have experienced this power of large consumers in driving energy system changes. In the United States, as in Japan, telecommunications and IT firms have begun to generate their own on-site renewable power, coupled with battery storage in some cases.

Like IT and telecommunications firms, manufacturing companies also can play a role as potential electricity producers if they have access to the grid. Relationships with the electric utilities and the government impact this potential, as demonstrated by the grid access challenges discussed in chapter five. If government policies enable manufacturers to sell their excess power, these firms can support socio-ecological resilience by providing localized electricity. They also can enhance social and economic resilience through their role in supply-demand load balancing, conservation of energy resources as "prosumers" – roles as both producers and consumers of power – and potential electricity cost reductions. These features can hold particular salience in nations with agro-industrial prosumers and rural communities unable to access a centralized grid (United Nations Industrial Development Organization, 2015).

The media's relationships with the government, the energy sector and the public represent a third set of stakeholder relationships that indirectly influence energy system resilience, according to the interview data. Existing studies indicate that government-media relations do not directly alter energy policymaking. However, interviewees' comments indicated that the media plays a crucial role in shaping the public's attitude toward the government, government policies, and the electric utilities. As a result, the media also impacts the government's relationships with the electric utilities. The interview data suggests that the media's influence on public opinion wields particular importance after shocks occur. The media's role as the conduit for conveying information thus strongly influences transparency and communication between the government and all other groups, as well as the energy sector's communication with the public. When media agencies align with particular stakeholder groups or political parties, as many do in Japan and other places around the globe, the information received by these groups may differ, exacerbating divergences in risk perceptions and resilience priorities.

The media also plays a role in gauging public trust in the government and the energy sector. As shown in chapters three through five, governments and the energy sector can use media polls as tools to understand public risk perceptions and resilience priorities. On the other hand, the media also shapes this trust, these risk perceptions, and these priorities. In Japan, the media largely did not highlight the nuclear accidents in the 1990s and early 2000s, said some interviewees, which preserved public trust and perceptions of zero risk. Other interviewees noted that the media relied on revenue from advertisements by the electric utilities, leading them to withhold criticism when accidents occurred. The Fukushima disaster altered this dynamic, opening the door for media criticism of nuclear safety and the relationships between the electric utilities, the regulators, and METI (e.g., I10, June 2013). As time has passed, media coverage of the NRA has supported the new regulator, contributing to a return of public trust in nuclear regulation. Some government interviewees such as G11 also noted that the government also can leverage the media to resurrect trust in the electric utilities. Public trust in energy technologies, the energy sector's operation of them, and the government's ability to oversee and regulate them also depend on the amount of information the media provides, as well as the technical explanations needed to enable public understanding.

Japan's narrative sheds light on how this trust influences the government's ability to support innovation to improve incumbent technologies and introduce new ones, particularly when disasters occur.

Innovating from Disasters

Examples of energy system vulnerability to shocks exist around the globe. At a national level, the United States has experienced similar shocks, including the 1970s oil crises, the 1979 Three-Mile Island nuclear accident, the 1989 Exxon-Valdez oil spill, and the 2010 Deepwater Horizon oil spill. We can see regional parallels in more recent shocks that include the 2018 destruction of Puerto Rico's power grid by Hurricanes Maria and Irma, followed by the 2020 earthquake. Mainland U.S. shocks include the 2021 winter storm-induced power outages in Texas and 2021 hacker-led shutdown of the Colonial gas pipeline. In Asia, Typhoon Haiyan led to a loss of 6.3 billion hours of electricity in the Philippines in 2013, and domestic terrorism fomented long-term power outages in Pakistan in 2015 (Owens, 2020). In South America, drought triggered Venezuela's power crisis that began in 2017. European nations have faced several close calls that narrowly averted widespread multinational outages, most recently the split in the synchronized European power grid due to a Croatian substation technological malfunction in 2021 (Appunn, 2021; Starn et al., 2021). Previously, in 1999, France lost one-fourth of its extra high voltage transmission lines, 180 high-voltage transmission lines, and more than 100 substations due to Cyclones Lothar and Martin, leaving almost 3.4 million households without electricity (Eurelectric, 2006).

These shocks and others have yielded diverse energy policy outcomes, ranging from unchanged energy systems to dramatic transformation. France has maintained its centralized energy system. despite bureaucratic delays in system repairs due to this centralized control (Eurelectric, 2006). Japan's similar difficulties regarding pacing of responses to nuclear incidents offer lessons on accident response and the roles of transparency and communication across energy facility operators and responsible government agencies. Recent Japanese policy movement toward supporting distributed generation also can inform responses to this type of institutional setback to engineering resilience.

Venezuela has remained reliant on vulnerable hydropower and fossil fuels (IRENA, 2021). Japan's narrative reveals the resilience challenges of such system lock-in.

Meanwhile, the Puerto Rican local government shifted from initial interest in rebuilding its prior system toward a phased transition away from imported fossil fuels and toward renewable energy (EIA). This trajectory resembles Japan's post-Fukushima movement toward replacing inefficient coal plants with renewables.

Like Japan's narrative, each of these shocks can reveal contributing factors emerging from stakeholder relationships and resilience priorities, as well as risk perceptions. The lessons from Japan discussed in previous chapters can help us to identify and assess these factors in these cases and others from the past, present and future. We also can apply Japan's lessons to examine how these factors shape responses that promote or hinder each form of energy system resilience in these other cases and places.

The 1970s oil crises triggered Japanese policymakers' cooperation with the electric utilities to innovate out of the existing oil dependent energy system. This policy innovation reframed Japan's energy system around nuclear power as solution to energy security, economic stability, and environmental concerns such as air pollution and climate change. The government and utilities also collaborated on technological innovations to advance nuclear power deployment, coupled with cooperation on policy and technological innovations on an open fuel cycle to address nuclear waste challenges and uranium imports. This collaboration provides a model for stakeholder cooperation to leverage a shock as an opportunity for innovation toward increased energy system resilience. This cooperation on policy and technological innovations continued throughout the 1990s and early 2000s, focusing on advancing nuclear fuel reprocessing, as well as new reactor designs to improve passive safety and achieve greater economies of scale (Kadak, 2017).

However, the conflict over regulatory oversight, setbacks from accidents, and efforts to avoid unsettling a risk averse public inhibited some incremental innovations that could have addressed safety concerns and degradation of aging reactor components. These issues also led to suppression of innovation on other technologies that could have complemented nuclear power. Japan's post-oil crises trajectory thus provides lessons on encouraging incremental innovation toward resilience through acknowledgment of existing challenges to a chosen technology. Additionally, Japan's policy shift toward reliance on nuclear power, coal and natural gas demonstrates the need to build flexibility and diversity into energy policy planning and investment incentives, which make room for revised priorities and new technology innovations. These efforts can avert energy system lock-in that inhibits innovation and all forms of resilience from national to local levels.

The Fukushima disaster spurred innovation both within and away from Japan's incumbent energy system. We already have examined some of the government's and utilities' incremental innovations to build resilience within Japan's existing energy system after the Fukushima disaster. These include policy and regulatory changes to advance Japan's nuclear safety culture, heat pump designs to enhance energy efficiency, and carbon capture, utilization and storage (CCUS) research and development to decarbonize fossil fuel use.

Innovation Examples from Japan

While changes in national policies to incorporate new energy sources have moved slowly, the Fukushima disaster has generated local innovations developed by local governments, electric utilities, and other entrepreneurs to build local energy system resilience. Examples highlighted by former NGO Japan for Sustainability include rooftop solar leasing models in Kanagawa and Miyagi Prefectures, a public-private partnership for solar aggregation in Nagano Prefecture, Toyota's electricity production partnership with a local community and the utility company, and Fukushima's planned transformation to a solar and wind hub. Now adopted across the nation, Kanagawa's model began with rooftop leasing for solar on local government facilities. The prefectural government then initiated a matching program for private buildings, followed by matching land leasing, as well as rooftop leasing for aggregated residential clusters (Japan for Sustainability, 2015). These features of the model promote socio-ecological and economic resilience.

Miyagi Prefecture innovated on Kanagawa's model, applying it to public housing for disaster evacuees who had lost their homes. In a public-private partnership, the municipalities lease the rooftops to the power generation companies, and residents receive free electricity from the panels when blackouts occur (Japan for Sustainability, 2015). This model could be adapted for low-income housing in the United States, and potentially for the increasingly common refugee facilities around the world.

Nagano's Renewable Energy Shinshu-net also addresses economic and socio-ecological resilience risks through cooperation, economies of scale, financing, and transparency and communication. A collaborative network of citizens, businesses, universities and administrative bodies concluded a three-party agreement with power generation companies and the prefectural government. The program utilizes dispersed power generation by organizing large and small rooftops of public and private buildings in clusters distributed across the prefecture. Part of the prefecture's electric power sales revenue covers the project's cost. Renewable Energy Shinshu-net released the project manual to the public to promote deployment, and the public also has access to data on the amount of electricity generated at different installation angles at a solar power generation laboratory. The prefecture conducts tours of solar power installation sites during several stages of installation, as well as after completion (Japan for Sustainability, 2015). This empowerment of local communities to understand and engage in energy system transformation embeds consumers in promoting system resilience.

Japan's first regional emergency power system, F-Grid Ohira, Miyagi Limited Liability Partnership (LLP), also involves local community partnerships for electricity and heat supply and demand optimization to build socio-ecological resilience

(Toyota, 2015). The grid connects businesses with privately owned power generators such as Toyota, as well as the electric utility and local government facilities.
An onsite gas turbine provides power to Toyota factory, which uses heat generated
from the gas turbine to dry the paint on finished vehicles. VEGi-Dream Kuri-
hara also uses the waste heat in to cultivate peppers in its greenhouse. At times
when the Toyota factory doesn't need as much power, electricity is transferred to
local restaurant chain Skylark to power refrigeration (Sato, n.d.). During power
outages, local utility Tohoku Electric Power Company can purchase power from
Toyota for provision to emergency centers. F-Grid also employs battery storage for
emergency power, utilizing eight plug-in hybrid vehicles as external power sources
and charging/discharging systems (Toyota, 2015).

To achieve its goal of 100% renewable electricity by 2040, the Fukushima prefectural government received funding from the government-supported Development
Bank of Japan and Mizuho Bank to construct 11 solar and 10 wind farms by the
end of March 2024. Siting focuses on abandoned, contaminated farmland (Ueda
and Kurimoto, 2019). As of the end of fiscal year 2020, renewables accounted for
43 percent of the prefecture's energy consumption (Balmer and Ozawa, 2022).
While the influx of renewables builds the prefecture's socio-ecological resilience,
some consumers remain concerned about electricity prices, reflecting potential
conflict over economic resilience perspectives.

These local examples offer models for community-level partnerships to respond
to disasters with technological and financial innovations that build all forms
of resilience. They also highlight the role of institutional support in promoting
cooperation on such innovations. This support can take the form of policies that
provide an enabling environment for innovations, as well as regulations that facilitate their deployment while protecting the public from any negative externalities.
Japan's case has shown us that building flexibility to adjust to new knowledge on
these technologies – including refinements as well as challenges that require further innovation and regulation – is crucial to sustaining all forms of energy system
resilience. Japan's narrative illuminates how variations in resilience priorities and
perspectives can generate cooperation on or conflict over energy system changes,
enabling or disabling innovation. Thus, these variations determine whether resilience priorities serve as catalysts for or barriers to energy system adaptation when
shocks occur.

We can apply these models and lessons to other nations and communities challenged by crises that have threatened their energy systems, including natural disasters, pandemics, accidents, and geopolitically induced resource shortages and
price disruptions.

Global Applications

Following the Fukushima disaster, many nations' governments revamped nuclear
safety regulations to promote resilience in their existing energy systems. For example, the French electricity supply continues to feature nuclear power, which provides approximately 70 percent of France's electricity as of March 2022 (World

Nuclear Association, 2022). In 2012, French nuclear regulator Autorité de sûreté nucléaire (ASN) released a National Action Plan requiring safety upgrades to all reactors (Autorité de sûreté nucléaire, 2012). The U.S. Nuclear Regulatory Commission (NRC) also issued plant-specific orders and requests for information as a result of hazard reevaluations following the Fukushima disaster (United States Nuclear Regulatory Commission, 2021). The Chinese and Indian governments also introduced new regulations and safety assessments, with plans to continue nuclear power expansion using advanced nuclear technologies with enhanced safety features.

Other nations have announced movement away from nuclear power in response to the Fukushima disaster. The German government had been heading toward eliminating nuclear power from the electricity mix prior to the Fukushima disaster. Following a brief period of policies extending nuclear power use, the disaster expedited this movement to decommission Germany's nuclear reactors. The Belgian government also made plans to close the nation's nuclear plants by 2025; the Italian government ceased plans to resurrect nuclear power, and the Spanish and Swiss governments decided against new nuclear plant construction (Paillere and Donovan, 2021).

Like Japan, numerous U.S. states and localities have experienced energy system crises due to natural disasters. The January 2021 power crisis in Texas, precipitated by an unprecedented series of snowstorms, parallels the characterization of Japan's March 11 earthquake and tsunami as a black swan event. As in Japan, risk perceptions and resilience priorities contributed to the crisis. Perceptions of minimal risk from cold weather led to a lack of winterization of the state's energy infrastructure, creating engineering resilience vulnerability. The power grid in Texas is not connected to other states, which created a similar power transfer challenge to the one Fukushima experienced due to Japan's 50–60 hertz bifurcated national grid. The prolonged cold temperatures froze all of Texas' energy infrastructure – natural gas, wind, coal, and nuclear – causing blackouts and skyrocketing electricity rates.

Policy responses to the crisis in Texas have addressed some of these challenges, but not all, and some not adequately. The state government's focus on the energy industry's economic resilience priorities precipitated legislation that enabled natural gas utilities and electric cooperatives to recoup losses through ratepayer-backed bonds. This focus creates an economic resilience challenge for consumers. To address engineering and social resilience, the legislation also requires power plants to weatherize, but not natural gas infrastructure owners. This omission perpetuates engineering resilience risk, just as Japan's regulatory challenges did. The crisis in Texas was compounded by close relationships between energy companies, ERCOT and state officials, as well as the distance between consumers and ERCOT's Board of Directors, one-third of whom did not live in Texas.

Japan's lessons on innovating from disasters include applications to Texas. Membership in transmission operator ERCOT already includes consumers, cooperatives, generators, power marketers, retail electric providers, investor-owned electric utilities, transmission & distribution providers & municipally owned electric utilities. If ERCOT could promote transparent communication and collaboration across these groups, it could serve as an innovation hub for building greater economic, engineering, and socio-ecological resilience for all stakeholders, including cooperation on infrastructure planning and demand-response measures.

Puerto Rican energy stakeholders also can glean lessons from Japan's trajectory. Like Japan, Puerto Rico is prone to strong storms, and a fossil fuel-based energy system has faced engineering, socio-ecological and economic resilience vulnerabilities. One week after Hurricane Maria ravaged Puerto Rico in 2017, 95 percent of the population had no electricity. One month after the hurricane, 88 percent remained without power. Three months after Maria departed, 45 percent of the population – more than 1.5 million people – remained without electricity (Owens, 2020). Almost 7 months after the hurricane, between 100,000 and 200,000 residents remained without electricity (Owens, 2020). The local government originally planned to rebuild the grid as it was prior to the hurricane, despite warnings that the existing infrastructure posed challenges to engineering resilience. The Puerto Rico Energy Public Policy Act of 2019 has set the stage for a transformation of the local energy system, with milestones to achieve a grid powered by 100 percent renewables by 2050 (Puerto Rico Energy Public Policy Act, 2019). A study group comprised of the U.S. Department of Energy's Office of Electricity, five national laboratories, funders, local implementation agencies, and a stakeholder advisory group is conducting a study, Puerto Rico Grid Resilience and Transitions to 100% Renewable Energy (PR100), from 2022–2024 to determine plans to achieve these milestones. Japan's locally driven innovation models can provide examples of collaboration that could benefit the study group's analysis. Japan's gradual energy system lock-in also provides lessons on development of flexible policy and regulatory frameworks and infrastructure investments structured to prevent future lock-in and adaptability to respond to shocks as Puerto Rico develops its new system.

Other examples of energy shocks abound around the world, including the 2013 blackout in the Philippines due to Typhoon Haiyan; the 2015 blackout in Pakistan from a cascading power failure after separatists blew up two transmission towers; and the 2021 hacker-induced shutdown of the U.S. East Coast Colonial Pipeline. Lessons from Japan can inform energy system recovery, resilience-building and innovation after these types of catastrophic events and others.

Most recently, Russia's reduction of natural gas exports to the European Union since 2021 has resulted in price hikes and power shortages, exacerbated by Russia's political maneuvering aligned with its invasion of Ukraine. Reminiscent of Japan's situation after the 1970s oil crises, these effects highlight European reliance on an unstable supplier, pointing to the need to diversify natural gas suppliers, as well as a need for further diversification of electricity and heat sources. As Japan's trajectory demonstrates, collaboration within and across EU nations can support this shift in resource procurement and choices, as well as innovations to facilitate it and bolster all forms of resilience.

Japan's narrative thus provides insights for innovating from disasters through cooperation based on transparent risk communication and development of shared resilience priorities. However, collaboration on innovation toward energy system resilience should not begin with disasters. In addition to revealing the importance of stakeholder cooperation on innovation in response to shocks, Japan's case shows us that we need to identify ways to collaborate to achieve our collective energy system resilience goals before shocks occur in order to avert them, mitigate their effects, and adapt and rebound as quickly and effectively as possible. Japan's energy system trajectory also reveals lessons on ways to build resilience into nascent and evolving energy systems.

Building Resilience into Energy Systems

As discussed in chapters one and two, the standard definition of resilience centers on a system's ability to withstand shocks and resume operation. Systems designed with this definition in mind can be inherently resistant to change. Emphasis on operational continuity also can generate regulatory capture that weakens engineering resilience. In addition, this definition of resilience can create clashes across stakeholders' economic resilience priorities, as we observed in the conflicts between Japanese regulators, policymakers, utility companies, and the public since the 1990s. As such, resilient systems defined in this way can stifle innovation and further resilience-building, even when disasters occur. Adding additional facets of socio-ecological resilience, such as sustainability and flexibility, to resilience definitions and priorities can enable a variety of stakeholders to envision systems that can withstand shocks and adapt to address risks, weaknesses, and new challenges. Economic resilience then becomes integrated with these definitions, incorporating social and environmental costs, along with avoided costs of damage from future shocks. Japan's trajectory from the oil crises through the post-Fukushima disaster period offers examples of ways to build such resilience into energy systems, as well as lessons on challenges that emerge from not doing so.

After the 1970s oil crises, as discussed in chapter three, Japanese policymakers, utilities and consumers cooperated to shift the energy system by diversifying electricity sources away from oil and toward nuclear power, coupled with conservation and energy efficiency measures and programs. These efforts promoted socio-ecological and economic resilience by reducing reliance on unstable imported resources, emissions, and economic risk. Concurrently, nuclear regulations developed to support engineering resilience.

As Japan's post-oil crises energy system developed, the shared focus on infrastructure expansion and economic resilience centered on investment in this infrastructure contributed to the government's and utilities' difficulties in responding to future shocks to Japan's energy system (Sklarew, 2018).

As discussed in chapter four, during the 1990s and early 2000s, nuclear accidents and safety violation scandals did not catalyze changes in Japan's energy system. They also did not yield significant policymaking process change or impactful regulatory change. Instead, the policies fostered continuity of operations, as well as preservation and expansion of a nuclear-based energy system, without addressing engineering and socio-ecological resilience challenges. Interviewees' comments suggest that the utilities and many politicians and bureaucrats viewed preservation of nuclear reactors' operating capability as central to economic resilience, as well as socio-economic resilience focused on the three Es, with emphasis on energy security and decarbonization. This perspective clashed with regulators' focus on engineering resilience. As time passed, emerging nuclear waste disposal challenges and technological difficulties divided the politicians and bureaucrats. Some officials perceived these safety and environmental concerns as a threat to system resilience, necessitating a shift away from nuclear power as a baseload electricity source. Others prioritized the role of energy security in system resilience, viewing nuclear power as the key to freedom from fossil fuel imports and the answer to climate change mitigation. Concurrently, lack of risk communication perpetuated public acceptance of a nuclear-based energy system without recognition of safety risks. This combination contributed to a decline in all forms of resilience, culminating in the Fukushima disaster and short-term responses to it.

The creation of the NRA and its new regulations aim to facilitate a future return to prior operations through enhanced engineering and social resilience measures that enable reactor restarts, safe operation, and an ability to withstand future shocks. While these incremental changes build a more resilient energy system, holistic resilience requires more. Moving beyond a mere return to prior operations requires embedding economic priorities in the context of engineering and socio-ecological resilience goals. This integration would transition the goals of policymakers, regulators and utilities from regulatory compliance to achievement of socio-ecological, engineering and economic resilience in a holistic way, enabling innovation and adaptation. In this context, the delays to Japan's nuclear fuel reprocessing facility completion and the associated costs may be viewed as necessary results of prioritizing combined socio-ecological, engineering and economic resilience goals. Retired nuclear and coal plants also may be viewed from this perspective, rather than merely as stranded investments. Similarly, grid access for renewables producers and other new entrants, an increasingly salient challenge in Japan and many other locations, is reframed as necessary for achievement of these communal resilience goals. Concurrent with the incremental shifts in Japanese policy and regulation that frame a return to nuclear reactor operations, decarbonization goals have precipitated a transformative policy shift from older coal plants to renewables, coupled with innovations on carbon management technologies.

By demonstrating the ways in which shocks can create rifts or synergies across stakeholder groups' risk perceptions and priorities, Japan's narrative can help to explain current and future energy policy conflicts and inform domestic and international energy cooperation. As energy stakeholders innovate to resolve challenges to resilience, a holistic perspective will foster collaboration and transparency across policymakers, regulators, energy producers, and consumers of all sizes, as well as the general public. Achieving these integrated resilience goals also requires willingness to modify or even abandon technologies and solutions that do not achieve them.

As such, Japan's narrative reveals the importance of the roles of policymakers' and regulators' relationships with the electric utilities and the public, as well as these groups' energy system resilience goals. We have observed how these relationships, risk perceptions, and resilience priorities influence whether shocks elicit a dramatic shift away from the existing energy system in order to build a more resilient system, as demonstrated in collaboration across policymakers, utilities and the public to shift Japan's energy system away from oil and toward nuclear power and coal after the 1970s oil crises. Relationships, risk perceptions and resilience goals also can preserve the status quo, embodied in policymaker-utility support for Japan's policy changes to promote nuclear power and retain public acceptance during the 1990s and 2000s period of sequential nuclear accidents and scandal. Communications of zero risk compromised resilience by inhibiting incremental innovations to mitigate these risks, while generating public acceptance based on this myth of zero risk. Finally, we have seen how relationships, risk perceptions and resilience priorities can elicit incremental changes to build resilience within the existing energy system, as appears to be the case following the Fukushima disaster. The accident injected tension into relationships between policymakers, regulators, the electric utilities, and the public. It also shifted these groups' resilience goals further out of alignment, as some policymakers and utilities remain focused on energy security and economics, while emphasis on environmental considerations has declined. Other policymakers and the public have prioritized environmental concerns as inextricably linked to safety and resilience. At the same time, the disaster elevated perceptions of safety risks for all groups, while increasing uncertainty regarding utilities' and renewables producers' investment risks. The gradual emergence of renewables, rise and planned decline of coal, and planned return of nuclear power reflect a combination of compromises on these various stakeholders' risk perceptions and resilience priorities.

These three periods in Japan's energy policymaking trajectory demonstrate how building resilience into energy systems requires stakeholder cooperation, recognition of diverse groups' resilience priorities and risk perceptions, and willingness to adjust or transform these systems to achieve holistic resilience. As traits inherent to energy systems, infrastructure, interrelatedness and complexity, institutional support, momentum, and risk and uncertainty will emerge naturally as these systems develop. Resilience involves leveraging these traits to prevent system lock-in and promote adaptability.

Infrastructure and Interrelatedness

Japan's experiences demonstrate the roles of infrastructure and the energy system's internal interconnections and linkages with other systems in promoting or weakening resilience.

As previously mentioned, while energy infrastructure investments are required for system resilience, they must be embedded in the broader context of the resilience goals they support. Resilient infrastructure withstands shocks, and it also adapts to new vulnerabilities. This framing requires coordination and transparency across policymakers, infrastructure developers and system operators, which can enable reduction of investment risks and promote all forms of long-term resilience.

Japan's trajectory reveals how infrastructure and interconnections within an energy system's components can support or challenge resilience. As discussed in chapters four and five, the Japanese government's planned linkages between nuclear power production and nuclear fuel reprocessing infrastructure aimed to build engineering and socio-ecological resilience by addressing energy security and nuclear waste challenges. However, the 1990s-2000s accidents and the Fukushima disaster exposed vulnerabilities of this interconnectedness, which the government and energy industry must address. Similarly, the aforementioned power transfer challenges Japanese utilities experienced during the Fukushima disaster demonstrated the resilience advantages of interconnected grids. Conversely, these same interconnections may open the potential for cascading power outages, as the United States and other places have experienced. Recognizing this tradeoff and addressing it through infrastructure design can build greater system resilience.

Shocks to energy systems also reveal the interconnectedness of energy with other sectors. Both the oil crises and the Fukushima disaster precipitated energy system failures that led to increased electricity prices. Both the price increases and energy conservation measures affected the manufacturing industry, raising product prices for consumers. The Fukushima disaster also affected food production and sales through soil contamination and long-lasting risk perceptions, as discussed at the end of this chapter. Energy system development thus requires comprehensive examination of linkages between chosen energy sources and other parts of the energy system, as well as other sectors and systems. This evaluation can contribute to policies that can help to build system resilience by addressing the ripples shocks can cause in these interconnected systems.

On the other hand, the energy system's interconnections with other sectors also can promote resilience, in particular through infrastructure complementarities. For instance, in Japan, the United States, and elsewhere, electricity sector synergies with the IT and telecommunications industries have emerged as integration of transmission networks and cables has progressed. These synergies have enhanced all forms of resilience by reducing prices for electricity producers and consumers and enabling new entrants that include renewables producers. Integration of these systems also enables access for remote communities. Energy and water system interconnections offer another opportunity for resilience-building synergies. In a growing number of communities around the world, systems for drinking water and storm water also produce hydropower, as turbines installed in the pipes utilize the inherent water pressure (Sklarew and Sklarew, 2017). Institutional support for these types of synergistic innovations can enhance energy system resilience, if coupled with mechanisms to prevent institutional lock-in that would weaken such resilience.

Institutional Support

Japan's energy system narrative offers insights on features that can foster flexible institutional support. We can define the first of these as regulatory realism without capture. Government documents and much of the literature analyzing the Fukushima disaster attributed problems to regulatory capture and cooperation between safety regulators and the electric utilities. Interviewees' comments revealed a completely different, but equally problematic relationship. The scandal and accidents that occurred because of the conflict and battle for clout between Japan's electric utilities and safety regulators revealed that such conflict can cause as much damage as capture.

Several institutional design features can facilitate an environment of cooperation and information exchange without regulatory capture. Government and electric utility interviewees broadly agreed than a regulator independent from the government's policymaking functions can regulate more effectively. This view is echoed by international organizations such as the IAEA and the IEA in their assessments of a range of national energy systems. At the same time, effective communication between regulators and the electric utilities remains necessary. Japan's regulatory challenges of the past several decades have demonstrated that energy system resilience requires input from regulated entities in order to create effectual, realistic regulations, while avoiding both regulatory capture and complete isolation from these firms. Conversely, poor communication between the regulators and the regulated can lead to ineffective regulations that contribute to shocks and inhibit resilience. Isolation of regulators from regulated firms also hinders development of effective regulations and firms' ability to comply, weakening resilience and inhibiting cooperation and development of shared resilience goals. Many interviewees highlighted transparency as the key to solving this problem while building public trust.

Government, electric utility, and public opinion interviewees highlighted the need for more transparent energy policies. However, the Fukushima disaster revealed that the government and the public define transparency differently. While the government has focused on increasing the transparency of information conveyed about energy policies, citizens seek transparency of the process and considerations behind the policies. This dichotomy has appeared in other places around the world.

In Japan, this disconnect has yielded government measures to explain energy policies to the public in order to regain trust. These efforts have not generated public trust, since the public is seeking greater openness in the process and explanation of the priorities that shape the policies. Japan's narrative thus illuminates the need for formal stakeholder engagement mechanisms such as an effective public comment process and advisory group representation, which can build trust and support energy system development and transitions. Public access to minutes from advisory group meetings and NRA meetings with utility companies has improved process transparency, but the public's zero risk tolerance has complicated the effects on trust in both energy technologies and the government's ability to oversee them. This dilemma highlights the need to achieve public acceptance of an energy system's realities, including challenges and shared agreement on tolerable levels of risk.

Risk and Uncertainty

Transparent communication of challenges and risks can shape resilience goals and the potential for cooperation on innovations to solve these challenges and risks, building holistic energy system resilience. Japan's story of safety risk communication failure and its negative effect on public trust demonstrates the need for regulators, policymakers, and electric utilities to share and convey realistic risk expectations and trade-offs with each other and the public. A lack of transparency regarding energy technology risks – including safety, but also energy security, environmental and economic risks – leads to public distrust when these risks reveal themselves through shocks.

Japan's situation also reveals the role of financial risk in preserving incumbent systems and preventing energy system transformation. Electric utility interviewees indicated that their firms prefer to maintain the incumbent system as long as it compensates them for their financial investments. The risks and uncertainty of transitioning from an incumbent system thus can limit innovation. As we observed in chapter 5, institutional changes resulting from the Fukushima disaster injected financial uncertainty that has challenged the electric utilities' long-term investment decisions. This effect provides lessons for utilities around the world as they develop their integrated resource plans.

The oil crises and the Fukushima disaster did spark innovation both within and outside Japan's incumbent energy system, reflecting the role of institutional support in fostering innovation by alleviating risk and uncertainty. Examples include funding and policy incentives for battery storage and hydrogen research and development, as well as energy efficiency incentives such as such as the Top-Runner program. The local innovations previously described in this chapter also emerged from risk-mitigating local government partnerships with private sector firms and the public.

Innovation in Japan also emerged from the promise of financial gain due to public demand. For instance, interviewees indicated that they innovated on efficient heat pumps in response to consumers' interest in more efficient products that would lower their electricity bills after the Fukushima disaster. This promise of a market for energy innovations also mitigates risk, as long as regulatory and policy frameworks support them.

Integrative solutions to risk can mitigate uncertainty and leverage energy system interconnectedness with other systems. For instance, in addition to deploying solar power on contaminated farmland, public-private partnerships could enable agrivoltaics on operational farms. Agrivoltaics involves the deployment of solar panels on agricultural land, enabling emissions-free, on-site electricity production to power irrigation pumps and farm equipment, while also shading water-stressed plants and grazing animals. Institutional support for agrivoltaics in the form of tax incentives and regulatory frameworks can promote its expansion. In Japan, the New Energy and Industrial Technology Development Organization (NEDO,) a METI subsidiary, released guidelines on design and construction of co-location of solar panels with crops and livestock in late 2021 (New Energy and Industrial Technology Development Organization, 2021; Bellini, 2021).

Japan's case thus provides several lessons on building resilience into existing energy systems. It also provides lessons on innovating out of unsustainable energy systems that challenge resilience.

Transitioning Out of Unsustainable Energy Systems

Unsustainable energy systems may reveal their vulnerabilities when disasters or other sudden shocks occur, such as the oil crises, the Fukushima disaster, or other geopolitical, natural or technological energy-related catastrophic events. Energy system weaknesses also may emerge gradually, as during Japan's 1990s-2000s nuclear accidents, the COVID-19 pandemic, seasonal weather patterns, and other longer-term events and trends. In addition to informing places coping with sudden energy system shocks, Japan's lessons can inform other nations and communities that face resilience challenges from reliance on fluctuating energy sources. As climate change exacerbates flooding and drought patterns, nations like Venezuela and Brazil, as well as communities in the western United States, discover vulnerabilities associated with large hydropower dependence. Diversifying away from lock-in of one primary electricity source will enable all forms of resilience as these unpredictable weather and climate effects increasingly challenge these communities' energy systems.

The oil crises revealed the social and economic resilience vulnerabilities of Japan's energy system in the 1970s. In particular, the shocks highlighted the challenges of system interrelatedness, as well as the risk and uncertainty associated with a system heavily reliant on imported fuel sources. The oil crises also challenged institutional support for the existing system and stalled its momentum. Japanese policymakers' clout over and cooperative relationships with the electric utilities and the public, combined with alignment of resilience priorities, supported the shocks' pressure for a transition away from an oil-based energy system. This shift was further catalyzed by these groups' shared view of reliance on imported oil for baseload electricity as a threat to energy system resilience. Top government officials and utility companies encouraged the public to view nuclear power as the key to a resilient Japanese energy system, bolstering energy security and providing a more environmentally friendly option compared to fossil fuels. These relationships and mutual resilience perspectives thus enabled the Japanese government's transformation of Japan's energy system. At the time, this evolution built greater economic, socio-ecological, and engineering resilience.

The Fukushima disaster revealed unsustainable vulnerabilities in Japan's transformed system, as discussed earlier in this chapter. These include locked-in infrastructure investments, complementary locked-in policy planning, unacknowledged safety risks, and long-term environmental challenges. These vulnerabilities emerged during the 1990s -2000s accidents and scandal, but they remained unaddressed until after the Fukushima disaster occurred. In its aftermath, Japan's national energy policies and utility company plans have moved toward transition.

This transformation is slowed by some of these same vulnerabilities, particularly those related to prior investments, revealing the roles of relationships, resilience priorities and risk perceptions in the pacing of system changes.

The cases around the world mentioned earlier in this chapter have resulted in varied responses to shocks, ranging from relative stasis, as in Texas, to system transition, as planned in Puerto Rico. Japan's case teaches us that efforts to preserve an unsustainable energy system can exacerbate existing challenges, weakening the ability to adapt to shocks, and thus undermining system resilience. Slow transition can enable private sector investment planning, building economic resilience. Japan's case shows us the need for transparent communication of specific timelines for transition stages to promote public trust and support, enable energy industry actors to plan infrastructure investments effectively, and foster development of effective regulatory frameworks. At the same time, slow transition pacing also can exacerbate existing resilience vulnerabilities and create new ones. These challenges can include continued reliance on unsustainable energy sources, as well as advancement of policies supporting the unsustainable aspects of the existing system. Germany's energy transition parallels this challenge arising in Japan, as the slow German shift to renewables, coupled with reduction of nuclear power, has increased reliance on coal and natural gas.

Local innovation out of energy systems may move more quickly than innovations at the national level in some places, as evidenced by examples from Japan described earlier in this chapter. Government interviewees say that this local movement stems from the belief that renewables innovation will create jobs. MOE is making efforts to create an environment conducive to such innovation. Concurrently, METI is encouraging the electric utilities to position themselves as innovators, rather than incumbents threatened by innovation. The public has indicated a willingness to pay for this innovation through higher electricity prices, because they believe renewables will make the energy system more resilient. This set of perspectives suggests that cooperative relationships between policymakers, regulators, electric utilities and the public can enable innovation to arise from external shocks if these groups' priorities and risk perceptions align to promote cooperation on energy system change. If their priorities and risk perceptions are aligned to preserve the status quo, little innovation will result.

Japan's experience also offers some specific insights on how transitions out of unsustainable energy systems are influenced by public trust in an energy technology and in the government's ability to oversee it. Japan's case suggests that if public trust in the government is coupled with distrust in an incumbent energy technology, trust in the government combines with this technological distrust and enables a shift away from the existing system if the government chooses transformation. This scenario emerged from the oil crises. Public trust in the government and distrust of the energy technology also can permit continuation of the existing energy system if the government prefers the incumbent system. This scenario occurred after the 1990s and 2000s shocks. During this period, the public gradually lost some trust in both nuclear technology and the government's ability to manage it. As a result, when the Fukushima disaster occurred, the public already had begun to distrust the existing energy system. The disaster depleted public trust in both nuclear technology and the government's ability to regulate it. This double distrust catalyzed public calls for a new system and a new policymaking process, suggesting that the loss of public trust in both the government and the technology also opens the possibility for energy system change. Conversely, as Japan's regulatory challenges have revealed, this lack of public trust simultaneously can hinder government efforts to transform the energy system, since the public doesn't trust the government to create good policies or effectively regulate new technologies.

The public's distrust of Japan's energy policy process after the Fukushima disaster has generated calls from NGOs, and even some government officials, for process reform. Suggestions include more opportunities for public involvement, some devolvement of policymaking to local governments interested in distributed generation, and introduction of more transparency measures in the policymaking process. Deliberative polling, described in chapter five, offers one example of such innovation. Policy process innovation after a shock offers the potential to build cooperation across groups while redistributing clout, along with some responsibility for energy policy results. These types of changes can build resilience in a nation's policymaking process and in the energy system itself, enabling movement out of unsustainable systems.

These lessons from Japan can facilitate smooth transitioning out of unsustainable energy systems after energy-related shocks occur, building more resilient systems that can address future shocks more effectively. These insights from Japan also prove useful when energy systems reveal weaknesses during shocks not directly related to energy.

Implications for Post-Pandemic Energy Innovation and Resilience

The COVID-19 pandemic embodies both a short- and long-term shock to global supply chains. Their interconnectedness with energy systems has led to pandemic effects on national to local energy system resilience through alteration of energy resource production and consumption patterns, as mentioned in chapter 1. The energy system traits that affected Japan's responses to the three sets of shocks described in this book also influence energy policy responses to the pandemic's effects. Japan's lessons on transparency and communication, risk perceptions and uncertainty, and resilience priorities can foster improved energy system resilience and innovation as communities around the world grapple with the pandemic's ongoing consequences.

Japan's trajectory has shown us the resilience challenges and benefits of energy system infrastructure investment and system interconnectedness when shocks occur. The pandemic created energy system resilience challenges based on interconnectedness with component supply chains. As a result of predictions of reduced demand during the pandemic, insufficient production of components needed for energy infrastructure, such as polysilicon for solar panel manufacturing, drastically increased pricing of this infrastructure (Rivero, 2021), even as demand for solar installations increased. Just as the 1990s-2000s nuclear accidents could have served as opportunities for Japanese development of more resilient infrastructure, the pandemic offers a chance to prepare for future component shortages through diversification of supply sources and innovation on energy infrastructure designs. As Japan's Fukushima disaster experience has taught us, even as the pandemic subsides, an eventual return to the prior energy system exactly as it was prior to the shock does not build resilience, since future shocks can yield the same devastating effects if no system adaptation occurs to prevent them.

This ability to adapt relies on institutional support. We examined Japanese policies developed to protect against future supply chain shocks after the oil crises. Conversely, we observed how Japanese policies to preserve existing infrastructure during the 1990s–2000s period of accidents hindered such adaptation. Building a more resilient energy supply chain that can respond to pandemic-induced issues requires support and coordination from all levels of government in nations around the world. Communication and transparency between stakeholder groups within and across nations can promote cooperation to identify and address supply energy chain vulnerabilities and build resilience.

We can extrapolate from Japan's lessons on transparent communication of risk to the broader context of pandemic-induced energy risk and uncertainty. Demand for electricity and oil plummeted globally during pandemic lockdowns, triggering energy price instability that affected both producers and consumers (International Energy Agency, 2021). Government and utility bidirectional communication with consumers regarding energy resource supply and demand fluctuations, along with related price volatility, can enable more effective electricity load balancing, as well as measures to preserve producer investments while promoting energy justice for low-income consumers struggling to pay electricity bills. This communication thus can mitigate risk and uncertainty regarding energy supply, demand and pricing, promoting economic resilience, and socio-ecological resilience. It also can enable innovation on policies, infrastructure, and supply chain design to protect against such uncertainty when future shocks occur.

The resilience priority alignments and shifts that emerged from shocks to Japan's energy system offer lessons for pandemic-induced changes to priorities that indirectly affect energy system resilience. Public health and safety priorities rose to the forefront during the height of the pandemic, shaping government policies, consumer behavior, and producer investment decisions. This priority shift and resultant changes led to some of the previously discussed effects on energy systems: fluctuating energy demand, mismatches with supply, and volatile pricing. Japan's case teaches us that misalignment of resilience priorities and lack of communication of these priorities across stakeholder groups can create new challenges this hinder system resilience. It also demonstrates that cooperation on resilient energy system transformation can emerge from aligned resilience priorities across stakeholder groups. In the context of the pandemic, such alignment needs to occur regarding energy producers' and consumers' economic resilience priorities, which would foster supply-demand balance and energy justice. As Japan's case has demonstrated, energy conservation and efficiency also can play a crucial role in promoting both of these goals, especially in periods of unpredictable supply after-shocks occur. Employing these tools can help to reduce supply and price volatility and enable more predictable demand.

Japan's trajectory also suggests that stakeholders' resilience priorities need to absorb lessons from shocks. While the pandemic has begun to subside in many places around the world, ensuing shocks, such as the aforementioned Russian invasion of Ukraine, have revealed a continued lack of global energy system resilience and misalignment of stakeholders' resilience priorities across sectors and nations. To address global energy supply chain challenges, the focus on socio-ecological resilience needs to extend from the community level to international partnerships.

Interconnectedness of sectors and systems, as well as local to international institutional influences, has framed both the pandemic's effects on energy and Japan's energy system trajectory, suggesting the need to consider energy system resilience in a broader context. Energy system stakeholders' resilience priorities combine with those of stakeholders in these other sectors and places.

Broader Resilience and Innovation in the Food-Energy-Water-Climate Nexus

Japan's case reveals that socio-ecological and economic resilience of energy systems is intertwined with resilience of water and food systems, as well as climate change effects.

Energy systems are interconnected with water and food systems. Production, transport, and storage of food require energy, as do water transport and sanitation. Energy production uses water and can affect its quality. In addition, land use tradeoffs occur between food and energy production. These interconnections can create challenges that precipitate or exacerbate disasters. They also can generate synergies or integrative solutions that promote resilience. Energy systems utilizing fossil fuel resources and large hydropower dams impact climate change through greenhouse gas emissions. Conversely, climate change affects energy infrastructure through the potential for damage from extreme weather and natural disasters. Energy infrastructure failures such as the Fukushima disaster affect food and water quality. We can apply Japan's energy system trajectory lessons in the broader context of resilience in the food-energy-water-climate nexus, a concept that has evolved to describe these sectoral interconnections since it emerged globally from the Bonn 2011 Conference: Water Energy and Food Security Nexus – Solutions for the Green Economy and the World Economic Forum's publication on the nexus in the same year (e.g., World Economic Forum, 2011; Bazilian et al., 2011; Dodds and Bartram, 2016; Janssen et al., 2020).

In Japan, public awareness of the economic resilience interconnections between energy, food, and water emerged during the 1970s oil crises, when conservation measures included restrictions on heating of water for household use in response to heating fuel and electricity price increases.

The 1990s-2000s nuclear accidents largely did not impact food or water systems, while social resilience linkages between energy and climate change effects garnered attention, promoting nuclear power as a carbon-free source.

By contrast, the Fukushima disaster resulted in water, soil, and food contamination in Fukushima Prefecture and surrounding prefectures, including excessive levels of radioactive iodine and cesium in soil, food, and water. Testing of food and water in Fukushima Prefecture beginning five days after the accident found contamination of "tap water, raw milk, vegetables, mushrooms, fruit, nuts, seaweeds, marine invertebrates, coastal fish, freshwater fish, beef, wild animal meat, brown rice, wheat, tea leaves and other foodstuffs" (Hamada et al., 2012). Testing found soil contaminated with high levels of cesium in Miyagi, Ibaraki, Iwate, Yamagata, Tochigi, and Chiba prefectures one to five weeks after the accident (Yasunari et al., 2011). Further water contamination challenges arose from water outflows from the damaged reactors. TEPCO estimated that over 11,000 tons of water containing excessive levels of radioactive iodine and cesium flowed from the Fukushima Daiichi reactors into the Pacific Ocean during the three months following the accident[1] (Hamada et al., 2012).

These ecological effects created social resilience challenges for residents, as well as economic resilience challenges for the farming and fisheries industries. Agricultural exports to other parts of Japan and other nations expanded the groups affected by these challenges to include the entire nation, as well as importers of Fukushima-grown food products. On March 22, 2011, the U.S. Food and Drug Administration (FDA) issued an import alert for milk, milk products, fresh fruits, and vegetables produced in Fukushima, Tochigi, Ibaraki, and Gunma Prefectures. They expanded the alert to include seafood products, as well as additional prefectures: Aomori, Chiba, Iwate, Miyagi, Nagano, Niigata, Saitama, Shizuoka, Yamagata, and Yamanashi. The FDA deactivated Import Alert #99–33 in September 2021, citing "an extensive analysis of Japan's robust control measures that include decontamination, monitoring and enforcement; after reviewing the results of 10 years of sampling food products from Japan; and after determining a very low risk to American consumers from radioactive contaminated foods imported from Japan" as justification for deactivating the alert (U.S. Food and Drug Administration, 2021).

In addition, the government's decision to discharge over one million tons of stored, treated wastewater from the Fukushima reactors, into the Pacific Ocean, has raised social resilience concerns among some Japanese stakeholders and in nations adjacent to the Pacific Ocean. The water contains high levels of tritium and traces of radionuclides.

As climate change induces more extreme weather events and natural disasters, energy system resilience must include adaptation to changing infrastructure risks and their potential effects on water and food. Public and governmental risk perceptions regarding energy's ecological connections with food and water remained relatively untouched by the oil crises and 1990s-2000s accidents, despite an emerging focus on climate change effects from energy use. The Fukushima disaster brought these food-energy-water connections to the forefront, altering risk perceptions across stakeholder groups. These changes to perceived risks drove public concerns regarding consumption of contaminated food and water. Based on annual polls of over 5,000 residents, conducted by Japan's Consumer Affairs Agency since 2013, consumer reluctance to purchase food products from Fukushima, Iwate, and Miyagi prefectures peaked in 2013, at 14.9 percent (Maeda, 2022). The highest percentage of consumers avoiding Fukushima-made products appeared in 2014, at 19.6 percent. The 2015 survey found that 67 percent of respondents expressed concern regarding the origin of purchased foods, and 34 percent of these indicated that this focus emerged from a desire to avoid food contaminated by radioactive material (Hongo, 2015). In the 2022 poll, this figure dropped to 6.5 percent (Maeda, 2022).[2] A post-disaster food safety risk perceptions study by Reiher (2017) finds that inadequate information on radiation in food exacerbated residents' anxiety regarding radioactive food.

Public distrust in the government's ability to oversee energy infrastructure operations expanded to include oversight of food affected by the disaster. Reiher (2017) finds this distrust evidenced by formation of citizen monitoring groups for radiation in food. New Japanese public awareness of the potential for energy-related accident impacts on food and water safety, coupled with this distrust in government oversight of energy infrastructure and management of these risks, catalyzed some of the local injunctions against nuclear reactor restarts mentioned in chapter 5. Communities reliant on Lake Biwa, which supplies drinking water to approximately 14 million residents, became concerned about the potential for contamination from future nuclear accidents (Johnston, 2016).

This awareness of energy-related risks to food and water expanded the Japanese public's socio-ecological energy system resilience priorities to include linked water and food system resilience priorities. Local and national government officials in Japan also recognized these connections, and they found themselves caught between consumers' socio-ecological resilience priorities and agricultural producers' economic resilience goals. When the Fukushima disaster occurred, the Japanese government did not have food and water radiation contamination regulations in place, revealing a safety culture gap regarding linkages between energy, food, and water. This absence of standards for radioactivity in food also reflected a lack of nexus-oriented social resilience in energy and food systems. One week after the disaster, the Ministry of Health, Labor and Welfare (MHLW) established provisional standards, and one year later, the ministry approved standards opposed by farmers and other producers as too stringent (Reiher, 2017). Reiher's research reveals a lack of stakeholder input, resembling the NRA's initial revision of nuclear safety standards.

Like the previously described energy regulation difficulties, Japan's food safety challenges highlight the role of regulators and regulation in mitigating resilience risks. Combining these food risks with the water contamination resulting from the accident demonstrates the need for regulatory frameworks to measure food and water risks associated with energy system risks. Taken together, these food-energy-water challenges also suggest a need for coordination across regulatory authorities responsible for energy, food, and water safety to assess and address cross-sectoral risks in an integrated way.

These food-energy-water challenges emerging from the Fukushima disaster parallel and broaden the previously discussed transparency and communication lessons for energy sector stakeholders. In the context of the food-energy-water-climate nexus, transparency and clear risk communication remain central to public trust. TEPCO's mid-2013 announcement of contaminated water leakage from the damaged Fukushima Daiichi reactors into the Pacific Ocean escalated public concerns regarding the accident's effects on water (Prime Minister of Japan and His Cabinet, 2013). TEPCO revealed that in order to avoid worrying the public, the company had postponed announcement of the leak until they confirmed the amount of water leakage. The delayed communication produced the opposite effect, deepening public distrust in the utility and government-utility management of energy infrastructure and its effects on water. This situation reflects the challenge of balancing timely provision of information with collection of accurate and complete information prior to dissemination.

The government's post-disaster communication on radioactivity in food provides similar lessons on provision of timely and detailed information to the public. Concurrent with food safety regulatory changes, government communication with the public focused on rebuilding trust in agricultural products without conveying the processes used to monitor radioactivity in these products (Reiher, 2017). A decade after the disaster, Japanese policymakers continue to prioritize building consumer trust in order to promote the agricultural sector's economic resilience (Walravens et al., 2022). The aforementioned 2022 Consumer Affairs Agency poll found that 46.1 percent of respondents still want the government to provide more information on food safety, including inspection results (Maeda, 2022).

Japan's lessons on risk communication and resilience priorities can inform energy, food, and water stakeholder interactions from local to national levels around the world. Transparent communication of energy's relationships with food and water, as well as connections to climate change, enable energy, food, and water sector stakeholders to incorporate consideration of integrated risks and synergies from each of these sectors into their resilience priorities. This integration will more effectively align these diverse, connected groups' resilience goals. This alignment can create an environment enabling cooperation on synergistic innovations to solve resilience risks across these sectors, promoting economic, engineering, and socio-ecological resilience that spans food, energy, water, and climate.

These lessons also apply to a broader nexus of other systems interconnected with energy, including health, IT and telecommunications, manufacturing, and others. Japan's narrative thus provides insights on how stakeholder relationships and resilience priorities can bolster or inhibit holistic resilience of energy systems in the context of a network of integrated systems. Local to national communities across the globe can apply these lessons in determining paths to collaboration on innovation and resilience-building in these interconnected systems before, during, and after shocks.

Notes

1 According to Hamada et al. (2012), who cite data from the *Report of Japanese Government to IAEA Ministerial Conference on Nuclear Safety – Accident at TEPCO's Fukushima Nuclear Power Stations* transmitted by the Government of Japan's Nuclear Emergency Response Headquarters (2011), TEPCO estimated that "520 tons of water containing 4.7 PBq (a total level of ^{131}I, ^{134}Cs and ^{137}Cs) was released between April 1 and 6, 2011"; "10,393 tons of water containing 150 GBq was released between April 4 and 10, 2011"; and "250 tons of water containing 20 TBq on May 11, 2011."
2 According to Hongo (2015) and Maeda (2022), Japan's Consumer Affairs Agency conducted the surveys online survey and received valid responses from 5,176 people in their 20s through 60s. Respondents are residents of Iwate, Miyagi, Fukushima, and Ibaraki prefectures; the Tokyo metropolitan areas consisting of Saitama, Chiba, and Kanagawa prefectures; two Kansai prefectures, Osaka and Hyogo; and Aichi Prefecture, which spans the Kansai and Chubu regions.

References

Appunn, K. (2021) 'Shutting down nuclear and coal – can Germany keep the lights on?' *Clean Energy Wire*. 17 May. https://www.cleanenergywire.org/news/shutting-down-nuclear-and-coal-can-germany-maintain-supply-security-renewables-alone

Autorité de sûreté nucléaire. (2012) *National Action Plan of the French Nuclear Safety Authority*. December. www.ensreg.eu/sites/default/files/post%20stress%20tests%20National%20Action%20plan%20ASN%20France.pdf.

Balmer, E., and Ozawa, H. (2022) 'Fukushima Forges Renewable Future After Nuclear Disaster.' *The Japan Times*. 9 March. www.japantimes.co.jp/news/2022/03/09/national/fukushima-renewable-energy-future/.

Bazilian, M., Rogner, H., Howells, M., Hermann, S., Arent, D., Gielen, D., Steduto, P., Mueller, A., Komor, P., Tol, R.S.J., and Yumkella, K.K. (2011) 'Considering the Energy, Water and Food Nexus: Towards an Integrated Modelling Approach.' *Energy Policy*, 39, 7896–7906.

Bellini, E. (2021) 'Japan Releases New Guidelines for Agrivoltaics as Installations Hit 200 MW. *PV Magazine*.' 13 December. www.pv-magazine.com/2021/12/13/japan-releases-new-guidelines-for-agrivoltaics-as-installations-hit-200-mw/.

Dodds, F., and Bartram, J. Eds. (2016) *The Water, Food, Energy and Climate Nexus: Challenges and an Agenda for Action*. London: Routledge.

Eurelectric. (2006) *Impacts of Severe Storms on Electric Grids*. Task Force on Power Outages.

Hamada, N., Ogino, H., and Fujimichi, Y. (2012) 'Safety Regulations of Food and Water Implemented in the First Year Following the Fukushima Nuclear Accident.' *Journal of Radiation Research*, 53 (5), 641–671.

Hongo, J. (2015) 'Nearly One in Five Japanese Reluctant to Buy Fukushima Food.' *The Wall Street Journal*. 11 March. www.wsj.com/articles/BL-JRTB-19444.

International Energy Agency. (2021) 'COVID-19 Impact on Electricity.' January. www.iea.org/reports/covid-19-impact-on-electricity.

IRENA. (2021) *Energy Profile: Venezuela (Bolivarian Republic of)*. 29 September. Abu Dhabi: International Renewable Energy Agency.

Janssen, D.N.G., Ramos, E.P, Linderhof, V., Polman, N., Laspidou, C., Fokkinga, D., and de Mesquita e Sousa, D. (2020) 'The Climate, Land, Energy, Water and Food Nexus Challenge in a Land Scarce Country: Innovations in the Netherlands.' *Sustainability*, 12 (24), 10491.

Japan for Sustainability. (2015) *Japan for Sustainability Newsletter No. 152.* April.

Johnston, E. (2016) 'KEPCO Loses Challenge to Takahama Injunction.' *The Japan Times.* 17 June. www.japantimes.co.jp/news/2016/06/17/national/crime-legal/kepco-fails-suspend-injunction-takahama-nuclear-plant/.

Kadak, A. (2017) 'A Comparison of Advanced Nuclear Technologies. Columbia/SIPA Center on Global Energy Policy. March.

Maeda, J. (2022) 'Poll: Record Low 6.5% Hesitant to Buy Food Items From Fukushima.' *The Asahi Shimbun.* 23 March. www.asahi.com/ajw/articles/14572562.

New Energy and Industrial Technology Development Organization. (2021) *Guidelines for Agrivoltaic System Design and Construction* (営農型太陽光発電システムの設計・施工ガイドライン2021年版). 12 November.

Nuclear Emergency Response Headquarters, Government of Japan. (2011) *Report of Japanese Government to IAEA Ministerial Conference on Nuclear Safety – Accident at TEPCO's Fukushima Nuclear Power Stations.* 15 September.

Owens, C. (2020) 'The Blackout Report: The 11 Biggest Blackouts of All Time.' 7 December. www.theblackoutreport.co.uk/2020/12/07/11-biggest-blackouts/.

Paillere, H., and Donovan, J. (2021) 'Nuclear Power 10 Years After Fukushima: The Long Road Back.' *International Atomic Energy Agency.* 11 March. www.iaea.org/newscenter/news/nuclear-power-10-years-after-fukushima-the-long-road-back.

The Prime Minister of Japan and His Cabinet. (2013) 'Press Conference by the Chief Cabinet Secretary.' 23 July. https://japan.kantei.go.jp/tyoukanpress/201307/23_a.html.

Puerto Rico Energy Public Policy Act (No. 17–2019). (2019) 11 April. https://aeepr.com/es-pr/QuienesSomos/Ley17/A-17-2019%20PS%201121%20Politica%20Publica%20Energetica.pdf.

Reiher, C. (2017) 'Food Safety and Consumer Trust in Post-Fukushima Japan.' *Japan Forum,* 29 (1): Trust and Mistrust in Contemporary Japan. Published online 28 October 2016, Taylor & Francis Online, 53–76.

Rivero, N. (2021) 'Here's How Supply Chain Issues Are Affecting Renewable Energy Projects.' *World Economic Forum.* 4 November. www.weforum.org/agenda/2021/11/supply-chain-problems-solar-power-renewable-energy/.

Sato, K. (n.d.). *Community Development With a Core Facility for Ensuring Peace of Mind.* Toyota. www.toyota-global.com/sustainability/social_contribution/vision/smiles/the-f-grid-concept/.

Sklarew, J.F. (2018) 'Power Fluctuations: How Japan's Nuclear Infrastructure Priorities Influence Electric Utilities' Clout.' *Energy Research & Social Science,* 41, 158–167.

Sklarew, J.F., and Sklarew, D. (2017) 'Empowering Resilience in Energy and Water Systems: Addressing Barriers to Implementation of Urban Hydroelectric Micro-turbines.' The CIP Report, July 2017. Center for Infrastructure Protection & Homeland Security, George Mason University.

Starn, J., Parkin, B., and Vilcu, I. (2021) 'The Day Europe's Power Grid Came Close to a Massive Blackout.' *Bloomberg.* 27 January. https://www.bloomberg.com/news/articles/2021-01-27/green-shift-brings-blackout-risk-to-world-s-biggest-power-grid#xj4y7vzkg

Toyota. (2015) 'Japan's First Regional Emergency Power Supply System Commences Operation.' 22 October. https://global.toyota/en/detail/10001641.

Ueda, S., and Kurimoto, S. (2019) 'Fukushima to Be Reborn as $2.7bn Wind and Solar Power Hub.' *Nikkei Asia.* 10 November. https://asia.nikkei.com/Business/Energy/Fukushima-to-be-reborn-as-2.7bn-wind-and-solar-power-hub.

United Nations Industrial Development Organization. (2015) *Industrial Prosumers of Renewable Energy: Contribution to Inclusive and Sustainable Industrial Development.* Vienna: UNIDO.

United States Nuclear Regulatory Commission. (2021) 'Plant-Specific Safety Enhancements After Fukushima.' 7 December. www.nrc.gov/reactors/operating/ops-experience/fukushima.html.

U.S. Food and Drug Administration. (2021) 'FDA Response to the Fukushima Daiichi Nuclear Power Facility Incident.' 21 September. https://www.fda.gov/news-events/public-health-focus/fda-response-fukushima-daiichi-nuclear-power-facility-incident

Walravens, T., O'Shea, P., and Ahrenkiel, N. (2022) 'Let's eat Fukushima': Communicating Risk and Restoring 'Safe Food' After the Fukushima Disaster (2011–2020).' *Japan Forum*, 34 (1), Special Issue on the Merits of the Mundane. Published online 15 March 2022, Taylor & Francis Online, 79–102. DOI: 10.1080/09555803.2022.2046131

World Economic Forum. (2011) *Water Security: The Water-Energy-Food-Climate Nexus*. World Economic Forum Initiative.

World Nuclear Association. (2022) Nuclear Power in France. March. www.world-nuclear.org/information-library/country-profiles/countries-a-f/france.aspx.

Yasunari, T.J., Stohl, A., Hayano, R.S., and Yasunari, T. (2011) 'Cesium-137 Deposition and Contamination of Japanese Soils Due to the Fukushima Nuclear Accident.' *PNAS*, 108 (49), 14 November. www.pnas.org/doi/10.1073/pnas.1112058108.

Index

Taylor & Francis Group
an **informa** business

Taylor & Francis eBooks

www.taylorfrancis.com

A single destination for eBooks from Taylor & Francis
with increased functionality and an improved user
experience to meet the needs of our customers.

90,000+ eBooks of award-winning academic content in
Humanities, Social Science, Science, Technology, Engineering,
and Medical written by a global network of editors and authors.

TAYLOR & FRANCIS EBOOKS OFFERS:

A streamlined
experience for
our library
customers

A single point
of discovery
for all of our
eBook content

Improved
search and
discovery of
content at both
book and
chapter level

REQUEST A FREE TRIAL
support@taylorfrancis.com

Routledge
Taylor & Francis Group

CRC Press
Taylor & Francis Group

For Product Safety Concerns and Information please contact our EU
representative GPSR@taylorandfrancis.com
Taylor & Francis Verlag GmbH, Kaufingerstraße 24, 80331 München, Germany

www.ingramcontent.com/pod-product-compliance
Lightning Source LLC
Chambersburg PA
CBHW050349270326
41926CB00016B/3655